بسم الله الرحمن الرحيم

"In the name of Allah, the most Gracious, the most Merciful"

The <u>Lies</u>

About

Muhammad

The <u>Lies</u>

About

Muhammad

**An Answer to the Robert Spencer book
"The Truth About Muhammad"**

Moustafa Zayed

Table of Contents

Chapter Seven (169)

Chapter Eight (213)

Chapter Nine (262)

Chapter Ten (330)

Index of Answers to Allegations (390)

This book is about the truth, the truth that always enlightens and guides to the straight path.

If this book does so for you, please thank Allah, the one mighty God, for the woman who I owe everything to: My late mother who had always been the blessing of Allah upon me.

I dedicate this book to her.

I miss her greatly.

Moustafa Zayed

Appreciation

The author would like to express his deepest appreciation to:

Mr. El Sayed Maaty, senior translation reviser of the UN for his most valuable help editing this book.

M. Zayed, for her limitless support in every aspect of producing this book cover to cover.

May Allah give them the best reward of helping bring the truth of his religion and his prophet, and for helping me personally.

Moustafa Zayed

"Allah does not forbid you to deal justly and kindly with those who did not fight you for your religion and did not drive you out of your homes. Verily, Allah loves those who deal justly" [8]

"It is only in regards to those who fought you for your religion, have driven you out of your homes, and helped to drive you out, that Allah forbids you to take them as allies. And whoever takes them as Allies, then those are the oppressors" [9]

Holy Quran, Surat (Al Mumtahina) Ch (60), verses (8-9)

لَا يَنْهَاكُمُ اللَّهُ عَنِ الَّذِينَ لَمْ يُقَاتِلُوكُمْ فِي الدِّينِ وَلَمْ يُخْرِجُوكُمْ مِنْ دِيَارِكُمْ أَنْ تَبَرُّوهُمْ وَتُقْسِطُوا إِلَيْهِمْ ۚ إِنَّ اللَّهَ يُحِبُّ الْمُقْسِطِينَ (8)

إِنَّمَا يَنْهَاكُمُ اللَّهُ عَنِ الَّذِينَ قَاتَلُوكُمْ فِي الدِّينِ وَأَخْرَجُوكُمْ مِنْ دِيَارِكُمْ وَظَاهَرُوا عَلَىٰ إِخْرَاجِكُمْ أَنْ تَوَلَّوْهُمْ ۚ وَمَنْ يَتَوَلَّهُمْ فَأُولَٰئِكَ هُمُ الظَّالِمُونَ (9)

Why this book?

I could have gathered all the known fabrications and lies about Islam or Prophet Muhammad (PBUH) and answered them one after the other in an indexed way. Why choose the Robert Spencer book "The Truth About Muhammad" to answer and refute its claims and accusations, page by page and paragraph by paragraph?

I wanted to show how far the intentional fabrications against everything Muslim have gone, and in details of its process and how it is done.

I wanted to demonstrate how parts or full Holy Quran verses are omitted when their translations don't fit the author's Allegations, how only well-known fabrications and unreliable sources are used to support the most extreme of opinions, and worse, how sometimes zero evidence whatsoever is the basis of the weirdest of claims.

This is not some difference in opinions, tastes, or clash of cultures, but deliberate fabrications, relying mostly upon well- known untrue stories and a myriad of the weirdest illogical conclusions.

It is all, however, means to an end. How convenient it is to fabricate the weakest connection between a minority I hate and some horrible crime, and then provoke the court of public opinion to execute that minority for me!

By reading what Mr. Spencer is ringing the alarming bells for, you would think that the Iraqis had already occupied Miami, Afghanistan is wreaking havoc in California, while the Palestinian war machinery is crushing the bones of the poor children of Poland and Germany!
My contention here is not that Mr. Spencer is an incapable writer, quite the contrary, he is, and I might add, he is very creative as well! Only I question if he is an advertiser who doesn't care how defectively dangerous the product he is fiercely marketing to people is, since it may be a lucrative piece of business to him.

But as a proud Muslim American myself, this defective product is not some bad-tasting brand of gum, but the same propaganda of the fascist anti-anything-Muslim, and hate-mongering that set up my American people to have our treasury pillaged for trillions of dollars

14

paying for a fictitious war against a country that had done nothing to us; a war that is still going with hundreds of thousands of innocent civilian victims most of which are Muslims. This is hate mongering that puts America on a clash course with one quarter of the population of the planet.

Today it is the Muslims, tomorrow it will be the Chinese, the day after tomorrow it will be the World War fought with just sticks!

All along we were paying by the trillions, are paying the trillions, and if not awakened, will still be paying the trillions.

Find out for yourself why it is done, how it is done... just once!

Moustafa Zayed

Preface

Whoever you are, I am inviting you to tap into your common sense and to be just and fair, as simple as that. Fairness is crucial, because the task at hand is to uncover if Robert Spencer, as a leading representative of the "let's hate anything Muslim" tide, is truthful, objective, and unbiased, or the total opposite.

If I have 100 dollars in cash and 40 in debts, and you asked about my financial well being, and someone answered, "He owes 40 dollars," then he certainly misled you even though he has stated a fact.

However, if I owe not one penny and someone claims repeatedly that I have nothing but debts, then our subject case gets in the absurdity mode. I don't want to ruin your conclusions, but to sum up Robert Spencer's claims about Islam in one simple analogy:
"Shaquille O'Neal is such a poor, short, white guy!"

In a religion where the last Prophet of God (PBUH) set the condition for believers to enter paradise to:
"**Spread peace amongst yourselves,**" our author, with laughable logic, statements conjured up out of thin air, and questionable sources, can see nothing but hatred and violence in Islam.

The same last Prophet of God, who did the greatest act of mercy in the history of mankind by forgiving the entire city of Mecca including the Pagans and their leaders who killed, tortured and starved his companions while relentlessly conspiring to kill him.

The same Prophet who would kneel down to tilt a pot of water till a cat finished drinking, and forbade his followers to have stand-still conversations while imposing their weights on the backs of their horses.

The same Prophet of God who invited the local Christians to perform their prayers inside his Mosque and guaranteed the repairing of their churches out of the Muslim's treasury, is the same Prophet Mr. Spencer described by his book subtitled "Founder of the world's most intolerant religion"!

But when we will refute the author's claims; we will not do that by just stating our opinion, since it is not about my individual ideology against his. We will bring evidence from the most reliable and accurate sources of the Prophet's quotation, Islamic history, and history in general. But most surely, in addition, we will even use basic logic to show the reader the absolute and known truths to the average Muslim that Mr. Spencer denies his readers. Yet, still not only our logic but that, and the testimony of some of the brightest thinkers in the history of the West as well.

After Muslim scholars have founded the science of verifying testable evidence by which we know which quotations of the Prophet and his biography are doubtlessly correct and which ones are not, Mr. Spencer miraculously picks the well-known, fabricated ones out of Ibn Is'haq, and ignores the main 6 trusted references of the Prophet's quotations that cover the same incidents.

Mr. Spencer overwhelmingly uses Ibn Is'haq's biography of the Prophet, which is well known to contain all the stories he had heard about the Prophet - the correct and the fabricated ones without discrimination as per Ibn Is'haq himself - who admitted that "only Allah knows which one is correct."

Throughout his book, the author subtly divides humanity into an east and west. And while any bit of logic dictates that there is no monopoly on human decency by any race, religion, or nation on earth, you will constantly get the notion that the east - represented by Islam and Muslims (in the eye of the author) - is guilty till never proven innocent, to the limit that sometimes he makes the east guilty of incidents that were historically, mainly committed in what he collectively calls "the west." So be aware and beware.

Throughout the book Mr. Spencer uses old techniques that are effective sometimes with simple minded and half ignorant people. One simply states a few, undeniable facts, then out of nowhere slips you an absurd assumption that has no relation to truth, logic or sometimes even the subject at hand, and then quickly moves to the next paragraph!

This is the street, this is a car, this is a building, and this is the flying, blue elephant!

You will read in Mr. Spencer's book some baffling terminologies. Two examples:

The first is, whenever the subject is about Islamic, Arab or Middle Eastern documented and authentic history, the author will never call it history, and rather he calls it "traditions"! And while the term "Christian tradition" is not one that Mr. Spencer had invented himself, yet manufacturing or reflecting what that term entails upon Islam is anything but being truthfully objective. Muslim scholars who founded the process of verifying testable evidence of the companions who lived the events by the minute and quoted Prophet Muhammad (PBUH)'s sayings and life with astounding accuracy, in the author's perspective, could never have been trusted with their own history! It has to be the account of somebody else who agrees with what the author wants it to be; otherwise it is all old tales that, over time became "traditions"!

Within the context of Islam, the word tradition is tricky when translated. A core fundamental belief in Islam is the belief in the Holy Quran and the tradition of the Prophet (PBUH) as a perfect human example of how we should live our lives. What the Prophet (PBUH) has ordered Muslims to do becomes an order as respected and followed as an order in the Holy Quran itself.

How the Prophet did things also becomes a preference and a reference to Muslims in the similar situation. The word "Sunnah" translated here to "tradition" is strictly the tradition of the Prophetic orders and behavior, and absolutely cannot be confused with the common meaning of an Egyptian, American or any historical or cultural tradition for that matter, yet that is the confusing technique the author uses almost every time he uses the word "traditions" with Islam.

The second example is certain categorizations of Muslims with expressions manufactured by some in the media that have no translation or even comparison in the Arabic language or in Islam! A glaring example is **"Jihadist,"** which is another made up flavor of what the

18

media used to call the "Mujahideen" in Afghanistan when they were supported by the CIA to freedom fight the Russian occupation in the 1980s. Jihadist should be the translation of an Arabic word pronounced "Jihady," only there is no such a word in either Arabic or Islam - this is a word you read over a hundred times in his book - Jihadist!

What is Jihad in Islam?

Jihad in Arabic means to strive: in Islam, that is striving for the sake of God. It has many forms. Jihad can be done with your money, knowledge, or power, and in the case of war, with fighting in your nation's army for the sake of God, not Halliburton.

"To believe in Allah and his messenger, and to make Jihad for the sake of Allah with your monies and your own selves"
Holy Quran, Surat (Al Saff) Ch. (61) No (11)

"الساعي على الأرملة والمسكين ، كالمجاهد في سبيل الله ، أو القائم الليل والصائم النهار"

"The sponsor of a widow or a needy person, is like the one making Jihad for the sake of God, or Praying at night, and fasting at day"
(Prophet Muhammad (PBUH))
*Narrator: Abou Hurayra. **Reference**: Saheeh Al Bukhary, **Number**: 5353.*
***Degree**: Correct.*

أن جاهمة جاء على النبي صلى الله عليه وسلم ، فقال : يا رسول الله ! أردت أن أغزو ، وقد جئت أستشيرك ؟ فقال : هل لك من أم . قال : نعم ، قال : فالزمها فإن الجنة تحت رجليها

When a young man (Jahema) wanted to join the Muslim army, the Prophet asked him if his mother was alive; when the young man said yes, the Prophet ordered him:

"Go and keep her company, for paradise is underneath her feet"
i.e. serving his mother supersedes joining the army.
*Narrator: Moawea Ibn Jahema Alsalmy. **Reference**: Al Albany of Saheeh Alnasaye, **Number**: 3104. **Degree**: Correct/Good.*

19

Yet, the only kind of Jihad Mr. Spencer dedicates himself to, is the military kind, which in Islam is almost equivalent to military draft in America. When the Muslim nation is under attack or a population is oppressed, in danger, or prohibited from receiving the message of God when they don't have the freedom to decide for themselves, it becomes a religious obligation to all men able to fight to join the Army. What did I just say? Is there such a thing as an American man called "drafty," describing his ability to be drafted to the army? No. The same applies in Arabic and Islam.

Historical facts:

1- In all the battles that the Prophet fought, two offerings of peace were given ample time before battle, and when it was rejected, the Prophet and his army would fight man to man, even when they were severely outnumbered (which occurred most of the time). Ahead of anyone else, the Prophet was always in the front line of battle, sacrificing himself for the sake of God and the righteous cause of stopping oppression. Army to army, face to face, and in broad daylight:

"Then fight (Muhammad (PBUH)) in the Cause of Allah, none is tasked except for yourself, and incite the believers to fight along with you, so it may be that Allah will stop the evil might of the infidels. And Allah is Stronger in Might and Stronger in punishing"
Holy Quran, Surat (Al Nissa) Ch (4) No (84)

فَقَاتِلْ فِي سَبِيلِ اللَّهِ لَا تُكَلَّفُ إِلَّا نَفْسَكَ ۚ وَحَرِّضِ الْمُؤْمِنِينَ ۖ عَسَى اللَّهُ أَنْ يَكُفَّ بَأْسَ الَّذِينَ كَفَرُوا ۚ وَاللَّهُ أَشَدُّ بَأْسًا وَأَشَدُّ تَنْكِيلًا (84

2- No call for Jihad or fighting was ever declared by any Muslim subgroup at the time of the Prophet or even under his approval. Jihad as per the Prophet of Islam and as per God doctrine in the Holy Quran is a call to the entire nation by the leader of the Muslim nation to a one army battle. **"And fight in the Way of Allah those who fight you, but do not transgress the limits. Truly, Allah does not like the transgressors"**
Holy Quran Surat (Al Baqara) Ch (2), No (190)

(وَقَاتِلُوا فِي سَبِيلِ اللَّهِ الَّذِينَ يُقَاتِلُونَكُمْ وَلَا تَعْتَدُوا ۚ إِنَّ اللَّهَ لَا يُحِبُّ الْمُعْتَدِينَ (190

Having said that, what is the best kind of Jihad in Islam?

"The best Jihad is a word of truth to a tyrannical ruler"
(Prophet Muhammad (PBUH))
Narrator: Abou Aumama. **Reference:** *Saheeh Al jamee,* **Number:** *4954.*
Degree: *Correct.*

3-   Did anyone or any Muslim group ever violate the rule of Jihad and used it as an excuse to commit violence? Of course some did. Why? Because, people will always break the rules and commit crimes; don't humans do that anywhere anyhow mostly for made up excuses? Is it a crime in Islam? Yes. Why? Please refer back to No 1, 2 and 3.

In the same example you will constantly see the notion that the author supports real fascism-propaganda doctrines like: "Watch out they live amongst us", pre-emptive strikes, and oppressing people for their ideology, identity, race, ethnicity, or worse, their intentions that the author and his peers claim advance knowledge of. At the same time, he accuses his best friends - the "Jihadist warriors" of his imagination - of potentially wanting to do the same when they take over the west!

So is it that a brand of fascism is better than the other, or is it that the author and the agenda that he represents are desperately trying to terrify us of a scarecrow that can only be seen in their own mirrors?

Finally, I apologize for being sarcastic at times, but that is what screaming misinformation does to you!

ACCORDING TO ISLAM:

Islam means to surrender all matters to the One and only Mighty God (Allah).

Islam is the religion of Abraham, David, Moses, Jesus and all the Prophets and messengers of the one mighty God.

21

You are not a Muslim if you don't believe in all of God's Prophets.

Muhammad (PBUH), who is a descendant of Ismail son of Abraham, is the last Prophet of God (Allah) who brought the completed religion and the Word of God unaltered, as the last Prophet of God to mankind and the world.

The Holy Quran is the book of God that contains the text and Word of God that was "truly" given - to the letter - to all Prophets of God since Adam, Abraham, and all the way to Muhammad (PBUH) (PBU all of them).

The Holy Quran is the Prophethood miracle of Muhammad (PBUH).

In the Holy Quran the word Muhammad (PBUH) is mentioned 4 times.

The word Eissa (Jesus) (PBUH) is mentioned 25 times.

The word Moses (PBUH) is mentioned 131 times.

Pictures or illustrations of Muhammad (PBUH) and his first followers are forbidden; only following the message of God should be praised.

There are no holy men or high priests in Islam, only scholars respected for their knowledge of the book of God, tradition of Prophet Muhammad (PBUH), and Islamic law. Such knowledge is available for any Muslim to gain.

There are no middlemen between Muslims and God.

Jesus is a Prophet of God created by a Word of God and from His spirit.

Virgin Mary is the greatest woman that ever lived and will ever live; Read Holy Quran Chapter (19) (Maryam).

The biggest sin of Islam is Atheism or associating a partner with God.

The Five Pillars of Islam are:

*To certify that there is no God but Allah, and that Muhammad (PBUH) is his worshipper and messenger.

*Praying to God five times a day.

*Paying charity (Zakah) to the poor, which is 2.5% annually of unspent assets.

*Fasting daily for the holy month of Ramadan.

*Pilgrimage to Mecca once in your life if you are physically and financially sound.

People were created to worship God, in everything they do.

Life is a test where following the Word of God and Islamic law provides dignifying, safe, prosperous life, while preparing for the eternal afterlife. On Judgment day, if one's virtuous deeds outweigh his sins, he enters Heaven, and if vice versa, he will enter Hell fire.

Before Judgment day, Jesus (PBUH) will descend from Heaven, Kill the Anti-Christ, and spread peace on earth till God inherits the earth and what is on it.

Notes from Moustafa Zayed:

*We will copy the titles of Mr. Spencer's paragraphs as is.

* According to Islamic manners, "Peace be upon him" or (PBUH) is a phrase of respect to be mentioned after the name of Prophet Muhammad (PBUH) and all Prophets.

*Allah is the name of the One Mighty God of Abraham, Moses and Jesus (PBU all of them) in the Old Testament and according to the current New Testament.

*MZ refers to a comment by Moustafa Zayed.

* We added the "Index of Allegations" at the end of the book, so if you are looking for the refutal of a specific allegation, you can have a quick reference to the page that addresses that specific allegation. There are about 154 of them!

*Mr. Spencer never debated a true Muslim scholar; I invite him to a fair public debate anywhere, anytime, and about any topic of Islam.

*Finally, please borrow Mr. Spencer's book from the library and don't buy it, my hope is that none of us want to support fascism with book purchases.

Acknowledgment

The Seerah of Ibn Is'haq

Ibn Is'haq authored a biography of Prophet Muhammad (PBUH) that included the life of the Prophet before the beginning of his Prophethood, some of the Ignorance era before declaring his Prophethood, then (after his immigration to Mecca), his life in Medina, his battles, and his sent missions till his death (PBUH).

Ibn Is'haq's method of event chorography and narration is not completely clear, as his writings didn't reach us except through quoting him in the books of the scholars who came after him. The closest of which is "Tahzeeb Al Seerah" of Abdel Mlik Ibn Hesham. Please note that there is no such thing as a complete biography of Ibn Is'haq to begin with, but only the excerpts of later scholars who quoted some of it.

Ibn Hesham, however, stated that he purified the narrations of Ibn Is'haq by writing:
"...And I left some of what Ibn Is'haq had narrated that is not of the quotations of the Seerah of the Prophet of Allah (PBUH), that which the Holy Quran never mentions, that is no reason of this book, an interpretation of, or a witness to it"

Also Ibn Hesham stated that he: "also left what Imam Bukaey - his teacher of the correct quotations of the Prophet and his Seerah- didn't certify as correct "

In the Seerah (Biography of the Prophet) of Ibn Hesham, he quotes Ibn Is'haq at times, and sometimes he quotes himself.

Ibn Is'haq's method was based on narrating the events the way they reached him, whether with proofs, weak proofs or no proofs at all. He, for example, relied upon unknown sources; in some instances he would say: "Some people with knowledge told me" or "Some people in

25

Mecca told me." About some of his narrations, he would describe his sources by "As they claimed" or "As they remembered".

In many of his narrations, when he didn't know whether the narration was true or a fabrication, he would say, "Only Allah is more knowledgeable about the truth of that." He also, when faced with several narrations of the same incident, would mix the related proofs of which narrators - if any - all together without discriminating which one of them is the narrator for which quotation.

Ibn Is'haq was like a man who gathered every dollar he found: the real money and the counterfeit. Then later, others came with mechanisms that filtered his real dollars from the fake. Mr. Spencer ignores all the real dollars and looks almost exclusively inside Ibn Is'haq's bag and picks only the counterfeit ones!

"He was Caesar and Pope in one, but he was Pope without the Pope's pretentions, and Caesar without the Legions of Caesar: without a standing army, without a bodyguard, without a palace, without a fixed revenue; if ever any man had the right say that he ruled by the right Divine, it was Mohammad, for he had all the powers without its instruments and without its supports."

R. Bosworth Smith, "Mohammad and Mohammadanism", London 1874

Chapter One

"Why a biography of Muhammad is relevant today"

On page one, the author wrote:
"Islamic law, (which includes death penalty for Christian converts)..."

*First of all, Christians were an absolute minority in Arabia at the time of the Prophet (PBUH). All notions that Islam was there to appease Christians, attack them, or specifically target Christians whether positively or negatively, are just not true.
Tolerance is the overriding principal of Islamic law in dealing with non-Muslims, and again, Christians were an absolute minority in Arabia.

The author tries to constantly make it a Muslim VS. Christian case to imply falsely that anything Muslim is automatically and violently anti-Christian, which is not only wrong but the absolute opposite of the truth.

<u>Historical facts:</u>
1) The first scholar of any religion to identify Prophet Muhammad (PBUH) as a Prophet of God (Allah) was the Christian scholar Warqa Ibn Nawfal, who was a member of Khadija's family (the Prophet (PBUH)'s wife).

2) Under the author's own Chronology on page (XI) and on the year 615, he wrote:
"Friction with the Quraysh causes Muslims to leave Arabia for Abyssinia."

*The author fails to mention that of all places to flee to from the oppression of the pagans of Mecca; Muhammad (PBUH) ordered his followers to go there for it was ruled by, "**A righteous Christian king**."

3) In the tenth year of Hijra, the Prophet, as the most powerful man in the Arab Peninsula at the time, received the Christians of Najran in his Mosque. There, he allowed them to perform their prayers and pledged to give them the rights that Muslims had, and even promised to repair their old churches out of the Muslim treasury. The cost wouldn't even be considered a debt upon the Christians! This tolerance and civility in the seventh century is unheard of, even according to today's standards. Was it just an isolated incident, for it was the Prophet himself, or was this Islamic law in general?

"May Allah keep the rule of the Turks forever...they take the Jizyah tax and they never interfere with religions whether their people are Christians, Jews or Samarians, but the Cursed Polish are never content with the taxes and fees from their brethren in Christ, even though they serve them willingly, yet they put them under the authority of the unjust Jews, the enemies of Christ, who never allow them to build churches or leave them priests who know the secrets of their religion." *Makarius, the Patriarch of Antakya, (14th century).*

This telling quote not only shows the inherent tolerance in Islam of all non-Muslims, but also indicates the level of prejudice against Jews at the time in non-Muslim lands.

4) For those who do not know that Islamic law never mandated killing Christian converts or even any other converts for their religion, race, gender or ethnic background, let us examine the following:

If being a Muslim means automatically that you are anti-Christian, how is it that Islam is the only non - Christian faith that believes in the immaculate birth of Jesus (PBUH) and Virgin Mary, glorifies and testifies for them (PBU both of them)?
How is it that the Muslims' Holy Quran is the only Holy Scripture in the world (including any Gospel you may have), that has an entire chapter named after Virgin Mary, glorifying and describing her as the greatest woman that ever lived and will ever live?
Read Holy Quran, Surat "Maryam" (Ch. 19), and "Al Omran" (Ch. 3)

How is it, according to Islamic law, that if you do not believe in all God's prophets, Jesus (PBUH), or in his original Gospel, you cannot be a Muslim?

On page four and after the author quoted two modern Muslim scholars about the merciful and forgiving nature of the Prophet (PBUH), he quotes one of them:
"Islamic traditions include a number of instances of the Prophet having the opportunity to strike back at those who attacked him, but refraining from doing so." - Ibrahim Hooper of CAIR

Yet the author then wrote:
"But the international riots and murders committed over these cartoons - universally explained by the perpetrators as revenge for the alleged insult on Muhammad - suggested that Hooper's view was by no means universally accepted by Muslims."

*Is it logical that isolated incidents can be considered a universally accepted tendency of the 1.6 billion (and growing) Muslims? Hundreds of thousands of drivers drive through red lights, endangering themselves and the public every year. Does that mean that Americans universally do not accept or adhere to traffic laws? And even if all Muslims are hypothetically outraged about a dirty attack against humanity's last Prophet of God, what is the relation between that and "the truth about Muhammad " himself?

On pages 4, 5 and 6, the author quotes individuals representing outlawed organizations that some characterize as terrorist and others as freedom fighter. Such organizations, regardless, have no scholarly status of any respectable weight in Islam, or Islamic jurisprudence (Fiqh). You want to research the American constitution, then read it or quote it for us. You want to learn about who Thomas Jefferson really was, then read an authentic biography of his, or at least read what the man historically had done, said or authored. But then why would you go and quote someone who could possibly be a Charles Manson, to tell us who Jefferson "truly" was?

I can only perceive, if you do so, that demonizing or at least altering the truth about Jefferson is your ulterior motive.

On pages 6, 7, 8, 9 and 10, the author makes several illogical and historically untruthful assumptions:

1-That Quranic texts, since they are in Arabic, are not understood by Muslims even if they were translated to their native language from Arabic, and asserts that it is similar to the difficulty of a King James Bible translation!

2- That there is a raging intellectual battle between peaceful Muslims and what he calls Jihadist terrorists about a somewhat mystical historical Muhammad who is yet to be clearly fully discovered, and that the outcome of such an imaginary battle will be determined by discovering who he really was!

*Historical facts:

1- Prophet Muhammad (PBUH) is not only the most quoted man in history, but also the most accurately biographed man in history.
   Is the author looking for where the sun has been historically shining every day, as well?
2- Except for a few letters in the beginning of some chapters in the Holy Quran, (their meaning has not been revealed yet) almost every verse in the Holy Quran is either understood or interpreted by the companions of the Prophet (PBUH) and later Muslim scholars.
3- Some of the verses that have multiple meanings are mainly the ones that describe pure scientific phenomena of God creations. For example, the verses about the phases of the human embryo were not fully understood till the invention of electronic microscopes; then, it became one of the most glaring scientific miracles of the Holy Quran, as per how accurately God had described a fetus's stages of growth 1400 years ago.
   Read Holy Quran- Al Mouminoun (The believers) Ch. (23) No (12-14)

So if the author is trying to discover a mystical historical Muhammad (PBUH) 1400 years after his prophecy had begun, contradicting the

31

ocean of continuous certain knowledge about him, then he could only be looking for another Muhammad other than Muhammad (PBUH) the Prophet of Islam, or just attempting to alter the "truth" about the Prophet and the fundamentals of the religion of 1.6 billion Muslims all together.

On Page 13, the author states:
"Criticism of Muhammad or even Islam is not and should not be considered equivalent to anti- Semitism. Islam is not a race."

*First of all, technically an Anti- Semite is one who hates Arabs, for they are the largest Semite race on earth - pushing 400 million- vs. their genetic cousins, the other group of Semites, - between 15 to 17 millions- the Jews. As a matter of fact the number of Muslim men who carry the names of Jewish Prophets - in Islam they are Prophets of God, Islam, and are respected as Muhammad (PBUH) himself (PBU all of them) - are more than four times the entire Jewish population in the world! It is interesting however, that Semite as a term, was originally for the language itself and not for people, i.e. an Anti-Semite should be someone who hates Hebrew as a language!

As we explained in the preface, while the author apparently is against anti- Semitism, he runs to affirm that attacking Islam or the Prophet of 1.6 billion Muslims cannot be compared to attacking Judaism or a highly revered figure of the Jews. So our champion of civil rights here indicates that religious profiling and discrimination is somewhat acceptable compared to racial discrimination, in the matter fact may be preferred in the eyes of Mr. Spencer if you just have the excuse of a tendency to hate Islam and Muslims.

So if you can create any excuse for your hate, is it acceptable?
What is the stark difference then, if there is any, between Mr. Spencer and his self-proclaimed "Jihadist" fascist terrorists?!

The author then asserts that the teachings of Prophet Muhammad (PBUH) must be ones that persuade his followers to commit violence, because - he throws the names of his Jihad terrorists - these people or organizations use the name and the teachings of Muhammad (PBUH) as their excuses for their actions.

So if the teachings of Muhammad (PBUH) are "truly" as such, why not show them to us, translate them correctly and within the correct historical context, so we can see for ourselves?

If Mr. Spencer is a hate mongering, oppressive fascist - hypothetically speaking - and he misuses the tenets of the American constitution of civil rights and freedom of speech to further his evil causes, would that be the fault of George Washington, Thomas Jefferson, the constitution, or the entire American population?

On the same page 13, about the Danish cartoons controversy, the author wrote:

"The Danish cartoons controversy indicated the gulf between the Islamic world and the post-Christian west on matters of freedom of speech and expression"

*I believe what really alarmed the author is the unity in the outcry of the Muslim world against ridiculing the last Prophet of God (PBUH). The author definitely has the right to wonder why the Muslims reaction wasn't like that in the west when Jesus (PBUH) is depicted sometimes in the most offensive of ways. But he is absolutely wrong when he indirectly expects that Muslims should blindly adapt to the habits of others as a beacon of light or a reference and guidance as to how to evaluate right from wrong, especially when it comes to their Prophet of God.

If the author himself would slander or libel any one of 300 million Americans, he would be subjecting himself to be sued for hefty damages. But when you know that the ultimate symbol of righteousness and perfect manners for 1.6 billion people is Prophet Muhammad (PBUH) and still go ahead and offend them all by offending him, intentionally I might add, then why would you be surprised of the reaction? Personally I don't know which nation or group that can come to England for example and dictate to the English how to react as a nation to an unacceptable insult to the entire British population?

33

How would you then justify that you offend the Muslims, the Prophet of God, and then criticize the worldwide Islamic rejection to that insult while requesting that all Muslims should adhere to some other culture's behavioral model?

Had the cartoonists published similar offensive cartoons in any Muslim country attacking Jesus (PBUH), instead, they would have been prosecuted and jailed just the same as if it was an offense against Muhammad (PBUH) himself...

And while we are at the subject: **You will never find one book, article or word about Jesus (PBUH) in any Muslim country, but of praise and reverence, for he is a mighty Prophet of God and of Islam. You will never find one similar book to Mr. Spencer's like the one we are refuting, attacking Jesus (PBUH) or any Prophet of God in any Muslim country.**

What you will also never find is Mr. Spencer mentioning this glaring and absolutely relevant fact anywhere in his "truth" finding campaign of "Let the Christian west hate anything Muslim" crusade.

In the "real" decency of Islamic law, there are limits to some things, because not everything is unlimited. Structural pillars of societies are not to be tampered or joked with. You can live in the building of society, do whatever you want in your privacy, walk on your hands in the lobby to your apartment if you want, but when you are seen sledge hammering one of the pillars that support the entire building, then it is everyone's duty to stop you. Even from a pure secular stand point, the universally collective moral opinion of the Muslim world is that such cartoons were an outrage, what more freedom of speech or expression you could want from them if freedom of expression is really what you are for?

Marching in the streets, however, causing material damage to others who didn't draw any cartoons or personally offend the Prophet, and certainly the horrible crime of causing death to the innocent, are against all fundamental laws and manners of Islam. And while these incidents are not acceptable by Islam or the Prophet himself had he been alive at the time, humans of any race anywhere, at moments of anger, will always take things to extremes. The most Islamic reaction to the cartoons in my opinion was that some Muslims boycotted every company whose products were advertised on any media that published the cartoons, which is what I call the civil freedom that all people should be aware of: the freedom of voting with your dollar.

Some Muslims used it most effectively.

Finally, to whoever describes the dirty cartoons as a part of the civility of freedom of speech, I remind them with the fact that only animals leave their droppings and filth openly anywhere.

"Death to blasphemy"

On page 14, the author mentions the murders of multiple individuals who, by the author's own admission, offended and intended insults to Islam and Muslims in Holland.

I am sure that the reader has guessed by now that a main theme of the author demonizing Muslims is imposing on Islam and all Muslims the guilt of any crime committed by the absolute few for whatever reason, with the excuse that the criminal is a Muslim who claims he did it in or for the name of Islam.

It is really baffling. People everywhere with any ethnic, religious, economic background commit the most horrible of crimes every second and sometimes for the most stupid and bizarre of reasons, yet when the killer is a Muslim committing the crime of taking a soul without justice, which the author knows is punishable in Islamic law by death, the author would run and cry, "see, he is a Muslim." Yes, he is. And if it is a crime, then he is a Muslim criminal, like there is a Jewish criminal, a Hindu criminal, an Argentinean criminal and a hate-mongering criminal!

What fascinates me is the only group in the world that believes blindly in the laughable notion that "the criminals and killers always tell the truth", and constantly quote them is Muslim-haters!

Mr. Spencer will not stop day or night quoting the committers of the most horrible of crimes, impose their insanity sometimes as a unique ideology, then paint the entire religion of Islam and its billion and a half followers with the same brush! Should I count how many serial killers all over the world killed thousands of innocent souls for no reason whatsoever, and then claimed that God ordered them to do so?

Did you hear Muslims call them Christian, Jew or atheist fascists, or even a crime of religion?

"Defending freedom of speech"

Reading page 15 and 16, it was hard to contain myself from grinning when the author wrote:

"…And it is not my intention to insult Muhammad, to deride him, to lampoon or mock him, or to write anything except a scrupulously accurate account of what he said and did about some key issues."

*Such a quest has also been a personal endeavor all my life. The only difficulty I faced personally is the shear greatness of the amount of material about the life of the great Prophet of God (PBUH) for as we mentioned earlier, he is not only the most quoted man in history but also the most accurately quoted and biographed.

So if this is the same task the author takes, then one of us is in for a major surprise, for one of us is seriously wrong, and my contention is that he already knows it!

"General notes"

On page 16, the author makes the most bizarre statement I heard in a long time (and I have heard a lot). He wrote:

"Holy Quranic verse numeration is not standard"!!

*What?! For 1400 years not one verse number of any verse of the Holy Quran has ever changed from the exact way that it was revealed to Prophet Muhammad (PBUH) by arch-Angel Gabriel before his passing, and the author is now quoting us from a Holy Quran translation that has "different numbers"?

"Excuse me for I will intentionally confuse you and alter the truth going forward", is all I understood from what the author wrote.

"The eastern churches in Asia were already separated from the rest of the Christian world which was not to support them in any way considering them heretics of the religion. Therefore the sheer existence of these churches today is in itself a strong evidence of the general tolerance of Islamic governments towards them"

Sir Thomas Walker Arnold, the most prominent orientalist in history

Chapter Two

On page 20, the author wrote:
"The Holy Quran is, according to Islamic tradition, a perfect copy of an eternal book- the umm al-kitab or mother of the book – that has existed forever with Allah"

*Before we answer, I want to remind the reader again that there is no such a thing as "Islamic tradition" there is the "Prophet's tradition". The author's statement is not true, for "Umm al-kitab" was never the name of the Holy Quran but a name of the first chapter of the Holy Quran known by "Al-Fatiha" or "The Opening." The name the author needed to know for the eternal copy of the Holy Quran is "Al-Lauh Al-Mahfooz" which means "The protected tablet."

Later on page 20, the author indicates that in chapter 48: verse 27 (Al-Fateh) he has made a discovery! Which is:
"(while it is an undeniable fact of Islam that every word in the Holy Quran is a Word of God to all Muslims): how is it that God then says "In Shaa Allah" which means God willing?"

*The answer is that it is obvious that Mr. Spencer either didn't read the entire Holy Quran, or believes his readers never did, because what he thinks is a discovery is all over the Holy Quran in many ways, where God speaks about himself as, "Allah", "your God", and "he is the most merciful," "powerful," "able," "all-knower", and more. It is a feature of God's revelation of referring to himself as an infinite entity, in plural for praise in many cases, and repeated throughout the Holy Quran often, even in a form like "he who created for you…"
I urge Mr. Spencer to read more than just one verse or chapter of the Holy Quran, or at least assume that we did!

On pages 20 to 24, the author criticizes the narrative of the Holy Quran that it is not self explaining of some of the verses, and criticizes having to depend on the historical tradition of the quotations of the Prophet (PBUH) and historical statements of his companions.

*If the Holy Quran was the current Bible, for example where most of its chapters were written sometimes a hundred years after the incidents covered, and in the form of stories about Jesus (PBUH) and Biblical Prophets, then some verses of the Holy Quran may need some self explanation to fit into such format. But the Holy Quran was memorized verbatim as it was revealed by Arch-Angel Gabriel to the Prophet (PBUH), then kept to date the same exact way.

For example when someone today says, "The damage that Katrina caused was devastating," we would all, today, know exactly what he is talking about. The most important thing for humanity - 1400 years from now - is if the speaker was God himself then what he had said should stay exactly the same to the letter. People later then, however, can refer to authentic historical sources to learn the historical context of what happened when Katrina hit. The Word of God that is the Holy Quran, was never altered, changed, and still is in its original language, but most importantly, this is how God said it and how he forever wants it kept and given to mankind. At the same time, there is no disconnection between the historical contexts of the verses, the occasions of revealing them, and an ocean of "uninterrupted" authentic historical context about them.

Then, the author takes an example with Surat (Al-Tahreem) Ch. (66) which covers an incident between the Prophet and his wives.

*Here is what really happened. The Prophet (PBUH) was the kindest to his wives, and it was he (PBUH) who said:
"Your best, are your best to their women" i.e. their mothers, wives, daughters and sisters.
Narrator: Abu Hurayra. **Reference:** *Al Tarmazy,* **Number:** *1162.* **Degree:** *Correct/Good.*

39

The Prophet's wife Hafsa once got jealous that he brought another wife into her house in a day that he specified earlier for her. In caring for Hafsa's feelings, the Prophet swore not to come near the other wife (Mariyah the Copt,) and in caring for the effect of that oath on Mariyah, the Prophet (PBUH) asked Hafsa not to tell anyone about his oath, but she went ahead and told his wife (Ayesha). Before we get into the verses of the Holy Quran revealed for this specific incident, we need to know that Allah made it so that the Prophet in certain situations be corrected and advised about certain matters, to give us a practical human example of matters we need to pay attention to, be affirmed about, or make them specifically clear to mankind. One of these instances is when Allah revealed to Muhammad (PBUH) that to care for the feelings of one wife cannot be at the expense of the "Halal" or the lawful right that Allah had given another wife upon the Prophet (PBUH). Allah revealed to the Prophet that Hafsa didn't keep her promise to the Prophet and told Ayesha. In addition, Allah showed in the following verse to the Prophet and all of us that when you take an oath - breaking an oath is a major sin in Islam-, then later you discover that that oath would entail disobeying God or oppressing someone's right, then in obedience to Allah you can break that oath, by paying for feeding 10 needy persons as expiation. The following Verse promised the wives of the Prophet that if they make more materialistic demands on the Prophet and burden him, then Allah can exchange them for better wives in everything.

Here is what Mr. Spencer wrote about the incident:

"In this scenario the revelation of Sura 66 concerns only his wives jealousy (or perhaps Muhammad's bad breath) and his oath to stop drinking honey"

I have no further comment!

"Hadith"

On page 24, the author defines Hadith - pronounced correctly as "Hadeeth" - as "traditions of the Prophet" (PBUH), which is not true. Hadeeth is the collected sayings or quotations of the Prophet (PBUH) and the narrations of events that show his behavior. The tradition of the

Prophet (PBUH) is "Sunnah" or the behavioral example of his biography including his sayings, of which the majority of Muslims are described as (Sunni) or followers of the traditions of the Prophet (PBUH).

On page 25, the author quotes the Muslim scholar Ahmed Von Denffer - a German Muslim – that:
"there is an agreement between Muslim scholars that the contents of Sunnah are also from Allah".

*Which is not true also. Parts of the Sunnah are from Allah, especially the worshipping details and the correct quotations of the Prophet (PBUH). In the Holy Quran, Allah says:

"..And whatever the Messenger gives you, take it, and whatever he forbids you, abstain from it.."
Holy Quran, Surat (Al Hasher) Ch. (59) No (7)

(7) ... ۚ وَمَا آتَاكُمُ الرَّسُولُ فَخُذُوهُ وَمَا نَهَاكُمْ عَنْهُ فَانْتَهُوا

So Islamic law is derived from both sources, only when it comes to the Sunnah, it is only the sections where the Prophet ordered or asked us to do or not to do things, either verbally, by gesture or even by just not opposing an issue. For that matter if the Hadeeth is correct and authenticated, then Allah tells us in the Holy Quran:

"And he doesn't utter of self desire"
Holy Quran, Surat (Al Najm) Ch. (53) No (3)

(3) وَمَا يَنْطِقُ عَنِ الْهَوَىٰ

Having said that, there are many parts of the Seerah (Biography of the Prophet) and the tradition of the Prophet that are not parts of the Sunnah of the (Halal and Haram) or what is allowed and what is forbidden; an example is the personal preferences of the Prophet (PBUH) in certain foods, clothes, travelling routes to take vs. others, etc. which the Prophet (PBUH) himself did, but never ordered Muslims to do or not to do.

41

The author then continues to an absurd fabrication, when he claims in the next paragraph that in the huge amount of information about the Prophet (PBUH), there is no way to know what is correct and what is not!!

*Really!!

Imam Al Bukhary, the author of the legendary reference "Saheeh al Bukhary" of the correct Hadeeth (quotations of the Prophet), had memorized over 300,000 Hadeeths of the Prophet with the chain of who said the Hadeeth last till who heard it from the Prophet himself first.

He identified 60,000 correct Hadeeth that he certified were correct, then used the most ingenious and rigorous way of authenticating a historical quote by researching and memorizing the detailed biographies of 2500 companions and followers of the Prophet. He even travelled to their towns, so when someone says that a person heard the quotation from another, he would filter it to their credibility, the possibility of the two individuals meeting each other in person, and chronically, all the way to how many other credible sources confirming the same text to the letter.

The same rigorous authentication - testable evidence - founded for the first time in history by Imam al Bukhary, was pursued by the great six Hadeeth scholars, Ahmed, Muslim, al Turmezy, Ibn Majah, al Nasaey, and Ibn Daoud, covering hundreds of thousands of Hadeeths and narrations of the Prophet's biography. The science of Hadeeth actually had come to the level that almost every Hadeeth of hundreds of thousands of Hadeeths are already rated by their levels of authenticity. The ratings are: 1) Correct, 2) Good, 3) Weak (may be correct but we have weak verification of it) and, 4) Fabricated, probably by the "truth-seekers" of its time!

Now - with all that accurate account of every word, event, even gesture of the Prophet, comes our truth-seeker Mr. Spencer, 1400 years later to tell us that it is impossible to tell what is authentic and what is not!

The author comments later about the six Hadeeth references that they are not authentic but that the "Muslims generally regard as trustworthy" as if the Muslims have no documented history, but strictly what they consider trustworthy tales of folklore!

On page 28, the author claims that:
"Many incidents in the Prophet's life, including ones that became influential in Islamic history, have no other sources"

*What are these mystical source-less incidents that were never heard by the hundreds of companions who narrated - as eye witnesses - hundreds of thousands of the quotations and biography of the Prophet (PBUH)? More importantly what "many incidents" as per the author statement, which were so influential in Islamic history that the Prophet (PBUH) never mentioned to any of his companions? Are they many and so influential that the Prophet (PBUH) never cared to mention to any companions so there are no sources for them?! How it is that Mr. Spencer is the only one who received a unique knowledge of these "hidden-sources incidents from the others for 1400 years"? Is this even logical to a five year old, in seeking the "truth about Muhammad"?

On page 30, after the author had quickly mentioned earlier the actually most used book of Seerah (Biography) of the Prophet (PBUH) which is Seeraht Ibn Hisham, he goes back and forth about how the stories of Seerat Ibn Is'haq were criticized by early Muslim scholars, and then desperately names people like a current Pakistani army general, to validate Seerat Ibn Is'haq for us!

The author then decides to rely first on the unreliable Ibn Is'haq account, then relies last upon the most trusted sources of the Seerah and tradition of the Prophet (PBUH) which are the two Hadeeth books of Al Bukhary and Muslim, but also instead decides to rely upon Martin Ling's biography of the Prophet (PBUH) which is in many ways a good translation. But as true Muslim scholars know, it has also many grave errors about other incident, or maybe that is why Mr. Spencer has chosen it?

"Historical fact and Muslim belief"

On page 30, the author, on his own, jumps without any reasoning or historical fact to the little irrelevant conclusion that:
"Historical certainty is not easy to ascertain with a text as sketchy as the Holy Quran, as overwhelmed with false information as the Hadeeth"!!

* Holy Quran is the only Word of God that is still in its original language, not altered and not changed for over 1400 years with one copy in the hands of 1.6 billion people. The memorization of the correct Hadeeth of the Prophet was never interrupted for one day nor skipped generations like other scriptures, and to date, is all categorized into an accurate account of what is fabricated, what is accepted, what is good, and what is absolutely authentic. Yet the author can see nothing but sketchiness and false information!

Actually, I challenge Mr. Spencer to find me one man in history that is accurately quoted and biographed word for word in over 40 volumes just between the two references of Al Bukhary and Muslim alone. They are absolutely authentic, even by the admission of the author himself. The real truth is that the man Mr. Spencer claims of portraying the truth about, is already the most quoted and accurately biographed in history: The truth about Prophet Muhammad's every aspect of his life is a glaring sun and second to none.

On page 31, the author claims that there are some indications in Islamic History that the Holy Quran was altered!

* Remember the author claims that the "alterations" are many, and if that is true, in such a crucially important topic, it might crumple the foundation of Islam, yet he comes up with one laughable account with a comment of some early Muslim scholar that the Holy Quran - which contains many amazingly accurate predictions of future scientific discoveries - had a verse that spoke of the statement of Muslim Martyrs, in paradise, who were satisfied by their reward as God was pleased with

44

their righteous deeds! Posing the question that Judgment day didn't happen yet, so how can such a statement be made?

Again, Mr. Spencer does nothing but tell us either that he never read the Holy Quran, or he is just hoping that he writes for people who never read it just the same!

The Holy Quran even has dialogues between Believers and infidels on Judgment day about the joy and disappointment between the two parties; accurate description of Paradise and hell fire in the day that never happened yet. Do I need to remind that Allah, who has no limitations of time, distance or anything against His will, is the One whose word is the Holy Quran's? So when he describes to us what will happen in the future of his rewards to the righteous, through the words of his satisfied believers in paradise, in the author's words, that will be an indication that his word is altered?! In the Holy Quran:

"The event (Judgment day) of Allah had already happened, so don't hasten it"

Holy Quran, Surat (Al Nahl) Ch. (16) No (1)

أَتَىٰ أَمْرُ اللَّهِ فَلَا تَسْتَعْجِلُوهُ ۚ سُبْحَانَهُ وَتَعَالَىٰ عَمَّا يُشْرِكُونَ (1)

If you look at the verse, the question begs that how has the event already happened, and yet Allah is asking us not to hasten it?

The answer is that the future of anything already had happened in the realm of the knowledge of Allah. It was already written in the "Al Kitab Al Mubeen" before even creation started billions of years ago.

Does Mr. Spencer think that God doesn't know what will happen in the future? And you call that supposition "historical"?!

The author later names some anti-Islam orientalists, and then states that their opinions differ sharply from "the received wisdom" of Muslim scholars of Hadeeth.

*Are Muslim scholars, who are most knowledgeable about their history and strict rules of its subject religion, wrong, because some known non-Muslim haters of Islam and their theories are sharply different than theirs?

Watch how the author describes absolute Islamic knowledge by "received wisdom" as if it is some mystical inherited cultural tales or rituals that people may utter or practice and receive from older generations as is without questioning. So if the scholars who are unparalleled historically in their genius and integrity are Muslims, then it is a fallible "received wisdom" and if the fabricators are Islam-hating orientalists, then they are trustworthy historians? And if there is - naturally - a sharp difference of opinions, then it is the Muslim scholars who are doubted!

Welcome to the roller coaster ride of Spencer land!

On pages 31 and 32; if you thought that the author started to totally lose it before, you thought wrong! In the last pages the author goes to the assumption (are you ready?) that Muhammad (PBUH) may not have even existed!!

And the reason is that some people - unnamed as usual - thought, supposed, and may have scratched their heads in wonder about the fact?!!

In his head scratching, star gazing pretend, Mr. Spencer innocently wonders if that "mythical" figure Muhammad (PBUH) was conjured up! Why then did the Muslims keep some embarrassing stories – according to what the author's whole book is about - and not just omit them if the whole account is made up?

The answer that begs to jump out of his own question is: because these stories are twists of a real event that Muslims carried, and memorized, uninterrupted, of the life of the Prophet for 1400 years, without "Spencering!"

It is worth mentioning, that not only that the knowledge of the Seerah and quotations of the Prophet are second to none in the history of mankind in their accuracy and abundance, but it is also an uninterrupted - not for one half a day - knowledge throughout history, where no one man or even one group had a monopoly on such knowledge that was available at all times for students of the religion to learn. That fact is Just an evidence of the mercy of God upon all of us, for there are no more Prophets to guide mankind after God's last Prophet Muhammad (PBUH).

"I have studied him, the wonderful man, and in my opinion far from being an Anti-Christ, he must be called the Savior of Humanity."

Sir George Bernard Shaw, in "The Genuine Islam," Vol. 1.

Chapter Three

On page 34, the author wrote:
"One of these Gods, "Allah," not yet identified with the lone God of Islam, may have been the tribal God of the Quraysh"

*In the Holy Quran Allah reveals what the idolaters of Mecca have said about the Idols they were worshipping:
"And we didn't worship them for anything but that they would get us closer to Allah".
Holy Quran, Surat (Al Zomar) Ch (39) verse (3)

وَالَّذِينَ اتَّخَذُوا مِنْ دُونِهِ أَوْلِيَاءَ مَا نَعْبُدُهُمْ إِلَّا لِيُقَرِّبُونَا إِلَى اللَّهِ زُلْفَىٰ ۚ (3)

So the Arabs before Islam knew Allah, only like many nations in the region before them, they modified the straight path to their Creator to yield to their desires or to the benefit of their powerful elite. In our case they used the excuse of trying to get closer to the one mighty God Allah by worshipping idols, which is what destroys the monotheistic core of worshipping God to begin with.
One of the glaring truths about all the Biblical Prophets is that they all worshiped the One Mighty Allah. The average western reader may automatically say I never heard of that name, and he mostly would be correct, only because, some don't have a vested interest in telling him the fact.

If we read throughout the Old Testament - not the Holy Quran - and ask the Torah scholars what was the name of God in the Old scriptures, they will tell you it is pronounced "Allah-aim".

"Aim" here is plural for praise; note that it is also the last part of the Father of Prophets name "Ibrah-aim" - Abraham - (PBUH) as pronounced in Hebrew. So what is the name of God in the Old

49

Testament? Allah.

Please notice the author's remark of "Lone God of Islam" as if Allah of Islam has nothing to do with Allah of the Bible.

In the New Testament Jesus (PBUH) on the cross cries (In Aramaic) **""Elohi, Elohi, lama sabachthani?"** or "My God, My God why have you forsaken me?"
Mark 15:34, Weymouth New Testament

Even though according to the Word of God in the Quran, Jesus (PBUH) was never killed nor crucified but was raised to heaven, the text shows clearly the word Allah as the name of God (when called to, it is pronounced "Elahi")

In addition to the fact of the majority of Prophets and messengers of God who passed through the Arab Peninsula, Egypt and Palestine, the author, with the whiff of a pen, decided on his own that the Arabs never heard of the name of God identified by all the Old Testament Prophets, which is Allah or "Allah-aim" and when the pagans of Quraysh said that we worship these idols to get us closer to "Allah", the author decides for them, the Prophets, and us, that Allah is not Allah!

To be fair here, this is an old biased orientalists' trick. So when the Muslims explain that the fundamental of their religion is that it is the same true religion of the Biblical Prophets, and that it is about worshipping the same One Mighty God Allah; God of Abraham (PBUH), the answer would say, that "Allah" is not 'Allah-aim" and that it is a new name of another God that belongs only to the Arabs!

On page 34, the author explains that Quraysh had a major influence on the tribes of Arabia so when they rejected Muhammad (PBUH)'s religion all tribes did the same, and when Quraysh accepted Islam they all followed"

*Another untruthful statement:
If that's the case, then which other tribe had another major influence upon Quraysh itself to influence it to accept Islam? What evidence at all

50

that may support that statement? The Muslim army was powerful enough that Quraysh surrendered without even attempting to raise one sword, so what other tribe that could have had a bigger army and influence than the Muslims had?

One of the major astounding achievements of the Prophet of God (PBUH) was his ability to bring people to worship their creator and fear him in dealing justly with their brothers in humanity.

A glaring example is the case of the two major tribes of Aous and Khazraj in Medina, who were ever battling each other to the most unthinkable of extents - in the next paragraph the author adds "Blood feuds were frequent"- but when the Prophet (PBUH) guided them to Islam, they not only stopped fighting each other, but united and became one tribe of one family of Islam, a story that was repeated all over the world. The author implies here that the entire Arab Peninsula's conversion to Islam was just a matter up to Quraysh's rejection or approval of the message of Islam, and not because of the Prophet's (PBUH) message or because of the tenets of Islam itself.

On page 36, the author brings a translation of the verse in Surat (Al Saff) - where Jesus (PBUH) says (his translation):
"I am the Messenger of Allah (sent) to you, confirming the law (which came) before me, and giving glad tidings of a messenger to come after me whose name shall be Ahmad"
Holy Quran Surat (Al Saff) Ch (61) verse (6)

*The translation is flawed and I might add intentionally so, for how is it that the translator would omit the entire sentence Jesus (PBUH) had actually said in the Holy Quran in the very same verse "**confirming what is between my hands of the Torah**"?

Here is the correct translation :
"**And Jesus, son of Maryam said: "O Children of Israel, I am the Messenger of Allah to you, confirming what is in between my hand of the Torah, and giving glad tidings of a Messenger to come after me, whose name shall be Ahmed.**

51

But when he (Muhammad (PBUH)) came to them with clear proofs, they said: "This is plain magic"
Holy Quran Surat (Al Saff) Ch (61) verse (6)

وَإِذْ قَالَ عِيسَى ابْنُ مَرْيَمَ يَا بَنِي إِسْرَائِيلَ إِنِّي رَسُولُ اللَّهِ إِلَيْكُم مُّصَدِّقًا لِّمَا بَيْنَ يَدَيَّ مِنَ التَّوْرَاةِ وَمُبَشِّرًا بِرَسُولٍ يَأْتِي مِن بَعْدِي اسْمُهُ أَحْمَدُ ۖ فَلَمَّا جَاءَهُم بِالْبَيِّنَاتِ قَالُوا هَٰذَا سِحْرٌ مُّبِينٌ (6)

Some would say that Mr. Spencer doesn't speak Arabic and it is the translator's fault; I would then ask, how is it that these horrible translators keep almost exclusively appearing in Mr. Spencer's books? Does he know only them for some reason?
Or is it because in our case here, it is in today's Bible that Jesus (PBUH) said :

"I am not sent but to the lost sheep of the house of Israel"
King James Bible, Mathew 15:24
Is it that the author doesn't like the same truth to resonate between parts of the Bible and the Holy Quran?

On page 37, the author writes about two separate incidents. The first is a warning from the Christian monk Buhaira to Muhammad (PBUH)'s Uncle Abu Talib, to protect him from the Jews and not tell them about his nephew, because they will do him harm. The second is a story about a Jew who has seen the seal of Prophethood between Muhammad (PBUH)'s shoulders - when he was a child - and cried that the last Prophet is not a Jew and that the new Holy Scripture will be taken from the Israelites. (The seal of Prophethood is a dark mark the size of a piece of grapes between the shoulders of the Prophet (PBUH)). Then oddly enough, the author adds that the Jew stated that Muhammad (PBUH) would fight the Jews and kill their scholars! Then the author adds from his history manufacturing facility that the Jewish man's statement is:

"A rather revealing statement as an early Muslim view of the Mission of Muhammad (PBUH)"!

52

*Was Buhaira a Jew-hater, or wrong for warning Abu Talib against the Jews knowing about Muhammad (PBUH) as the new Prophet of God?
Let's inspect that; what happened to the last Prophet before Muhammad (PBUH)?

A faction of the Jews believed in him and another faction rejected him. Then what happened later? Was he killed by Muslims? No, some of the Jews who rejected him - and Jesus (PBUH) was a Jew himself - conspired to kill him, and according to the overwhelming narrative of the Christianity of today, he was killed by these Jews! According to the Holy Quran he (PBUH) was raised to heaven and was never killed - So what do you think some other similar faction of the Jews, might do to an Arab, not even a Jew, who comes with the same message from God? Send him flowers and chocolates?!

In the second incident the author summarizes the Mission of Muhammad (PBUH) by a statement of a Jewish man who cried hearing about the coming of Muhammad (PBUH) because he was an Arab not a Jew, so now, should the Mission of Islam or any other religion be identified by a statement of a crying fanatic of another religion?!

On pages 37 and 38, the author makes the old false claim that a Muslim or Islam is automatically anti-Jewish. And while the same claim was made for centuries against some writings in the Bible itself, truth -seekers like Mr. Spencer won't mention most of the time the obvious same fact in Biblical writings and in the Holy Quran.
The fact is that all Jewish Prophets were only sent to the Jewish people.

What does that mean? The meaning is that the believers of these Prophets were Jews who worshipped God and Jews who obeyed His messengers, but guess what else? The enemies of these Prophets, who fought them, killed them and angered God, were naturally also Jews.

53

So I ask any of the truth-seekers to put themselves in the position of the scriptures and tell us how to describe or criticize the later kind of Jews. Are they of a different species, Chinese, Aliens from outer space, or are still also Jews? It is simply like going to a maximum security prison in France and when asked about the nationality of all the criminals inside, you answer: they are all French. Someone would come after and state that you must be a French hater, as if the subject matter or the context in which the statement was made, which is the thing that matter the most in any objective evaluation of a statement, should never be considered or even mentioned.

In the Holy Quran, God Says:
"And whoever wishes to believe should believe, and whoever wishes to be an infidel should be an infidel"
Holy Quran, Surat (Al Kahf) Ch (18) verse (29)

فَمَنْ شَاءَ فَلْيُؤْمِنْ وَمَنْ شَاءَ فَلْيَكْفُرْ (29) ۚ

"So remind; you are not but a reminder"(21)
You are not to control them"(22)
Holy Quran, Surat (Al Ghashya) Ch (88) verses (21-22)

فَذَكِّرْ إِنَّمَا أَنْتَ مُذَكِّرٌ (21)

لَسْتَ عَلَيْهِمْ بِمُصَيْطِرٍ (22)

The most fundamental aspect of inviting people to Islam is to inform them of the truth that their Creator had revealed for them, and do that in the most polite and lenient way. What they decide afterwards is their own decision, at least for it is their own responsibility and it would be only them who would answer for it to God on Judgment day, not me, you, or even the Prophets themselves.

On page 38, the author writes:
"It should be a matter of history that there is no record of Christians expecting a Prophet in Arabia 540 years after the death of Jesus"

*What about the Arabs' own records for the incidents at the time? And what about that Christianity and its Gospels were born and written in the Middle East? The author, as we explained in the previous chapters, considers history, credibility and objectivity only to be attributed to people who agree with his own ideology, so if I hate or oppose the ideology of a certain math teacher then 1+1 cannot be accepted to equal 2 anymore, because it is stated by the teacher I don't like! This is a known ideological disease called "generic fallacy."

What he is so strongly implying here - not to my surprise any more - is that the events that the historians of the Middle East and Arabia declared and carried through the centuries which they experienced firsthand, and which were never opposed at the time by even the biggest haters of Islam, our truth-seeker will never consider them a matter of history!

The author then goes to the end of the paragraph stating that the Pope at the time of the Prophet (PBUH) - as if the Pope had control or telepathic knowledge of factual events in Arabia at the time - didn't mention any thing that was expected to happen in Arabia! And since the Arabs - according to Mr. Spencer - are deaf, mute, and not aware of what happens in their societies and history, they had no history of Christianity! And if they did, only the Pope might have known about it all the way from Rome! The author lastly, states that Christianity at the birth of the Prophet "was well established and seeking neither new Prophets nor new heresies."

*Just the notion that the sending of a Prophet or a message of God is validated only by what the "old establishment" leaders sought or accepted is just laughable. I would also like to say specifically to the last quote, that maybe what happened all over Europe later, of saint worshipping, selling Indulgences (forgiveness documents), splitting into warring factions, inquisitions and burning women on the stake by the millions, must have then been done by the Muslims, because the Roman church was innocently busy being well established and innocently not expecting "new Prophets nor new heresies"!

As far as the claim that Christianity was not awaiting the coming of a new Prophet, my answer is; why ask the clairvoyant pope?

I would instead go and ask Jesus (PBUH) about what Christianity was awaiting at the time. **In the King James Bible**:

"And the book is delivered to him that is not learned, saying, read this, I pray thee: and he says, I am not learned"
Isaiah 29:12

"And I will pray the Father, and he shall give you <u>another Comforter</u>, that he may abide with you forever" (the last Prophet)
John 14:16

"Howbeit, when He the Spirit of Truth is come, <u>He will guide you into all truth</u>. For He shall not speak of Himself, but whatsoever He shall hear that shall He speak; and He will show you things to come. He shall glorify me; for He shall receive of mine, and shall show it unto you things to come"
John 16:13

I might add that the current translation of "the spirit of truth" is totally erroneous, for in the original Greek text, you will find that the corresponding word to the "spirit of truth", is the Greek word " Paraclete" which actually has nothing to do with the word "spirit" or even the word "truth". It means literally **"the praised one"** and if our truth-seeker never have mentioned the meaning of the Arabic word **"Muhammad"** to you yet, let me give you its literal translation; It is **"the praised one"**.

"Khadija"

On page 38, the author says "Muhammad's boyhood was relatively uneventful"

* Till Muhammad (PBUH) had reached 40 years of age and received the first revelation from God, if you walked in Mecca and ask where is the " truthful honest" any one in the entire town would point to

56

Muhammad (PBUH). Even before he knew himself to become a Prophet, he was never seen fornicating, drinking, or doing any act of ill manners to even be mentioned later by his worst enemies. If that is what the author means by "uneventful," then we thank him for the due praise.

The author then claims two major fabrications.

The first; that "without Khadija Muhammad might never have become a Prophet"!

*Another flying blue elephant example! How could it be possible that the author would fabricate something like that and not even care to comment on which magic he used to conjure it with?

Was Khadija another Prophet who granted Muhammad (PBUH) his Prophethood? Was she a super genius comparative religions professor who dedicated her Harvard career to cooking him up a religion?

Did he receive God's revelation through her? I am just trying to pull my eyebrows back down at the moment.

The second claim; is that Warqa Ibn Nawfal had known about Muhammad (PBUH)'s Prophecy for 15 years before the first revelation to the Prophet, which is not true.

The authenticated correct history tells us that Muhammad (PBUH) was so shocked and trembling of fear seeing the greatness of Arch Angel Gabriel (PBUH) for the first time, so Khadija went to Warqa and told him about what happened, and he immediately identified Muhammad (PBUH) as the awaited Prophet of God.

On page 40, the author shows several descriptions of the Prophet, but then shows the incident when the Prophet (PBUH) advised his companions of dying their beards with Al Henna (a hair dye and treatment), then the author tells us the shocking truth that:

"Al Mujahideen" dye their beards the same way like the Prophet !

Guilty your honor!! It is all in the dye!! So if I wear a suit and a beard like you, Mr. Spencer, would that turn me into a truth-seeker?

57

On pages 40 and 41, the author tells the story narrated by Ayesha about that what he (PBUH) seen were "dreams" and a truth descended upon him when the Holy Quran was revealed to him for the first time! The story is absolutely true and absolutely not! It is true and narrated as such in the ultimate reference of Saheeh Al Bukhary, only as how the process of Muhammad (PBUH) seeking his creator started. In the beginning he would see visions in his sleep that later happened exactly the same way, after which he would tend to stay in open areas alone, then he chose to meditate in the cave of Hiraa alone. What is wrong is that the author narrated the story as if the actual revelations of the Holy Quran to the Prophet were in the form of visions in dreams!

Muhammad (PBUH), and for years, used to go to the cave of Hiraa to meditate in seclusion, and was not worshipping or praying to Allah at the time.

One night in the holy month of Ramadan, Gabriel (PBUH) appeared to him and asked him to read, he answered "I am not learned," the angel asked him to read again and for three times Muhammad (PBUH) would repeat the same answer: then, the first revealed Sura in the Holy Quran was recited to the Prophet by Archangel Gabriel:

"Read, In the Name of your Lord Who has created all that exists [1] He has created man from a leech like clot [2]"
Holy Quran, Surat (Al Alaq) Ch (96) verses (1-2)

اقْرَأْ بِاسْمِ رَبِّكَ الَّذِي خَلَقَ (1)

خَلَقَ الْإِنْسَانَ مِنْ عَلَقٍ (2)

In itself the verse is a scientific miracle of the Holy Quran of accurately describing the fetus in its Microscopic early stages 1400 years before a microscope is invented!

Why then, would the author confuse his reader about the sequence of events of one of the most major events in the history of Islam?

Jesus (PBUH) will tell you why, when he (PBUH) said:
"And the book is delivered to him that is not learned, saying, read this, I pray thee: and he says, I am not learned"
King James Bible, Isaiah 29:12

Probably to confuse you and never allow you to draw a connection if you read that part of the Bible about the fundamental fact of how the first revelation of the Holy Quran was made to Muhammad (PBUH), the evidence of the coming of Muhammad (PBUH), and how the word of God will be revealed to him in today's Bible, is hid from the American reader.

The author later brings the authentic event of Gabriel (PBUH) descending and revealing himself to the Prophet (PBUH) and describing the true story as:
"This is the famous first revelation of the Holy Quran"

On page 43, the author tells the true story of the meeting between the Prophet and Warqa Ibn Nawfal after the first revelation, contradicting the fabricated story he brought just 5 pages ago on Page 38; that Warqa learned about Muhammad (PBUH) Prophethood from Maysara 15 years earlier!

On Page 44, the author brings a story of a test Khadija had done to see if Arch Angel Gabriel is truly an Angel! When the Prophet (PBUH) had told Khadija that he was to be the Prophet of God, her answer was that she absolutely believes that he was a Prophet of God:
"By Allah, Allah will never let you down, for you treat your family well, carry the weak, give to the have not, help with the hardship of righteousness, care for the weak and the needy, honor your guests, and you are the truthful honest"
Narrator: Ayesha. Reference: Saheeh Al Bukhary, Number: 3. Degree: Correct.

59

But when you go back to the author, why would Khadija test any angel's existence?

Now comes the appalling statement of the author:
" Muslim hardliners to this day insist upon the veiling of women because of, among other things, this underlying assumption: the sight of an unveiled woman is so distressing, so deeply sinful, that it causes even the angels to flee"!!!

Where is it in the Holy Quran or the Hadeeth of the Prophet, even the weak ones, that there is any mention that the creation of Allah of the women who are our mothers, daughters, sisters and wives is so distressing or sinful that Angels flee from it? Even if there was such an ignorant hard liner - of the religion of Islam itself - who might have made up such a statement, what is the relevance of it to Islam itself?

Islam is the religion of which, for the first time in history relieved women of the abhorrent original sin concept, and gave women their God given rights some of which they are deprived from even till today in some countries. In the Holy Quran:

"Then Satan made them (both) **slip from Paradise, and got them out from where they were"**
Holy Quran, Surat (Al Baqara) Ch (2) verse (36)

فَأَزَلَّهُمَا الشَّيْطَانُ عَنْهَا فَأَخْرَجَهُمَا مِمَّا كَانَا فِيهِ ۖ (36)

So Allah, in the Holy Quran, states that both Adam and Eve were deceived by Satan out of Paradise.

I can quote you Christian, Jewish or whatever men who claim that they talk to God on a daily basis, or just had coffee with angels; can anyone in his right mind evaluate any aspect of Christianity and similarly Islam, whether major or minor, through the insane statements of such people?

60

The Prophet (PBUH) in answering one of his companions' question of whom was most deserving of the man's companionship, each time the man asked the Prophet further, "then whom," the Prophet said: **"Your mother, then your mother, then your mother, then your father"** (Prophet Muhammad (PBUH))
Narrator: Abou Hurayra. **Reference:** *Saheeh Al Bukhary,* **Number:** *5971.* **Degree:** *Correct.*

Or when the Prophet (PBUH) said:
"The best of you are the best to their women" i.e. mother, wife, sisters, and daughters. (Prophet Muhammad (PBUH))
Narrator: Abu Hurayra. **Reference:** *Al Turmezy,* **Number:** *1162.* **Degree:** *Correct/Good.*

Then comes the author with his imaginary nameless "hardliners" to tell us about how or how not our own mothers and daughters are perceived in Islam!

"The Suicidal Despair Returns"

On pages 44 and 45 under, the author is trying to portray God's last Prophet, and the perfect example of mankind as a suicidal maniac, then he ends the paragraph - to give credibility to his story - by verses of the Holy Quran which are in Surat (Al Muddather) Ch. 74, verses 1-7, in which it is well-known to be given to the Prophet in relation to the first encounter of the Prophet with Gabriel (PBUH), when he returned home to see Khadija for the first time, shaken to his bones saying:

"Wrap me with covers, wrap me with covers"
(Prophet Muhammad (PBUH))
Narrator: Jaber ibn Abdu Allah. **Reference:** *Saheeh Al Bukhary,* **Number:** *4954.* **Degree:** *Correct.*

The verses told the Prophet that his message is to warn mankind and inform them with the message of their Creator:

61

(1) O, you (Muhammad (PBUH)) enveloped in cloth.

(2) Arise and warn.

(3) And Say your God is Greater.

Holy Quran, Surat (Al Muddather) Ch (74) verses (1-3)

يَا أَيُّهَا الْمُدَّثِّرُ (1)

قُمْ فَأَنْذِرْ (2)

وَرَبَّكَ فَكَبِّرْ (3)

Have we read in the verses anything about committing suicide every day? Did we get – may be - a hint of an advice about staying alive as a requirement, because if you were dead, you will not be able to perform your duties as the last messenger of God to mankind?

Then in the last paragraph the author claims that a woman from Quraysh - obviously not a Muslim - had said that when Gabriel didn't appear for some time to the Prophet that:

"His Satan had deserted him"

*Never mind that the most trusted interpretations of the verses of the Holy Quran with pin point "true" historical accuracy, state that what the infidels of Quraysh had said was "His God deserted him."

An example is the respected interpretation of the Holy Quran of Ibn Katheer (Tafseer Ibn Katheer) of the verse in Surat (Al Doha).

In the Holy Quran:

"Your God (O, Muhammad (PBUH)) has neither forsaken you nor resented you"

Holy Quran, Surat (Al Doha), Ch (93), verse (3)

مَا وَدَّعَكَ رَبُّكَ وَمَا قَلَىٰ (3)

But let's inspect this; a nameless, non-Muslim woman, obviously a hater of the Prophet and Islam, who never saw the revelation to the

Prophet either false or correct, never saw God, angels or Satan, makes a comment that no one heard or cared for, and we hear it for the first time from the author. Which researcher would even care to consider it, and what scholar would even waste ink rejecting it? And by which wild imagination could this be used to learn any truth about the incident? The answer is, if the goal is to show the last Prophet of God palling with Satan while being a suicide maniac, then our truth-seeker had no choice to use this as a one worthless source for him. Is it a new case of "cause fabricates the means?" You be the judge.

Finally, here is what unbiased objective researchers say:

"Muhammad received most of his messages from Allah through an angel, whom Muhammad believed to be the Arch Angel Gabriel. For almost two years, Muhammad was afraid to share the messages with anyone other than his wife, Khadija. Eventually, the angel ordered Muhammad to "Recite!" Muhammad finally obeyed the command and, at the age of 42, began his ministry. Incidentally, Jesus referred to a future Prophet numerous times in the New Testament, with a term "paraclete," used to describe the next messenger from God. This term is often translated as "comforter," but it is more probably translated as "advocate" or "counselor."

Christians assert that the advocate is the Holy Spirit, an intangible entity connoting the spirit or Word of God. However, the passages related to the advocate plainly reveal that Jesus was describing a flesh and blood person, not a ghost. Moreover, when the Greek word "Paraclete" is translated into Arabic, the world becomes Ahmad (i.e. Muhammad). In sum, Muslims think Jesus foresaw Muhammad. As an impartial seeker of the truth, I must agree with the Muslims. Indeed, Jesus even predicted how the next prophet would receive and share God's message.

"I have much more to tell you, but you cannot bear it now. But when he comes, the spirit of truth, he will guide you to all truth. He will not speak on his own, but he will speak what he hears, and will declare to you the things that are coming.

He will glorify me, because he will take from what is mine and declare it to you."
Gospel of John, Chapter 16: 12-14.

The Oracle Institute in its research book, "The Truth", page 148

"Islam can be considered a break off Judaism and Christianity, and some considered it as such for according to the opinion, that Islam completes them. Fair researchers however say that Islam is the third of the major three religions that complete each other collectively from the same one source"

"To sum it up, Prophet Muhammad brought a monotheistic religion 9 centuries before any Christian brings monotheism into Christianity (Unitarians). No Prophet before or after had such a complete victory like that of Muhammad."

George Sarton, the prominent historian (1884-1956)

Chapter Four

"Muhammad revelations and their sources"

Let's get to the bottom line first!

This entire chapter is desperately dedicated to the attempt of discrediting the Quran as the final unaltered Word of God. That is what the Spencer dance is all about, so, before we even attempt ourselves to shine the truth on the heap of allegations in this chapter, we will first put to eternal rest any illusions about the Quran not being the final true Word of God.

Let's assume that I would come to you today in the year 2010 and tell you that the creator, not only of our planet, but the one creator of a universe that is 13.8 billion light years wide - light can spin planet earth 14 times over in less than a second! - had sent a final messenger with His book of guidance to all mankind, and in it He not only provides the ultimate wisdom for mankind to live the most joyful, satisfying and fulfilling life, but also provided undisputable proofs scientific and other wise, that he is the creator and most knowledgeable above all his creations; from the atom all the way to the stupendous galaxies in the depth of space. What would you say to that?

The answer would most likely be, "Prove it!"

1- In Surat (Al Mouminoon) (The Believers) Ch (23) Verses (12-14) the most accurate description - even with today's superior knowledge of embryology - of how insemination happens between a sperm and a woman's egg and its phases of growth till a fetus becomes a born baby, are in this Surah (Quran chapter) revealed 1400 years ago!

The description is not only so accurate but also so descriptive in a way that was not revealed by modern science till the advent of electronic microscopes few decades ago. There is no possible explanation that this

66

was in the Quran 1400 years ago other than that the word of the Quran is the word of the creator of mankind.

"And indeed We created man out of an extract of clay (12). Then We made him as a Nutfah (A mix of the sperm and woman egg) **in a safe lodging** (the womb of the woman) **(13). Then We made the Nutfah into a leech like clot, then We made the clot into a piece of chew, then We made out of that piece of chew bones, then We clothed the bones with flesh, and then We brought it forth as another creation. So Blessed is Allah, the Best of creators (14).**
Quran, Surat (Al Mouminoon) (The Believers) Ch (23) Verses (12-14)

وَلَقَدْ خَلَقْنَا الْإِنْسَانَ مِنْ سُلَالَةٍ مِنْ طِينٍ (12)

ثُمَّ جَعَلْنَاهُ نُطْفَةً فِي قَرَارٍ مَكِينٍ (13)

ثُمَّ خَلَقْنَا النُّطْفَةَ عَلَقَةً فَخَلَقْنَا الْعَلَقَةَ مُضْغَةً فَخَلَقْنَا الْمُضْغَةَ عِظَامًا فَكَسَوْنَا الْعِظَامَ لَحْمًا ثُمَّ أَنْشَأْنَاهُ خَلْقًا آخَرَ ۚ فَتَبَارَكَ اللَّهُ أَحْسَنُ الْخَالِقِينَ (14)

Please note two things:
A- The amazing description of the phase "piece of chew," see Fig. 2, p 114, where now, when we look at it with an electronic microscope, it looks exactly like a piece of dough with a teeth mark, as if someone bit or chewed into it! What look like teeth marks is nothing but the beginning of the human backbone line from which ribs later branch out.

B- Describing the clot as a "Leech," see Fig. 1 and 3, p 119 and 121. Not only does the clot look like a leech, but it latches to the uterus wall and sucks nutrients out of it like a leech does: exactly the same!

C- In Dr. Moore's 2007 embryology reference, it was introduced that now scientists believe that bones are created first in the fetus then it is clothed later by flesh tissues. The creator had told us so 1400 years ago:

"Then We clothed the bones with flesh".
Quran, Surat (Al Mouminoon) (The Believers) Ch (23) Verses (14)

فَكَسَوْنَا الْعِظَامَ لَحْمًا (14)

Are these facts mentioned in any scriptures before the revelation of the Holy Quran?

Did the "Truth-seeker of the sources of the Quran" care to mention this glaring, like the sun, and amazing truth to his readers? Not once.

2- In Surat (Al Anbyaa) (The Prophets) Ch (21) Verse (30)

The "Big Bang" theory was revealed in 1925 and turned our perception of the creation and the beginning of the universe upside down. It stated that the universe was a massive matter then it exploded outward initiating the beginning of the universe as we know it. Let's look at what the Creator - praises be only to Him - had said about His creation.

"Haven't the infidels known that the heavens and the earth were joined together as one piece, and then We tore them apart?"
Quran, Surat (Al Anbyaa) (The Prophets) Ch (21) Verse (30)

أَوَلَمْ يَرَ الَّذِينَ كَفَرُوا أَنَّ السَّمَاوَاتِ وَالْأَرْضَ كَانَتَا رَتْقًا فَفَتَقْنَاهُمَا (30)

The greatness of the verse doesn't stop there, but the creator continues to tell us in the same verse about that which NASA is spending half a billion of dollars today looking for on planet Mars; they are looking for the only source and proof of life in the universe; water.

"And We have made from water every living thing. Will they not then believe?"
Quran, Surat (Al Anbyaa) (The Prophets) Ch (21) Verse (30)

وَجَعَلْنَا مِنَ الْمَاءِ كُلَّ شَيْءٍ حَيٍّ ۖ أَفَلَا يُؤْمِنُونَ (30)

Will they?

The "Big Bang" theory continues to explain that planets and stars were not formed immediately out of the huge explosion, for in the beginning the universe was in a smoke state then later areas of that smoke got so dense that stars and planets started to form from. Let's see what the creator said about that.

In Surat "Fussilatt" Ch (41) verse (11)

"Then He settled towards the heaven when it was <u>smoke</u>, and said to it and to the earth: "Come willingly or unwillingly." They both said: "We come, willingly"
Quran, Surat "Fussilatt" Ch (41) verse (11)

ثُمَّ اسْتَوَىٰ إِلَى السَّمَاءِ وَهِيَ دُخَانٌ فَقَالَ لَهَا وَلِلْأَرْضِ ائْتِيَا طَوْعًا أَوْ كَرْهًا قَالَتَا أَتَيْنَا طَائِعِينَ (11)

Can you imagine on your own that the planets and earth were originally smoke? No, only He who created the universe, heavens and earth billions of years ago could possibly know that.

The latest evolvement of the theory regarding the current condition of the universe is that it is still expanding, as if the initial explosion still echoing at the edges of the universe.

In Surat "Al Zaryat" Ch (51) Verse (47)

"With powers, we did construct the sky, and Verily, We are expanding it"
Quran, Surat "Al Zaryat", Ch (51) Verse (47)

وَالسَّمَاءَ بَنَيْنَاهَا بِأَيْدٍ وَإِنَّا لَمُوسِعُونَ (47)

Never mind that no one at the time - seventh century - even knew the existence of half of the planet, but who other than the creator of the universe would not only know the scope of its creation and existence, but in addition the changing condition of its size and edges?

Then comes the several times in the Quran when the creator swears by the towers in the skies and heavens; see Fig. 5, p 123. Many old interpretations of the Quran tried to explain the greatness of these towers that Allah swears by, as may be constellation of stars, planets or more frequently as the final dwelling of the righteous in paradise. Then comes NASA, who recently and after receiving Hubble telescope images from the far depth of space into other galaxies; in the documentary "cosmic voyage" narrated by the Oscar award winner Morgan Freeman, NASA reveals to us these light-years-high "mysterious towers of gas" where gases get so dense inside giving birth to stars as if they were gigantic "Star nurseries" See Fig. 5 p 123!

In the Quran:

"And indeed, We have put towers in the heavens and We beautified them for the beholders"
Quran, Surat (Al Hejr) (The mind) Ch (15) Verse (16)

وَلَقَدْ جَعَلْنَا فِي السَّمَاءِ بُرُوجًا وَزَيَّنَّاهَا لِلنَّاظِرِينَ (16)

"And by the heaven of the towers".
Quran, Surat (Al Borooj) (The towers) Ch 85 Verse (1)

وَالسَّمَاءِ ذَاتِ الْبُرُوجِ (1)

With a plethora of other proofs, in the subject of the universe and its creation alone, we can dedicate an entire multiple volume book on the scientific miracles of the Quran.

*In Surat (Al Roum) (The Romans) Verses (2 -4):

"The Romans have been defeated (2)
In the lowest land, and they, after their defeat, will be victorious (3)
Within few years ... (4)"
Surat (Al Roum) (The Romans) Ch. (30) Verses (2 -4)

70

غُلِبَتِ الرُّومُ (2)
فِي أَدْنَى الْأَرْضِ وَهُمْ مِنْ بَعْدِ غَلَبِهِمْ سَيَغْلِبُونَ (3)
فِي بِضْعِ سِنِينَ ۗ لِلَّهِ الْأَمْرُ مِنْ قَبْلُ وَمِنْ بَعْدُ ۚ وَيَوْمَئِذٍ يَفْرَحُ الْمُؤْمِنُونَ (4)

Why would Muhammad (PBUH) if he is the author of Quran, get out of his own way and predict that the Romans not only will be defeated first, but then within 9 years will be victorious again? What if the opposite happened, the events never happened at all, or happened in a reversed sequence? And if it wasn't miraculous enough that it did happen exactly as God who knows the future had already told in the Quran, then look at the description of how the defeat of the Romans will happen in the lowest earth. Modern scientists then came with satellite scanning technology to tell us that the site of the battle where the Muslims had defeated the Romans - first - by the shore of the Dead Sea in today's Jordan - is typographically the lowest point on the surface of earth!
One can puzzle himself till the day he dies on the question "How is it possible that Muhammad (PBUH) knew that 1400 years ago?"
Or one can simply realize that it is impossible for anyone but the creator of heavens and earth to foretell these facts, for he is all knower of the planet He created and the future?
In the Quran there are hundreds more of similar undeniable proofs.

Now let's see what Mr. Spencer, is claiming about the subject!

As the old adage says, "The first word of the poem is blasphemy"!

"Borrowings from Judaism"

In the first paragraph on page 47, Mr. Spencer starts this chapter by stating that there is a:
"most severe and lingering challenge to Muhammad's claim to be a Prophet."

*If we can call this a challenge! He claims that there are similarities between Judaism, Christianity and Islam, that there are

71

similarities between Judaism and Islam in Monotheism, and basic laws. Then the blue elephant of a statement comes flying - as usual - about the Jewish tribes around Mecca; that Muhammad (PBUH) respected them and sought their approval of his Prophetic mission!

*Mr. Spencer - in writing - is making such a serious accusation. An accusation that the world's second largest religion came through the approval of the leaders of another religion and through the pursuit of the Prophet of Islam to its leaders!!

With that unbelievably weird claim, would the author show us any supporting evidence to even attempt to slow us down in refuting this claim? Not one iota! Did he have the audacity to throw such a claim up in the air then just move to the next paragraph?
Yes he did.

*What would a Prophet of God do?
Should he destroy the message of all Prophets - of the same God - before him?! Did David, Joseph, Moses, and Jesus, may peace be upon all of them, do that about laws, and messages, of Prophets that were sent before them?
As per the Bible Jesus (PBUH) said:
"I am not sent but unto the lost sheep of the house of Israel"
King James Bible, Mathew 15:24

Does this mean that Jesus (PBUH) is not a Prophet of God for his mission was to bring the lost sheep of the house of Israel back to the mosaic laws, i.e. upholding the true religion that was revealed by Moses before him?

If God is One, and who has no partner (Monotheism) which is the number one fundamental pillar of Islam and truly for all of the Abrahamic religions, where does it say that Muhammad has to denounce the oneness of God (Monotheism) as proof of his new Prophethood? If God, as mankind evolved did not send Prophets after messengers after

72

Prophets to support his eternal message of his oneness, and enhance his previous laws to mankind, what would be the need then for all those Prophets and messengers one after the other?

Why send Moses after Abraham? Why then send Jesus to begin with, after all the Old Testament Prophets and messengers were sent with all their Scriptures and laws?

In the next paragraph the author - again - wonders why the stories of Prophets in the Quran are similar to the ones in the Bible and the Old Testament!

*The same one mighty God, who has sent all Prophets and messengers, has sent his last Prophet; what should his last Prophet Muhammad (PBUH) now claim as proof of his Prophethood and that he is the last messenger of the same Mighty God? Should he claim that Moses (PBUH) had parted the Pacific Ocean instead of the Red Sea? Or that David (PBUH) was defeated by Goliath?

A minimum of common sense would be the absolute opposite, meaning that if the stories of the Quran were totally dissimilar to the Bible about the same events, then that would have raised questions - with non-Muslims - yet majority of the stories are generally the same, and in itself is another confirmation among hundreds of them, that he is the last Prophet (PBUH) of the same One Mighty God of all Prophets and messengers sent before him, completing and enhancing the same message of God once and for all.

*Dissimilarities in the Quran (M.Z)

When comparing the stories of God's Prophets in the Quran to the ones included in the Bible we would generally find that the common thread is the same, yet there are unmistakable differences:

1-The stories in the Quran are purified from the man-made fabrications and accusations against the Prophets of God. Please review the beginning of this chapter proving the Quran as the undeniable Word of God. A glaring example is some of the fabrications like those in the story of David (PBUH) where he was accused of sending one of his army leaders to his death in battle so he can marry his wife - that is a Prophet of God they are talking about - or that Lot (PBUH) had an incestuous relationship with his daughters, etc.

In the Quran, the honor and the record of God's Prophets, the best humans that ever walked the earth, was restored once and for all. Examples in the Quran:

"Oh Family of David, do (righteous deeds) **thankfully, and few of my worshippers are truly the thankful"**
Quran, Surat (Saba) Ch 34, verse (13)

ۚ اعْمَلُوا آلَ دَاوُودَ شُكْرًا ۚ وَقَلِيلٌ مِنْ عِبَادِيَ الشَّكُورُ (13)

In the verse, David (PBUH) had made a schedule for his family to praise and worship God all day and all night, so there was always one person in his household praising God at all times. Prophet Muhammad (PBUH) says of David (PBUH):

"The best fasting was the fasting of my brother David, for he used to fast every other day and eat the next, and he never fled if confronted in battle" (Prophet Muhammad (PBUH))
Narrator: Abdu Allah Ibn Alaas. **Reference:** *Saheeh Al Tarmazy,* **Number:** *70.* **Degree:** *Correct.*

Can you imagine that this Great Prophet of God, who was commissioned by God to tell mankind right from wrong, is some man who lusts for another man's wife, plotting the death of her husband!

2- There are more stories and events that God revealed in the Quran about his Prophets that were never included in the Bible, as in the story of Moses in Surat (Al Kahf) (The Cave) (chapter 18), as well as others mentioned in the quotations of Prophet Muhammad (PBUH) in addition to him (PBUH) elaborating on some of these events in his quotations.

3- One of the most glaring parts of the story of Prophets that were never mentioned anywhere except in the Quran is the verse in Surat Younis (Jonas) where God talks to Pharoe of Moses after he has drowned and stating a historical fact that modern science had discovered recently.

In the late eighties, a group of French scientists performed tissue analysis on the mummy of what was believed to be the Pharaoh Ramses the second. The lead scientist (Maurice Bukaille) thought that he made the discovery of the century when he declared to his colleagues that the body of Moses's Pharaoh was saved and that it is what was believed to be the body of Ramses the second. He found sea salt all over the tissues, broken ribs and no skin scars as a result of drowning under a crushing water weight, and apparent rushed mummification of a stiff body at the time. Before the scientist raced to declare his discovery to the world, he was told by a colleague that Muslims knew that fact 1400 years ago. P.122

The body of the Pharaoh was saved! Is this mentioned anywhere else other than the Quran? In the Holy Quran:

"So this day, We shall save your body so that you may be made an example of (Sign from God) to those who come after you" *Quran, Surat (Younis) Ch (10) Verse (92)*

On page 49, the author brings the verses in the Quran that tells the story of Adam's two sons, Cain and Abel (Qabeel and Habeel in Arabic), where Cain killed his brother Abel, then Allah had sent a raven to bury a dead one before Cain to show him how to bury the body of his dead brother.

*In the Quran verses that told the aove mentioned story (27-31) are immediately followed by the famous verse No 32 that says:

"Because of that We ordained for the children of Israel that if anyone killed a soul not in punishment for killing another soul, or spreading mischief on earth, it would be as if he killed all mankind,

75

and if anyone saved a life, it would be as if he saved the life of all mankind. And indeed, there came to them Our Messengers with clear proofs, but, even then many of them continued to exceed the limits"

Quran Surat (Al Maeda) (The table) Ch (5) Verse (32)

مِنْ أَجْلِ ذَٰلِكَ كَتَبْنَا عَلَىٰ بَنِي إِسْرَائِيلَ أَنَّهُ مَن قَتَلَ نَفْسًا بِغَيْرِ نَفْسٍ أَوْ فَسَادٍ فِي الْأَرْضِ فَكَأَنَّمَا قَتَلَ النَّاسَ جَمِيعًا وَمَنْ أَحْيَاهَا فَكَأَنَّمَا أَحْيَا النَّاسَ جَمِيعًا ۚ وَلَقَدْ جَاءَتْهُمْ رُسُلُنَا بِالْبَيِّنَاتِ ثُمَّ إِنَّ كَثِيرًا مِّنْهُم بَعْدَ ذَٰلِكَ فِي الْأَرْضِ لَمُسْرِفُونَ (32)

Here the author really dazzles us, when he wonders:
"There is no stated reason why this injunction against murder follows the story of Cain and Abel"

*Can you believe that after telling the story of the first murder in the history of mankind; a brother killing his own brother, Mr. Spencer wonders why the following verse condemns murder?! As bizarre as that sounds, we'll see why he said that.

The author runs to bring a story about the mentioning of the raven in the Talmud - which was gathered in the second century B.C - implying that Muhammad had copied it from the Jews!
And by that he pushes smoke on a gun that was never fired, and more importantly, when none was shot to begin with!

The author then goes back to his previous question as to why the Quran - God for that matter - doesn't always explain everything in it in details, which we have answered already in this book. The author imagines that the explanation of the Quranic verse as to why killing one person is like killing all mankind and vice versa, can only be explained by the Talmud where the story of the two brothers is mentioned!
On page 49, he wrote:
"The voice of thy brothers bloods crieth" (Gen 4:10)
and because the word "bloods" was in plural not in singular, then on page 50 he adds:
"...suggests to numerous readers across centuries that the Quran author or compiler was depending on the Jewish source"

76

*Did the Verse in the Quran contain one word about "blood" either way? No.

Then on page 50 he explains again that the Talmud refers to the killed brother as a seed of many people to have been born yet, so by killing him, it is like killing his lineage as well, and that is the connection.

*I will not use the fact that the Quran is the true unaltered Word of God which Biblical stories should actually be verified by, but I will follow the same logic the author has been trying to use.

Was the seed of killed Abel the seed that would have produced mankind? No, we are here, me and you and another 6 billion people; yes he was killed, yet none of us obviously came from his seed.

Is it mentioned anywhere that Cain didn't carry his own seed or that he was impotent in any way so he never had any children; hence the death of his only brother was like killing all mankind? No.

Is there any undeniable proof that Adam (PBUH) didn't have any other sons or daughters who reproduced? No.

Then that cannot be what God meant in the Quran when he said killing one is killing all.

Did the author read the Quranic verse itself? It says **"We ordained for the Children of Israel",** the whole statement of God in this Quranic verse is a law ordained upon the sons of Jacob - Israel - (PBUH), that is tens of generations after Adam (PBUH) and his two sons to begin with!

But then what is the meaning of the verse in the Quran? And how is it that killing one man is like killing all? The meaning closest to the truth, is that killing a soul that God had created is such an abomination and transgression against God that it equals killing all mankind and vice versa. Some scholars also explain that, to the killed, meaning, in the point of view of the killed, the entire world had died, and to the saved soul then, the entire world was revived again. But then, these true Muslim scholars are never included amongst the author's nameless "numerous readers across centuries"!

77

The clear fact is that if a story is in the Quran and the Talmud as well, it means without a doubt that it did happen, more importantly that this is the normal thing if it did happen, for the one Mighty God would tell the same event, naturally, the same way in the multiple of scriptures, and the ultimate reference here is the Quran itself, the last unaltered Word of God.

"Tales of the ancients"

How about someone who commits a crime and goes public with what he believes a claim for his innocence, only to bring with it the overwhelming proof of his absolute guilt?

The author brings the verses in the Holy Quran that state what the infidels of Quraysh had falsely claimed about the Quran. They claimed that the Quran had tales like the tales of the ancients (old scriptures), that these tales have been dictated to Muhammad (PBUH) day and night, and that he was receiving help from others authoring it! Please note that Muhammad (PBUH) died illiterate, and didn't know how to read or write (MZ)

Is it amazing that the claims of the infidels That God mentions in the Quran are almost exactly the same claims Mr. Spencer just mentioned 14 centuries later in his previous paragraph?

Does he realize what he might be saying and quoting from the Quran about his ownself?

A side note: If you walked into Mecca before Muhammad's Prophetic mission and asked anyone; where is the "Truthful honest?" You would never be pointed to three or two choices of men; you would have always been pointed to one man that is Muhammad (PBUH).

Here we will quote the same verses the "author" quoted, only with an honest accurate translation.

"Verily, this we have been promised (resurrection) we and our fathers before (us), this is only the tales of the ancients"
Quran, Surat (Al Mouminoon) (The Believers) Ch (9) verse (83)

لَقَدْ وُعِدْنَا نَحْنُ وَآبَاؤُنَا هَٰذَا مِنْ قَبْلُ إِنْ هَٰذَا إِلَّا أَسَاطِيرُ الْأَوَّلِينَ (83)

(4) "Those who disbelieve say: "This (the Quran) is nothing but a lie that he (Muhammad) has invented, and others have helped him at it. In fact they have produced oppression and a fabrication"
(5) And they say: "Tales of the ancients, which he has written down, and they are dictated to him morning and afternoon."
(6) Say: "It (Quran) has been sent down by Him (Allah) Who knows the secret in the heavens and the earth. Truly, He is Most Forgiving, Most Merciful."
Quran, Surat (Al Furqan) Ch. (25), verses (4-6)

وَقَالَ الَّذِينَ كَفَرُوا إِنْ هَٰذَا إِلَّا إِفْكٌ افْتَرَاهُ وَأَعَانَهُ عَلَيْهِ قَوْمٌ آخَرُونَ ۖ فَقَدْ جَاءُوا ظُلْمًا وَزُورًا (4)

وَقَالُوا أَسَاطِيرُ الْأَوَّلِينَ اكْتَتَبَهَا فَهِيَ تُمْلَىٰ عَلَيْهِ بُكْرَةً وَأَصِيلًا (5)

قُلْ أَنْزَلَهُ الَّذِي يَعْلَمُ السِّرَّ فِي السَّمَاوَاتِ وَالْأَرْضِ ۚ إِنَّهُ كَانَ غَفُورًا رَحِيمًا (6)

And of them there are some who listen to you; but We have set veils on their hearts, so they do not understand, and deafness in their ears; and even if they see every one of the signs, they will not believe; to the point that when they come to you to argue with you, the disbelievers say: "These are nothing but tales of the ancients."
Quran, Surat (Al Anaam) Ch (6), verse (25)

وَمِنْهُمْ مَنْ يَسْتَمِعُ إِلَيْكَ ۖ وَجَعَلْنَا عَلَىٰ قُلُوبِهِمْ أَكِنَّةً أَنْ يَفْقَهُوهُ وَفِي آذَانِهِمْ وَقْرًا ۚ وَإِنْ يَرَوْا كُلَّ آيَةٍ لَا يُؤْمِنُوا بِهَا ۚ حَتَّىٰ إِذَا جَاءُوكَ يُجَادِلُونَكَ يَقُولُ الَّذِينَ كَفَرُوا إِنْ هَٰذَا إِلَّا أَسَاطِيرُ الْأَوَّلِينَ (25)

The author claims that in the following verses, Muhammad (PBUH) reacted with "fury", where there is no record of that furious reaction whatsoever. The author never mentions what is the source of that "fury" incident! The clear text in the following verses shows the well known and always declared fact that God, not Muhammad, may strike the infidels which clearly shows how baseless and false that "Fury" claim is. In the Holy Quran (our translation):

[10] **"And (O Muhammad (PBUH), do not obey every lying swearer.**
[11] **A slanderer, going about with obscenities,**
[12] **Hinderer of the good, sinful transgressor,**
[13] **Cruel, and moreover of illegitimate birth.**
[14] **(Do not obey him) even if he had wealth and children.**
[15] **When Our Verses (of the Quran) are recited to him, he says: "Tales of the ancients**
[16] **We shall strike him on the nose"**
Quran, Surat (Al Qalam) (The Penn) Ch (68), verse (10-16)

وَلَا تُطِعْ كُلَّ حَلَّافٍ مَهِينٍ (10)

هَمَّازٍ مَشَّاءٍ بِنَمِيمٍ (11)

مَنَّاعٍ لِلْخَيْرِ مُعْتَدٍ أَثِيمٍ (12)

عُتُلٍّ بَعْدَ ذَٰلِكَ زَنِيمٍ (13)

أَنْ كَانَ ذَا مَالٍ وَبَنِينَ (14)

إِذَا تُتْلَىٰ عَلَيْهِ آيَاتُنَا قَالَ أَسَاطِيرُ الْأَوَّلِينَ (15)

سَنَسِمُهُ عَلَى الْخُرْطُومِ (16)

"And those who disbelieved, say: "(O, Muhammad (PBUH) you are not a Messenger." Say: "Allah is Sufficient a witness between me and you and those who have knowledge of the Scripture too"
Quran, Surat (Al Raad) (The Thunder) Ch. (13), verses (43)

وَيَقُولُ الَّذِينَ كَفَرُوا لَسْتَ مُرْسَلًا ۚ قُلْ كَفَىٰ بِاللَّهِ شَهِيدًا بَيْنِي وَبَيْنَكُمْ وَمَنْ عِنْدَهُ عِلْمُ الْكِتَابِ (43)

"Those to whom We gave the Scriptures before it (the Quran), they believe in it (the Quran) and only the disbelievers would deny it"
Quran, Surat (Al Ankabout) Ch. (29), verses (47)

فَالَّذِينَ آتَيْنَاهُمُ الْكِتَابَ يُؤْمِنُونَ بِهِ ۖ وَمِنْ هَٰؤُلَاءِ مَنْ يُؤْمِنُ بِهِ ۚ وَمَا يَجْحَدُ بِآيَاتِنَا إِلَّا الْكَافِرُونَ (47)

One of the rampant practices of Muslim-Bashers is when they quote a part of a verse - often mistranslated - that fits the image they want to portray, they never quote you the verse before or the verse after, for that will give context and truth. The author, amazingly, didn't see a reason why to quote the verse that immediately follows!

"**And when it is recited to them** (people who have knowledge of the old scriptures)**, they say: "We believe in it. Verily, it is the truth from our Lord. Indeed even before it, we have been from those who submit themselves to Allah as Muslims"**
Quran, Surat (Al Furqan) Ch (28), verses (53)

(وَإِذَا يُتْلَىٰ عَلَيْهِمْ قَالُوا آمَنَّا بِهِ إِنَّهُ الْحَقُّ مِنْ رَبِّنَا إِنَّا كُنَّا مِنْ قَبْلِهِ مُسْلِمِينَ (53)

The next verse the author quoted is interesting! (Our translation):
"**And do not argue with the people of the Scripture** (Jews and Christians)**, unless it with the better way, except those who are oppressors amongst them; and say** (to them)**: "We believe in that which has been revealed to us and revealed to you; our God and your God is One (Allah), and to Him we have submitted as Muslims."**
Quran, Surat (Al Ankaboot) (The Spider) Ch (29), verses (46)

وَلَا تُجَادِلُوا أَهْلَ الْكِتَابِ إِلَّا بِالَّتِي هِيَ أَحْسَنُ إِلَّا الَّذِينَ ظَلَمُوا مِنْهُمْ ۖ وَقُولُوا آمَنَّا بِالَّذِي أُنْزِلَ إِلَيْنَا وَأُنْزِلَ إِلَيْكُمْ وَإِلَٰهُنَا وَإِلَٰهُكُمْ وَاحِدٌ وَنَحْنُ لَهُ مُسْلِمُونَ (46)

This is how the author translated the same exact above verse 46:

In page 51 he wrote:
"Those who did not convert to Islam should be reminded that Muslims, Christians, and Jews all worship the same deity" Quran 29 [46]"

*The entire first part of the verse "**And do not argue with the people of the Scripture** (Jews and Christians)**, unless it with the better way,**

81

except those who are oppressors amongst them", is totally and intentionally omitted!

Why the screaming mistranslation and misinformation? Because the beginning of the verse reveals an order from God to Muslims, to always communicate with leniency and peace with Christians and Jews, except - of course - when dealing with the oppressors amongst them, and that doesn't fit the image of a demonized jihadist Muslim that should kill a Jew or a Christian every day after breakfast! Not to mention that the word "convert" that the author concocted out of thin air in his translation doesn't exist in the verse to begin with.

I won't have to tell you why – again – the author chose not to include this verse that immediately followed!
"Those to whom We gave the Scriptures before it (the Quran)**, they believe in it** (the Quran) **and only the disbelievers would deny it"**
Quran, Surat (Al Ankabout) Ch. (29), verses (47)

47) فَالَّذِينَ آتَيْنَاهُمُ الْكِتَابَ يُؤْمِنُونَ بِهِ وَمِنْ هَٰؤُلَاءِ مَنْ يُؤْمِنُ بِهِ وَمَا يَجْحَدُ بِآيَاتِنَا إِلَّا الْكَافِرُونَ

Then the author quotes another verse which is always an easy one for Muslim-haters, yet refuting the misinterpretation is even easier with facts! Let's see what Mr. Spencer says about it?

On Page 51 he wrote:
"Allah even tells Muhammad to consult with the Jews and Christians if he doubts the truth of what he has been receiving: "And if thou (Muhammad) art in doubt concerning that which we reveal unto thee, then question those who read the scripture (that was) before thee. Verily the truth from thy lord hath come unto thee. So be not thou of the waverers" Quran 10:94" "

*Here is the correct translation:

"So if you (Muhammad) **are in doubt concerning that which We have revealed unto you, then ask those who were reading the Book** (Old Scriptures before you)**. Verily, the truth has come to you from your**

82

Lord. So do not be amongst the doubters*
Quran, Surat (Youness) Ch (10), Verse (94)

فَإِنْ كُنْتَ فِي شَكٍّ مِمَّا أَنْزَلْنَا إِلَيْكَ فَاسْأَلِ الَّذِينَ يَقْرَءُونَ الْكِتَابَ مِنْ قَبْلِكَ ۚ لَقَدْ جَاءَكَ الْحَقُّ مِنْ رَبِّكَ فَلَا تَكُونَنَّ مِنَ الْمُمْتَرِينَ (94)

*Any word about "consulting"? No.

Any reason why the author would change a simple no second guess meaning of a word like "Ask" into "Question" as if Muhammad is doubtful, or is to inquire with a higher authority of learning?

Every single leading interpretation of the Quran - Ibn Katheer, Al Galalayn, Al Tabary, and Al Qurtoby - had the correct interpretation of the above verse evidenced by the correct context of the statements of the companions of the Prophet (PBUH). Why would the truth-seeker, ignore them all?

Here is the interpretation of the leading Muslim scholars:

God said in the above verses that the coming of Muhammad is foretold in the old scriptures - the original ones - and if Muhammad had doubts that his name and his imminent coming is there, he can go and ask the people of the old scriptures to "read" his name in their scriptures for him, so he may not have any doubt about it.

In the King James Bible (Muhammad's name is in the original Hebrew text):

"His mouth is most sweet: yea, he is "Muhamad'em". This is my beloved, and this is my friend, O, daughters of Jerusalem."
King James Bible, Song of Songs 5:16

Can things be simpler than the truth? Please note that in the English translation of the King James Bible the word "Muhammad" is translated to; are you ready? It is translated to "All-great and lovely"!!

In addition, the fact that, Qutada, a companion of the Prophet (PBUH) had stated that Muhammad never doubted or asked anyone of the people of the scriptures, the same confirmation came from the great scholar of the followers Saeed Ibn Gobair that Muhammad never doubted or asked. But then why the question from God, even though

83

God knows the faith strength of his Prophet and the future fact that Muhammad will never doubt or ask others about the mention of his name in the old scriptures?

Let's go to another conversation in the Quran with another great Prophet of God.

"And when Allah says "O 'Eissa (Jesus), son of Maryam (Mary) did you say to people: 'Worship me and my mother as two gods besides Allah?' "He will say: "Glory be to You, It was not for me to say what I had no right to say. Had I said such a thing, You would surely have known it. You know what is in my inner-self though I do not know what is in Yours: truly, You, only You, are the All-Knower of all that is unknown."

Surat, (Al Maeda) Ch (5) Verse (116)

وَإِذْ قَالَ اللَّهُ يَا عِيسَى ابْنَ مَرْيَمَ أَأَنْتَ قُلْتَ لِلنَّاسِ اتَّخِذُونِي وَأُمِّيَ إِلَهَيْنِ مِنْ دُونِ اللَّهِ ۚ قَالَ سُبْحَانَكَ مَا يَكُونُ لِي أَنْ أَقُولَ مَا لَيْسَ لِي بِحَقٍّ ۚ إِنْ كُنْتُ قُلْتُهُ فَقَدْ عَلِمْتَهُ ۚ تَعْلَمُ مَا فِي نَفْسِي وَلَا أَعْلَمُ مَا فِي نَفْسِكَ ۚ إِنَّكَ أَنْتَ عَلَّامُ الْغُيُوبِ (116)

Why would Allah ask Jesus this question? Surely he knows the answer! The reason is that yes, the question is asked to Jesus, but in actuality it is directed to us, readers of the Quran in all times, about the true nature of Jesus and Virgin Mary. Our verse in question is the same way; the statement is told to Muhammad, yet it is directed to us and to inform all of us.

So there is no "obstinacy from the people of the book that kept them from recognizing Muhammad" as the author claimed later, not to mention that the approval or disapproval of some or all of the minority Christians or Jews in the Arab Peninsula, made no difference in the exponential growth of Islam at any point in history. Today there are about 15 million Jews, and over 1.6 billion Muslims worldwide, as well as the Vatican stating that today there are more Muslims in the world than Catholics.

The author in the next Paragraph creates a conflict that never existed except in his imagined reasons, and to prove his claims, he uses the one great verse that ironically can only be used to hang his allegation by the neck! It is verse 110 in Surat Al Omran, Ch (3)

"You are the best nation that was ever brought out for mankind; you demand virtue and prohibit vice, and you believe in Allah. Had the people of the Scripture believed, it would have been better for them"
Quran, Surat (Al Omran) Ch (3) Verse (110)

كُنْتُمْ خَيْرَ أُمَّةٍ أُخْرِجَتْ لِلنَّاسِ تَأْمُرُونَ بِالْمَعْرُوفِ وَتَنْهَوْنَ عَنِ الْمُنْكَرِ وَتُؤْمِنُونَ بِاللَّهِ ۗ وَلَوْ آمَنَ أَهْلُ الْكِتَابِ لَكَانَ خَيْرًا لَهُمْ ۚ مِنْهُمُ الْمُؤْمِنُونَ وَأَكْثَرُهُمُ الْفَاسِقُونَ (110)

In this great Verse, God states one of the great known Islamic fundamentals, that no one is better than anyone except by fearing God in what they do, meaning that preference in the eyes of Allah, is based only upon an ethical standard, not gender, race, fake holiness, nor even just solely being a Muslim like the author attempts to convince you. Even believing in God - as Muslims - came third to the ethical standard of actual deeds. Can the author tell me with a straight face that a Muslim nation that doesn't demand virtue and prohibit vice could automatically be the best nation that was ever brought out to mankind according to this verse? Not even him!

The author ends this paragraph by stating his motto that Jihadists (his favorite people) around the world state that only by observing Islam, Muslims can be the best nation!

*Do we need unionists, vegetarians, or even his imaginary Jihadist crazies to inform us that God prefers the righteous Muslims over the not-righteous Muslims?!

"Borrowings from Christianity"

How easy it is to validate a fabrication by using laughable excuses like "some sources say," "others suggested that," " some charged," or "some modern scholars contend" without listing any source or telling who, when, or what those imaginary "some" are?

85

On page, 52, the first paragraph, the author wonders why that Warqa, the "Arab" scholar who is related to the Prophet's wife and who recognized Prophet Muhammad as the promised Prophet in the Bible:
"writes the Bible not in Hebrew but in Arabic".
*An Arab writing in Arabic, what a conspiracy!
The author explains the plot of Warqa not writing the Bible in Hebrew because:
"Might be to distance Warqa from the Jews, who, some charged were teaching Muhammad the Quran"

　　　*Just by saying that, the author is assuming that it was a fact that Warqa taught Muhammad and that all the narrators of the quotations of the Prophet knew this as a fact and that they all - in addition - conspired to cover it up! Who said that Warqa was a Jew? What we know is that he was Khadija the Prophet's wife's cousin and she was of course an Arab, if she was an Arab, then what would that likely make her cousin?
First of all, would an Arab writing his Bible in Arabic be a wonder?
　Secondly, and regardless, all accounts indicate the passing of Warqa shortly after the first revelation to Muhammad by Arch-Angel Gabriel.
Thirdly and most importantly, if Warqa acted as a volunteer private "author" to Muhammad of the magnificent Word of God that is the Quran, what was he waiting for, him or whatever Jew, Persian or even Red-Indian our author may claim to have taught Muhammad the Quran? What was he waiting for to declare himself a Prophet of God instead of Muhammad? Can Muhammad (PBUH) - God forbid - possibly lie to people about the truth of his Prophethood, yet his imaginary teachers and writers who are feeding him the lies - according to some sources! - won't tell the supposed truth that they are the actual writers and origin of it all! Why give the glory to Muhammad and not keep it for their ownselves?

　　　The author then quotes the following verse: (our correct translation, not his)

86

" **And indeed We know that they** (polytheists and pagans) **say: "It is only a human being who teaches him** (Muhammad) **The tongue of the man they refer to is foreign, while this** (the Quran) **is a clear Arabic tongue"**

Quran, Surat (Al Nahl) Ch (16) Verse (103)

وَلَقَدْ نَعْلَمُ أَنَّهُمْ يَقُولُونَ إِنَّمَا يُعَلِّمُهُ بَشَرٌ ۗ لِّسَانُ الَّذِي يُلْحِدُونَ إِلَيْهِ أَعْجَمِيٌّ وَهَٰذَا لِسَانٌ عَرَبِيٌّ مُّبِينٌ (103)

While the word Ajami in the Arabic text means "foreign," the author ventured to tell the Arabs the meaning of their own vocabulary by saying that "Ajami means Persian or Iranian"!!

Never mind that in Arabic the word "Ajami" means anything foreign to an Arab; does the author know that there was no Iran or Iranian at the time of the Prophet? Even nowadays Iranians speak Persian, so is the author saying that all foreign languages of the world at the time to the Prophet other than Arabic were only Persian?

That is like someone saying that a word coincidentally means the same in English or American!

The author quotes the Word of God in the above verse, but does he read his own English?

God says in the Verse, that how could a non-Arab teach the most complex and most fascinating text in the Arabic language ever read? And I repeat the same question to the author!

The author in page 53, ventures to say that Warqa's confirmation to Muhammad's Prophetic mission "has been a source of embarrassment to Muslims."

*Why is it an embarrassment?!

In most of the verses that we mentioned in this chapter and the ones the author himself quoted, God states many times that the coming of Muhammad as the last Prophet of God was mentioned in the Old Scriptures.

"Those who follow the Messenger, the Prophet who can neither read nor write, whom they find written with them in the Torah and the Injeel (Gospel)"
Quran, Surat (Al Aaraf) Ch 7, Verse (157)

الَّذِينَ يَتَّبِعُونَ الرَّسُولَ النَّبِيَّ الْأُمِّيَّ الَّذِي يَجِدُونَهُ مَكْتُوبًا عِنْدَهُمْ فِي التَّوْرَاةِ (157)

So when a Christian scholar confirms and attests to the fact, why is it an embarrassment to Muslims? Can anyone tell us at least from the point of view of Muslims themselves?

Had that been enough of a circus ride for one chapter already? No. The author quotes his invisible hidden sources saying that "some modern scholars contend that Warqa actually rejected Muhammad"!

*A second ago the Muslims were embarrassed by Warqa confirming Muhammad as a Prophet, now it is the opposite; Warqa has now rejected Muhammad?!
And if he did, who said that every Christian and Jew of the Arab Peninsula did believe in Muhammad? And if one Christian rejected him, does that mean that the rest of the population would follow? Did they?
The author then claims the possibility that the account of Ibn Hisham was specifically corrupt when it came to the story of Warqa, then moves to why there are no details of the conversion of Warqa to Islam, even though - in his opinion - it "would have been a momentous event"!

*No Hadeeth (quotations of the Prophet) scholar worth his weight would argue that the Seerah (biography of the prophet) of Ibn Hisham without a doubt is heavens higher of credibility than the remnants of the Seerah of Ibn Is'haq, and while the reader will soon discover for himself that the author overwhelmingly uses Ibn Is'haq's well known fabricated stories, the author comes here and criticizes the credibility of the story of Warqa according to Ibn Hisham!

As we said earlier, most narrators verify the passing of Warqa shortly after the first revelation to Muhammad. The overwhelming majority of the religion of Islam as Quran, quotations and laws was not even revealed when Warqa passed away. At that junction of time then, believing in the one mighty God and his messenger - confirming him for that matter- was all that was needed to be accepted by Allah for one to be a Muslim.

A side note (MZ):

In painful details, the quotations of the Prophet's all over Islamic history references, describe the event of the Prophet's uncle Abu Taleb totally refusing Shahada and dying a non-Muslim. Abu Taleb, who raised and sponsored the Prophet, never accepted Muhammad's pleas on his death bed to declare Shahada (declare the oneness of God and that Muhammad is his Messenger so he becomes a Muslim before his passing) and instead listened to his pagan friends' pleas not to change his ancestors' religion before his passing. The event that saddened Muhammad enough to be the occasion for Allah to reveal the great verse:

"You do not guide whomever you want, but it is Allah who guides whomever he wills"
Quran Surat (Al Qassass) Ch (28) Verse (56)

إِنَّكَ لَا تَهْدِي مَنْ أَحْبَبْتَ وَلَكِنَّ اللَّهَ يَهْدِي مَنْ يَشَاءُ ۚ وَهُوَ أَعْلَمُ بِالْمُهْتَدِينَ (56)

What Warqa, Christian, Jew or atheist becoming or never becoming a Muslim that can be compared to the Prophet's own uncle and sponsor?

That was the Prophet's uncle and sponsor refusing the guidance of God and dying a non-Muslim, yet for Muslim scholars; it is always about stating the truth, only the truth: "momentous" or otherwise.

On page 55, the author goes to the one issue that separates Pauline Christianity from both true Christianity and Islam, which is the nature of Jesus (PBUH) and the claimed crucifixion.

In the Quran, Jesus (PBUH) is a mighty Prophet of Islam; he is created from the Holy Spirit and by a Word of God given to Virgin Mary (PBUH), yet it is the most major of sins to call him God or associate him, Virgin Mary, anyone, or thing with God.

The really odd situation is when Mr. Spencer who spearheads the ideology that anything Muslim is anti-Christianity, totally ignores the many more powers and miracles that God gave Jesus (PBUH), stated in the Quran in addition to those mentioned in the Bible, and resorts to the Infancy Arabic Bible that indicated some of the same miracles of Jesus (PBUH) mentioned in the Quran.

A side note (MZ):

Some go as far as counting about 100 different Gospels, yet the Encyclopedia Britannica researchers state that there are at least 26 different Gospels of which the Roman Empire church had chosen only 4 in Today's Bible. I will leave the historical question to Christian scholars: Did the Roman Empire determine what the word of God is?

The infancy Gospel which is unique in describing the infancy of Jesus (PBUH) in more details than the others, is what Mr. Spencer is talking about and which he will later describe as heresy! According to whose evidence I, really want to know?

*According to the author's logic, since the Infancy "Arabic" Bible is associated with what he calls "Christian heretical groups" then it is all wrong and so is any similarity in it to the truth in the Quran, he then adds:

"Muhammad's experiences with Christian heretical groups may also explain his view of the crucifixion of Christ"?!

*(M. Z).The one great miracle of Jesus (PBUH) that is only told in the Quran

It is the miracle of the just born Jesus (PBUH), talking and defending Virgin Mary when confronted by her people. Here are the verses in the Quran that describes how it happened:

[27] **"Then she brought him** (just born Jesus) **to her people, carrying him. They said: "O Mary, Indeed you have brought a mighty sin.**
[28] **"O sister of Aaron, your father was not a man who commits adultery, nor was your mother an unchaste woman."**

90

[29] Then she pointed to him. They said: "How can we talk to one who is a child in the cradle?"

[30] He (Jesus) said: Verily I am a servant of Allah, He has given me the Scripture and made me a Prophet;"

[31] And He has made me blessed wherever I be, and has enjoined on me Salah (prayer), and Zakah (obligated charity), as long as I live."

[32] And dutiful to my mother, and did not make me an unblessed arrogant.

[33] And peace be upon me the day I was born, and the day I die, and the day I shall be raised alive!

[34] Such is Jesus, son of Maryam. The statement of truth, about which they dispute"

Quran, Surat (Maryam) (Mary) Ch (19) Verses (27-34)

فَأَتَتْ بِهِ قَوْمَهَا تَحْمِلُهُ ۖ قَالُوا يَا مَرْيَمُ لَقَدْ جِئْتِ شَيْئًا فَرِيًّا (27)
يَا أُخْتَ هَارُونَ مَا كَانَ أَبُوكِ امْرَأَ سَوْءٍ وَمَا كَانَتْ أُمُّكِ بَغِيًّا (28)
فَأَشَارَتْ إِلَيْهِ ۖ قَالُوا كَيْفَ نُكَلِّمُ مَنْ كَانَ فِي الْمَهْدِ صَبِيًّا (29)
قَالَ إِنِّي عَبْدُ اللَّهِ آتَانِيَ الْكِتَابَ وَجَعَلَنِي نَبِيًّا (30)
وَجَعَلَنِي مُبَارَكًا أَيْنَ مَا كُنْتُ وَأَوْصَانِي بِالصَّلَاةِ وَالزَّكَاةِ مَا دُمْتُ حَيًّا (31)
وَبَرًّا بِوَالِدَتِي وَلَمْ يَجْعَلْنِي جَبَّارًا شَقِيًّا (32)
وَالسَّلَامُ عَلَيَّ يَوْمَ وُلِدْتُ وَيَوْمَ أَمُوتُ وَيَوْمَ أُبْعَثُ حَيًّا (33)
ذَٰلِكَ عِيسَى ابْنُ مَرْيَمَ ۚ قَوْلَ الْحَقِّ الَّذِي فِيهِ يَمْتَرُونَ (34)

*Naturally any similar miracles or events in that infancy Arabic Bible would also be true since it is mentioned in the ultimate reference, the Quran, the true Word of God. Yet, apparently to the author, more Jesus (PBUH) power and miracles in the Quran, that are not mentioned in today's Bible; miracles that add to the reverence of Jesus (PBUH), are now something to be fought and discredited!

Normally we would display the truth of the event and prove, as usual, that the disagreement of the author with the Word of God in the Quran is his own failure. This time, however, we will not show why a miracle of Jesus (PBUH) is also mentioned in the author's "Infancy Arabic Bible", but instead we will show the reader the utmost important fact as to why such a miracle was not mentioned in the selected Gospels that make today's Bible.

1- Read what Jesus said first when he talked in the cradle: **"I am the servant of Allah"**, immediately Jesus (PBUH) says what kills the controversy that may send billions of people astray, **"I am not God, but I am a servant of God, then he made me a Prophet, gave me powers and ordered me to pray, give charity and be dutiable to my mother."**
The beginning of his statement simply ends the whole argument.

2- Has anyone ever asked the question as to why no one wondered how was it possible that at the time that an adulterous woman would be stoned to death as per the Torah law, a high-profile young girl would walk in with what seems to be her illegitimate baby, yet her people would let her walk free and unscathed? How is it possible that she could ever survive that encounter?
Not to mention the fact that she wasn't just another girl from a distinguished family, but probably the only female allowed to worship God in an all male servant temple, and was sponsored by another Prophet of God Zackary (PBUH) - her aunt's husband - and engaged to another man, Joseph the carpenter, who could have avenged his honor himself. How could she survive all that? Escaping to Egypt can never be the answer because they saw her face to face, and they could have dragged her to the temple or just stoned her right then and there.
The only possible answer is the truth.
Her baby spoke in the cradle and rendered them all mute, defending the honor of his mother, the purest woman that ever lived and will ever live, and then stating his status as a Prophet of God and his mission on earth. That is the only reason why Virgin Mary (PBUH) had survived the impact of her people seeing her with an out of marriage baby.

"The Crucifixion"

The next appalling statement by the author is clearly telling of what might be his concept of God!

On page 55 Mr. Spencer wrote:

"It would have been wrong for Allah to allow one of his Prophets to die in shame and humiliation, so Allah substituted someone who looked like him before he was placed on the Cross."

*Did the author say that God gets embarrassed?

Did the author say that God gets wronged?

Did the author say that God changes what he had decided for his Prophets in response to what humans do, or say, to avoid being" wrong"?

In the Holy Quran Allah says:

[40] "So I swear by the Lord of the east and the west that surely We are Able"

[41] "To replace them by better (people) than them; and our powers are unprecedented"

Quran, Surat (Al Maarej) Ch 70, Verses (40-41)

فَلَا أُقْسِمُ بِرَبّ الْمَشَارِقِ وَالْمَغَارِبِ إِنَّا لَقَادِرُونَ (40)

عَلَىٰ أَنْ نُبَدّلَ خَيْرًا مِنْهُمْ وَمَا نَحْنُ بِمَسْبُوقِينَ (41)

This is Allah in the Quran, not just in this chapter but almost in every chapter of the Quran, above and beyond any might. This is what Muslims believe. Where did the author come up with such a statement, not to mention attributing it to Islam?!!

Oddly enough the oldest copy of any known Bible, which is known as "Codex Sinaticus," - around 300 AD - has just been compiled and published in Latin. It has though one significant difference from today's Bible: there is no mention what so ever of the Crucifixion of Jesus (PBUH).

Maybe because the truth is what was already given to mankind on a silver platter in the Quran, that Jesus (PBUH) was raised to heaven and was never killed nor crucified?

"And they neither killed him nor crucified him, but it was made to look like that to them..."
Quran, Surat (Al Nissa) Ch (4) Verse (157)

(157) ۞ وَمَا قَتَلُوهُ وَمَا صَلَبُوهُ وَلَٰكِنْ شُبِّهَ لَهُمْ

And the verse continues:

"And those who differ about it are in doubt of it"
Quran, Surat (Al Nissa) Ch (4) Verse (157)

(157) ۞ وَإِنَّ الَّذِينَ اخْتَلَفُوا فِيهِ لَفِي شَكٍّ مِنْهُ

The author concludes that the verse can only mean that Muhammad (PBUH): "encountered squabbling groups of Christians and intended to present his revelation as a final resolution to the matter"!

*By that dreamy statement, the author is telling us that throughout history there was no disagreement about how the claimed crucifixion and resurrection of Jesus (PBUH) happened except at the time of the Prophet Muhammad (PBUH) where, there it was, the first and last fighting of "rival groups of Christians", and that Muhammad - now being the ultimate Christianity judge - created that revelation just to settle their squabbling for them!

So the Quranic statement, according to the author, has nothing to do with the fact that he truly was never killed nor crucified, but instead related to an imaginary local Christian rivalry - that was never mentioned in the entire history of Islam - and that Muhammad was the one to put it to rest not even being a Christian himself!

Does the author know that the story of the resurrection varies significantly between the four Gospels within today's Bible? Never mind the 22 other Gospels that the Church decided not to include in the Bible to begin with, then, and to date?

Example: In the Gospel of Mark the crucifixion happened the day <u>after</u> the Passover meal was eaten (Mark 14:12; 15:25), on the other hand, according to the Gospel of John the crucifixion happened in the day <u>before</u> the Passover meal was eaten. (John 19:14)

Now the author tells us that that major Christian dilemma was just a seventh century Christian-Arab matter that was settled by the prophet of Islam!

On Page 56, the author notices that the stories of the Prophets that he has been quoting from various Gospels are not identical to the ones in the Quran and adds an interesting explanation to it:

"One need not assume that Muhammad had actually read the heretical Christian material that seemed to have influenced the Quran"

*What an intelligent observation from the author knowing that Muhammad died an illiterate man! The author adds later that Muhammad then must have heard them recited!

Would that be all of them, including all the heretical ones in a non-Christian Arab Peninsula?

He adds that Muhammad - supposedly - now being the world's illiterate super comparative religious genius authored the events of the Quran about God's Prophets! These are God's Prophets who spanned thousands of years, including details never mentioned in the Old Testament, the New Testament, and the heretical ones as well!

My dear reader, if you are not already tired of me refuting this over and over, I beg your pardon, for I am!

Another embarrassing mistake - I hope it is not intentional like the many others - when the author addresses the verse in the Quran when Virgin Mary returned to her people and the Quran quoted what her people had addressed her by:

" **Oh, sister of Haroun (Aaron)**"
Quran, Surat (Maryam) Ch (19), verse (28)

95

The author wrote:

"...And appeared to some Muhammad contemporaries, that Muhammad confused Mary the sister of Moses and Aaron with Mary the mother of Jesus"!

*The joke is not that the author, as usual, never mentions the names of these contemporaries that no one had ever heard of - let's hope his coming book won't be called the "truth" about contemporaries! - the joke however, is the fact that the author made up that confusion because he is "apparently" ignorant of a wide spread Middle Eastern way of honoring people who have names similar to relatives of Prophets or great men. For example, Ali Ibn Abi Talib, the cousin of the Prophet and the great companion, was the father of Al Hassan Ibn Ali, so any one whose name is Hassan in many of the Arab countries is honored mostly in dialogue by being called Hassan Aba Ali, or the one whom Ali is his father, etc. In the case of the people of Virgin Mary, who thought she gave birth to an illegitimate child, they talked to her in the meaning of, "How could one with such an honorable name do that?"
Here is the immediate continuation of the verse that the author conveniently dropped out of his translation of the verse!

"Oh, sister of Haroun, your father was not a man who used to commit adultery, nor your mother was an unchaste woman"
Quran, Surat (Maryam) Ch 19, verse (28)

يَا أُخْتَ هَارُونَ مَا كَانَ أَبُوكِ امْرَأَ سَوْءٍ وَمَا كَانَتْ أُمُّكِ بَغِيًّا (28)

The author adds after that, that a Christian man asked Muhammad about it, and that the Prophet who had a "ready answer" answered him with the same answer we just explained.
Muslim historians of the biography of the Prophet never mentioned the incident with a Christian man, but actually it was one of the companions of the Prophet who asked him the question.

Look at the author's ridiculous way of describing the answer of God's Prophet as "ready answer"! How can one tell the truth in the eye of a truth-seeker who by the way witnessed nothing?! Should one stutter

96

to make the answer look not-ready and by that it would be truthful? Or is it the ignorant calling God's Prophet confused?

"Other borrowings"

On page 57, the author expands - again - on indirectly praising Muhammad as the utmost genius and most knowledgeable human that ever lived. Everywhere in chapter four of his book, the author has not been only claiming that Muhammad, the illiterate man, in a desert with no schools or libraries, had just amazingly gained superb knowledge of the entire body of Jewish and Christian scriptures that are not even in Arabic - suddenly after the age of forty - but in this paragraph he goes even further!

He questions the vivid details and description of paradise "Jannah" in the Quran that are not found in any of the Biblical scriptures including the heretical ones! And his explanation is:

Muhammad is also a "Guru" of the Persian scriptures and Hinduism as well! He quotes another truth-seeker of a book named "Sources of Islam" who says:

"Zoroastrians and Hindus…bear the most extraordinary likeness to what we find in the Koran and Hadeeth."

*In addition to the fact that both sects are practiced in two totally foreign languages – Persian and old Hindi - to Muhammad (PBUH), but notice that all the elements of the description of Paradise in the Holy Quran are the basic earthly environment elements of any time; rivers of the nicest drinks, beautiful spouses, gold, pearls, emeralds, the best of weather, food and fruits, and simply utmost pleasure and happiness just for the wishing.

What did the author and his friend expect? Lower tax rates?!

The fact that other non-Abrahimic communities had dreams or vision about an eternal life or another paradise is the normal thing to expect, what is even more natural is that the elements of these dreams would have been mostly elements of the things that anyone utmost desires in his current life, even today; the beautiful spouses, gold, pearls, pleasures etc. which would be similar to some of what God had promised the righteous

97

in Paradise. Ibn Abbas, who was one of the closest companions to the Prophet, said that "The similarity between what Allah had promised in "Jannah" and our earthly things is just in the names. Gold is not the gold and pearls are not the pearls"

How would the Quran describe paradise to the humans of the seventh century? That it has huge plasma TV screens, race cars with no polluting exhaust and super fast internet?! Would it be the same even to people who will live centuries from now?
It has to be in the same elements of the same basic natural desires that we, all mankind, can relate to, in the 7th century, today and in the future.

Yet the purpose was also for our limited comprehension to have some grasp of a hint of the wonderful paradise truths that we are incapable of comprehending: God says in the quotation of the Prophet:

"I (God) prepared for my righteous worshippers, what an eye has never seen, an ear has never heard, nor a human heart has ever felt"
(Prophet Muhammad (PBUH))
*Narrator: Abu Hurayra. **Reference**: Saheeh Al Bukhary, **Number**: 4779.*
Degree: *Correct*

But why there is no similar accurate description in the Bible like those in the Quran and the Quotations "Hadeeth" of the Prophet? Prophet Muhammad is the only Prophet of God (and human being, for that matter) who was ever raised by God to heaven in the journey of "Israa and Miraaj" to see both paradise and hell fire with his own eyes and come back to tell us. He also is the only Prophet of God who had seen the other mighty Prophets, talked, prayed with them, and described them to mankind.

While we are at the subject, we just wonder, as to why our author and Mr. Tisdal the author of the book "Sources of Islam" never tell us as to why Muhammad - the world's ultimate comparative religions borrower, according to them - didn't borrow "Vinayaka" the Hindu's God of a human body and an elephant head, from Hinduism?! Or added "Ahuramazda" the ultimate divine character of the Zoroastrians, to the revered figures of the Quran as well?

May be because they are atheists and that the One Mighty God who revealed the Quran to Muhammad and all mankind condemns paganism?

In the matter of fact, just the name of the book "Sources of Islam" (when The Holy Quran and the correct Hadeeth of the Prophet are before everyone like a glaring sun), reminds me of the story when people noticed a man in the street circling a light post at night searching the ground over and over again. When asked, the man explained that he was looking for his wallet that he lost in his backyard, and when people wondered why wasn't he looking for it in his backyard; he explained that it was dark there!

Muhammad was an illiterate man, but revealed to us what was revealed to him by God.

"And he doesn't utter of his desire, he is not but revealing what is revealed to him"
Quran Surat (Al Najm) (The star) Ch 53, Verses (3-4)

Or as Jesus says according to the Gospel of John:
"Howbeit, when He the Spirit of Truth is come, He will guide you into all truth. <u>For He shall not speak of Himself, but whatsoever He shall hear that shall He speak</u>; and He will show you things to come.

He shall glorify me; for He shall receive of mine, and shall show it unto you"
King James Bible, John 16:12 - 14

How painfully relentless the truth is when one's goal is to cover it at any cost.

"Revelations of convenience"

The next topic is something that I always use as an example of the extent of misinformation and apparent fabrication that some go to just to smear the honor of the last Prophet of God.

On page 59, the author comments on how the Quran was revealed to the Prophet:

"Some of the other difficulties Non-Muslims have had with accepting Muhammad as a Prophet come from the circumstances of many of the revelations he received. As we shall see, quite often during his Prophetic career he received revelations that answered critics, or solved a disputed question, or gave his particular perspective on a series of events"

*Let us ask ourselves what, to the contrary, a revelation from God should be about? Is it to ignore questions and pressing issues? Complicate and cause vague disputed questions? Or should it adapt and promote the prospect of atheism over the truth of righteousness a Prophet of God is revealing?!

The author, then, adds in his total disrespect for God: "...these revelations seemed to manifest Allah's anxiety to grant his Prophet his heart's desires"

*The author claims that the One Mighty God has anxieties and that the author, of all people, had special knowledge of the desires of the Prophet of God that no one obviously knew!

The puzzling question here: what are the desires that the author is referring to? All his life the Prophet could have had any earthly desire he could have wanted; all that pales, however, in comparison with what he was offered by Quraysh's leaders, just to abandon his message which exceeded any man's imagination. The Prophet of God was never a man

100

seeking any desire but that which to satisfy his creator by delivering His message. We'll see that clearly, shortly.

Not even the most imaginative of Islam-haters can find one iota even of an old lie that dared to attempt touching Muhammad and his decent mannerism, even before he was revealed as the last Prophet of God. There are no accounts whatsoever that he fornicated or had any illegitimate relationship with any woman, even when doing so was the norm for a young strong man from one of the noblest families of Quraysh. Of all Meccans, he had the title "the truthful honest." He (PBUH) married his wife Khadija at the age of 25, never married any other woman nor had a one iota of a relationship with another woman for another 25 years till Khadija died, and at the time he was 50 years old. 10 years of that quarter-century marriage period, Muhammad was a Prophet of God who could have still married whomever he wanted, including the wealthiest, most beautiful women in the Arab Peninsula offered to him by the leaders of Mecca. Their offer was in addition to all the money and leadership he could have asked for, in return for his abandonment of "his new religion," yet he refused. Refused, I might add, from a position of weakness and persecution, and not a position of strength, which sheds more light on the verse in the Quran:

"And you are truly but with great manners"
Quran, Surat (Al Qalam) (The Pen), Ch (68) Verse (4)

وَإِنَّكَ لَعَلَىٰ خُلُقٍ عَظِيمٍ (4)

After the death of Khadija, (his first and only wife for 25 years) his migration to Madina and the beginning of Islam's spreading to new tribes and corners of the Arab Peninsula were the reasons Muhammad started marrying into some of these tribes with the permission of God, to strengthen alliances and invite them to Islam. Marrying into a family from another tribe was an element of peace and respect between the two at the time. In the case of the Prophet, it was also an honor for that tribe

101

or the family of the bride. Some of his marriages happened for totally different reasons, yet it was also about respect and honor.

During the early battles of Islam, many of the companions of the Prophet died fighting for the sake of God, leaving behind widows who were mostly old and poor.
To honor the widows and the legacy of their late husbands, the Prophet usually asked his companions to marry and care for them, and they mostly did. The ones that sometimes the companions didn't want to marry, the Prophet went ahead and married them. The total marriages of the Prophet were 13, 9 were simultaneous ones.
Of all marriages only two wives were able to carry a child, and only two out of the thirteen were also what people may have described as attractive. Here are the facts about the next story our author is about to tell us:

Zaynab Bint Jahsh was the Prophet's cousin, he had known, seen her all his life, and if he wanted to marry her he could have married her a thousand times over. Even though she opposed it initially, Prophet Muhammad was the one who persuaded her to marry his former servant Zayd Ibn Haritha. Prophet Muhammad started a marriage between a servant / former slave and his cousin whom they both (Muhammad and Zaynab) belonged to the noble tribe of Bani Hashem. The reason was to show people and set a practical example that there are no classes in Islam and that no one is better than another except by fearing God. If Muhammad wanted his cousin as a wife, why would he, of all people, encourage her to marry his former servant?

The marriage didn't last long because Zaynab kept looking down upon her husband, who kept complaining to the Prophet till the Prophet, found no other solution but to accept their divorce. The Prophet, in that case, didn't ask his companions to propose to her for marriage for he was the one who convinced her to marry Zayd against the old traditions of the tribe to begin with, and because she was of his own family; in Islam, your relatives are more deserving of your virtue. So after the legal

102

waiting period of 3 months following her divorce, the Prophet married Zaynab. Is there more proof than God himself telling us why in the Quran?

"..So that (in the future) **there may be no difficulty to the believers marrying the wives of their adopted sons when they divorce them after marrying them and Allah's Command is fulfilled."**
Quran, Surat (Al Ahzab) (The Pen), Ch (33) Verse (37)

لِكَيْ لَا يَكُونَ عَلَى الْمُؤْمِنِينَ حَرَجٌ فِي أَزْوَاجِ أَدْعِيَائِهِمْ إِذَا قَضَوْا مِنْهُنَّ وَطَرًا ۚ وَكَانَ أَمْرُ اللَّهِ مَفْعُولًا (37)

Here is the same story, only it is Mr. Spencer narrating! On page 59:

"Prophet Muhammad had an adopted son by the name of Zayd Ibn Haritha, who was married to Zaynab Bint Jahsh, and both of them never wanted to marry each other because Muhammad insisted " to show the equality of all believers" for Zaynab "was from a notable family" - the author never tells us that she is the Prophet's cousin for obvious reasons (MZ) - " while Zayd was a freed slave" the author quotes the verse (our translation) - "It is not for a believer, man or woman, when Allah and His Messenger have decreed a matter that they should have any option in their decision. And whoever disobeys Allah and His Messenger has indeed strayed an apparent stray"

*First of all, adoption is forbidden in Islam; in the Holy Quran:

"Name them to their fathers, it is more just that way to Allah"
Quran, Surat (Al Ahzab) Ch (33), Verse (5)

ادْعُوهُمْ لِآبَائِهِمْ هُوَ أَقْسَطُ عِنْدَ اللَّهِ (5)

And while sponsoring an orphan or a widow has one of the greatest of rewards in Islam, an orphan can never carry the name of his sponsor for there are many inheritances and legal rights that rely upon who is biologically related to whom. Zayd was a servant of the Prophet before Islam; his parents came to the Prophet and offered to pay him money and let their son travel with them. The Prophet (PBUH) refused to take any money from them and offered for them to take their son without forcing Zayd. Zayd was so grateful for the treatment he had received from the Prophet that he refused adamantly to go back to his parents. "Muhammad's son" was something that Muhammad declared before his Prophethood; while everyone knew who he really was, it was also a nickname given by the people of Mecca to the oddity of Zayd - not Muhammad - preferring the Prophet over his own parents. All that happened before the Prophethood of Muhammad. After Muhammad (PBUH) became a Prophet, Allah forbade adoption. Then Zayd became what he always was: a companion and a former servant of the prophet of God.

Second of all, look at the absurdness of our author giving this paragraph the title of "Revelations of convenience." It is the Prophet himself who revealed the verses to mankind; had it been an embarrassment, why mention it all to begin with if - according to the supposition of the author - the Holy Quran was all up to Muhammad, to conveniently say whatever he wanted to say in it!

Zayd came to the Prophet and asked him to allow him to divorce Zaynab, and the Prophet told him to keep his wife and fear Allah, and who told us that? God himself in the Quran:

"And when you who we bestowed our favor upon you and you upon him, said to him (Zayd) "Keep your wife, and fear Allah..." *Quran, Surat (Al Ahzab) Ch (33) Verse (37)*

وَإِذْ تَقُولُ لِلَّذِي أَنْعَمَ اللَّهُ عَلَيْهِ وَأَنْعَمْتَ عَلَيْهِ أَمْسِكْ عَلَيْكَ زَوْجَكَ وَاتَّقِ اللهَ.. (37)

In the continuation of the verse, God blames Muhammad for not being supportive of the divorce that both parties are demanding, for God had foretold Muhammad that Zaynab was to be his wife in the future; while Muhammad was concerned that some of the people would try to make it a backbiting issue against the Prophet. God ended that part of the verse with the fact that the Prophet considered what people might say

and God is more deserving of any consideration.
The verse continues:

"...And you did hide in yourself that which Allah will make manifest, you did fear the people whereas Allah is more deserving that you fear Him. So when Zayd had accomplished what he wanted (i.e. divorced her), We gave her to you in marriage, so that (in the future) **there may be no difficulty to the believers marrying the wives of their adopted sons when they divorce them and Allah's Command is fulfilled."**
Quran, Surat (Al Ahzab) Ch (33) Verse (37)

وَتُخْفِي فِي نَفْسِكَ مَا اللَّهُ مُبْدِيهِ وَتَخْشَى النَّاسَ وَاللَّهُ أَحَقُّ أَنْ تَخْشَاهُ ۚ فَلَمَّا قَضَىٰ زَيْدٌ مِنْهَا وَطَرًا زَوَّجْنَاكَهَا لِكَيْ لَا يَكُونَ عَلَى الْمُؤْمِنِينَ حَرَجٌ فِي أَزْوَاجِ أَدْعِيَائِهِمْ إِذَا قَضَوْا مِنْهُنَّ وَطَرًا ۚ وَكَانَ أَمْرُ اللَّهِ مَفْعُولًا (37)

God also states that He manifested that marriage for Prophet Muhammad to clear any doubt that not only can a noble woman marry a freed slave, but also that the best of men who is the Prophet himself, can marry the divorcee of a freed slave.

Another purpose is to affirm that there is no adoption in Islam, evident by the fact that Allah wouldn't allow a marriage of a father in law to his former daughter in law: unless Zayd was not any son of Muhammad.

If it is truly a revelation of convenience, why reveal the verse all together to begin with if it is something that is authored by Muhammad and not the Word of God? In itself this is a proof after the thousand proofs already in the Quran, that it is God's Word and that Muhammad, "the truthful honest," is His Prophet who delivers the message of God as is. Let's look at the appalling claims of Mr. Spencer about the matter.

On page 60, and naturally without a reference or a source of an incident that never happened, the author fabricated a quote for Zayd: "Zayd, saddled with a marriage he had not wanted, saw his way out. He went to see Muhammad and echoed Zaynab's language: "Messenger of God, I have heard that you came to my house. Why didn't you go in, you are who are dear to me as my father and mother?" Then he got to the

105

point, "Messenger of God, perhaps Zaynab has excited your admiration, and so I will separate myself from her." Muhammad told him, "Keep thy wife to thy self and fear Allah" (Quran 33:37)"

*Not only that Zayd never said that, but the truth-seeker uses an old trick to bring a fabrication and give it the authentication of another truthful statement he attaches at the end.

When we say Zayd never said that, we say that not because there is no record in any of the major references that he ever said that, but also due to the fact that it is totally forbidden "Haram" for a man to enter another man's house while he is not there, and then to have Zayd asking the Prophet of God "why didn't you go in?" is beyond laughable. The author naturally didn't have a source or a reference to the laughable story, but added a verse in the Quran that is irrelevant to the fabricated story the author has just put before it (the correct translation is listed above), so some may think the whole story is in the Quran!

A side note (M.Z):

In the entire body of all the correct quotations and biography of the Prophet, there is no expression ever of (excite your admiration) that the author uses as a saying of Zayd; if you ever see that expression in Arabic it would be in contemporary writings and as an expression originally translated from English literature! English as a language was formed around the end of the 12th century! Five centuries after the passing of the Prophet!

Zayd came to the Prophet repeatedly complaining about Zaynab looking down upon him, and asked for a divorce several times, but what was the Prophet's answer in the Quran?

"Keep your wife and fear God."
Quran, Surat (Al Ahzab) Ch (33) Verse (37)

3- The author never mentions that Zaynab was the Prophet's cousin - the daughter of his aunt! - That intentional omission was obviously necessary for him to imply that the Prophet fell in love with her beauty when he saw her the first time in the house of Zayd. The Prophet never entered the house of Zayd while Zayd wasn't there. The author also never mentions that the Prophet could have married her a thousand times over for every time he saw her before her marriage to Zayd.

4- On page 61, the author quotes Zaynab, boasting about the fact of her marriage to the Prophet: "You were given in marriage by your families, while I was married (to the Prophet) by Allah from over seven heavens." Where is the scene caught by the author's custom-made-time-machine video camera, recording the way the Prophet looked, turned, and felt seeing his cousin for the hundredth time when he was over 50 years of age? The same Prophet that the day he died, had over 124,000 followers and was the most powerful man in the Arab Peninsula, and all he had in his house were few pieces of stale bread, and some oats.

And it is him (PBUH) who said:

"I was only sent to complete the most noble of manners"
(Prophet Muhammad (PBUH))
Narrator: *Abu Hurayra* **Reference**: *Al silsilah Al Saheeha* **Number**: *45.* **Degree**: *Correct*

That is the Prophet Mr. Spencer is talking about!

On page 61, the author narrates for us the story of "Ifk" or the "false accusation."

Ayesha, the wife of the Prophet, was in the convoy of the Muslim army. When they stopped for a break, she dropped her necklace and went looking for it. The helpers of the convoy thought that she was still inside the Hawdaj, which is a small compartment carried on the camel back, and took her camel with the departing convoy. When Ayesha came back, she found the convoy had already left, so she went back to her original camel-stopping location, where sleep took over her. A delayed Muslim fighter by the name of Safwan Ibn Al Moatal noticed her when he saw a person sitting from afar. When he got closer he saw Ayesha asleep and recognized her, so he gestured to her to ride on his camel to catch up with the convoy, while he walked aside.

When they got close to the convoy, a man by the name of Abdullah Ibn Salool, who is well-known as "the leader of hypocrites," started a rumor about a possible affair between the Prophet's wife and Safwan.

Abdullah Ibn Abi Salool was known for plotting feuds against Islam and the Prophet every way he could, yet publicly he declared he was a devout Muslim. Ayesha later learned from another lady what the people were saying, so she asked the Prophet to stay at her parent's house. The Prophet always consulted with his companions even in a matter that was that personal. The majority stated what he already knew: that she was of the most honorable women of Quraysh, and that the fighter Safwan was an honorable man who never entered the house of the Prophet without the Prophet being there.

Then 10 verses were revealed to the Prophet by Arch-Angel Gabriel, declaring the innocence of Ayesha and the plot of the hypocrites against Islam and its Prophet.

On page 61 the author wrote:
"Since the order for veiling meant that no one could look at her or speak to her"

*Not true. The veil is for the woman's attire; in Islam a veiled woman can talk to anyone as long as they are not in seclusion, are in public, and for a daily life necessity.

On page 62 the author added:
"Ayesha had been alone with a man who was not her husband, for some that was enough to begin circulating ugly rumors about her"

*The author, relying on a confused translation, makes a big mistake, which I admit is easy to fall into when reading the text describing the incident. The author had the word "Manzel" which in contemporary Arabic means "home," confused with its original Arabic meaning of "stopping location." So when Ibn Al Moatal Saw Ayesha, they were both in the open desert in the same location where her camel in the convoy stopped earlier and not in a 'house"; I do not need to explain

108

to the reader that standing in an open desert with someone can be anything but called in isolation or alone. A fundamental mannerism of the Arabs at the time was to help someone who was stranded like Ayesha; imagine if that person was the wife of the Prophet of God herself.

When Al Moatal saw her, he brought her attention by waking her up yelling the "Isterjaa" phrase: "We are from God and to him we will return." Ayesha covered her face and never spoke a word with him. Most importantly is the paragraph of Ayesha's story that none other than the author himself showed in the same page, where Ayesha states:
"He dismounted from his camel and made it kneel down, putting his leg on its front legs and then I got up and rode on it"!!

When the camel kneeled down and Ayesha rode it, was the man riding his camel that he dismounted from, inside the room of a closed building?? How could anyone deduce that "Ayesha had been alone with a man who was not her husband"? Did he mean by alone, outside in the open desert?
And it continues, on page 63 the author comments:
"Muhammad evidently believed the rumors"

*Where did the author get that Muhammad "evidently" believed the rumors?! It is really amazing to me how that any third grader may accept to read Mr. Spencer's books filled with these comedic statements.

Muhammad's treatment to Ayesha was different. The Prophet wouldn't be a human being if it wasn't, yet who said the Prophet believed the rumors?! Did the Prophet say I believed the rumors? Did he divorce her? Did any of his companions even say I think that the Prophet believed the rumors? Even Ibn Salool the hypocrite of his time, never said that the Prophet believed the rumors. Where did "Ibn Spencer" then get that from? I am really puzzled as to the how extremely low Mr. Spencer's perception of his readers IQ is.

Let's look at what the Prophet really said and believed about the whole matter. The Prophet addressed the matter to all Muslims in his famous statement (Khotba) about the Issue:

"Oh, Muslims, who would give me my excuse for a man whose harm had reached my home, and by Allah I never learned about my wife but virtue and they have mentioned a man who I never learned about but virtue, and who never entered my home except with me"
(Prophet Muhammad (PBUH))
Narrator: Oruwa Ibn Al Zubair. **Reference**: Saheeh Al Bukhary, **Number**: 7369. **Degree**: Correct   **Narrator**: Ayesha. **Reference**: Saheeh Al Bukhary, **Number**: 4141. **Degree**: Correct

Oddly enough our author brings the same statement of the Prophet on the following page! The Prophet clearly, in black and white, says, I do not believe the rumor and just one page earlier the author comments "evidently Muhammad believed the rumor"?!

I ask Mr. Spencer, what does his word "evidently" mean; does it mean it becomes 100% different from one page to the next? I am really curious to be introduced to the new revelation of the meaning proposed by the author.

Ayesha prays to Allah to reveal her innocence and Allah with his mercy upon her reveals 10 verses in Surat (Al Noor) (The Light) that declared her innocence.

Then, another major embarrassing fabrication! The author not only quotes the 10 verses in a mutilated self-serving translation, but also he removes 5 entire verses completely out!

Here is the correct, complete translation:

[11] Verily! Those who brought forth the slander are a group among you. Do not consider it a bad thing for you. But it is good for you. Unto every man among them what he earned of sin, and the one who had the greater share of it, his will be a great torment.

110

[12] Why then, did not the believers, men and women, when you heard it (the slander) think good of their own people and say: "This is an apparent lie?"

[13] Why did they not produce four witnesses? Since they have not produced witnesses! Then with Allah they are the liars.

[14] Had it not been for the Grace of Allah and His Mercy upon you in this World and in the Hereafter, a great torment would have touched you for what you have meddled yourselves into.

[15] When you propagate it with your tongues, and utter it with your mouths that which you have no knowledge of, you think it is a little thing, while it is with Allah great.

[16] And why did you not, when you heard it, say? "It is not right for us to speak of this. Glory is to Allah. This is a great lie."

[17] Allah advises you to never repeat the like of it, if you are believers.

[18] And Allah makes His lessons plain to you, and Allah is All-Knowing, All-Wise.

[19] Verily, those who like abominations to spread among those who believe, they will have a painful torment in this World and in the Hereafter. And Allah knows and you do not know.

[20] And it is for none other than the Grace of Allah and His Mercy upon you. And that Allah is full of kindness, Most Merciful.
Quran, Surat (Al Noor) (The Light), Ch (24) Verses (11-20)

Here is the translation of Mr. Spencer, on page 66:

"Why did they not produce four witnesses? Since they produce not witnesses, they verily are liars in the sight of Allah. Had it not been for the grace of Allah and His mercy onto you in the world and the hereafter an awful doom had overtaken you for that whereof ye murmured. When ye welcomed it with your tongues, and uttered with your mouth that whereof ye had no knowledge ye counted it a trifle. In the sight of Allah it is very great. Wherefore, when ye heard it, said ye not: it is not for us to speak of this. Glory be to Thee (Oh, Allah)! This is awful calumny. (Quran 24:11-20)

111

Half of the 10 verses are hidden from the reader; specifically the ones that show the general ethical purpose of revealing the verses. I ask the reader to compare and decide for him or herself.

"The consequences"

On page 67, the Author comments on the incident; he wrote:
"It seems as if Allah's solicitude for his Prophet takes the Quran, which is supposed to be a universal message applicable to all people in all times and places, into some rather surprisingly localized area"!

*Now you know why the author intentionally omitted half the verses from the last page. Here are the missing verses:

[11] Verily! Those who brought forth the slander are a group among you. Do not consider it a bad thing for you. But it is good for you. Unto every man among them what he earned of sin, and the one who had the greater share of it, his will be a great torment.

[12] Why then, did not the believers, men and women, when you heard it (the slander) think good of their own people and say: "This is an apparent lie?"

[18] And Allah makes his lessons plain to you, and Allah is All-Knowing, All-Wise.

[19] Verily, those who like abominations to spread among those who believe, they will have a painful torment in this world and in the Hereafter. And Allah knows and you do not know.

[20] And it is for none other than the Grace of Allah and His Mercy upon you. And that Allah is full of kindness, Most Merciful.

Another question; did the author omit verse no. [11], for it scared him personally?

Clearly, Allah in verse [18] tells all Muslims that the whole issue is a lesson that Allah wanted to make clear to all Muslims.
The lesson is backbiting and tarnishing people's reputations unjustly, falsely, and without proof.

112

Then Verse [19] is about those who like to spread rumors to falsely promote as if there is a consensus of wide spread abominations in society - sexual misbehavior in our example -and that those will receive severe punishment from God.

Is backbiting and throwing false accusations at people a localized area in the universal human experience?

Let me ask our truth-seeker; why did you author this book that I am refuting? Because you wanted to praise God, Islam and the Prophet of God?! Is throwing all these accusations, misinformation, and fabrications about the last Prophet of God a localized area to you and not universal enough for a population that spans 1.6 billion Muslims in over 57 countries? Are extra-marital affairs and their consequences including the innocence of a falsely-accused woman or man, a trivial matter in any time, place or level of any society?

The author then moves to another area (that is the trade mark of misinformation about Islam), which is the mandate of four witnesses to the crime of adultery. God had put a severe condition to punishing a man or a woman with the crime of adultery, why?

Because the punishment that God put to it fits it as an irreversible cancer of societies, which is death to a married man or woman who commits adultery, yet the law is very strict in accepting the witnesses who have to be four, and further, the four have to simultaneously testify that they saw the intercourse as clear as a pen inserted into an ink Pot.

This criterion is so difficult to apply, that in the first 1000 years of Islam this punishment was only executed a whopping three times upon adulterers!

The three incidents were for adulterers who insisted on admitting their crime and weren't even caught via the rules! Having stated that, how then would the author like it if the four witnesses rule was not there, that a woman would come and claim that - for example - the author raped her, should he be killed because she said so?

What should a married woman do if a single man claimed that she had an affair with him? He would be punished by lashing and expulsion from the same city, and she should then be killed? Is that fair? Probably every terminally ill person would then have all his enemies executed by just admitting he had sex with them!

The punishment in Islam in itself is obviously similar to many in Islamic law; more of a deterrent to future violations than a vengeance of any sort. God's law or Islamic law is not vindictive, but it is purposefully preventive.

"And in punishment, there is life for you, O, you who comprehend so you may fear God"
Quran, Surat (Al Baqara) (The Cow) Ch (2) Verse (179)

وَلَكُمْ فِي الْقِصَاصِ حَيَاةٌ يَا أُولِي الْأَلْبَابِ لَعَلَّكُمْ تَتَّقُونَ (179)

The author brings an incorrect statistic that in Pakistan 75% of women prisoners are jailed because they falsely claimed they were raped! Just use your logic, my reader, if that was the case and the number is that staggering, which woman, then, in her right mind would even bring it up? Not to mention that now, the author claims that jails are filled with them! No thefts, murders, violence or embezzlements? All are busy being raped?!

In Islamic law, if there is any undeniable scientific evidence that a woman was raped like bruises coupled with correct DNA testing, then a man can be executed for the crime. And that is the correct Islamic law applied to the matter in many Islamic countries today.

I also want to bring the reader attention to the only sand box those Islam-bashers/fabricators like to play in, which is tent villages in the rural areas of Afghanistan and Pakistan.

Areas where, abject poverty and illiteracy, in general and of Islamic law sometimes, is what stares you in the face, yet Islam-haters can only see that these horrible local conditions must be Islam and the other 1.6 billion Muslims must be all the same!

I would have loved to take Mr. Spencer and his likes in a tour to New York's South Bronx for example, and claim that this is America; its quality of life, social relationships, crime level and economy, but I am

114

the first one to testify that this is not America, the same as his bizarre Afghan/Pakistan misinformation tales have nothing to do with Islam itself.

Our author brings up another misinformation subject about women rights in Islam. A case study of a Saudi girl who was in a compromising position in a car with a young man; both were attacked by several men who raped her. While the men received various punishments for the rape crime - even though there was no other four witnesses to their crime! - using regular evidence and the victim identifying them. The western media roared against the court also applying punishment upon the girl, why? Islam-haters have portrayed the girl's punishment as if it was because she was raped or as a result of her testifying against the rapists!! The girl's punishment was, however, for being in a car with a man foreign to her, and what is the purpose of that rule in Islam? So that society is protected from the ills of adultery and for a woman to be protected from a compromising position where she might be
- for example - raped!
It is like trying to hold up someone with a gun, and then to be held up with a machine gun by other criminals.
Being a victim in the second crime doesn't make you innocent of the first. The king of Saudi Arabia interfered himself, not yielding to "international pressure" as the author would like to say, but in saying that the physical harm she received by the rapists in itself was enough punishment for her.

The author then brings a verse trying to prove that Islam restricts a woman's testimony "Particular in cases involving sexual immortality." The author, as usual, doesn't bring the complete verse; we will bring his quote of a proof first.
On page 68 he quotes the Quran:
"Call in two witnesses from among you, but if two men cannot be found then one man and two women who you judge fit as two witnesses, so that if either of them commits an error, the other will remember" (2:282)"

Here is the beginning of the verse that the author intentionally omitted:

115

"O, you who believe, if you owed a debt to be paid at a determined date then write it down..."
Quran, Surat (Al Baqara) (The cow) Ch (2) verse (282)

يَا أَيُّهَا الَّذِينَ آمَنُوا إِذَا تَدَايَنْتُمْ بِدَيْنٍ إِلَىٰ أَجَلٍ مُسَمًّى فَاكْتُبُوهُ (282)

The entire verse is about recording debts, so feuds can never be generated between believers if one party claims a dispute in the terms of the debt agreement!

Where is the particularity of Islamic law and in this verse in restricting a woman testimony as Mr. Spencer claimed:

"Particular in cases involving <u>sexual immortality</u>"?!!

The case is only particular in Mr. Spencer's outright fabrication.

*A brief note about women rights in Islam (MZ)

Islam gave women unprecedented rights in the seventh century and even according to today's standards.

While this is not enough a space to detail all these rights that our mothers, daughters, sisters and wives are most deserving of, I would like to comment on the two points Mr. Spencer addressed:

On page 68, he quoted verse 282 in (chapter 2 (the Baqara) (the Cow)) that we mentioned above:

"Call in two witnesses from amongst you, but if two men cannot be found then one man and two women who you judge fit as two witnesses, so that if either of them commits an error, the other will remember" (2:282)

*Some would rush to say Aha, see; one male witness is equivalent to two women witnesses. Yet the rule is obvious and clear, God didn't mandate two men because one man is half a witness but, and in the same part Mr. Spencer quoted, "So that if either of them commits an error, the other will remember" (2:282)

The difference here is that, it is fine for two men to witness, but if we substitute one woman for one man, then for witnessing a contract a woman would be forced to a conversation where she may be obligated to communicate with a foreign man to her in order to remind each other, which is forbidden in Islam. So unless we make a rule that only a husband and a wife, a brother and a sister, can testify to replace a set of two men witnesses then there cannot be witnessing with only one man! The way God mandated it is such that if one forgets then the two women can independently remind each other without having to communicate and comingle with a man who may be foreign to them. On the contrary and more importantly, in the real rule regarding infidelity (a spouse accusing the other of infidelity) a wife's testimony is exactly the same against her husband's; and you will not hear about that from our author!

2- Unless it is something made by Sony, there is no such a thing that I am aware of called "Muslim legal manual", page 68! And there are no restrictions on women testifying in most of the cases including murder.

3- Islam-bashers would tell you that a daughter in Islam inherits half of what her brother inherits. The "Aha" would break out again, see;
a woman is half a man in Islam!

The rule is absolutely correct but they don't quote you - as usual -
the rest of the law, that a woman, in Islam, by the law; inherits her father, her husband, her son and her brother, even in certain cases, her grand children. A simple example is that her grandfather who is the father of her deceased parent would inherit less than her, even though he is a man and a first degree relative to the deceased, so is a woman now more than a man in Islam!?

Islamic inheritance laws are totally irrelevant to the gender of the individual. The amount of inheritance is determined by three factors:

1. The closeness of the relationship to the deceased.
2. The generation the individual belongs to (parents or children)
3. The degree of responsibility of sustaining the rest of the family.

When you calculate the probabilities of a woman's potential inheritances, you will find that she inherits exactly like a man inherits. Is that all? No. Islamic law mandates that the father, the brother or the husband is responsible financially for the female, so the males' monies are theirs and hers, yet her inheritance which is potentially equal to her counterpart male, is always only hers!

"Modern embarrassment"

The author goes back again to the issue of Zaynab! The most amusing thing is that Mr. Spencer, of all people, starts to blame some objective Muslim writers and non-Muslims like Karen Armstrong for focusing on things and ignoring others!
While in the same breath he ignores what Karen Armstrong stated - he even quoted her - that Zaynab was the Prophet's cousin, and that the Prophet had seen her all his life!

*The real embarrassment here is that for the Prophet who, for the sake of God, refused everything that this world could offer all his life and died with just the clothes on his back, is to call him a man of desire. And of all the women, money and power he was offered just to take another path other than the path of God, if one miraculous woman would have shockingly dazzled him to be totally the opposite of the man of heavenly manners that he always has been, it would definitely not be his cousin whom he has seen a hundred times and whom he himself persuaded to marry his former servant. Was she the wife that God blamed the Prophet in the Holy Quran that he refused to support Zayd in divorcing her and asked Zayd to fear Allah and keep her?
Ayesha said that she hadn't seen any women facing the lack of materialistic things in life as much as the Prophets wives. The prophet wasn't a man of this world where anything could move him away from the path of righteousness.
On the contrary I do think definitely Mr. Spencer by now is extremely embarrassed!

.

Leech-like clot

علق

"The leech like clot" Fig.1

المُضغة

(ثُمَّ مِن مُضغةٍ مُخَلَّقةٍ وَغَيرِ مُخَلَّقةٍ لِنُبَيِّنَ لَكُم وَنُقِرُّ فِي الأَرحامِ مَا نَشَاءُ إِلَى أَجَلٍ مُسَمّى) [الحج: 5].

The Piece of chew

"The piece of Chew" Fig. 2

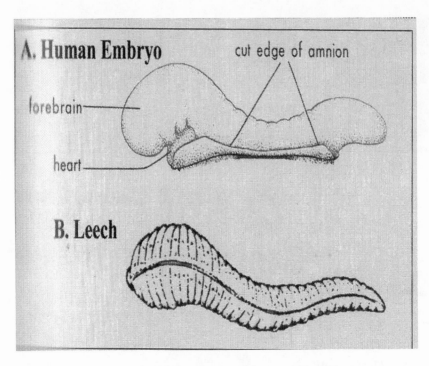

A. Human Embryo — cut edge of amnion

forebrain

heart

B. Leech

"A comparison between a leech and a human clot" Fig. 3

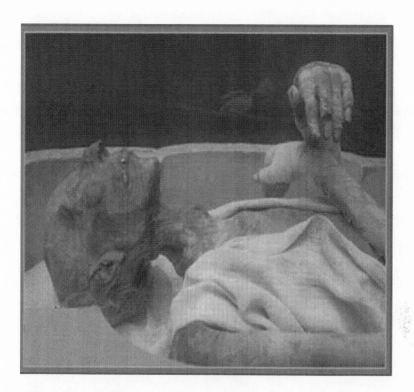

"Moses's pharaoh; notice the stiffness of the left hand raised with the shield to protect him from the falling mountain of water" Fig. 4

"The towers in the depth of space" Fig. 5.

"I scrutinized, studied and contemplated the holy scriptures that are produced by theology, and for what was in them of tampering I didn't find the wisdom I sought... and such laws do not secure happiness to humanity..., and I scrutinized the Holy Quran from every angle, and found great wisdom in every word of it...and whoever claimed that the Holy Quran is of Muhammad (PBUH)'s invention, then he had closed his eyes to the facts, for this claim ridicules mind and wisdom..and I declare that Muhammad is a great role model that is not possible to find again, secondly...Oh, Muhammad, the book you have spread is not of your invention, and denying its divine source is nonsense...and based on that I have all respect for your greatness while bowing to your spiritual presence"
Bismarck (1815-1898); Uniter of Germany and one of the most prominent wise men of 19th century Europe.

Chapter Five

The author starts this chapter by narrating for us the beginnings of Islam and Muhammad (PBUH) initiating his tribe (Quraysh) invitation to Islam.

Whether he was aware of it or not, the author quotes for us what we already displayed in the previous chapters, which is the fact that Muhammad (PBUH), whom his people gave him the nickname "the truthful honest," was a man that his worst enemies would certify that he had never told a lie in his entire life.

Muhammad (PBUH) called his people and asked them if they would believe him if he warned them of an army behind the mountain that was about to come and attack them. The author reports on page 74 what Quraysh had said:

"Yes, for we have not found you telling anything other than the truth".

Abu Lahab was the Prophet's uncle and probably the most active hater of Islam. A chapter was revealed in the Holy Quran - (Al Masad) Chapter (111) - dooming him and his wife to hell fire and that they will die as infidels.

A well-known remark about Chapter (Al Masad) and Abu Lahab, is that if he had any intelligence, he would have accepted Islam (even falsely) to prove the Word of God wrong and cast doubt on it, yet he and his wife died exactly as the verses had foretold they will.

The event in Islamic history that the author tries to throw vagueness on here, is how Abu Lahab died. He died 7 days after the victory of the first battle of Badr of the overwhelmingly outnumbered Muslims over the infidels of Quraysh. Abu Lahab died of an infectious disease called (al Adasa) at the time. Even his own sons were scared to come near his corpse, till people blamed them for leaving his body to rot for over three days. He was later washed by throwing water at his corpse from afar, and then he was thrown in a hole in the ground where he was covered by rocks.

While the story of the perishing of the sworn enemy of Islam, understandably, had been mentioned in a majority of "Seerah" - biography references - of the Prophet, here is what the author says about it on page 74:

"A Hadeeth informs us that Abu Lahab "indeed perished." The Hadeeth does not record the manner of his death, but one possible cause may be ruled out: at this point the Muslims were not targeting their enemies for violent attacks"

1. *It is well-known how Abu Lahab had died, why would the author then claim that there's only one hadeeth that addresses his death? And if that one hadeeth does not tell the details, then who said that there are no other Hadeeths that address it or that it is never recorded in history?
2. As supposedly an opposite to the enemies of Muslims may be attacking Muslims gently with love and by throwing roses at them, the author's notion here is that crazy Muslims attacking their innocent enemies violently might have been the cause of Abu Lahab's death!
3. As usual the author doesn't give us any reference to that one hadeeth!

Even in such a known incident of Islamic History, the vagueness of the author's genetically violent crazy demonized Muslim had to be fogged in here.

Saad Ibn Abi Waqas was one of the early companions of the Prophet's. He and other companions were praying in one of the glens of Mecca, where the author himself said on Page 75:

"They were praying and rudely interrupted. The companions of the Prophet blamed the polytheists for their rudeness and it escalated when Saad hit one of them and wounded him. This was the first blood to be shed in Islam."

*People, peacefully praying, not bothering anyone, and not imposing themselves upon anyone, are interrupted rudely as the author himself said, and violently we add, then one of them stood up to one of the intruders and engaged him. In any civilized court of law, this is an incident of self-defense, yet how is this narrated objectively by the author? On page 75, he wrote:

"Though the Muslims were only a tiny band at this point, violence connected with the new religion began early"!

So the victim of violence and persecution is "connected to violence" and, the author adds that it began "early"!

*One crucially important observation here is that Mr. Spencer who gave us a splitting headache about stuffing any trivial matter into his scare crow of "all Muslims are violently crazy" narrative, never mentioned even one iota of one letter about the torture and the killing of some of the best companions of the prophet in cold blood on the hands of the pagans of Quraysh. The reason of course is to show that any Muslim's defensive action is always and forever nothing but sheer violence, and on the contrary of all humans, Muslims cannot be acting in self defense for they are always violent till never proven human.

The original "fierce crazy jihadist warriors" that Mr. Spencer is deafening our ears about were scared to their core when Bilal the former African slave and great companion of the Prophet showed them his mutilated back by the whipping torture of his master just to abandon his belief in God! I ask Mr. Spencer to forgive me for that may not be totally "linked to violence" like all his irrelevant tales!

Bilal, however, was one of the lucky ones as Abu Bakr bought him from his master and freed him. Many others like the famous family of Yasser were not that fortunate and were killed by the pagans after torturing them. We need another book just to cover some of the atrocities committed by the pagans of Quraysh against the early Muslims.

In the next paragraph the author goes further into claiming that our English is so bad, and that we may not know the difference between the words "warn" and "threaten." On page 75, while he himself says

126

about the Prophet that:

"He confined his activities to preaching, although his preaching threatened the pagan Meccans with annihilation."

*When somebody tells you "beware of a certain danger", a fast coming car, a flood, or a plague, is he threatening you? Or just warning you to avert a looming danger? How is it then, that that person would be threatening you, when what he says is the exact message of your God in His final Word to you?

The author claims that quoting God's warning to his creations is a personal threat from a Prophet to his people. A, B, C of Islamic History is the appalling killing, persecution, torture, and starvation of the early Muslims and companions of the Prophet on the hands of Quraysh's elite and powerful. That amazing pillar of the whole narration of the Prophet's Meccan era is nowhere to be found with Mr. Spencer. On page 76, the author writes:

"As Muhammad began to attack them and their gods with increasing vehemence; they began to see Islam and its Prophet as a threat. In due course, they began to strike back."

I could not imagine that the author would reach as low as claiming that all that Quraysh had done to the poor, powerless, early Muslims was a "strike back" to an imaginary verbal denunciation that Muhammad (PBUH) had against their gods.

Was there any strike first by the Muslims for Quraysh's strike back? Or was the persecution of the early Muslims the "preemptive strike" of its time?!

In the following paragraph, the author himself shows how persecuted the Muslims were to the limit that the Prophet had asked them to flee to Abyssinia (today's Ethiopia), to escape Quraysh's persecution and of course, as we mentioned in our comment on Chapter One, the author, in the same paragraph, doesn't mention that Prophet Muhammad (PBUH) chose Abyssinia because it was ruled by

"a righteous Christian king" (Al-Najashy).

The incubator of some of the first followers of Islam by the choice of the

Prophet of Islam was a Christian king in a Christian land. But to our honest author, this is not a relevant fact in seeking "the truth about Muhammad"

Is it that, because it does not fit the author's genetically crazed Muslim who is anti-anything-Christian scenario, facts are never told?

When Al Najashy, the Abyssinia king died, Prophet Muhammad (PBUH) Performed a Muslim absentee burial prayer upon him as a Muslim.

On page 76, the author writes:

"On one occasion, Muhammad (PBUH)'s anger and frustration over his failure to convert the Quraysh boiled over."

*Reversing facts is really amazing here, as it is well-known that it's Quraysh's anger and frustration over their failure to hinder the exponential increase of the number of Meccans accepting Islam was the cause of the persecution and the torture of the early Muslims. Here, the author claims the false opposite and again, uses it as if Prophet Muhammad (PBUH) failed to have his tribe accept Islam to the limit that he mistranslates his warning of the demise of the polytheists by punishment of God, as if Muhammad (PBUH) was threatening to slaughter them if they did not believe in his message!

On page 76, the author quotes:

"O Quraysh! By him who holds my life in His hand, I bring you slaughter." He then adds, "This was one prophecy of Muhammad that would indisputably prove true."

*When Prophet Muhammad (PBUH) died, he had over a hundred and twenty-four thousand followers in the Arab Peninsula, not to mention almost 1.6 billion followers today. The frustration, the anger and the failure to speak of when it comes to the amazing spread of Islam throughout history, has always been that of the infidels and Muslim-bashers not being able to stop the tide of the true religion of God.

128

But then what is the cardinal rule regarding conversion of non-Muslims to Islam? In the Holy Quran:

"There is no compulsion in religion"
Holy Quran, Surat (Al Baqara) Ch. (2) Verse (256),

لَا إِكْرَاهَ فِي الدِّينِ ۛ (256)

And the verse,
"Guiding them is not up to you, but it is Allah who guides whomever He wills"
Holy Quran, Surat (Al Baqara) Ch. (2) Verse (272)

لَيْسَ عَلَيْكَ هُدَاهُمْ وَلَٰكِنَّ اللَّهَ يَهْدِي مَنْ يَشَاءُ (272)

On page 77, the author brings us a rare quote that speaks about a major part of the essence of Islam as an ideology and as a way of life. He quotes one of the early Muslims who gave the pledge of Aqaba to the Prophet:

"We gave allegiance to the apostle that we would associate nothing with God, not steal, not commit fornication, not kill our offspring, not slander our neighbor, not disobey him in what was right; if we fulfilled this, paradise would be ours; and if we committed any of those sins, we should be punished in this world, and this would serve as expiation; if the sin was concealed until the day of resurrection, then it would be for God to decide whether to punish or to forgive."

*Aside from the fact that the author never comments on the glaring exceptional ethical quality of the fundamentals of Islam, the author brings us a weird assumption. He then adds:
"There was nothing in this pledge about warring for Islam."!

*My question here to the author is that when the Holy Quran wasn't even all revealed yet, who said that every law in Islam had to be included in that man's pledge? Does any American citizen or soldier of any country for that matter, when he gives his allegiance to his homeland, does he include in that pledge, that he - for example - will be faithful to his wife? And then, if he does cheat on her, is it an odd thing to happen for it wasn't mentioned in his allegiance to the nation?!

*On page 78, the author shows a classic example of non-Muslims who are mostly not well-versed in the Arabic language, making massive translation errors whether intentionally or unintentionally.
The word "Fitnah" mainly expresses an act or a condition of suffering, so if Fitnah is applied upon someone then it means he is harmed or tortured, if it happens between people then it means a feud that may lead to bloodshed, and if it is from Allah then it also means an ordeal but in a context of being a test by God.
Our author abandons all the possible meanings of the word and uses a contemporary slang expression of the word that is used to express that if a woman is stunningly beautiful she is a "Fitnah" meaning a heart break to look at!
For example in the Holy Quran:

"**Verily, those who applied Fitnah upon the believing men and believing women** (by torturing them and burning them)**,
and then do not turn in repentance, then they will have the torment of Hell, and they will have the punishment of the burning Fire**"
Holy Quran, Surat (Al Brooj) (the Towers), Ch (85) verse (10)

إِنَّ الَّذِينَ فَتَنُوا الْمُؤْمِنِينَ وَالْمُؤْمِنَاتِ ثُمَّ لَمْ يَتُوبُوا فَلَهُمْ عَذَابُ جَهَنَّمَ وَلَهُمْ عَذَابُ الْحَرِيقِ(10)

But then read the explanation of the following verse that the Author brought on page 78. In the Holy Quran:

"**And fight them until there is no more Fitnah (feud) and the religion would be that of Allah. But if they cease, let there be no**

130

transgression except against the oppressors"
Holy Quran, Surat (Al Baqara) (the Cow), Ch (2) Verse (193)

وَقَاتِلُوهُمْ حَتَّىٰ لَا تَكُونَ فِتْنَةٌ وَيَكُونَ الدِّينُ لِلَّهِ ۖ فَإِنِ انْتَهَوْا فَلَا عُدْوَانَ إِلَّا عَلَى الظَّالِمِينَ (193)

*The author wrote that the meaning of the verse is "Fight them so there will be no more seduction"!

Then in the following paragraph the author twists the meaning of: "so that the religion would be that of Allah" 180 degrees.

The apparent meaning that explains itself is, "Fight those who torture you to convert you from your religion so the oppression stops and your religion would be only the religion of Allah - i.e. so you keep your religion -, and if the oppressors stopped then do not transgress against any but the transgressors"

And here is what the author wanted to finally write: On page 78:

"Later, Islamic law based on statements of Muhammad would offer non-Muslims three options: conversion to Islam, subjugation as inferiors under Islamic law, or warfare"!

*So let's put this gigantic nugget of misinformation in its eternal waste-basket rest:

1- In the middle of the seventh century, there were no borders, diplomacy, or UN peace keeping troops! You are constantly being attacked by or you are attacking your neighbors. This was the rule, unless there was a signed treaty, and even those never lasted long. Attacks were sudden and violent without any warning and for taking it all or losing it all.

2- 500 years before the dark ages Muhammad (PBUH) gave his enemies 3 options, two were for peace and one was man to man, army to army, kill or be killed for the sake of God. Centuries before Muhammad (PBUH) and after him, were there any army offering such alternatives before battle, if any at all? None.

3- The first option: become a Muslim and then you will have our rights and our obligations. In Islamic law there are no classes or discrimination before the law based on any background, race, religion, or color.

131

4- The second option is "you can keep your religion under Islamic rule." Had any winning army till 8 centuries later offered that to the defeated if they even let them live? Check out the crusaders, the Mongolians before you stop by the Inquisitions.

Now, let's enjoy the truth about non-Muslims' "subjugation as inferiors under Islamic law" as our author describes it.

Non-Muslims had every right and obligation that Muslims had before the law; not only is this shown in the Holy Quran (as well as all over Islamic law references and throughout 1400 years of history), but here is a very well-known example:

Ali Ibn Abi Talib, the khalifa (the ruler) at the time, lost his shield in a battle where it was picked up by a Jewish man. One day, when Ali saw his shield with the Jewish man in the market, he asked for its return, the man refused and claimed that it was his. Here is what the "intolerant, violent Muslim ruler" did: Ali brought himself and the Jewish man to the Islamic court and stood before judge "Shoraih" who by coincidence was a black African. What was the "subjugating" Islamic law ruling?

The judge ruled the shield to the Jewish man, for Ali had only his sons - the grandchildren of Muhammad (PBUH) - as witnesses and in Islamic law they are all considered one entity, so the shield was given to whoever had possession.

So what did the "anti non-Muslim subjugator violent Muslim ruler" do? He accepted the ruling of the law of God and left his own shield to the man!

Of course if it was a story in some comic book about Ali scaring a baby Alien from Mars it would have been worth it for Mr. Spencer to narrate it, but the truth, or a well known event like that which is repeated thousands of times throughout the history of Islamic rule? Never.

Was there any difference in the eyes of Islamic law between a Muslim and a non-Muslim? Yes there was! And here is the screaming "discriminative subjugating inferiority" of a non-Muslim in a Muslim land. A non-Muslim in a Muslim land is called "Zemmey."

Here is the agonizing discrimination that seems to bring tears in the eyes of Mr. Spencer; are you ready?

A Zemmey is exempt from being drafted to the Muslim army!

Here are the savage Muslims denying the Zemmeys the basic civil right of being potentially killed or amputated in battle!

As their tax duty to their community, like the "Zakah" tax every Muslim pays, and for that privilege, a Zemmey would pay a whopping Jizyah tax of one Dinar a year, (less than one hundred dollars today) and that is for Muslims and their sons to defend them and the entire society.

But then, Does all Zemmies (non-Muslims) pay Jizyah?

Not the rabbi, not the priest, not the women, not the children, not the old, but only men who can fight and join an army!

Has there been enough "subjugation and discrimination" yet?

No, by paying that amount (Jizyah) the Zemmey has a right in the Muslim treasury (today's social services) which is the right that a Muslim has by paying his own obligated tax (charity) to the Muslim treasury. The Muslim, however, pays 2.5% of his unspent assets, meaning that a Muslim pays more depending on the assets he has, but the "inferior" Zemmey pays just that one dinar for the same right, even if the Zemmey was much wealthier.

Here is another well-known example that shows how the law of God was applied:

The ruler of Sham (today's Syria, Jordan, Palestine and Lebanon), Obaida Ibn Al Jarrah - a close companion to the Prophet - collected the Jizyah from the Zemmeys of today's Syria only to come back and refund it to them - for the first time in taxation history - explaining that his army was called to another country and, that he couldn't defend the land and couldn't accept their tax to the Muslim treasury without providing the Muslim government's duty to its citizens, yet he promised that if they were attacked he would bring a faction back to defend them regardless!

How important is the well treatment of non-Muslims in a Muslim ruled land? Here are the protection rights of non-Muslims stated by Prophet Muhammad (PBUH) himself:

hoever oppressed a Zemmey, took from his rights, or took
..om him unjustly, then I am his opponent on judgment day (then the
Prophet pointed to his own chest), **verily whoever killed a Zemmey of
Allah and his messenger, then paradise will be forbidden for him,
and its scent is felt from a seventy year ride"**
Reference: Ibn Hajar al Aslam, **Source:** *Muwafaqat Al Khabar,* **Number:**
184/2. **Degree:** *Good*

Show us a leader in modern history that said that to his population
majority and actually applied that protection to his Zemmeys.

Was that good treatment temporary or maybe limited to just a few
centuries after the passing of the Prophet?

Let's move to Europe 400 years after the passing of the Prophet and for
an additional 800 years later in the Muslim Andalus - today's Spain and
Portugal – which was the most civilized, advanced, and prosperous
nation in the entire world then, under Islamic law.

Muslims, Christians and Jews prospered together in perfect harmony. It
is worth mentioning that in a country like England, Jews were banned
even to enter or exist in it for over 350 years, before even thinking about
granting them any rights.

When the Inquisitions prevailed, where did the Jews of Andalus escape
for their lives to?

They fled to the nearest Muslim countries.

Some objective historians even admit that throughout the history of
Islamic rule, it was Islamic law's exceptional tolerance to Non-Muslims
that kept Judaism as a protected faith in Muslim lands, where if it was up
to the abhorring prejudice against Jews that was the norm outside the
Muslim states then, Judaism would have been a thing of the far past
today.

Let's take another example to show the absolute fairness, mercy, and
civility of the law of God, which is Islamic law, versus what we take for
granted nowadays as far as man-made laws, specifically in regards to
minority civil rights.

134

Islam gives you the full rights and obligations of a born-Muslim citizen for just saying the certification of Islam (God is one and Muhammad (PBUH) is His Messenger).

Let's say you are a newcomer to the United States of America - which has some of the most tolerant immigration laws in the developed world today - and have a green card, not even if you were an illegal immigrant. You don't have the right to vote, you don't have the right to Medicaid till you're in the country for five years, and civil rights and anti-discrimination rights do not apply to you because you're not a citizen yet.

Can we compare objectively and see the difference for ourselves?

"The Satanic verses"

One of the most well-known fabrications about Islamic history that had wide notoriety, is the famous case of a third-class English writer by the name of Salman Rushti, supposedly a Muslim from an Indian descent, who published a book attacking Islam, Prophet Muhammad (PBUH) and claiming that some of the verses that Muhammad (PBUH) recited to his people were dictated to him by none other than the devil himself!

Naturally, Mr. Spencer would not overlook a juicy fabrication like this one. On the following pages, he paints for us a more dramatic picture that describes even the most inner of personal thoughts and feelings of Prophet Muhammad (PBUH). All of which Prophet Muhammad (PBUH) never expressed what Mr. Spencer claims to have personal knowledge of! And as usual, he does not tell us about the miraculous sources that he used in describing the Prophet's personal thoughts, feelings, and even intentions.

Mr. Spencer paints for us a premise of Prophet Muhammad (PBUH)'s frustrating failure to have his people accept Islam, and as we explained in the previous pages that this is absolutely the opposite of the truth, where men and women, children, and old men and women were accepting Islam left and right, on every level in Mecca. And because of

135

that exponential growth of the number of new Muslims - Muhammad (PBUH) died leaving behind 124,000 followers, which is equal to 8 million people in today's populations - Quraysh started a relentless campaign that spared nothing trying to stop "the new religion" at any cost.

It is really amusing that the next incident that Mr. Spencer tries to narrate in his "Satanic tale" is Quraysh coming to Prophet Muhammad (PBUH) and offering him that they will all worship Allah, the God of Islam, for an entire year, if Prophet Muhammad (PBUH) would agree to worship their gods (lat and Uzza) for a similar period! And before we confirm that that offer actually was made, and was recorded in most of the Seerah references, I would go to the simple question; if Mr. Spencer's premise was correct, and that:

"Muhammad was frustrated over his inability to convert his own people, the Quraysh to Islam" (page 78)

*How is it then that Quraysh and all its leaders would come to the lone persecuted Muhammad (PBUH) and offer to worship Allah for a year, just for him to reduce his campaign for the new religion a bit?!

Quraysh's offer was true. Yet, Allah has revealed the famous verses that every Muslim knows:

"O, you infidels! (1) I do not worship what you worship (2) and you are not worshipping what I worship (3)."
Holy Quran, Surat (Al-Kaferoun) Ch (109), Verses (1-3)

قُلْ يَا أَيُّهَا الْكَافِرُونَ (1)
لَا أَعْبُدُ مَا تَعْبُدُونَ (2)
وَلَا أَنْتُمْ عَابِدُونَ مَا أَعْبُدُ (3)

So, Prophet Muhammad (PBUH) rejected their offer, and that was the end of that offer in every verified reference that we know of. The fabrication starts, where they say that, instead, the devil revealed verses to Prophet Muhammad (PBUH) that it is now okay for him to

136

worship the idols of Quraysh so he can then accept their offer!! And guess what else they claimed? Muhammad (PBUH) "satanically" ordered his followers to do so!! What is most amazing is that the story doesn't tell us of any objection or questions from the companions of the Prophet about a statement that literally destroys the Islam, in its core, that he has been teaching them all along!!

Not only has this never happened, but a six-year old child couldn't believe that Muhammad (PBUH) would totally destroy the number one pillar of his entire message, that is "God is one with no partner".

Naturally, none of the companions of Prophet Muhammad (PBUH), or any credible Islamic reference had ever mentioned a hint of this ever happening.

On page 79 and 80, the author uses a reference of Ibn Is'haq's account, which not only is not a reliable source of the biography of the Prophet, according to the ultimate reference of historic credibility as far as the Prophet's biography, Al-Bukhary and Muslim references, but many of the hadeeth mentioned in Ibn Is'haq, are either weak or fabricated. Ibn Is'haq himself wrote that only Allah knows which one of his narrations are true. No wonder he is Mr. Spencer's favorite source.

The whole incident is so far-fetched that it's as if someone claimed that Ronald Regean not only called the American nation for a historical speech just to publicly give his allegiance to the Soviet Union, but that also no American had objected to that ever, not by even voicing one word of opposition against it!

What is satanic here is the extent that fabricators and Islam-haters are willing to go to, even at the expense of seriously ridiculing themselves.

Why is the Seerah of Ibn Is'haq Mr. Spencer's favorite reference?

A side note: the Seerah of Ibn Is'haq (MZ)

Why didn't our truth-seeker, if he was really looking for the truth, use the 100 times more reliable Ibn Hisham or Al Tabary at all so far, never mind often?

Is it that if you are looking for the "satanic" stories, and weird illogical tales, your best chance would only be with Ibn Is'haq?

137

Had Ibn Is'haq been alive today as a historian, few hundred years into the future, the Spencer of that future time would have narrated how a native born Kenyan socialist became the president of the United States of America based on a story in Ibn Is'haq's reference!

"The Night Journey"

The author discusses the "Israa and Miraj" journey when Muhammad (PBUH) was ascended through the levels of heaven on the back of a heavenly creature (winged small mule-like animal called the Buraq) till he reached as close as he was allowed into the highest heaven.

Note from Moustafa Zayed: This is a second reminder to the reader about the term "Islamic tradition" that the author uses so loosely. The word "tradition" as translated of the word "sunnah" means only the tradition of the Prophet himself, his sayings, his behavior, his approval, and his orders of what to do and what not to do. The author uses "Islamic tradition" for the western reader as if it is an amalgamation of historical cultural habits or some men of religion generational practices that are accumulated overtime, and not what it is as the Word of God and the orders of God to us through His last Prophet quotations.

On page 85, while the author briefly narrates some details of the heavenly journey of Prophet Muhammad (PBUH), he almost does not mention the most important detail of the whole journey, in which Muhammad (PBUH) talked to God Himself from behind a veil, and where the order of prayers for Muslims was given to the prophet for the first time.

Look at how the author almost erased the entire talk and order from God to Muhammad (PBUH) to establish prayers. On page 55, the author writes:
"In the seventh heaven, Muhammad meets Abraham, has further visions, and receives the command that the Muslims pray 50 times daily."

*In the prior entire page and a half before this paragraph, on page 85, the author showed in details the supernatural aspects of the journey, meeting with other Prophets of God, yet when it comes to the most important part of the journey, which is talking to God Himself from behind a veil, our truth-seeker narrates that by saying, "has further visions"!

When Muhammad (PBUH) came back and told the tribe of Quraysh what happened, naturally, they did not believe him, and doubted the credibility of the story. So Prophet Muhammad (PBUH) was given a supernatural vision by God, where he saw the farthest mosque (Aqsa), as if it was right before him. They challenged him as to how many doors were in the farthest mosque, and through his vision, he counted the doors, and answered them correctly (eight doors). Further, a caravan on its way back from Jerusalem to Mecca, was described by the Prophet accurately as it was when it arrived back in Mecca. Yet, here's our author again; on page 86 he writes:

"Evidently, however, his descriptions of Jerusalem were not altogether convincing."

*If it is "evident," then where is the evidence?

Where is the evidence that Prophet Muhammad (PBUH)'s description was either not accurate, or his description of the caravan was flawed? The author could not even find in any of his far-fetched, weak references or even one count of anyone saying that the number that Muhammad (PBUH) told of the doors was wrong. 8 cannot be 9 or 20; it is either absolutely correct, or absolutely wrong. There's no room for perception, conviction or opinion when it comes to a number! And for that, there's no one account "satanic" or otherwise that the number which Muhammad (PBUH) had mentioned was not the correct number.

The same way, had his description of the caravan was wrong, flawed, or inaccurate, we would have heard about it. Even in other instances, some of the infidels of Quraysh went as far as claiming that he was a magician, reciting poetry, telling other nations tales, or that the Prophet was crazy, but even none of these infidels could challenge the accuracy of the eyewitness details that Prophet Muhammad (PBUH) had

139

given describing the caravan or the correct number of the doors of the Farthest (Aqsa mosque).

What does the word "evidently" mean to the author? I just wonder.

In the following paragraph, on page 86, the author flips a very well-known incident to its total opposite. He claims that Muslims reverted from Islam because of the incident and because they did not believe it. And immediately, attaches to his claim, the well-known incident when infidels of Quraysh (not Muslims as he claimed), asked Abu Bakr, the lifelong companion of the Prophet, if he was to believe that someone could go to Jerusalem and come back on the same night. Abu Bakr said he would not believe it, yet when they told him that it was Muhammad (PBUH) who said that, he said:
"If Muhammad had said it, then I believe it."

To the one who does not know the details of the incident with Abu Bakr, and the way the author narrated it, he would think that it was Muslims who reverted from Islam, who tried to trick Abu Bakr to state that he does not believe the Prophet, yet they were infidels all along, and this conversation happened before Muhammad (PBUH) accepted the Quraysh challenge and stated the number of the doors of the Farthest Masjid, and the description of the soon-to-arrive caravan, by which he rendered them all mute.

On page 87, the author goes further to claim that:
"Later Muhammad seems to have retreated from the claim that this was a bodily journey."

*What does the word "seems" mean? Did Prophet Muhammad (PBUH) say, "I retract my statement and my journey was not bodily?" Or did he?
Well, we know that the Prophet did not. So what does the word "seems" again mean to the author? Having said that, let's look at what Allah himself had said in the holy Quran about the journey:

140

"Praises be to him who traveled his servant from the Haram masjid to the Farthest Masjid at night so we can show him some of our miracles. It is truly He who is the All hearer and All seer"
Holy Quran, Surat (Al-Israa) Ch (17), Verses (1)

سُبْحَانَ الَّذِي أَسْرَىٰ بِعَبْدِهِ لَيْلًا مِنَ الْمَسْجِدِ الْحَرَامِ إِلَى الْمَسْجِدِ الْأَقْصَى الَّذِي بَارَكْنَا حَوْلَهُ
(لِنُرِيَهُ مِنْ آيَاتِنَا ۚ إِنَّهُ هُوَ السَّمِيعُ الْبَصِيرُ (1)

The verse clearly states that the travel was in person of the prophet and not a vision or a dream. Needless to say the prophet never contradicted the Quran, not to mention that it was he himself of all people who knew that it was a bodily journey!

The author follows by a fabricated statement from Ayesha, the Prophet's wife, when she said that:

"The body of the Prophet stayed while God ascended the Prophet's spirit."

In the event that which by the power of God, all veils of time, distance, and dimension were dropped to his Prophet, is it mightily difficult to believe that God could have taken His Prophet through and showed him all that in a fraction of a second of our time, while to the human consciousness he was still there? Even to make it simple; is it too difficult for God to make Muhammad (PBUH) appear in two places at the same time? He proved to every one without a doubt that he has seen the farthest Mosque and the caravan that was travelling from there.

50 years ago, if someone claimed that he can push in a little square in a piece of metal, and immediately he could talk and even video chat with anyone on the face of the planet, he would have been certified as a lunatic on the spot. Yet that is the smart phone that we all have access to now. That amazing invention is but a creation of man not God and within just few decades of improvement. It is not even just a matter of if you do believe or not, it is actually if you understand the limitations of your comprehension against the infinite abilities of God; or simply not.

Why then, when it comes specifically to when veils of time, distances, and dimension, were preached for the Prophet, that the author would go to a fabricated statement of the Prophet's wife, who was not a witness to the journey and the incident - that night the Prophet was at the house of Oum Hanye his cousin - and was in a dimension, a time, and a place, totally different from where the Prophet was? It's almost like the author's next question may be, "And how much mileage was there on the Buraq meter?!"

"I like Mohammed for his hypocrisy-free nature. With clear and sound words he addresses the Roman Tsars and Kings of Persia. He guides them to what he loves for them in this life and in the eternal life."
English writer, Thomas Carlyle.

Chapter Six

On page 90, Mr. Spencer describes parts of the Holy Quran of 1.6 billion people, the final Word of God, and the most powerful text that mankind had ever read.

No objective scholar, regardless of his religion or native language who studied the language of the Holy Quran, that didn't swear by its depth, complexity, and the fact that no human had ever written at its levels. Here is the statement of Mr. Spencer about the Holy Quran:
It is "discursive" and "prosaic"!

*One of the most evident features of the Holy Quran as a whole text is that it has the same DNA of writing throughout its text, so whether it is a short verse in a short Chapter or the longest ones for that matter, it is the same language and miraculously expressive writing structure.

Because the chapters revealed in the Medina of the Prophet were longer than the chapters revealed in Mecca, the author describes the ones revealed in Medina, with the same divine intensity and wisdom, as "discursive" and "prosaic."
I am glad the author didn't go as far as also complaining that there are no pictures in the Holy Book!

And as if that introduction to chapter six was not unobjective enough, even from a well-known Muslim-hater like Mr. Spencer, the next paragraph is even more ridiculous.

Mr. Spencer claims that the longer chapters of the Holy Quran, revealed in Medina after the emigration of the Prophet and the early Muslims to it from Mecca, were that long because they have detailed laws of Islam of which he says were "copied" from the Jews of Medina!
He further claims that that copying was because Muhammad (PBUH) interacted with them! As if Mecca had no Jews!

And as usual, the author is relentless in tiring us of pointing to him and the readers about the fact that he makes up these unbelievably far-fetched statements that defy any logic, then flips facts 180 degrees, sometimes several rounds without one iota of proof, reference or even somewhat objective speculation: worse, without even attempting to put any explanation as to from which planet did he come up with these statements.

Here's one for you on page 90:
"from nearly the beginning of his Prophetic career, Muhammad was strongly influenced by Judaism situating himself within a roster of Jewish Prophets"!

*The author explains - it seems that this is his only proof of this laughable statement - further by the fact that Muhammad (PBUH) forbade his followers from eating pork, and that he and his followers were praying several times a day.

As we explained before, a core fundamental belief of Islam is to believe in all the Prophets of God equally, and that the laws of God - the true ones - are almost all the same, because the message of the oneness of God itself is the same. Islam is the whole message of God, purified, completed, and enhanced. So for the Muslims to be Muslims, worshippers of God - not just representing any race, creed, tribe, or man-made ritual - should they have invented new recipes of how to eat pork? Should God's last Prophet, Muhammad (PBUH), who's an Arab from the noblest family in the Arab Peninsula, and a descendent of Ishmael, son of Abraham (PBUT), who both are not Jewish, should he forbid praying to God several times a day because Jews did pray to God, otherwise he is all of a sudden Jewish himself?
When did Muhammad (PBUH) ever make a statement, at any time that could in any far-fetched way be explained as that he considers himself a Jew, or part of a "Roster" of Jewish Prophets? Never.

Is Mr. Spencer the same author who wrote in his same book that an Arab scholar warned the Prophet's uncle not to tell anyone about the

145

Prophethood mark between the shoulders of infant Muhammad (PBUH) and specifically not to tell the Jews about it, otherwise they will hurt him?! Now, according to the "author," Prophet Muhammad (PBUH) is a Jew himself, or a Jew-wannabe?

As we mentioned earlier, the Holy Quran, like the Old Testament, is filled with the harshest criticism of the Jews who disobeyed and fought Prophets of God, who were Jewish themselves. How then could that statement be even fathomed?
And it is not about Prophet Muhammad (PBUH) being a Jew, or Chinese, or even African-American for that matter, it is to me about ridiculing facts, history, even the intelligence of the reader of the same book in which the author contradicts himself, and blatantly misleads his readers.

"The covenant between the Muslims and the Jews"

On page 91, the author takes a stab at the Zemmey issue again, claiming that a fundamental principle of equality between all Muslims is not as such. He writes:
"The document begins by declaring that all Muslims, whether they are Meccan or Medinan, are a single united community - another principle that Muslims have affirmed throughout history, although it would not always be uniformly upheld once non-Arabs began to join the Ummah."

*The two greatest figures in Islam after Prophet Muhammad (PBUH) are the two following caliphs: Abu Bakr and Omar, yet Omar described Bilal the companion of the Prophet, as "our master." Bilal was a black, freed slave. Two of the closest companions and advisors of Prophet Muhammad (PBUH) were Salman, the Persian, and Suhaib, the Roman.

In the first human rights declaration in history, of which Prophet Muhammad (PBUH), in his farewell pilgrimage, declared that:

"Your God is One, and your father is one, there is no preference of an Arab over a non-Arab or a non-Arab over an Arab; No white

146

man is better than a black man, and no black man is better a white man, except by fearing God."
(Prophet Muhammad (PBUH))

Narrator: *Jaber ibn Abdullah*. **Reference**: *Ghayat Almuram/AlAlbany*, **Number**: *313*. **Degree**: *Correct*

Fearing God, mind you, is something that no man can measure about another man, only God can.

In the following two pages, the author loosely translates a peace agreement for the people of Medina, including the Jewish tribes, and as usual, at the end, there comes his famous flying blue elephant out-of-thin-air statement; on page 92, he writes:
"The Jews agreed to fight alongside the Muslims 'except in the case of a holy war.'"

*There is no "holy war" in Islam. "Holy war" is a definition of the word "Crusade." Defining "jihad" as "holy war" is like someone accusing you of his own ills. Throughout the Holy Quran, the quotations of the Prophet and Islamic Law; peace is to be sought at the dearest of costs.

"And if they lean towards peace, then lean towards it."
Holy Quran, Surat (Al Anfal) Ch (8) Verse (61)

وَإِن جَنَحُوا لِلسَّلْمِ فَاجْنَحْ لَهَا وَتَوَكَّلْ عَلَى اللَّهِ ۚ إِنَّهُ هُوَ السَّمِيعُ الْعَلِيمُ (61)

"And fight for the sake of Allah those who fought you, and do not transgress, for Allah does not like the transgressors."
Holy Quran, Surat (Al Baqara) (The Cow) Ch (2) Verse (190)

وَقَاتِلُوا فِي سَبِيلِ اللَّهِ الَّذِينَ يُقَاتِلُونَكُمْ وَلَا تَعْتَدُوا ۚ إِنَّ اللَّهَ لَا يُحِبُّ الْمُعْتَدِينَ (190)

"And Allah had spared the believers the war."
Holy Quran, Surat (Al Ahzab) Ch (33) Verse (25)

وَكَفَى اللَّهُ الْمُؤْمِنِينَ الْقِتَالَ ۚ وَكَانَ اللَّهُ قَوِيًّا عَزِيزًا (25)

147

And as we explained the meaning of "jihad" in the first chapter of this book; it is when a Muslim exerts exceptional effort for the sake of God, whether by his money, by his life, or by his knowledge. In the case of a foreign invasion, then Jihad is joining the Muslim nation army to fight for the sake of God. If it's a drought, a famine, or poverty, then one can gain the same reward by charity and supporting the poor. If it's facing illiteracy, then one can do that by giving his time and knowledge to teach people for the sake of God, etc.

A Crusade or holy war is probably the label under which Mr. Spencer stands in his hatred against everything Muslim; it is a European expression that has nothing to do with Islam, but as we displayed repeatedly, it's his label, it is his war, it is his expressions, and there is nothing holy or Islamic about any of them.

"The conversion with Abdullah and tensions with the rabbis"

In the following pages (94-95), the author forces in phrases by the former Jewish Rabbi Abdullah Ibn Salam cursing the Jews to finally frame it into what he wrote on page 95:
"The idea of Jews and Christians as sinful renegades from the truth of Islam would become a cornerstone of Islamic thought regarding non-Muslims."

*And as he did in chapters three and five when he claimed that the coming of Muhammad (PBUH) as the last Prophet of God was never mentioned in Christian scriptures, he tries to do the same and claims that contrary to what is stated in the Holy Quran; that the Old Testament had no mention of the coming of Prophet Muhammad (PBUH), and for that, I'd like to dedicate to him, in today's Old Testament, the mention of Prophet Muhammad (PBUH) by name, as pronounced in Arabic "Muhammad"!

In the Song of Songs, chapter 5-16:

"His mouth is most sweet: yea, he is <u>altogether lovely</u>. This is my beloved, and this is my friend, O, daughters of Jerusalem."
King James Bible, Song of Songs 5:16

As bizarre it may be, the translators of the original Hebrew text translated the name mentioned in the Song of Solomon's verse; not as it is pronounced but to English, i.e. if someone's name is "Aswad," which means "black," they would just go right ahead and translate the name. So his name is not "Aswad" anymore, his name is now Mr. "black"! In our case, they even mutilated the translation of the name as far as they could. The Hebrew name of which they translated to "altogether lovely" is pronounced "Muhammad'em". And as we explained before that the "em" or "aim" is Hebrew plural for respect and praise. So, the name of Prophet Muhammad (PBUH) is mentioned exactly the same and as pronounced in the Torah. And even though names should be written and translated as they are pronounced, the bizarre attempt to translate the name should at a minimum be done correctly, i.e. the name should have been "the praised one." They translated it to the weird, "altogether lovely"!

I advise the author to go have a Hebrew-speaking person read it for him several times till it sinks in!

Then on page 95, the author tries to slip in one of his fabrications; this time it is a major one. On page 95, he wrote: "Muhammad composed for the Muslims a brief prayer known as the Fatiha that became the corner stone of Muslim prayer."

*It is the two possibilities of two disasters, and each one is worse than the other! The first would be that our truth-seeker, who claims to enlighten us about Islam, does not know that "The Fatiha" is the first chapter in the Holy Quran revealed by Archangel Gabriel to Prophet Muhammad (PBUH).

149

The second possibility is that our truth-seeker thinks that it is some sort of supplication composed by Prophet Muhammad (PBUH) for prayers! Did Muhammad (PBUH) or any of his companions even remotely mention that Muhammad (PBUH) had composed the Fatiha? Ever?!

At the end of the page, the author brings about the translation of the Fatiha and ends it amazingly with the reference, Holy Quran 1:1-7. Meaning, that he acknowledges that it is a part of the Holy Quran, which is so puzzling that on the same page the author claims it is a prayer composed by Muhammad (PBUH), and ends the page with quoting it as a chapter of the Holy Quran! Is it a worst case of cut and paste without distinction? I have no further comment.

The author quotes that specific chapter (Al Fatiha) Ch. (1) in the Holy Quran, to reference to the last three verses where a Muslim prays to God to bestow upon him the straight path other than the path of those who angered God or the path of those who went astray. And before he ran to tell us the most common interpretation that explains which two paths were these, he runs even faster to certify that the interpretation of Ibn Kathir is the most respected interpretation of the Holy Quran, and quotes a scholar by the name of Ahmed von Denffer to cut the way back on us, when he says that the two other paths that a Muslim avoids are the paths of former Jews and former Christians!
Before we answer that, we just want to politely ask the author this: if Ibn Kathir "represents a broad mainstream in Islamic tradition" (pg. 96), how is it that we are on page 96, almost half of your book, and you never quoted Ibn Kathir even once to this point?!
Maybe he never quoted Ibn Kathir because there's nothing "satanic" about the leading mainstream Islamic scholar!

*We have explained before that in Islam, the followers of the Prophets of God who followed the orders of the Prophets and obeyed God are in Heaven, Christians, Jews and those before them, and that they before Allah on Judgment Day are as good as any pious Muslim. Yet, Christians and Jews who were given holy scriptures who altered the

Word of God and associated their man-made theology with God, i.e. disobeyed God, fought His Prophets and His true believers, will be punished severely by God, and just exactly the same, the rule applies to any Muslim who may do the same. This is not only simple basic Islam but also simple logic as well.

Al-Fatiha specifically identifies those Christians and Jews, versus maybe Hindus. Atheists or Pagans, because Christians and Jews, like the Muslims, received true Prophets of God, and original scriptures, and some of them corrupted it to their likings, interests, and desires, and then claimed that that was the religion of God. A Muslim prays to God daily, not to fall into these devastating paths and potential pitfalls. At the end of the paragraph, the author adds: "a fact that the believer should be aware of, so that he avoids them" (pg. 96).
And I would naively assume here the good intentions of Mr. Spencer, that by "them," he means the deviated paths of certain theology and not all Christians and Jews as human beings themselves!

In Islam, it is the ideology of disobeying God that you should disassociate yourself with at any cost, a Muslim as ordered by Prophet Muhammad (PBUH) cannot judge the faith, intentions or the fate on Judgment Day of any human being, no matter who he is.

Is the Holy Quran the first scripture that warned of people claiming that they are pious and religious, even though you want to stay away from their ideology as far as you can? Let's ask Jesus (PBUH):

"Many will say to me on that day, 'Lord, Lord, did we not prophesy in your name and in your name drive out demons and perform many miracles?'
Then I will tell them plainly, 'I never knew you. Away from me, you evil doers!'
King James Bible, Mathew, Chapter 7:22-23

151

Was Jesus an anti-Christian and "avoiding them was a cornerstone of his ideology"?! Absolutely not.

What do you think Moses said to the Jews whom, after he saved them from the Pharaoh of Egypt, parted the red sea, and went to get God's Commandments for them, chose to worship a golden cow?
Did Moses ask the pious Jews to follow the path of the Jews who worshipped the cow, or were they to avoid their path and abomination at any cost?

*Please note that it is telling that the verses in Al Fatiha, technically didn't point to the two previous Abrahimic religions of Christianity and Judaism at all, instead it pointed to the sin itself, angering God and going astray, which are sins some Muslims or non-Muslims do, just the same and for that they will receive the same punishment of God.

"The Hypocrites"

The author addresses the issue of the hypocrites of Medina who were Muslims in the open, yet as he described, they were a fifth column within the Muslim community. The author again enjoys intentionally, not differentiating between the warnings that Prophet Muhammad (PBUH) told everyone about the severe punishment of hypocrites on Judgment Day, and narrated it as if it was a threat of a punishment that the Prophet himself will inflict upon them! On page 96, he wrote:
"Muhammad also received revelations attacking the hypocrites for dishonesty, warning them of the dreadful punishment that awaited them."

*This is a major and important point, for it is about one of the greatest human and civil rights in Islam. One historical incident will shed enough light on how individuality and personal beliefs are protected in Islam.
Osama Ibn Zayd was one of the companions of the Prophet who went in a faction of the Muslim army to fight another faction of infidels who attacked Muslims.
During the battle, Osama Ibn Zayd overcame one of the warriors and

152

managed to throw the infidel on the ground, throwing his sword away. When Osama raised his sword to finish the infidel exactly like the infidel was trying to do to him, the infidel yelled the certification as if he just became a Muslim. Naturally, Osama Ibn Zayd did not believe him, hit him with the sword and killed him, yet he felt bad about it. So he told Prophet Muhammad (PBUH), who was shocked, and asked Osama:

"He did say I certify that there is no God but Allah, and still you went ahead and killed him?" Osama answered, "Oh Prophet of Allah, he only said it in fear of my sword." Prophet Muhammad (PBUH) replied,

"Did you split his heart open to see inside it if he had truly meant it or not?" (Prophet Muhammad (PBUH))
Narrator: Osama Ibn Zayd. *Reference: Saheeh Muslim,* **Number***: 96.* **Degree***: Correct*

So a sworn infidel warrior battling and attacking Muslims in the one moment before his death declares his Islam, and the Prophet of Islam himself forbids that his faith be judged. Can anyone Muslim no matter who he is, judge any Muslim, further, punish him for suspecting his claimed flawed faith?

According to the tenets of Islam, hypocrisy is to be avoided at any cost as a major sin. Yet, it is another major sin to call somebody a hypocrite, when the Prophet himself denies himself the right to judge what's in people's hearts, not to mention taking action against someone based on suspecting that he's a hypocrite.
Was it just this one previous quotation of the Prophet?

"I was not ordered to dig into people's hearts or to split their insides open to see what's in it." (Prophet Muhammad (PBUH))
Narrator: Abu Saeed Al Khodry. **Reference***: Saheeh Al Bukhary,* **Number***: 4351.* **Degree***: Correct*

"The Nakhla raid"

Here the author moves to the subject of how Muslims treated civilians in their battles. Instead of showing the general rules that are very clear and precise, stated by Prophet Muhammad (PBUH) himself in his quotations and in Islamic Law, or the ton of historical records about the matter, the author chose a very exceptional unique condition that wasn't even factual but hypothetical in one Muslim soldier's question to the Prophet.

So what are the general rules in a war for Muslims in dealing with enemy civilians and specifically women and children?

When sending orders to Khalid Ibn Alwaleed, the great military leader, Prophet Muhammad (PBUH) made it clear in the message:

"Tell Khalid not to kill a woman or a servant."
(Prophet Muhammad (PBUH))
Narrator: Rabah Ibn Rabee. **Reference**: *Saheeh Abi Dawood,* **Number***: 4351.*
Degree*: Correct*

1. After a battle, Prophet Muhammad (PBUH) was angered by the sight of one woman of the enemy killed by an arrow. He repeated his explicit orders that women and children were not to be harmed whatsoever, and added, pointing to the body of the woman, **"she was not fighting"** meaning that the only condition that a woman would be fought in battle is if she actually carried arms and fought.

2. The general rule is mentioned in the Holy Quran itself:
    "And fight for the sake of Allah those who fought you, And do not transgress, for Allah does not like the transgressors"
    Holy Quran, Surat (Al Baqara)(The Cow) Ch (2) Verse (190)

Meaning that you may fight only enemy combatants, but no civilians whatsoever, even if they were able to be drafted as soldiers. For example, a strong male servant, who is not wearing a soldier uniform, carrying arms, or attacking Muslims, cannot be killed in battle.

3. There is no need to mention that children and old men or women are included in the same rule. But then what are the exceptions?

1. If any individual from the above did actually carry arms and fought against Muslims. For example, a woman, a teenager, an old man, or anyone who did actually fight the Muslim army, then these people should be fought like any other soldier of the enemy, because simply, they are.

2. Another exception, which is not only a rarity, but might have never happened, is that when there's a war that continues into the night, battle is raging, and Muslim soldiers, because of the condition of the night, could not differentiate between soldiers and civilians, then if it happens, that civilians were hurt, Prophet Muhammad (PBUH) explained that these soldiers have not violated the ethics of Islam, because it was out of their control.

*Our author leaves the entire glaring, precise rules of not to hurt civilians mandated by God and His Prophet which are unparalleled in the world then and to date, and goes to the exception of a hypothetical question of Muslim soldiers to Prophet Muhammad (PBUH) and shows it as if it was the general rule itself, not the exception. On page 97, the author quotes his favorable source of Ibn Is'haq:
"and was asked whether it was permissible to attack al-mushrikun (unbelieving) warriors at night with a probability of exposing their women and children to danger. The Prophet replied, 'They (i.e. women and children) are from them (i.e. al-mushrikun). "

*Would have that soldier asked that question, had it been that the rule was not to hurt civilians, specifically women and children? Here is the statement of the author. On page 98 he wrote:

"From then on, innocent non-Muslim women and children could legitimately suffer the fate of male unbelievers."!
*Why resort to the possibility of the "Could" when dealing with documented historical events? What battle did it actually happened that innocent non-Muslim women and children "did" suffer the fate of male

unbeliever warriors? The answer is never! Was the fate of these "male unbelievers" as such because they were "unbelievers" or because they were actually combating "male soldiers"?

The same author that was in pain saying that Muslims do not engage in battle without warnings and without offering three possibilities to their enemy, two of which include no battling, is now looking only at the extreme exception of war at night, which is a rarity at that time, in an already ongoing battle, making a hypothetical question of a soldier, as if it was the general rule of dealing with civilians at war!

Did the author find one incident after that question of the soldier, in any of his corrupted, convoluted stories, that there was such a battle where not only Prophet Muhammad (PBUH), but even any of the companions, said explicitly that let's go attack enemies at night without warning and it is okay to attack women and children as well? Never.

That hypothesis can only be found in a God-fearing Muslim soldier's question to the Prophet of God who had already prohibited the harm of any innocent civilians.

The author moves to an incident that he describes as "notorious." When Prophet Muhammad (PBUH) sent Abdullah Ibn Gahsh and other companions to strictly gather information in a place called "Nakhla" (Palm). When the companions went there, they discovered a caravan that had some of the infamous Quraysh leaders. Despite the fact that the Prophet had asked Abdullah Ibn Gahsh to only gather information, and the fact that the time was within the three sacred months that Arabs forbade fighting in, they engaged them in a fight.

The author runs to Abdullah Ibn Gahsh telling the other companions - before they discovered the caravan - that whoever does not want to die as a martyr can go back before we can go ahead with our mission, and immediately the author calls it:

"just as modern day jihad terrorists."!

*Even though they were going into a mission to gather information so their potential demise logically and clearly cannot be other than if they were caught and killed by the enemy, the author, as we explained in our introduction to the book, decided - on his own - that to be a martyr in Islam, it means only that you go and kill people, compared to Christianity, where according to his own definition, it would be "suffering onto death at the hands of the unjust for the sake of the faith." So if you are a Muslim and went on an intelligence-gathering mission, where you would potentially be killed and martyred, you were nothing but "modern day jihad terrorists." But if you were a Christian doing the same thing, receiving the same fate, then that is true martyrdom!

The author stated the fact that most of the people with Ibn Gahsh were immigrants. But he did not say what that may mean. An immigrant at that point of time is one who literally survived killing, torture, and starvation, under Quraysh's oppression, and made it, barely alive, to Medina, mostly with the clothes on their backs. So, when they saw the caravan, and they did not have any idea that they will ever meet that caravan - in addition to the fact that it was not planned, and was an absolute coincidence - they couldn't stop themselves from fighting back and avenging themselves.

The author himself, in narrating what he thought was a "modern day jihad terrorist attack!!" provided us the proof that attacking the caravan was not something that Ibn Gahsh and his companions had planned at all! He wrote that the Prophet:
".. gave Abdullah a letter with an order that he was not to open it until he had travelled for two days."

*So neither the Prophet, nor the companions with Ibn Gahsh knew that the caravan would be there at that exact time. Yet with the abhorring torture and persecution that some of the people of the caravan had applied upon Ibn Gahsh's helpless Muslims companions, the companions could not help but go ahead and fight them.

The Prophet's orders were just to gather information. Then, the question becomes: what happened then when the Prophet discovered that they disobeyed his orders and fought the caravan?

The Prophet got angry and asked them:
"Didn't I order you not to fight in the forbidden months?"

So not only did they not confine themselves to the news-gathering mission, but they also violated the general rule of not fighting in the forbidden months. Can this, in any logic, be categorized by anything remotely close to a planned attack? Did the author even call the Quraysh persecuting, torturing and killing Muslims, an act of terror to begin with? Or is it just the Muslim victims standing up to oppression and avenging themselves, a wrong thing, not to mention - according to Mr. Spencer - the only wrong thing around?

The people in the caravan were not innocent baby girls. They were armed fighters carrying their daggers and their swords, as was the custom of the majority of the men of Quraysh. The question here really is, had the result of the fighting been the opposite, meaning that the Muslim group were defeated and killed, what would have the author called the infidels of Quraysh then? "Peace advocates"?

If the Muslims were a Jewish militia in Nazi Germany, who accidentally found a Nazi convoy that they thought they had a chance in overcoming, would they have walked away, throwing post cards of well wishing at them? But then, if that militia had engaged the Nazis and killed them, would our objective author have called it a "modern day terrorist attack"? Would the militia conceivably then leave all the guns, ammunitions and supplies for the next Nazi faction to come collect them, or would they have seized them to fortify themselves with?

The author then quotes the verse that was revealed and addressed that incident in Surat Al-Baqara, but quoted us the wrong verse number. On page 99, he quotes it as "(Holy Quran 2:214)", where it is actually verse number 2:217.

In the verse, after the Prophet had blamed his companions for fighting, Allah relieved the companions, stating to all Muslims that even though fighting during the forbidden months was a big sin, yet the infidels of Quraysh that the companions of the Prophet fought, had committed the worst of all sins, torturing helpless Muslims just for the Muslims worshipping God, and forcing them to change their religion of worshipping the One Mighty God. In the verse, God had also stated that torturing people and exposing the believers to "Fitnah" (torture) is a sin that is much worse than the sin of battling in the forbidden months.

The fact that God had forgiven Ibn Gahsh and his companions, even though within the context of God stating that what they did was wrong, but the much lesser wrong than what the caravan infidels had committed against them, forced the author not end the topic without bringing his flying mammoth back again! At the end of page 99, he wrote:
"... this was a momentous incident, for it would set a pattern: good became identified with anything that redounded to the benefit of Muslims, and evil with anything that harmed them without reference to any larger moral standard. Moral absolutes were swept aside, in favor of the overreaching principle of expediency."

*I honestly have a pressing innocent question; is the author talking about Muslims, or the Republican Party?!

Victims of some of the worst oppression in history accidentally met their oppressors and fought them man to man within the fairness of *kill or be killed*, and they won. Is that an "overreaching principle of expediency"? And if the author has the audacity to call it that, what would the author have called it if whoever attacked the caravan were instead thieves who robbed for a living, went there intentionally to attack the caravan and rob it? What would have he said if everyone in the caravan was someone whom the thieves never knew, never oppressed, tortured, nor starved them? What would the author have called it then? An act of charity?!

159

The really amazing word of what the author wrote is, "anything"! The Prophet told them to gather only intelligence, the Prophet told them not to fight during the forbidden months, God Himself stated that it's a big sin to fight in the forbidden months, yet the companions could not help seeing their oppressors in the open, in an even plain field, away from their fortified positions in Mecca, without avenging what happened to them and their fellow Muslims. Can you call that, "moral absolutes were swept aside"?! Or maybe the moral thing to do - even though it was wrong to disobey the explicit orders of the Prophet - was to throw some selected sweets at the infidels. In the author's usual "Muslims are always terrorists regardless" convoluted absurdity!

"The break with the Jews and the change of qibla (direction for prayer)"

This time, the author brings his traditional convoluted statements right from the start. He writes:
"Muhammad continued to appeal to the Jews to accept his Prophetic status".

1. *Prophet Muhammad (PBUH) invited everyone to Islam, even the mercenary killer, "Wahshy" who was the one who killed his beloved protector, companion, and uncle, Hamza Ibn Abdel Muttalib. So Prophet Muhammad (PBUH) was not appealing specifically to any one group or race or creed; he was inviting all mankind to the straight path of God.

"And We have not sent you but as a mercy to all mankind."
Holy Quran, Surat (Al-Anbiyah) (The Prophets) Ch 21 verse (107)

وَمَا أَرْسَلْنَاكَ إِلَّا رَحْمَةً لِلْعَالَمِينَ (107)

2. Prophet Muhammad (PBUH) at this point had hundreds of revelations from the Holy Spirit (Archangel Gabriel), had prayed with all the Prophets of God in Jerusalem, was ascended nearest to the highest heaven with the power of God, and received - after talking several times to God - the orders of prayers to Muslims.

160

I ask the reader - in the eyes of Muhammad (PBUH) at this point - does he need any certification of his Prophethood whatsoever from any men on earth?

The author then quotes Prophet Muhammad (PBUH) asking the Jews, by the help and protection that God had afforded their true believers before in history that they search in their scripture for his name. While the author does not comment on the correct answer to that question, or even what the Jews had said, even in light of the Jewish rabbi Ibn Salam who already accepted Islam, I will - again - reiterate what's already in the Old Testament in Hebrew.

"His mouth is most sweet: yea, he is <u>"Muhamad'em"</u>. This is my beloved, and this is my friend, O daughters of Jerusalem."
King James Bible, Song of Songs 5:16

Then the author writes:
"The subsequent fortunes of the Jews of Arabia, however, indicate that this verse was not considered even in Muhammad's day to be an open-ended invitation to religion, pluralism, nor a call to Muslims to coexist peacefully as equals to non-Muslims."

*We already have answered how Jews throughout history were protected under Islamic law in Muslim lands; they were allowed to worship freely, and not only coexist, but thrive as well to the absolute contrary to how they were treated in Christendom, and we will not repeat the facts again.

On page 101, he writes:
"Around the time of the Nakhla raid, Muhammad began to give up on the idea that the Jews would ever accept him as a Prophet."

*The author revisits - again - the notion that Prophet Muhammad (PBUH) was seeking some sort of title or some position from the Jews, and not the fact that he was inviting them and everyone else just the same to the path of the One Mighty God.

161

Muslims up to this point in Islamic history were praying towards the Farthest Masjid in Jerusalem. God then revealed the verses that allowed the Prophet to pray towards the Kabaa directly. And while geographically, when you are in Mecca today and pray on any point of a 360 degree circle all around the Kabaa, meaning you are facing beyond the Kabaa every direction on Earth, you are correctly praying towards the Kabaa and your prayers are accepted. What that means is that while the Muslims in Mecca were praying towards Jerusalem, they were actually praying towards the eternal Qiblah direction of the Kabaa itself as well (being on the same line), and that is a geometrical scientific fact (look at any picture of Muslim prayers around the Kabaa).

On page 101, the author writes:
"Tawaef revelation even asserted that the Jews and Christians ("the people of the book") knew that the Muslims new direction for prayer was the correct one. (Holy Quran 2:143-144).

*The author twists the meaning of one of the verses of the Holy Quran about pious Muslims who believed in Muhammad (PBUH), and knew that what he brought to mankind was the truth. He twists that, without any proof, as if the verse meant that Christians and Jews of that period knew that praying towards Mecca was the truth!

The author, forcing the issue of changing the direction of Muslim prayers, into the subject of some of the Jews accepting Islam or not, is illogical, and the apparent proof is what he wrote himself on page 102 of the verse revealed when some of the Rabbis wanted the Prophet to bring back the direction of prayers towards Jerusalem, which the Prophet refused and the verse was revealed in Al-Baqara 2:142 that the west and the east both belong to Allah, the one mighty God.

*Let me ask the author here: at that time, in the 7th century B.C, was Judaism the religion of the majority of Jerusalem, or was it Christianity? Were all the holy sites in Jerusalem controlled by Christian Romans or by the Jews?
Let me ask another question: for a Jew who does not believe in Islam,

162

would he care and appeal to Muhammad (PBUH) that Muhammad (PBUH) would share their holy city with them as their direction of prayers, or is it better for them that Muhammad (PBUH) prays to another direction, or towards any other city?

God in Islamic Law loves those who share what they have with those who do not have, and sometimes I feel the urge to pick up the phone and call Mr. Spencer and share with him a wonderful new concept that would greatly benefit him: logic!

Our author ends the chapter with another incident that, again, full with discrediting his own logic and understanding. It is about a Jewish couple who committed adultery. they were brought to Prophet Muhammad (PBUH) by their Jewish leaders after they were caught. Apparently, the Jewish leaders of this tribe wanted to embarrass Prophet Muhammad (PBUH), or maybe test him.

The author, in narrating the same story, starts on page 102, with: "On one occasion, the Prophet of Islam challenged them over the appropriate punishment for the couple that had been accused of adultery."

*The true story tells us however that it is the Jewish leaders who brought the couple and came to Prophet Muhammad (PBUH) to ask his opinion, with an intention of obviously challenging and testing him. Prophet Muhammad (PBUH) answered their question, telling them that the order of stoning is written there in the Torah. One of the leaders started to read from the Torah, yet he put his hand on the part that ordered the stoning for committing adultery. The former Rabbi Ibn Salam was there and asked him to take his hand off the verse and reveal it, which he did. The Prophet blamed them for trying to conceal the orders and judgment of God.

God had failed them where they wanted to test the Prophethood of Prophet Muhammad (PBUH) himself. The author paints us a picture that leads to a final statement where he wrote, on page 102 describing the

163

stoning of the couple:
"Another Muslim remembered, "I saw the man leaning over the woman to shelter her from the stones""

    * Why didn't the man, if he had that Oscar worthy love for her, marry her, before he used her when he committed adultery with her, not to mention as usual that there is no record of that nameless Muslim man who "remembered"? It is well-known in Mosaic Law that the punishment of adulterers is stoning. In the matter of fact, naively, the author brings up the famous stoning story in the Gospel of John in today's Bible, where supposedly Jesus (PBUH) had said:
"Let he who is without sin cast the first stone". The obvious notion is to draw a fake comparison trying to deprive Islam of compassion.
And before I address that compassion issue, I want to ask the author; why would the Jewish leaders, according to the Biblical story, bring the adulteress woman to Jesus for anything other than punishing her? And why would anyone carry a stone for any reason related to the story other than stoning her? Because that was the Mosaic Law that the leader of that tribe thought that Prophet Muhammad (PBUH) did not know about. But don't take my word for it:

"If there is a man who commits adultery with another man's wife, one who commits adultery with his friend's wife, the adulterer and the adulteress shall surely be put to death"
King James Bible, Leviticus, 20:10

    Almost in a similar fashion, the leaders of the Jews as per the story included in the Gospel of John, wanted to embarrass Jesus (PBUH) who was preaching mercy and compassion, by bringing a woman who committed adultery. So if he let her go, then he violated a major law of Judaism, which will discredit him technically as a Jewish rabbi, and if he punished her, then supposedly that would have discredited his message of compassion as well. In either case, there was no question that stoning was a part of Judaic Law.

164

Stoning the two Jewish adulterers was an issue of these Jewish leaders applying their Torah laws or not. What Prophet Muhammad (PBUH) had told the Jewish leaders did not have any reflection upon Islam itself other than the fact that if they were testing Prophet Muhammad (PBUH) then he made them fail their own test.

Then our author writes on page 102:
"Not only does this episode reveal a sharp distinction between Jewish and Islamic concepts of compassion, but the contrast between Muhammad's teachings and that of Jesus."

In his book *Misquoting Jesus*, (the story behind who changed the Bible and why) the author, Mr. Bart D. Ehrman proved scientifically that the story in which Jesus said "Let he who is without sin cast the first stone" is not a part of the original Gospel of John to begin with, and most probably was a folklore story that a scribe wrote on the margin of the original manuscript, in which it was copied later onto another manuscript, mistakenly including it in the text itself. It is interesting to add that Mr. Ehrman currently chairs the Department of Religious Studies of the University of North Carolina at Chapel Hill, which is the department from which Mr. Spencer himself received his college degree!

On the other hand, and more interestingly, the author himself later in his book will admit to the unprecedented mercy and forgiveness the Prophet had shown, including forgiving the entire population of Mecca all their crimes and persecution against Muslims, when Muhammad (PBUH) entered Mecca and became its ruler.

Think about it:

1. Prophets of God do not get embarrassed when they know (from God) the ultimate wisdom of what to do. They advise, exactly as such, and do not fear any blame against the Word of God.

2. If a woman *was caught* committing adultery, then a Prophet of God would be the first one to apply the law of God, yet nobody in the that story said anything about the man that they caught her committing

165

adultery with, and why he wasn't brought to Jesus as well. Was the woman caught committing adultery alone?!

3.   The supposedly compassionate and merciful answer of Jesus in that story does not comply with the teachings of a mighty Prophet of God or any other mighty Prophet of God, whether in the old scriptures or in the Holy Quran. Did Jesus (PBUH) ever say it's okay to commit adultery? Did he ever say adultery is forgivable, and you can move on? Absolutely not.
It was he (PBUH) who said (in the Sermon on the Mount) *that if you just even looked at a woman and lusted after her then you have committed adultery in your heart.* What do you think Jesus would say then about committing physical adultery in itself with the woman?

Now, let's go to Islam, about which a few chapters ago, Mr. Spencer was in pain because it puts such difficult conditions to convict anyone of adultery. For stoning to be ruled, four simultaneous credible witnesses have to testify that they have seen the action.
We would also demonstrate the fact that, in the first thousand years of Islamic rule, the punishment of stoning under Islamic law was applied only three times! And these three incidents were after full, voluntary, insistent confessions of guilt by the committers of adultery, who were met with relentless attempts from the Muslims to try to find an excuse for them not to apply the punishment.
True mercy upon human beings is attained by applying the laws of God justly. Such rules are there to benefit them and protect them all.
The preventive, not the avenging way of the law of God in Islam, is to set a severe punishment to the corruptive crime as a deterrent to people committing it in the first place. Yet in this specific rule, setting conditions to convict and apply the punishment that are so difficult to meet, is in itself so merciful, that while protecting society from the destructive irreversible repercussions of adultery, it keeps such punishment at an absolute minimum.

166

Corrupting the laws of God, and concealing the right thing to do based on wane excuses and empty slogans of compassion and mercy, yet hypocritically behaving towards an outcome of the opposite, is what has always caused the suffering of mankind.

I hope Mr. Spencer is not helping.

"It is difficult to find, in anywhere other than Islam, what exceeds these advantages. This sincerity to the principal of the religion, and the simplicity of the fundamentals of the religion evident by the conviction of its Imams that inspires enthusiasm and conviction into others, are all the reasons that explains the success of Muslim preachers, which is expected however, for a well defined religion that is completely void of any philosophical complications; therefore it is within the grasp of the average individual, as it truly does possess a wonderful power to gain its way to people conscious'.

Edward Montier, the French orientalist, who translated the Quran to French

Chapter Seven

"War is deceit"

In this chapter, the author covers the beginning of the era when God had allowed the Muslims to fight the oppression of Quraysh and start to defend themselves militarily.

Before I move to comment on what the author wrote in the chapter, I cannot resist but comment on the title he chose for its beginning, "War is Deceit," which is an actual quotation from Prophet Muhammad (PBUH).
You don't have to be a mind-reader to see that the author is trying to bring a war tactic, actually the most principal of all war tactics, as if it is a personal trait of Prophet Muhammad (PBUH), Islam, or bluntly as if Prophet Muhammad (PBUH) himself is deceptive.

Maybe what we teach our soldiers and generals in West Point and all military colleges in the world, is that we should telegraph our goals and intentions for the next battle to the enemy, and make sure that the enemy is not confused about what we intend to do next! And if that, then Muhammad (PBUH), as a great military leader and Prophet of God, must - in the eyes of the author - be doing something wrong by concealing his plans from the enemy and actually hoping that the enemy would come to believe otherwise!

"The Battle of Badr"

In bolded capital letters, the author writes, on page 103: "As the Muslims' relations with the Jews steadily deteriorated, they reached their final breaking point with the Quraysh."

*The blue elephant began to fly early in this chapter! What relation was there between the Jews of Medina and Quraysh of Mecca at the time? And whoever said that the Jews of Medina were the decision-makers of Quraysh, so our author links Muhammad (PBUH)'s whatever relationship with the Jews with whatever breaking point there may be between him and Quraysh? There is no answer!

On page 104, the author writes:
"Muhammad received a revelation from Allah berating those Muslims who were reluctant to wage war for the Prophet of Islam."

*In Islamic Law, anything done for something other than the sake of Allah is totally reward less. Beyond any doubt, the most common quotation of the Prophet himself usually, in the preface of the mother books of Islamic Jurisprudence is:

"Deeds are rewarded by what they were done for, and every person will get what he intended. So whoever immigrated to a worldly gain or a woman to marry, then he immigrated to what he immigrated for."
(Prophet Muhammad (PBUH))
Narrator: *Omar Ibn Alkhatab* **Reference**: *Saheeh Al Bukhary,* **Number***: 1.*
Degree*: Correct*

Good deeds in Islam, no matter how great they are, are only rewarded by God on the Day of Judgment, if they were done purely for the sake of God, not for anyone else's. When we obey the Prophet of God, it is because the Prophet of God brings us commands to obey Allah Himself. You could never find someone Muslim in any reference - even in Ibn Is'haq - at any caliber of importance or status that would say, "I'm fighting for Muhammad," for, Muhammad (PBUH) himself would tell him that striving is only for the sake of Allah, and not for the sake of any person, even if it was the Prophet of God Muhammad (PBUH). God Himself talking to Muhammad (PBUH) in the Holy Quran, said:

"Then fight (Muhammad (PBUH)) in the Cause of Allah, none is tasked except for yourself"
Holy Quran, Surat (Al Nissa) Ch (4) No (84)

فَقَاتِلْ فِي سَبِيلِ اللَّهِ لَا تُكَلَّفُ إِلَّا نَفْسَكَ ۚ وَحَرِّضِ الْمُؤْمِنِينَ ۖ عَسَى اللَّهُ أَن يَكُفَّ بَأْسَ الَّذِينَ كَفَرُوا ۚ وَاللَّهُ أَشَدُّ بَأْسًا وَأَشَدُّ تَنْكِيلًا (84)

On page 104, the author misinterprets one of Prophet Muhammad (PBUH)'s miracles, when he wrote:
""And by God, it is as though I see the enemy lying prostrate.""

*What the Prophet said, was that he saw the future-dead leaders of Quraysh, whose fate was to die in the coming battle. The companions of Prophet Muhammad (PBUH), who heard him say that, and saw the locations that Prophet Muhammad (PBUH) pointed at, and specified which infidel of Quraysh would lie dead, in which specific spot; all of them certified that after the end of the battle of Badr, they walked around and saw exactly the same people lying dead in exactly the same spots that Prophet Muhammad (PBUH) foretold.

Again, the author invents intentions of the Prophet that the Prophet not only never expressed, are far-fetched, and intentions that defy even any logic. On page 105, he wrote about the fact that Quraysh's army outnumbered the Muslim army at the battle of Badr:
"Muhammad seems not to have expected these numbers and cried out to Allah in anxiety."

*Everyone at the time, even the youngest child in the Arab Peninsula, knew that Quraysh's numbers, might, and power were overwhelmingly superior to the small, newly-formed Muslim army. An army that was mainly made of Quraysh's poor and persecuted, who fled to Medina. Even when adding the Muslims of Medina itself to the Muslim army, they were still not a large army (at Badr the ratio was three to one against Muslims). The fact that Prophet Muhammad (PBUH) prayed and supplicated to God to give him aid, was because of

171

the fact that he already knew that Quraysh was much more powerful than the Muslims, and definitely not because, all of a sudden, he had a "Spencer" anxiety attack of a major surprise!

Then comes another major fabrication when, on page 105, the author wrote: "Some Muslim traditions say that Muhammad himself participated in the fighting; others, that it was more likely that he exhorted his followers from the sidelines."

Aside from the fact that we stated before, that there is no such a term or true references called "Muslim traditions," just the notion that Prophet Muhammad (PBUH) might've not participated in the battle of Badr - never mind the first and most crucial of all the battles Muslims fought - is an outright, abhorrent lie. Prophet Muhammad (PBUH) was a man of utmost honesty. His actions always paralleled his words and vice versa. Here is the account of the bravery of Prophet Muhammad (PBUH) and his ultimate sacrifice of himself first, before anyone else, as in the account of Ali Ibn Abi Talib:

"When the battles were at a climax, and the eyes reddened, we used to hide behind Prophet Muhammad, and always, no one was closer to the enemy than Prophet Muhammad himself."
Reference: Alnsaeey

It is worth mentioning here that Ali Ibn Abi Talib was one of the most powerful men of Quraysh and his nickname was "knight of the knights."

When Muslims fought, and when they were promised martyrdom, they fought in an army, in broad daylight, man to man, soldier to soldier, and in many cases - actually in most cases of all Islamic battles in the first 80 years after founding the Muslim state - Muslims were mostly the overwhelmingly outnumbered side, and the side with significantly less equipment.

172

Prophet Muhammad (PBUH) was not the kind of leader that would pound some table and yell in rage about patriotism, resolve and justice, then send the sons of poor minorities to the frontlines, while hiding, during the real war, behind far, and fancy fortifications. These were true battles, Muslims were the outnumbered side, and the side most likely to be annihilated, yet God had granted them victory, whether by defeating their enemy, or by granting them martyrdom.

I wonder, sometimes, in any country of the world: what do they call their "falling hero soldiers," what honorable stature do they award them, but also what speeches do their army generals motivate them with before battle? Or, may be in the eyes of our author, motivating and rallying your soldiers in battle, is only a crazy Jihadist warrior Muslim thing!

Muhammad (PBUH) not only participated in the entire battle of Badr, but almost always was in the front line till God had granted His worshippers, the outnumbered, the persecuted, and the oppressed, their first major victory.

On page 106, the author tries to show Prophet Muhammad (PBUH) as someone who is not forgiving. The excuse is him ordering a captured in the battle infidel, "Uqba" to be executed. The author tries to let us empathize with the little birdie Uqba, who pled to the Prophet: "But who will look after my children, oh Muhammad?"

*The author brought only the fact that this sweet Uqba used to throw camel dung, blood, and intestines on the Prophet of Islam, while he was praying in Mecca, maybe to imply that the Prophet ordered him to be executed just to avenge himself personally. Understandably, the author would not tell you, and my suspicion is, he would not even search for how many early Muslims Uqba had caused to be starved, tortured, and killed. Then, in a battle where all he wanted was to annihilate Islam and the Muslims, best kill Muhammad (PBUH) himself, he was captured. If Uqba would not be executed by a firing squad of any victorious army in the world, let the author tell us, then who?

Al Nadr Ibn al Harith was the only other infidel leader who was also executed in Badr, next to Uqba. In order to easily understand the reason behind the severe animosity of Uqba Ibn Mayeet and Al Nadr bin al Harith against the Muslims of Mecca, you may want to know they were partners in one of Mecca's major brothel and liquor houses. The virtues of Islam were devastating to their business of filth.

When entire Mecca and the tribe of Quraysh surrendered to the Muslim army few years later, Prophet Muhammad (PBUH) gave every single person amnesty, even people who committed crimes against the Muslims that were more horrible than Uqba; having said that, the people of Mecca did not raise a sword against Muhammad (PBUH) when he entered the city, unlike Uqba in Badr. Total number of infidels captured at Badr was 70. All were released except for the two.

The rest of the captured Quraysh warriors of Badr, some of which were heads of their tribes and glens, were set free to go back to their tribes after a famous debate and consultation between the Prophet, Abu Bakr, and Omar Ibn Al-Khattab which we will address in details later.

On page 106, comes another high-flying elephant that even surprised us! Abu Jahl, who was one of the leaders of Quraysh, and its army, was killed in the battle of Badr, yet Mr. Spencer has the audacity to tell us another story according to "another account" - which I'm growing accustomed that what he means by it, is just another blue elephant without any proof - he wrote:
"According to another account, two young Muslims murdered Abu Jahl as he was walking amongst people."!!

*So, Abu Jahl, the leader of Quraysh's earlier campaign to assassinate Muhammad (PBUH) and annihilate the Muslims, who just, in the previous page, the author himself quoted saying:
"No, by God, we will not turn back until God decides between us and Muhammad", and who was killed in the same battle, amazingly now was

174

not fighting and battling Muslims in Badr, and wasn't consequently killed in battle!! According to the author, "He was walking amongst people"!

According to what that "another account" suggests, it must've been a terrorist, jihadist Al-Qaeda, assassins who killed him! Because he was in the battlefield, just "walking amongst people" so peacefully and happily. Maybe because Abu Jahl forgot that he had some shopping to do, and had to pick up some stuff, walking around, browsing storefronts so innocently - amongst people -, till the crazy Muslim jihadists came and killed him while he unassumingly was awaiting God's decision between Quraysh and Muhammad, to be shown on CNN!

And as usual, that innocent, "another account" is never mentioned as to what it is, or which planet it is from.

Usually, I put the same titles that the author puts ahead of any paragraph, only this time the author puts an absurd, demeaning title that may be telling of what he truly believes about God himself.

His title is, "**Allah fights for the Muslims**" And I ask the readers and Mr. Spencer himself: is his perception of God, the one Mighty, the Creator of Heavens and Earth, is such that He needs to exert an effort to fight anything? That he cannot - in a blink - destroy the Earth and what's on it, and create another planet with another population? Or is it that Mr. Spencer truly believes in another thing or another earthly being, other than the One Mighty God that has the same flaws, limitations and needs that humans have?

In a following paragraph, Mr. Spencer deduces from the nature of warfare, horses, swords, and daggers, of 1400 years ago, that it is: "An Islamic practice - then and now - of beheading hostages and war captives"!!

175

*All those who were killed by the millions - 10 million in the religious wars in the middle-ages of Europe alone as per Voltaire's estimate - throughout history, apparently as per Mr. Spencer, were not killed by the sword but may be by the warriors' ill wishes for each other! Other than that, in Spencer land "then and now" and till the invention of the gun, a kill by the sword can only be a Muslim thing!

So, executing two war-criminal tyrants in battle, is now the overriding pillar of the religion of 1.6 billion people, because Mr. Spencer said so! Does it make it a lesser or more of a crime to the innocent victims, when killers murder them unjustly by a firing squad, lethal injection, or beheading? Not to mention that according to Islamic Law - which Mr. Spencer almost never quotes correctly - people who capture innocent civilians and kill them unjustifiably, are punishable by public execution as corruptors on Earth.

Let me ask Mr. Spencer, for he might, of all people, know the answer: If beheading is probably the most abhorring death to watch, then, for these criminals to specifically choose beheadings, videotape them and try to push them on TV stations and the internet worldwide, who then benefits and gains more public support out of killing their victims specifically that way? Is it Muslim-bashers, or is it 1.6 billion Muslims worldwide?

Throughout the rest of page 108, the author convolutes the verses in the Holy Quran, where Allah stated that it was His aid to the Muslims, neither Muhammad (PBUH), nor the abilities of the Muslims themselves that granted them victory; it was their piety and sacrifice for the sake of God that was deserving of Allah to grant them victory. The author jumps 1400 years to one of the militia leaders in Iraq resisting the American occupation, Al-Zarqawi and quotes him, repeating slogans about the victory that God grants the Muslims! And all of a sudden, our Prophet of Islam is not Muhammad (PBUH) anymore, and his quotations are not enough guidance for Muslims, Mr. Spencer chooses one whom he self-titled a "jihad-leader" and makes his quotes as if they were our own fundamental beliefs, and heavenly revelations as Muslims!

If anyone can pick the absolute few out of populations by the hundred millions, and impose his selection of criminals upon everybody's beliefs, then, it must be conceivable by the author, when somebody asks about the civility and the lawfulness of our American Constitution, that someone may quote him "Jeffery Dahmmer," for why bother with Thomas Jefferson or Lincoln any more when using the "Spencer" "always provoke hatred against them" logic.

And here is the pearl of wisdom that Mr. Spencer almost puts at the end of every title of a chapter. On page 109 he wrote:
"The Prophet, the most merciful, ordered (his army) to strike the necks of some prisoners (in the battle of Badr) and to kill them . . . . and he set a good example for us"

*Even though that is a quote of a Steven Stalinsky, but I would consider it as if Mr. Spencer believes in it, so I will answer them both.

1. It is only Uqba, and Al Nadr, two war criminals who were executed after the battle. If the Prophet of God judged the men as war criminals, should Muslims or even non-Muslims have a second thought or care about what Mr. Spencer may otherwise think of it?!
Can Mr. Spencer's opinion be worth a fly's weight against a final Supreme Court ruling, not to mention to then have the Muslims apologize for a ruling of non other than the Prophet of God himself? Is that what Mr. Spencer really thinks?!

2. At the time of the Prophet, and I'll for another five centuries after him; let's ask not only what did non-Muslims victorious armies do to their defeated enemy's generals, but even to the population of innocent women and children of the defeated army? I dare the author, Mr. Stalinsky, and their likes to even attempt to compare.

3. Mr. Spencer, in one public speech, in which he was defending the Crusades of all things, absurdly apologized for the Crusaders, who

177

immediately, after getting into Jerusalem, went to the nearest Synagogue that was built, protected, and freely worshiped in by Jews during the Muslim rule, and burned down the Synagogue with the innocent Jewish population alive inside; may be as an appetizer, before they went ahead and killed every living Muslim soul that they saw before them, not sparing the old, women or children, with a final tally of 70 thousand Muslims civilians killed within 6 days! On that day the Arabic phrase, "blood was up to the knees level," was coined.

Having learned that, let's stop here - to appease Mr. Spencer - and shed some tears over sweet Uqba!

"The problem of booty"

The author, as we are accustomed to, neglects a very important fact of the balance of power, between Quraysh's army at the battle of Badr in relation to the Muslim army. Quraysh had a thousand fully-armed warriors, but the Muslim army had about three hundred, not all with horses, and not all well-armed. The defeat of Quraysh's army in that size and that overwhelming outcome was a miracle by any objective military standard. The author, who is supposedly enlightening us about the truth of Islam, totally ignores the huge victory and its causes of the depth of belief of early Muslims and their willingness to sacrifice everything they had purely for the sake of God. But why do we want to learn that about Islam or Muslims? And why is it relevant to see how supportive and rewarding God is when you're that sincere to His cause against evil and oppression? Is all that any relevant to Mr. Spencer?

The author in this paragraph addresses some arguments that occurred between some of the Muslim fighters about their share of "the spoils of war," which is natural after years of starvation on the hands of the pagans of Quraysh, and after a huge victory the size of that of the battle of Badr. The author makes another far-fetched claim about a verse in Surat Al-Anfal, Chapter 8, No. 1.

178

The translation of the verse that the author himself quoted is: "They ask thee concerning things taken as spoils of war. Say: (Such) spoils are at the disposal of Allah and the Messenger."

*The verse simply and very obviously means that the decision of distributing the winnings of war is a decision of God and His Messenger. Where did the author get the following conclusion even if we were only reading his own translation?

On page 109, he wrote:
"Allah warns the Muslims not to consider booty won at Badr to belong to anyone but Muhammad"!

*Where did the author see the word "won"? In it or in any interpretation that is worth the paper it's written on? Even the author could not find this one weird interpretation, with Ibn Is'haq!
Weird enough that in the remainder of the paragraph, the author showed that the rule was that Prophet Muhammad (PBUH) would get only one fifth, and the rest of the soldiers would get four-fifths, which was the rule of Allah throughout the life of Prophet Muhammad (PBUH).
Again where did the author get, that it was all Muhammad's?

The one-fifth given to Prophet Muhammad (PBUH), even though he had absolute freedom to spend it whichever way he wanted, he actually spent it in the same function as the future Muslim treasury in the days after his passing i.e. for anything that generally benefits the Muslim community, the poor, needy, or defense efforts.

Anyone who knows the very least about Prophet Muhammad (PBUH), would know that he was never asked for any money or anything that he could give, that he did not give and more. Literally, he was the most generous man that humanity had ever seen:

"The Prophet of Allah was never asked anything for Islam that he didn't give"
Narrator: Anas ibn Malik. Reference: Saheeh Muslim, Number: 2312.
Degree: Correct

With all the winnings and all the gifts that was given to Prophet Muhammad (PBUH), he died with the clothes on his back, a bunch of oats in his house, and his ride outside, while the people of Medina, Muslims or non-Muslims, were enjoying unprecedented prosperity.

Even though we're in the middle of refuting Mr. Spencer's book, there's one incident that I will go ahead and narrate it myself.
One day, when Maghrib prayers (sunset prayers) time came, the companions of the Prophet were surprised to see him rushing outside the masjid to his home, and then came back later to lead the prayers. When they asked the Prophet about what made him rush back home that suddenly, he said that he remembered that he had a few dates after Asr (the afternoon prayers), that were beyond his needs for the day, and that he did not want sunset prayers to come, while he was still having something above his needs, that he could give away to the needy.

On page 109, the author mentions the Hadeeth where Prophet Muhammad (PBUH) had said:

"I have been given five things which were not given to any amongst the Prophets. One was that, "the booty has been made Halal (lawful) to me" and another one that the author would naturally jump onto. The author writes, "Allah made me victorious by awe." The author writes his unique interpretation on page 109:
"(By His frightening my enemies)"

"I was given victory by awe that is worth the rally of one month."
*Narrator: Jaber ibn abdullah. **Reference**: Saheeh Al Bukhary, **Number**: 335.*
Degree: Correct

What it means is that God would strike fear in his enemies' hearts that would be equivalent to their (retreat) of rallying and battling for a month. In the quotation that the author included, it says, "**Allah made me victorious**," which indicates that the victory is from Allah and the awe that Allah strikes in the hearts of the enemies of Islam, also comes from Allah, which is correct. Yet, through the unique prism of whatever goes, the author relentlessly looks even at the simplest words, and amazingly sees that it is Muhammad (PBUH) himself who is frightening his enemies, not that victory is from God, or that God is who strikes fear into the hearts of his religion's enemies!

The Issue of the Captives of Badr

The final nugget of truth the author brings to us at the end of this part on page 111 is this, he writes:
"The battle of Badr was the first practical example of what came to be as the Islamic doctrine of Jihad"

Let's first examine that "practical example" by the very facts of the incident, the author has intentionally omitted.

1- Seventy of Quraysh's warrior elites were captured, the ones who could pay an expiation were set free, and the ones who couldn't afford to pay were asked to teach 10 Muslims each, how to read and write as a condition for their release. The doctrine of "Jihadist warriors" was to release a warrior infidel who might come back to battle them again the next battle, if he would give ten Muslims the blessing of reading and writing. Such an amazing fact of appreciating the high value of enlightenment and education, in the seventh century, is not worth mentioning about Islam and its Prophet in the eyes of the author.

2- With the exception of two, Muhammad (PBUH) had released all 68 infidel warriors back to their tribes! How merciful and gracious to a battling enemy that treatment is! Can that be a part of the "Jihadist doctrine" Mr. Spencer?

Omar Ibn Al Khattab thought that they should all be killed for their

181

crimes and to deter Quraysh from oppressing Muslims anymore, yet Abu Bakr thought that if they are released, that would show the mercy of Islam and would have a profound effect on their tribes in the future when they are invited to Islam. The merciful advice of Abu Bakr was what the Prophet chose at the end.

3- As the companions of the Prophet had grown accustomed to learn about the Prophet of Islam, whenever there was a matter for the Prophet to judge and there were options to rule, that all could be accepted by God, without thinking, the companions knew the Prophet would always choose the most merciful of these options. Was that historical fact worth mentioning about Muhammad (PBUH)'s truth and "doctrines" of battle? Not to Mr. Spencer!

" Allah is gentle and loves gentleness, and he rewards for gentleness what he doesn't reward for harshness or anything else"
(Prophet Muhammad (PBUH))
*Narrator: Ayesha. **Reference:** Saheeh Muslim, **Number:** 2593. **Degree:** Correct*

4- Why would a Prophet of God consult any one to make a decision as major as releasing and setting his enemies free? Would any of the companions blame him for whatever choice he might have made, that was a revelation of God? Never. But it is the democracy of Islam that is built upon consulting with people of impeccable reputation and wisdom about the matter in question. One of the closest companions to the Prophet and narrators of his Quotations, Abu Hurayra said:

"I have never seen anyone one more consulting with his companions like Prophet Muhammad"
(Prophet Muhammad (PBUH))
*Narrator: Abu Hurayra. **Reference:** Ibn Katheer/Irshad Alfaqeeh, **Number:** 387/2. **Degree:** trusted narrators with discontinuity*

Not only did he set the example of consulting with his companions, but compared to anyone else at the time, he was the most consulting with his companions.

182

"God Blames Some Muslims"

An erroneous strategy that some of the Muslims applied when fighting the infidels of Quraysh in the battle of Badr, was that they thought that capturing the leaders of Quraysh in battles would be more beneficial to Muslims, so they avoided injuring them in battle in the face of these leader warriors of Quraysh themselves, striving to annihilate the Muslims. After the battle, three verses were released correcting that mistake (our translation):

"It is not for a Prophet that he should have prisoners of war until he had made a great slaughter (among his enemies) in the land. You (some Muslims) desire the good of this, but Allah wants (for you) the Hereafter. [67]
And Allah is All-Mighty, All-Wise. If it wasn't a previous ordainment from Allah, a severe torment would have touched you for what you took. [68]
So enjoy what you have gotten of booty in war, lawful and good, and be afraid of Allah. Certainly, Allah is most-Forgiving, Most Merciful. [69]"
Holy Quran, Surat (Al Anfal) Ch (8) Verses (67-69)

مَا كَانَ لِنَبِيٍّ أَنْ يَكُونَ لَهُ أَسْرَىٰ حَتَّىٰ يُثْخِنَ فِي الْأَرْضِ ۚ تُرِيدُونَ عَرَضَ الدُّنْيَا وَاللَّهُ يُرِيدُ الْآخِرَةَ ۗ وَاللَّهُ عَزِيزٌ حَكِيمٌ (67)

لَوْلَا كِتَابٌ مِنَ اللَّهِ سَبَقَ لَمَسَّكُمْ فِيمَا أَخَذْتُمْ عَذَابٌ عَظِيمٌ (68)

فَكُلُوا مِمَّا غَنِمْتُمْ حَلَالًا طَيِّبًا ۚ وَاتَّقُوا اللَّهَ ۚ إِنَّ اللَّهَ غَفُورٌ رَحِيمٌ (69)

In the verses, God orders the Muslims to fight the enemies of God at least like their enemies are fighting them, and while the infidel warriors are striving to kill the believers in God, so should the Muslims fight back to the end, without any consideration to any materialistic or political benefits that may arise from avoiding injuring them to capture them alive. What are the priorities and rules of engagement in modern warfare? Are they to secure the safety of combating enemies for the ultimate purpose of captivating them later? Or are they engaging the

183

enemy at all capacity/ force available, and when the dust settles, then deal with prisoners of war later?

Is the phrase "takes no prisoners" an Islamic, even Arabic term, or is it a western one?

While the author is using this verse to claim that Muslims are ordered to go for the kill all the time, which we have already proved is totally the opposite, many times over, I ask the reader to look at it from the same "practical example" the author claims it has shown us:

What had happened?

The Muslims had mercy upon 68 of their worst enemies, and even the one who couldn't pay expiation for his release were not killed, but set free after teaching Muslims how to read and write.

Before the author ended the topic with the statement he brought earlier, he misinterprets a famous verse in the Holy Quran. In the same Surat Al Anfal Ch. 8 (our translation):

"And prepare against them all you can of power, including steeds of war, to threaten the enemy of Allah and your enemy, and others besides whom you may not know but whom Allah does know. And whatever you shall spend in the Cause of Allah shall be repaid to you, and you shall not be treated unjustly"
Holy Quran, Surat (Al Anfal) Ch. (8) Verse (60)

وَأَعِدُّوا لَهُمْ مَا اسْتَطَعْتُمْ مِنْ قُوَّةٍ وَمِنْ رِبَاطِ الْخَيْلِ تُرْهِبُونَ بِهِ عَدُوَّ اللَّهِ وَعَدُوَّكُمْ وَآخَرِينَ مِنْ دُونِهِمْ لَا تَعْلَمُونَهُمُ اللَّهُ يَعْلَمُهُمْ ۚ وَمَا تُنْفِقُوا مِنْ شَيْءٍ فِي سَبِيلِ اللَّهِ يُوَفَّ إِلَيْكُمْ وَأَنْتُمْ لَا تُظْلَمُونَ (60)

Every major interpretation of the verse shows the same simple meaning that the verse itself tells us. Prepare as much as you can of military might for the purpose of deterring the enemies of God not to attempt to fight you. If this is not clear enough, then let's go to the immediately following verse, which is verse [61] to show the purpose of preparing that military might. (Our translation)

184

"But if they incline to peace, then you incline to it, and rely upon Allah. Verily, He is the All-Hearer, the All-Knower"
Holy Quran, Surat (Al Anfal) Ch. (8) Verse (61)

وَإِنْ جَنَحُوا لِلسَّلْمِ فَاجْنَحْ لَهَا وَتَوَكَّلْ عَلَى اللَّهِ ۚ إِنَّهُ هُوَ السَّمِيعُ الْعَلِيمُ (61)

Peace is the ultimate goal. Would the truth-seeker ever show you the immediate next verse that immediately follows and tells of the purpose of peace and the true context of whatever he quotes you? Never.

"The Qaynuqa Jews"

Another incident that shows the mercy of Prophet Muhammad (PBUH), is when he was resting under a tree, then an infidel warrior snuck upon him, raised his sword and was about to attack and kill Prophet Muhammad (PBUH), saying, "Who would save you from me today, Muhammad?" Prophet Muhammad (PBUH) said, "**Allah.**" Some power took over the warrior, when he dropped his sword, which Prophet Muhammad (PBUH) then picked up.

Prophet Muhammad (PBUH) who was not fighting and was not carrying his own sword, said to the man, "**Then who would protect you from me today?**" The man said, "No one." Prophet Muhammad (PBUH) offered him to become a Muslim, and to say the Shahada (The certification that God is one and Prophet Muhammad (PBUH) is his messenger). The man said, "No." Then the Prophet told him, that he was willing to spare his life - even though the man was a minute ago about to assassinate the Prophet in cold blood - if the man gave the Prophet a pledge that he will never under any circumstances attack Muslims again, or participate against them in battle. Prophet Muhammad (PBUH) sat free a man that has just tried to kill him in cold blood.
Narrator: Jaber ibn abdullah. Reference: Oumdat Altafseer, Number: 567/1.
Degree: Correct

The author tells the story exactly the same, as it was reported in the Seerah books, up till when the man said, "No one." After that, our Author, with his utmost integrity, did not allow the Prophet of mercy and Islam to let go an infidel assassin just like that. And, out of thin air, claimed on page 109:

"No one," said the warrior, and he recited the Shahada, the Islamic profession of faith ("There's no God but Allah, and Muhammad is his Prophet"), and became a Muslim."

So you, as an American reader who doesn't know the well-known incident, and came across the story that is recorded in most of the books of Seerah, and saw that Muhammad (PBUH) set his infidel assassin free, then that's not because Muhammad (PBUH) is merciful or tolerant with an assassin infidel, or any infidel whatsoever, according to our truth-seeker, but just because Muhammad (PBUH) under the sword, forced the man to become a Muslim to save his life!

The author now addresses the well-known incident with the Jews of Banu Qaynuqa.

What was the incident that caused the Muslim army to lay siege to the tribe of Banu Qaynuqa, for 15 days till they surrendered unconditionally? The cause is never mentioned by Mr. Spencer!

A Muslim woman went to buy gold from a Jewish gold merchant, and then some Jewish men tried to remove the woman veil which she refused. The shop owner tied the tail of her dress down so when she stood up to leave, her dress slipped off, exposing her body. When the woman screamed for protection, a Muslim man came to her rescue and killed the shop owner.

The crowd attacked the Muslim man and killed him. What the tribe of Banu Qaynuqa did according to the laws of the tribes at the time, was a major act of aggression against the Muslims. That made them the violators of the pledge and agreement with the Prophet, which the author strangely calls it "truce" even though they never fought against the Muslims before. This is in addition to the fact that the treaty was given by the Muslims in offering peace.

So the Prophet ordered the Muslim army to lay siege around them for 15 days till they surrendered. The Prophet ordered them to leave Medina taking all their properties with them except their arms. And just to compare apples to apples, I think the mention of the verses in the Old Testament (the holy scripture of the Jews) is in order here.

"Slay utterly old and young, both maids, and little children, and women: but come not near any man upon whom is the mark; and begin at my sanctuary. Then they began at the ancient men which were before the house."
"And he said unto them, Defile the house, and fill the courts with the slain: go ye forth. And they went forth, and slew in the city"
King James Bible, Ezekiel 9:6 -7

As a Muslim scholar myself who have read the Holy Quran, the last unaltered Word of God in its original language, I have to believe that this is an altered or mistranslated Word of God, for God never orders his Prophets to apply indiscriminate burning and killing to anyone, yet I brought in this verse as is, for context reference.

The Prophet in his first contact with them, has done his duty as a Prophet of God, offered them Islam and warned them of the punishment of God by not following the message of God (like what happened to Quraysh). The Prophet also reminded them that his coming was mentioned in their scriptures by name. The reply of that tribe was rude to say the least. They said that the Prophet should not rely upon the defeat of Quraysh for Quraysh doesn't know what war is, and that if they battled Muhammad he would learn that they are the true people (men).

The Prophet as usual declared to them the pledge, that they keep their expenses and religion like that of the Muslims keeping their own expenses and religion, and that they should not battle unless one party transgresses clearly against the other. Was that tolerant enough in the seventh century A.D?

What is the cause of the incident as told by our Mr. Spencer then?

The author jumps in the following paragraph to the Prophet laying siege to the tribe without mentioning the incident of the Muslim woman and the killing of the Muslim man who tried to protect her, as if not only it never happened, but as if the Prophet laid siege on the tribe because they refused to become Muslims, with months passing in between!!

The inevitable custom in battle, at the time - after the tribe had surrendered – is that all fighting men of the tribe would be executed, yet instead, the Prophet had yielded to an alliance of one of the Muslims who had business ties with the Jewish tribe who was

Abdullah Ibn Ubbay, who kept pleading to the Prophet not to hurt them, till he angered the Prophet. So what was the final "practical example"? The Prophet let them all leave alive.

A note from Moustafa Zayed:

The author evidently changed the real name Ibn Ubbay was known by, which is Abdullah Ibn Salool. Why, may be because he is the same one known to be the leader of the hypocrites who relentlessly conspired against the Prophet and Islam. Even the intercession of one of the most resentful men to all Muslims, was enough for the Prophet to have mercy upon them. We will see how mercifully the Prophet treated the man later. The author then brings the verse in the Holy Quran that was revealed afterwards (our translation):

"Oh you who believe! Do not take Jews and the Christians as allies; they are but allies of one another. And if any amongst you

188

takes them as allies then surely he is one of them. Verily, Allah guides not those people who are oppressors"
Holy Quran, Surat (Al Maeda) Ch (5) Verse (51)

*In three different verses in the Holy Quran, God orders the believers not to have the infidels as Allies (in (3-28),(4-139), and (4-144)), and these verses do not mention that they are infidels who may have declared war against the Muslims, just for being infidels, yet you cannot take them as allies. Naturally then, and without having to explain, that it is treachery to become an ally with your battling enemy. Then why does verse (51) above state that specifically for Jews and Christians? Obviously because throughout the Holy Quran and the quotations of the Prophet, Jews and Christians receive a special treatment other than all non-Muslims, so the verse had to specify that if some of the Jews or Christian were battling you or aiding your enemy, then you cannot take them as allies. The author himself told of the fact that verse (51) was revealed with the occasion of the battle with Banu Qaynuqa. The author of course made a minor change to the Arabic word (Aulia), meaning ally, to (Friend)! So the verse now is not addressing allies on a national level, but instead saying; never befriend any individual Jews or Christians!! And I let the reader be the judge of that!

Turkey had pled to the European Union for its membership, for decades, and I cannot find better than Jacques Chirac, the former French president's blatant statements about Turkey being a Muslim nation, as the reason not to agree to its membership. The real pragmatic question here is: should Muslim countries take France, for example, as an ally?

"Anger towards Jews and Christians"

In this paragraph, on page 114, the author, to our surprise, starts to address the historical event when Prophet Muhammad (PBUH) had welcomed the Christians of Najran in Medina. Yet when we looked into what he intentionally ignored of the historical event, we were not surprised at all! We have narrated the event earlier and any objective historian would focus at least on the core of the event, which is the

189

unbelievable tolerance for its time and even for our time, when a Prophet of God that is Muhammad (PBUH), opened the mosque of the Muslims for the Christian community of Najran to perform their prayers there, and gave them the pledge of having same rights and obligations of Muslims, and the unheard offer even in America today, the year 2010, where if their existing churches would start to fall apart, he would repair them from the Muslim treasury money, without considering it a debt upon the Christians. Even though Muslims believe that their man-made theology that says that Jesus is God is an absolute unforgivable blasphemy of associating a partner with the One Mighty God.

Narrator: Ibn Alqayem. **Reference:** *Ahkam Ahl el Zemah,* **Number:** *1/397.* **Degree:** *Correct*

Has anyone ever seen a religion or a religious leader that tolerant? Let us know, and then please, break the news to Mr. Spencer.

Out of that monumental telling-tale of Islamic tolerance, and coexistence with all people as long as peace, and people's rights are respected, Mr. Spencer saw only when Prophet Muhammad (PBUH) performed his duties as a Prophet of God to rectify man-made errors to the messages of prior Prophets, when he reminded them that Jesus was not God nor the son of God. Mr. Spencer, in spite of trying to focus on Prophet Muhammad (PBUH)'s opposition to the foundation of their belief, has never seen it fit to mention, that yet with that opposition to the Christians of Najran's faith tenets, it wasn't worth mentioning that the Muslims let the Christians worship inside their own mosque, and gave them rights as a minority of another religion that are not given to any minority in any country nowadays.

Do I have to remind the reader that the subtitle of Mr. Spencer's book "The truth about Muhammad" is "Founder of the world's most intolerant religion"?!

A side-note from Moustafa Zayed:
Just a few months ago, the civilized democratic nation of Switzerland

190

called voters to a nationwide-poll to vote on banning the traditional structure of Muslim mosques (minarets). The tolerant, democratic, highly-educated population voted by a percentage of 56% to ban Muslims from choosing the design of their own place of worship. It seems, however, that the nation-wide Swiss vote stemmed from the crisis of the overwhelming numbers of Muslim mosques with minarets that seemingly swept the landscape of the entire nation of Switzerland's architecture, with an unprecedented number of only <u>four</u> existing buildings as such! **This is the tolerance of manmade laws in the heart of Europe 14 centuries later!**

"Assassination and deceit"

The author starts this subject with a premise out of his own imagination. He wrote on page 115:
"After the Battle of Badr and the attack against the Qaynuqa Jews, the Prophet of Islam directed his anger at the Jewish poet Ka'b Ibn Al-Ashraf"

Maybe portraying Muhammad (PBUH) as an angry violent man, fits the deceptive image the author likes to impose upon the Prophet of God, yet, what source did the author rely upon to tell us that Muhammad (PBUH) was angry all the time - from Badr to the battle of Banu Qaynuqa and beyond - and what source - reliable or not - that even mentioned that any anger of battles was directed at one man? The answer is nothing whatsoever. The author is just saying that.

Another piece of misinformation is that Ibn Al Ashraf was only just a poet! Is the author saying that to make it a freedom-of-speech crime? Maybe he is!

The truth is that everyone around in Mecca was somewhat a poet. Poetry was the American football of its time. When you tell me today that there is an American kid who is interested in American football, you actually are telling me either you are talking about almost every kid in America

191

or you are just telling me nothing. Arabs were poets and if you weren't a poet yourself you have memorized huge amounts of poetry. Poetry was how people memorized their lineage, honorable victories of their tribe, and sometimes how they argued disputes. Yes, Ibn Al Ashraf composed insulting amatory verses about Muslim women, of which the laws of its time gave the right to the husbands to avenge their honor by killing the transgressor. Ibn Al Ashraf knew that when he publicized these verses about the honor of Muslim women, and their families knew it well!

What the author didn't tell you about our peaceful, just voicing-his-opinion poet, is that he was one of the provokers of the infidels in Mecca, that directed the torture, the starvation and the killing of early Muslims, and specifically was one of the leading instigators to push Quraysh and its leaders to go and destroy the Muslims in the battle of Uhud. Reducing a "Goebbels" to peaceful poet is just outright deceptive!

When Muhammad (PBUH) escaped from Mecca to Medina, he was actually escaping a plot to kill him in his own bed. Allah inspired him to let Ali, his cousin, sleep in his place, while he walked out the back door of his house, through the tribes' warriors surrounding his house to kill him. The miracle of the Prophet walking amongst them, while they stood like statues is another Miracle of Muhammad (PBUH), bestowed upon him by Allah himself. In the Holy Quran:

"And we blocked them from in between their hands and blocked what was behind them, so we made them blind so they do not see"
Holy Quran, Surat (Yaseen) Ch (36) Verse (9)

وَجَعَلْنَا مِنْ بَيْنِ أَيْدِيهِمْ سَدًّا وَمِنْ خَلْفِهِمْ سَدًّا فَأَغْشَيْنَاهُمْ فَهُمْ لَا يُبْصِرُونَ (9)

Our lovely poet was one of the conspirators. In Islamic law and any fair law for that matter, if someone gave himself the right to take your life, then he had given you the right to take his the same instant in self-defense, and the same goes for money, if someone allowed himself to take your money then he allowed you the right to take his for the same amount, whether he liked it or not, not to mention that Ibn Al Ashraf had committed suicide by putting a "wanted" sign over his head when he violated the honorable reputation of the Muslim wives.

This was a war mission with one of the leaders of the worst enemy to Allah and Islam, short of sending Ibn Al Ashraf a telegraph informing him that Ibn Maslama the Muslim soldier is travelling to kill him, the author writes on page 115:
"The Prophet of Islam again took the path of expediency over moral absolutes"!

  *What is the author saying here? When Ibn Maslama asked the Prophet to give him permission to offend the name of the Prophet publicly, so Ibn Al Ashraf would allow him to come closer to him, is that expediency? All martial arts and war tactics are about deceptive techniques to maximize chances for massive blows to the enemy and achieving victory. But when it comes to Muslims it is crying over moral absolutes vs. expediency.

Why not then fight Ibn Al Ashraf in a battle, man to man and face to face, like the Muslims and Quraysh did? The reason is that, a leader of the hypocrites like Ibn Al Ashraf, never participated in the battles, yet he publicly plotted and pushed for conspiracies to annihilate the Muslims, only from the safety behind closed doors. Is the moral thing to leave him to cause more damage to all Muslims, never mind defaming and insulting their women's honor, and the ultimate honor of the Prophet himself, just because the war instigator Ibn Al Ashraf was also a coward?

The most wanted dead or alive in the FBI list today, is a native born American by the name of Anwar Al Awlaki. Awlaki never committed an act of violence against America, so why is he on that list? Simply he is believed to have preached and instigated young men to commit terror crimes against the US. Even though that instigation was just by words and plotting, no one with any logical understanding would oppose the American authority's decision claiming that Awlaki was just a "poet" or

193

make the issue a freedom of speech one. But when it comes to Muslims - not to mention defaming Muslim women's honor - Muhammad can only be wrong and violent, when it came to sweet innocent "poets"!

On page 116, the author narrates the Prophet answers, to some of the Jews objecting the killing of their leader, he wrote:
"Reminded them of his misdeeds and how he has been instigating them and exciting them to fight with them (Muslims) and "harm them.
"The murder, in other words, came after intense provocation, a line to this day jihadists use to justify their actions"

*Why would it matter to the Prophet in any way, shape, or time that some one - we do not know who - would misuse a valid reason that the Prophet had, for something that is unjustifiable?

Was Ibn Al Ashraf, plotting, hurting and harming Muslims and their Prophet or not? Yes, he was, and the Jewish leaders didn't disagree with what Ibn Aashraf was doing either. Then who can blame the Prophet or Islam, if someone else, centuries later, would wrongly use that as justification for whatever wrong action or another?

Then, in my opinion, Mr. Spencer commits a crime. I would let the reader, with just what he had learned so far about Islam and the Prophet, judge what the author wrote on page 116:
"After the murder of Ka'b, Muhammad issued a blanket command, "Kill any Jew that falls into your power"
Is the author making such a blatant fabrication confusing his readers between the Inquisitions and Islam?

Can you imagine that the Prophet of mercy and Islam would order his people to kill everyone in a certain group of people indiscriminately? Women, children, old people, innocent people all the same?

The author intentionally uses a well-known corrupt story of none other than Ibn Is'haq himself, that not only is not narrated in any of the major

194

reliable sources of Seerah, but totally contradicts Islamic law, and everything the Prophet had taught Muslims, his entire historical behavioral record itself, and that of Islamic history after him.

As loyal, and strictly-obedient to God and His messenger, the early Muslims were - the author stated the fact many times in his book - there is not one iota of an account of any historical weight that states that any group of Muslims killed every Jew they met? Where are these massacres when Muslims grew by the day to be the most powerful nation in history for centuries? To the contrary, and throughout history, only under Muslim rule, and the protection of Islamic law could the Jews have lived, worship and prosper in peace.

The author at the end of the paragraph, draws a line of an extremist Canadian convert without any link to the issue at hand, then he brings up the killing of another enemy of God - Sufyan Ibn Khalid - whom the Prophet likened to the devil himself for the harm he was causing to the Muslims. The author poetically quotes the Prophet saying to the man who killed Sufyan, to take a staff and "walk with it to paradise."

Should the Prophet of Islam in rewarding the man for finishing his military mission, have given him a Purple Heart medal, another piece of brass to hang on his military uniform instead, or should he have just promoted him to general?!

Are there two universes that Mr. Spencer simultaneously looks at, one where anything Muslim is wrong and taken to the extreme opposite, and another universe, where the same exact thing is considered bravery for God and country that deserves nothing but our tears of pride?

"The Quraysh strike back"

The author comments on the next battle between the Muslims and Quraysh, which is the battle of Uhud. In his always amazing way of

195

contradicting himself by linking incidents that have absolutely nothing to do with each other, the author reports a question of a Muslim asking the Prophet before the battle. On page 117, he wrote:
"O apostle, should we not ask help from our allies, the Jews?"

In that question lays more contradiction than you could possibly imagine

A) Wasn't the author just a page ago, telling us that the prophet ordered any Jew to be killed?!! Now his companions are asking him to rely on the Jews as allies? Which one is a total fabrication Mr. Spencer?

B) The author is acknowledging that some of the Jews were allies of the Muslims, and the contradiction is even worse when the author, out of thin air, and after just reporting that question, immediately writes, on page 117:
"Or perhaps he was thinking of how bitter his relationship with the Jews had become."
Why does the author conclude that? Because - according to the Spencer logic - Prophet Muhammad (PBUH) simply said, "No, we do not need them"!

C) Were the Jews a part of the Muslim army in any previous battle against Quraysh? Absolutely not. So when the Prophet says, after a tremendous victory over Quraysh in Badr, and now with an army of a thousand Muslims, - I am paraphrasing (M.Z.) - "I do not need allies that I didn't get help from before, when I was much weaker". Does that at all mean now, that there's such a bitter relationship with these "allies"?

I am sure that the reader by now sees how the author keeps constantly and illogically, imposing the relationship between the Prophet and the Jews, upon many incidents that don't even relate to it.

The battle of Uhud was a unique battle in the history of the battles of the Prophet. As we mentioned before, and as the author himself had mentioned repeatedly, there are so many interpretations, references of Seerah that are far more respected than the scattered unfiltered account tainted with untrue stories, where Ibn Is'haq himself said:

196

"only God knows if they're true", yet the author quotes no one more than Ibn Is'haq. And I would add, as a Muslim scholar, that they are almost all the stories that were proven later by Muslim scholars to be untrue or outright fabricated, and failed the filter of being any reliable testable evidence.

You ask any Muslim who had any third grade classes of Islamic history, and he would tell you the actual events of the battle of Uhud as narrated accurately in every Seerah book, that totally contradicts, as usual, the story Mr. Spencer tells his readers.

Before the battle of Uhud, Prophet Muhammad (PBUH) positioned his army on certain strategic locations. On top of the mountain of Uhud, he had put a faction of archers and instructed them to always stay on top of the mountain and no matter how victorious the Muslims looked, to never leave their positions, unless he asks them to. In the beginning of the battle, Muslims advanced quickly and were winning the battle to the limit that sizable factions of Quraysh's army started to flee. When the archers saw that, they thought that Muslims have won the battle, so they left their positions and went down and totally disobeyed the orders of Prophet Muhammad (PBUH). When that happened, a remainder faction of the Quraysh army came back from around the mountain, cornered the Muslims and totally turned the tide against the Muslim army, to the limit that Prophet Muhammad (PBUH) himself was injured and was almost killed.

On page 118, the author brings a story about Ayesha, where he translated it as if the Muslims were confused and fighting each other. This again, is not true, even in an army the size of a thousand soldiers, Muslims knew each other individually, if not personally, then by name, prayed together, did business together, and lived together in the same small city of Medina. The entire city of Medina at the time was smaller than the main prophet mosque (Al masjid Al nabawy) of today's Medina. The retreat of some of the Muslim soldiers after the Muslim army started to get defeated, was chaotic and not organized. Yet, the term of a

197

supernatural intervention of Satan is just metaphorical meaning the devil may have tempted some of the Muslims to disobey the direct orders of the Prophet, being the main cause of their defeat, and not the physical effect of some evil supernatural powers!

The author never mentions the glaring reason why the Muslims were defeated; that it was directly because of some of the Muslims not following the Prophet's orders, to keep their positions during the battle. But as the author usually does, in the following few pages, we learn why.

Under the paragraph **"Assuaging doubts after Uhud"**, the author translates the verses that were revealed after the battle, blaming some of the Muslims and their lack of belief as a direct reason of their defeat, which is actually what happened! The author tries to make it look as if - God Forbid - God's revelations came as an excuse to justify the defeat, in spite of the fact that the author knows very well, like everyone else, the glaring cause for that defeat.

On page 119, the author narrates another untrue story. In Islamic law it is totally forbidden to mutilate or make an example of a dead body, as a matter fact, it is also as forbidden to offend or attack verbally a deceased person; the Prophet of God said:

"Do not curse the dead, for they have already been led to what they have done" (Prophet Muhammad (PBUH))
*Narrator: Ayesha. **Reference**: Saheeh Al Bukhary, **Number**: 6516. **Degree**: Correct*

I.e. what need is there for anything you might say, while the deceased is being judged by God?

Our author tells us here that after Muhammad (PBUH) had learned of the killing of his beloved uncle and companion Hamza:
"By God, if God gives us victory over them in the future we will mutilate them as no Arab has ever mutilated anyone"!

*What is recorded according to Ibn Is'haq, aside from its correctness or not, is that the Prophet had said when he saw Hamza's Mutilated body:

"If Allah will ever give me victory I will Mutilate 30 men from them"

The Quotation is weak (weak proofs of narrators) and is not reliable according to Hadeeth standards. The author may not tell you, or maybe he doesn't know, but my wild guess is that he wouldn't tell you any way; that Mutilation has been totally forbidden in Islam. In the Holy Quran Allah says to Muhammad (PBUH):

"And if you, then punish them with the like of that with which you were afflicted. But if you endure patiently, verily, it is better for the patient (126).
"And endure patiently; your patience is not but from Allah. And do not grieve over the Pagans and do not be distressed about what they plot" (127).
Holy Quran, Surat (Al Nahl) (The Bees) Ch (16) Verses (126-127)

وَإِنْ عَاقَبْتُمْ فَعَاقِبُوا بِمِثْلِ مَا عُوقِبْتُمْ بِهِ ۖ وَلَئِنْ صَبَرْتُمْ لَهُوَ خَيْرٌ لِلصَّابِرِينَ (126)
وَاصْبِرْ وَمَا صَبْرُكَ إِلَّا بِاللَّهِ ۚ وَلَا تَحْزَنْ عَلَيْهِمْ وَلَا تَكُ فِي ضَيْقٍ مِمَّا يَمْكُرُونَ (127)

Prophet Muhammad (PBUH) had forbidden mutilation totally and specifically after the revelation of the above verses.

I do not need to add, that Allah had granted Muhammad (PBUH) victory 9 times over with not one iota of an enemy mutilation account what so ever in any of the battles after Uhud. Prophet Muhammad (PBUH) never said I will do something - God willing- and did not do it and vice versa.

199

About Wahshy

Systematically, the same style of the author dealing with the highlights of Islamic history happens again; emptying them of their essence, and extracting a minor thread of them in a convoluted way that has nothing to do with the event itself, hoping for any imaginary support for his wane narrative. The author mentions the incident of Wahshy, the assassin and killer of Hamza, the Prophet's uncle.

The author never even comments on Prophet Muhammad (PBUH) - that he claims in the title of his book is the "Founder of the world's most Intolerant Religion"- as how he, who was so saddened over the assassination of his beloved protector and uncle on the hand of Wahshy, but yet he forgave Wahsy, and gave him complete amnesty when the Muslims took over surrendering Mecca?

When did it ever happen that a leader at the level of Muhammad (PBUH) with such a crucial victory over the worst of enemies, that he would pardon them all? When did it ever happen, that even beyond such astonishing forgiveness, that The prophet (PBUH) offers a full amnesty and pardon to the hired killer of his beloved uncle?

Tell us please, if we missed anything as tolerant, or even close to that, in the entire history of mankind!

"Assuaging doubts after Uhud"

Another flying blue elephant statement! The author writes on page 119:

"Since after Badr, Muhammad (PBUH) had frequently insisted that Allah Himself had been fighting for the Muslims".

*Not only that this is a total fabrication and not true, evidenced by the fact that the author himself could not even find any of his convoluted references to tell us where he got that statement from.

What is appalling to any Muslim, or any true believer of God in any faith, whether a Christian or a Jew, is the notion that the Mighty Creator of Heavens and Earth needs to fight anything, as if there's resistance or something that was impeding God's will that He needed to fight to overcome! This is not the first time in this book, that I really question the belief in God, if any, that Mr. Spencer has that allowed him to go as far as making these ridiculous, denigrating statements about God Himself.

In many places in the Holy Quran, God states that when his believers go as far as they can, sacrificing their lives, their money, and everything they have sincerely for the sake of God, that God aids them with victories, with invisible angels that fight along them, or simply by yielding the laws of nature and physics to make his believers victorious.

"And it is a right upon us to grant victory to the believers."
Holy Quran, Surat (Al Room) Ch (30) verse (47)

وَكَانَ حَقًّا عَلَيْنَا نَصْرُ الْمُؤْمِنِينَ (47)

On page 120, he writes:
"Again a pattern was set: when things go wrong for the Muslims, Muslim leaders inevitably insist it is because they are not Islamic enough."

*On the same page, and as we said just earlier, the whole page is attempts by the author to omit the fact that the disobedience of some Muslims in the battle of Uhud was the cause of defeat as stated by the Holy Quranic verses revealed after the battle and every reliable historical source possible, and yet Mr. Spencer tries to make it look like as if it is some pattern of finding an excuse for the defeat, in spite of a simple glaring historical fact.

On page 120, the author ignores the fundamental belief stated by the verse in the Holy Quran, when God had said:

201

"And whatever disaster that hit you is due to what your own hands have earned, and he forgives many of them."
Holy Quran, Surat (Al Shura) (consulting) Ch (42) Verse (30)

وَمَا أَصَابَكُمْ مِنْ مُصِيبَةٍ فَبِمَا كَسَبَتْ أَيْدِيكُمْ وَيَعْفُو عَنْ كَثِيرٍ (30)

This means, that if the Muslims are righteous, then the final outcome will be their reward from God, in this life and in the afterlife. However, when they disobey and commit sins, then they lose the protection of the righteous that God had secured for them, and by that, they make themselves susceptible to the ills of the consequences of their sins.

In the following paragraph, the author quotes a modern Muslim scholar; Sayyed Qutb, who was a theorist of the Muslim brotherhood, which the author solely, on his own, declared it a "modern Islamic terrorist group"! The Muslim brotherhood group today, occupies over thirty percent of the Egyptian parliament after the last public election, and almost none of its members in Egypt or in the Middle East were convicted of any terrorist attacks - they are often harassed by the ruling authorities with fictitious accusations, that are mostly not of any terrorism nature, just to hinder their popularity - the only military efforts to be mentioned for the Muslim brotherhood, was mainly fighting the Zionist occupation of Palestine, alongside the Palestinians around the 1940s and the 1950's as, freedom fighters fighting for their own homeland.

The right to defend your own country against a foreign occupation, which is the simplest of human rights, is a right that Mr. Spencer denies Muslims in their own home lands. While Islamic law clearly condemns suicide bombings - but according to Mr. Spencer - any other freedom-fighter in Iraq, Afghanistan, Palestine, is automatically a genetically demonized, Muslim terrorist jihadist warrior!

I do not know about Mr. Spencer, but I know as an American, if any foreign country ever dared to attempt to come to occupy any part of

America, and take the rights of my children in our homeland, I would fight them tooth and nail with every breath in my body, till I defeat them and send them back where they came from. And that is an Islamic principle, before any claims of patriotism. Yet if you are a Muslim defending your own country, in the eyes of Mr. Spencer, **then that will result in a sure condemnation, not for the invaders, but for Muhammad and Islam itself!**

On page 120, we notice that the author keeps repeating that the aid that God gives to his Muslim believers is "super-natural intervention."

By that, the author is imposing a mythical superstitious atmosphere over the revelation of the Holy Quran and God, specifically about the repeated Muslim victories over Quraysh. The author himself could not avoid that the Muslims were almost always outnumbered in their early battles, and severely less-equipped than their counterparts, and that by any means of objectivity, their victories were absolute miracles militarily.

Does the author believe that, that one weak, persecuted, chased man, who was a leader of a minority tribe, that was about to be annihilated by the army of the most tyrannical ruler on Earth, was someone who was claiming supernatural intervention excuses?

When God parted an entire sea, gave him safe passage for him and his people, and drowned the Pharaoh of Egypt and his army behind him; was Moses "setting up a pattern" that righteousness brings about miraculous support from God? Was he claiming Hocus Bogus supernatural intervention, or was there no "truth about Moses" in the mind of Mr. Spencer?

Did David miraculously defeat Goliath because David was much bigger and more powerful, or, with just his pure faith, sincerity, and sacrifice for the sake of God, and for that; God granted him the unimaginable victory?

203

The author ends the paragraph with a verse from the Holy Quran, 33:9 that we translate correctly as:

"It is He Who has sent His Messenger with guidance and the religion of truth to make it superior over all religions even though the infidels hate it [33]."
Holy Quran, Surat (Al Tawba) Ch (9), Verse (33)

هُوَ الَّذِي أَرْسَلَ رَسُولَهُ بِالْهُدَىٰ وَدِينِ الْحَقِّ لِيُظْهِرَهُ عَلَى الدِّينِ كُلِّهِ وَلَوْ كَرِهَ الْمُشْرِكُونَ (33)

The author here just switched the verse with the Chapter Number and quoted (Chapter 33 No 9)!

"The deportation of Banu Nadir"

It is clear by now that the author keeps imposing a false image of Prophet Muhammad (PBUH) hating and going after anything Jewish. My guess he is trying to reduce the Israeli Palestinian struggle into the false notion that it is just a thing the Muslims have against the Jews!

It is clear by narrating this event that the author is trying to make the confrontation between Muhammad (PBUH) and some of the tribes of Medina, a one-sided prejudicial affair.

Here is what happened:
Banu Nadir was one of the major Jewish tribes of Medina. They had a covenant with the Muslims of peaceful coexistence. Their leader Huayy Ibn Al Akhtab invited Prophet Muhammad (PBUH) to a meeting inside the territory of Banu Nadir. When the Prophet got there, he was received by some men of the tribe who asked him to wait by the wall of some house till Huyay Ibn Al Akhtab, and the rest of the tribe leaders came to meet with him. It was narrated that Prophet Muhammad (PBUH) received a revelation from Arch-Angel Gabriel that the tribe was planning to drop a large rock from the top of that house onto Muhammad (PBUH)'s head, killing him and making it look like an accident. Prophet Muhammad (PBUH) left immediately back to Medina, just before they were able to drop the rock and kill him. It was the entire

tribe's treason of not only breaking the covenant without any aggression or provocation against them by the Muslims, but by trying to kill Muhammad (PBUH) himself in cold blood when he was their guest.

On page 121, the author writes:
"Not long after the battle of Uhud, some members of a Jewish tribe, the Banu Nadir, conspired to kill Muhammad by dropping a large stone on his head as he passed one of their houses. Some Muslims learned of the plot and warned Muhammad (PBUH). Rather than appealing to the Nadir leaders to turn over the guilty men, Muhammad sent word to the Nadir: "Leave my country and do not live with me. You have intended treachery." "

*So here are the highlights of the author's story:

1. The plot was planned by "some members" of the tribe and not by the leaders of the tribe themselves, as if Muhammad (PBUH) - the most powerful man and leader of Medina at the time - accepts to visit tribes personally, without the knowledge and the invitation of the tribe leaders themselves.

2. The author implies that Muhammad (PBUH) learned about the plot from some Muslim men when he was in Medina without actually going to Banu Nadir and without being minutes away from his death.

3- The plot, according to the author, was to throw the rock onto Muhammad (PBUH) while he was passing, and not the truth of the leaders sending him men to specifically have the Prophet wait for them under the house of which a rock was prepared.

4. Muhammad (PBUH)'s life was not saved by a divine revelation from Archangel Gabriel, but by some Muslims who the Banu Nadir leaders naively had told - of all people - about their assassination plot, i.e. there was no divine protection from God to Muhammad (PBUH).

Even though every reliable source of Seerah, and later events confirmed that it was Huyay Ibn Al Akhtab, and the leaders of the tribe who plotted the whole incident, Mr. Spencer claims it was some Jewish men who conspired to kill Muhammad (PBUH). The author then innocently asks, and blames Muhammad (PBUH) that: "Rather than appealing to the Nadir leaders to turn over the guilty men".

What if the plotting men were the tribe leaders themselves, Mr. Spencer?! And they were.

Let's use simple logic here:

1. What invitation could possibly make the most powerful man and ruler of Medina that is Muhammad (PBUH) goes personally to visit Banu Nadir? Is it some man or some men who invited him, or is it most likely the leaders of Banu Nadir, specifically their leader Ibn Al Akhtab ?

2. If the author's claim was correct, and all the Muslim Seerah books were wrong, how the plotters who were to kill Muhammad (PBUH) would know which house he would be passing under at which time, to have an always ready man prepare a rock to throw onto Muhammad (PBUH)'s head? Unless, the plotters were so many as to put one man and one rock on most of the houses in Banu Nadir's territory and have these men camp there, waiting for the time that Muhammad (PBUH) would be passing by so the house he's closest to, would have a ready man on time to throw the rock and kill him! Is this even close to believable? Please, remember that Muhammad (PBUH) did not wander into Banu Nadir every day, not even every month.

3. What about this logical supposition; which is that only the leader of Banu Nadir can invite Muhammad (PBUH) where he would respond and actually come to visit them, and the simplest way to have him killed is to have men sent by the leaders to ask Muhammad (PBUH) to wait for the leaders under a specific house that they already had a rock on top of, ready to be pushed down to kill him? Which scenario is logical, simple, and looks practical to you?

Actually the latter scenario is exactly what happened, and what all-leading Seerah references do narrate, which in itself answers the

206

innocent blame that we just quoted the author asking Muhammad (PBUH), as to how come he didn't ask Banu Nadir about the men who plotted his own assassination. And the answer, of course, which you must have deduced by now, is that Muhammad (PBUH) did not ask the leaders of Banu Nadir to hand over the men, because it was the leaders of Banu Nadir and Ibn Al Akhtab himself, who plotted the whole incident then invited Muhammad (PBUH) to go there!

Above and beyond, it was the revelation given to him by Arch-Angel Gabriel himself, of who and what they were plotting to do.

Another fatal strategic decision by the leaders of the tribe - in addition to gambling the entire tribe's existence in Medina on killing a man who did nothing to them, and had a covenant of peace with them - was to decide to go to war with the Muslims when Banu Nadir broke the covenant.

I say gambling the existence of the tribe in Medina providing that it was the Islamic manners they were dealing with. Had it been a Roman leader or a leader of Quraysh they attempted to kill, it would have been gambling their entire lives, including their women, children and properties altogether.

The leader of the hypocrites Abdullah Ibn Salool, who claimed his Islam, and in hiding plotted against anything Muslim, learned of the breaking of the covenant between the Muslims and Banu Nadir. He wanted to push them against Muhammad (PBUH), claiming that he has access to two thousand fighters like him that will aid them with their battle against the Muslims. The second strategic disaster was that they believed him and accepted to go to war with Muhammad (PBUH). Muhammad (PBUH) issued his decision about that treason, which I want to remind the reader, a treason that was a plot to kill him personally while he was an invited guest at Banu Nadir. Muhammad (PBUH) ordered them to leave Medina, take all their possessions that they can carry, but leave their arms behind. He did not even, like the author suggested earlier, ask for the heads or the prosecution of the people who plotted the whole thing, and they were the leaders themselves. Muhammad (PBUH) told them to leave safely with their leaders and their possessions. But with the leader of hypocrites' promised support, Banu Nadir refused and fortified their positions where Muhammad (PBUH) had to lay siege around them. When that happened, of course the leader of hypocrites did not show up with one single fighter.

Banu Nadir had to surrender and accept Muhammad (PBUH)'s lenient judgment. History tells us of the unbelievable tolerance of the Muslims in dealing with Banu Nadir; the tolerance that the author is shedding tears for. Look at the Muslims when Huayy ibn Al Akhtab was riding out of Medina: he was the leader who inflicted the crisis upon his own people, and the one who plotted to kill Muhammad (PBUH). Huayy slaughtered one sheep and took its skin, filled it with his gold and while he was riding out of Medina yelled at the Muslims who were standing by, saying: "You see this? This is for raising the earth and slamming it down." Meaning that his own wealth that Muhammad (PBUH) allowed him to walk away with, will be used for nothing but fighting the Muslims. No one touched him, no one took a penny worth of that gold from him, while he walked freely out of Medina!

We will see later, that he went to Khaybar to plot again for a massive battle with Quraysh to annihilate Muhammad (PBUH) and the Muslims, which is well- known by The Battle of the Trench.

Let's see now how the author describes the treason of Banu Nadir and its leaders of blatantly attempting to kill Muhammad (PBUH) as their invited guest, which is the worst possible way to break a covenant, and I might add the most unethical and lowest of them all.

On page 121, our author wrote:
"With the displacement of responsibility onto the enemy that would become characteristic of jihad warriors throughout the ages, Muhammad told the Muslims, "The Jews have declared war.""

*Banu Nadir broke the covenant, tried to kill the leader of the Muslims, and the Muslims should not react to that?! And if that doesn't equate

208

declaring war against Muslims, then what does? May be when the last Muslim infant is slaughtered!?

Then still, with the most lenient judgment of letting the plotters go free with their most valuable properties, yet they defied all that and challenged the Muslims to battle!
Our author does not see that as a declaration of war!!

And worse, he claims that this is a jihadist warrior characteristic?!!

Did Banu Nadir reinforce the covenant of peace and behaved in a manner of trustworthiness, but it was the Muslims who were blindly aggressive and ungrateful?

Was the plot to throw roses at Muhammad (PBUH)'s head and shower him with perfumes, but it's that crazy jihadist warrior displacement of responsibility when the Muslims, without reason, acted as if Banu Nadir were trying to crush the last Prophet of God and the leader of the Muslims under a large rock?

And when all that treason is met with tolerance and leniency that was unparalleled and unprecedented in its time and our time, the Banu Nadir leaders fooled themselves again by believing the ridiculous claims of a known hypocrite, and instead of thanking God for the leniency that Muhammad (PBUH) had showed, they rudely defied the Muslims and asked them to do whatever they may do.

Since the beginning of this book, I thought I wasn't exaggerating with the logic-defying conclusions that the author kept making, which I likened to him constantly claiming that there's a blue flying elephant around. At this moment, I'm starting to see another pattern evolving of Mr. Spencer trying to fit that blue flying elephant into keyholes!

On page 122, the author comments on the war-tactic that Muhammad (PBUH) used justified by a revelation in the Holy Quran of burning some of the palm trees of Banu Nadir during the siege that he laid around them. The author asked innocently, as how is it that Islam forbids burning of trees, yet Muhammad (PBUH) himself does it, and accused what he calls "Muslim apologists" of supporting Muhammad (PBUH) for it.

*The author, as much as we disagree with all his misinformation and omission of facts, we know for sure has the mental capacity to differentiate between exceptional measures in a state of war, and civil laws.

Our own country, the United States of America, has thrown two hydrogen bombs on two Japanese cities with high population concentrations, incinerating anything alive around them, killing hundreds of thousands of innocent civilians, and leaving devastating radiation damage for decades. This is totally forbidden in Islam, even during a state of war, yet you would find true "apologists" that would justify that by the ultimate cause of trying to end a war and pushing Japan to surrender, but mainly the justification used would be that we were in a state of war with Japan.

The author knows, and we know that when somebody commits a crime that is forbidden by our own civil laws in America, we don't send the Pentagon to drop small nuclear bombs on the neighborhood that the criminal lives in. The reader knows that I don't have to explain again the difference between a state of war and civil law.

On page 122, the final nugget of every chapter comes when the author writes:
"The remaining Jews of Medina were next to receive the wrath of Muhammad."

*I just want to ask our author to define the "wrath of Muhammad" for us!

Did he strike the idea of killing his ownself in the minds of Banu Nadir to commit treason and for that bring a crisis upon their entire tribe?

Or was it that he was tolerant enough not to even execute the conspirators of the leaders of Banu Nadir who attempted to kill him personally in cold blood?

Was his wrath, to leave his worst enemy walk free, and by worst enemies I mean not the people that wish him harm or fiercely opposing him, but simply the people who plotted to crush his own skull?

Did he let them walk with their fortunes, which any logic could have predicted would be used to finance future battles against him? Yes he did!

I am blushing and innocently asking the author, what is the definition of "the wrath of Muhammad"?

The Spencers of the dark Ages

"The Europeans claimed that the messenger of Islam was a catholic cardinal whom the church ignored when they elected the new pope so he defected and formed a heretical faction in the east as revenge. The church considered him the biggest defector of Christianity where he was responsible of splitting half of humanity away from Christendom"

Hubert Herkimer, the German thinker

Chapter Eight

Before we cover the issues that the author brought up in this chapter, we need to clarify a general fact and understanding about how the Holy Quran was revealed.

There are two universal stages of revealing the Holy Quran.

The Holy Quran as a Word of God was written with God as a part of a universal book of creation. That book was there before God had created our universe. In it, is the Holy Quran as we exactly have it in our hands today to the letter, as well as every single iota of detail that would happen later in the universe? And by every single detail, we mean where every single piece of sand is and when, how, and where every tree leaf would fall down. In the Holy Quran:

"And everything We have recorded in an apparent Book."
Holy Quran, Surat (Yaseen) Ch (36), Verse (12)

وَكُلَّ شَيْءٍ أَحْصَيْنَاهُ فِي إِمَامٍ مُبِينٍ (12)

The first step of revealing the Holy Quran that already existed in "The Kitab Mubeen" is when God had revealed it and brought it down from the highest heaven, to Archangel Gabriel in the lowest heaven, which is called in the Holy Quran "Inzal," and it happened over one night in the holy month of Ramadan. In the Holy Quran, God says:

"**We have revealed it in the night of destiny."**
Holy Quran, Surat (Al-Qadr), Ch (97) Verse (1)

إِنَّا أَنْزَلْنَاهُ فِي لَيْلَةِ الْقَدْرِ (1)

The second process of revealing the Holy Quran is what is called in the Holy Quran, "Tanzeel." In the Holy Quran, God says:

"Verily, it is We Who have sent down the Holy Quran to you."
Holy Quran, Surat (Al Insan), Ch (76) Verse (23)

إِنَّا نَحْنُ نَزَّلْنَا عَلَيْكَ الْقُرْآنَ تَنْزِيلًا (23)

"Tanzeel" is the process that started with Archangel Gabriel, revealing the first verses of the Holy Quran to the Prophet in Ramadan in the cave of Hiraa, which is a process that continued for 23 years since then, till a very short period before the Prophet had passed away. Many people, who obviously are not aware of the fact, confuse the historical context and the occasion of which some verses were revealed, with a wrong perception that the verse was revealed specifically as a response to something that happened in the life of Prophet Muhammad (PBUH), which is not true.

Everything is known to God thousands of millennia before Adam was on Earth, and the occasion of revealing a verse in the Holy Quran is not the reason why a verse is revealed to the Prophet, but the occasion when God decided to reveal the specific verse to mankind. Does the verse cover a specific matter or issue that happened around the same time it was revealed? Yes, that is why that occasion was chosen to reveal the verse. The other major absurd perception that some impose based on that erroneous insight, is that it brings about a notion that - God Forbid - God does not have knowledge of what will happen, and that He responds with revelations as things happen and issues evolve. And since we're not talking generally, but specifically about the inclinations that Mr. Spencer keeps imposing upon us in his book, I have no other alternative but to reiterate, that God, because He is God, has no limitations. He does not have limitations of time, space, or knowledge. He's the All-Knower, most powerful above and beyond all his creations, and he is the sustainer of everything created, everything that ever happened, and everything that will ever happen.

"The Battle of the Trench"

On page 123, the author starts covering the battle of the Trench, in which Banu Qurayzah the last of Jewish Madina tribes - after banu Qaynuqa and Nadir Jews - had forged an alliance with Quraysh against Prophet Muhammad (PBUH). Quraysh, however, wanted more than just an alliance with the Jewish tribe. They asked the leaders of the Jews; on page 123, the author writes:

""Is our religion the best, or is his?" The Jews replied, as might be expected under the circumstances, that of course the pagan Quraysh religion was better." "

Here, the author simply is agreeing with these Jewish leaders denouncing the fundamental pillar of Judaism and the first Commandment of Moses - which is God is One, and that idol-worshipping is blasphemy - just to forge an alliance with the pagans of Mecca against Muhammad (PBUH)!

Compare the "under the circumstances" comment of the author to his own comment describing the incident when some Muslims fought their former oppressors when they met them by coincidence (the Nakhla incident) against the orders of the Prophet. The author commented on page 99:

"This was a momentous incident, for it would set a pattern: good became identified with anything that redounded to the benefit of Muslims, and evil with anything that harmed them without reference to any larger moral standard. Moral absolutes were swept aside, in favor of the overreaching principle of expediency."!

In chapter six - in addition - the author reported that Satan have deceived Muhammad (PBUH) supposedly to denounce monotheism, in the "satanic verses" story, which we proved was a fabrication. Yet, when these Jewish leaders denounce monotheism, which is the pillar of Judaism as it is in Islam, it's not expediency, there are no "Satanic

215

verses" for it, and it is only "as might be expected under the circumstances"!

The author then brings two verses that address the anger of God over these Jewish leaders, who declared they supported an alliance with idol-worshipers and pagans over the oneness of God, then another verse that persuaded the believers to give Prophet Muhammad (PBUH) full obedience by digging a trench across the entrance of Medina to protect the town and its people, as the Prophet prepared in anticipation of the pending Quraysh attack.

The author, on page 124, makes a weird comment:
"Such incidents reinforce the divinely commanded and exalted status of Muhammad among the Muslims."

At that moment in his book, and after more than half of the Holy Quran was revealed, it is really strange that the author would think that just this verse in chapter 24, was to reinforce some "divinely commanded and exalted status of Muhammad."   ·
Hundreds upon hundreds of verses were already revealed in the Holy Quran showing exactly the position and the status of the Prophet, that he is honored and praised by God, for the great manners given to him by God, that he is the servant of God, that people obey him not because it is him personally, but obeying the commands of god given to them by him as he does not utter of self-desire. And whatever he tells people to do and not to do, is the orders of God to be obeyed, and that his behavior is the perfect example for mankind.
At that point, before it and after it, and till the day he died, Prophet Muhammad (PBUH) knew his status with God, but compared to what he did, what he achieved, and what he was capable of doing, he was the most humble man that humanity had ever seen.
: in the Holy Quran, God ordered the Prophet to say:

"Say: I do not hold neither benefit nor harm to myself, except that which God had willed, and if I knew the unknown,

216

I would have brought upon me much of fortune and no harm would have touched me, I am none other than a warner, and a promiser of glad tidings to the people who believe."
Holy Quran, Surat (Al-Araf) Ch (7) Verse (188)

The author then jumps to the issue of the Danish cartoons that depicted the last Prophet of God in a way that offended all Muslims worldwide. Again, the author makes not only extremely illogical conclusions, but worse, bases them upon totally flawed perceptions to begin with. On page 124 he wrote:
"Many non-Muslims were puzzled by the fury of the Muslim reaction. At least some of that fury must be ascribed to the fact that in the Holy Quran again and again, Allah is quite solicitous of his Prophet, and ready to command what will please him."

*If Muhammad (PBUH), as per his abundant statements and behavior, was the utmost servant of God, then following the directives of Muhammad (PBUH), was following the directives of God, whom God himself had said about in the Holy Quran:

"..Whatever that the Prophet brought you, then take, and whatever that the Prophet forbade you to do, then abandon."
Holy Quran, Surat (Al Hasher) Ch (59) Verse (7)

وَمَا آتَاكُمُ الرَّسُولُ فَخُذُوهُ وَمَا نَهَاكُمْ عَنْهُ فَانْتَهُوا ۚ (7)

Which is naturally what any messenger-of-God's message is about.

This comment, again, is another denigrating comment about God Himself, which I cannot move on without exposing.
It is that the revelation of God and God's orders to all mankind in the Holy Quran are somehow according to what pleases and for the appeasement of Muhammad (PBUH)!

217

1. Was the pleasure of Muhammad (PBUH) and his personal gain, to be persecuted by Quraysh for 13 years, oppressed, hurt, and boycotted?

2. Was Muhammad (PBUH)'s refusal of every source of earthly pleasure that a human could ever want, offered to him by the leaders of Mecca, and refusing to abandon his message withstanding his hardship, a way of God entertaining him?

3. A chapter ago, our author empathized with a Quraysh war criminal Uqba, whom the Prophet ordered to be executed, when the author kindly brought us one of the things that Uqba used to do to the Prophet; throwing rotten camel dung and intestines on the back of the Prophet while he was praying to God, not to mention Quraysh sending kids throwing dirt and rocks at him as he walked till his feet bled. Was that constant persecution and much worse, a pleasurable appeasement from God to him?

4. What about 14 different attempts to kill the Prophet, some of which he was injured - in the battle of Uhud - and poisoned, which some attributed to his final illness?

   Wasn't Prophet Muhammad (PBUH) the most charitable giver of all his people till the day he died? Wasn't he the most afflicted of all his people, who lost his companions during the persecution in Mecca and in battles, more than anyone else? Wasn't he the one who escaped from Mecca to Medina, minutes away from being killed in his own bed by warriors representing all pagan tribes of Quraysh?

5. Weren't there 9 major battles that the Prophet went through fighting in the front line, risking his own life, and everything he's got; always for the sake of God? Can anything he has ever done in his life, be called a plethora of appeasement and custom- made pleasures for him?

Prophet Muhammad (PBUH) was the most obeying, sacrificing, afflicted and first in line for the sake of God, than any man that had ever lived. As Ayesha had described him:

"His manners were the Quran"

Narrator: Ayesha. **Reference**: Saheeh Al Jamee, **Number**: 4811. **Degree**: Correct.

On page 125, the author narrates in a mutilated way, one of the famous miracles of Prophet Muhammad (PBUH), where while he came down to help Salman the Persian to remove a big rock that blocked the digging of the trench the Muslims dug in Medina, to protect them against the imminent Quraysh invasion. The Prophet - and this is how the incident happened - hit the rock three times, each time one third of the rock broke out and the Prophet made a declaration of a vision that a major city will be opened for Islam. He mentioned three specific major cities; in Persia, a part of the Byzantine Empire in the East, and Yemen.

Before we bring the correct translation of the incident, I have two comments.
1. Where is the special appeasement of the Prophet, the author talked about earlier, that when there's a big rock being dug in a trench, he's the one that came down to break it and remove it? Mind you, that he (PBUH) was at the age of 57 then?
2. The narrator of the story that Mr. Spencer brought was Salman the Persian. Where is the second-class status that non-Arab Muslims received - claimed earlier by the author - when such a close companion to the Prophet was not only Persian, but he was also the source of suggesting the trench digging idea that the Prophet followed, and was what helped save the Muslims from the siege of Quraysh?

About Salman the Persian, Prophet Muhammad (PBUH) once held his hand and said:

" ..**If believing in God was at the highest height, a man of these would have reached it**" (Prophet Muhammad (PBUH))
Narrator: Abu Hurayra. **Reference**: *Saheeh Muslim,* **Number**: *2546.* **Degree**: *Correct.*

In the Seerah book, the story is narrated as follows:

"**A rock blocked the digging of the trench the Muslims were digging, so they called Prophet to break it. As we said, at the time the Prophet was 57 years of age helping the Muslims, while two rocks were tied to his stomach to help curb his hunger. The Prophet hit the rock three times and each time he would yell the name of a major city being opened for Islam. The first was Persia and its capital "Al Madayen" the second was the eastern Roman Empire and the third was Yemen and it is capital Sanaa. The companions of the Prophet cheered knowing all his visions came true and yelled "This is the truth that the Prophet of God had promised us" All the Prophet's predictions came true.**" (Prophet Muhammad (PBUH))
Narrator: A companion of the Prophet **Reference**: *Saheeh Alnasayee,* **Number**: *3176.* **Degree**: *Good.*

After the myriad of scientific proofs of the Holy Quran, the miracles, and the three visions of Muhammad (PBUH) in the story coming true, could Mr. Spencer comprehend yet that this is the last Prophet of God?!

The three cities that the Prophet predicted did become Muslim cities exactly the same way the Prophet had said. Hadn't he been the Prophet of God, why venture and risk the fact that making such predictions can potentially not come true, make him a liar and undermine his status of being the last Prophet of God? Why do it then?
Unless simply, he is the last Prophet of God, and it did exactly happen the same way the Prophet of God had been told of the future revealed to him by God.

On page 126, the author again justifies the treachery of the third Jewish tribe of Medina; "Banu Qurayzah" whom the author says: "…broke their covenant with the Prophet of Islam."

What justification the author would bring us this time for their treachery to the Prophet? :
"(Perhaps after reflecting upon the fate of the Banu Qaynuqa and Banu Nadir)."

The author himself admits that the Prophet didn't declare Banu Qurayzah enemies; even though news came that they broke their covenant with the Muslims, till the Prophet sent spies to confirm that that their alliance with Quraysh against the Muslims was actually happening.
On page 126, the author wrote:
"Muhammad sent spies among the Qurayzah to find out if what he was hearing was true."

The author goes into some details describing the siege that Quraysh had placed then around Medina, which went on for over three weeks. When the inclination for truce negotiations between the Muslims and Quraysh started to emerge, Prophet Muhammad (PBUH), the last Prophet of God and the one who does not utter of self desire, kept adhering to God, and his orders that were revealed in Surat "Al Shura":

"..**And those who responded to God, established prayers, consulted their matter amongst themselves, and from what we have blessed them with, they spend** (for charity)."
Holy Quran, Surat (Al Shura) Ch (42) Verse (38)

وَالَّذِينَ اسْتَجَابُوا لِرَبِّهِمْ وَأَقَامُوا الصَّلَاةَ وَأَمْرُهُمْ شُورَىٰ بَيْنَهُمْ وَمِمَّا رَزَقْنَاهُمْ يُنْفِقُونَ (38)

The Prophet, consulted with his companions, and expressed his opinion as to offer some of the Medina's valuable dates harvest to Quraysh as a part of a truce, where a companion objected - to the Prophet of God - stating his reasons, which is irrelevant to the more important fact that

221

Prophet Muhammad (PBUH) constantly consulted with his companions and in that case ended up abandoning his own personal suggestion, and accepting the reasons of that companion.

In many incidents, Prophet Muhammad (PBUH) accepted and answered the well-known question from his companions, commenting on some of his suggestions: "Is it the revelation or the consultation and opinion?"

In the battle of Badr, the famous Hadeeth when the Prophet asked his companions tells us:

"Give me advice as to which location to choose", then Alhabbab Ibn Al Munzer said to the Prophet: Is this a location revealed to you from God, so we do not go forward or backward from it? Or is it an opinion of war and tactics? **The Prophet replied: But it is an opinion of war and tactics**. Alhabbab answered: Then this is not a good location, let's go near the water supply for the people"
(Prophet Muhammad (PBUH))
Narrator: Ibn Al Araby. Reference: Ahkam Al Quran, Number: 391/1. Degree: Proven.

If it is a revelation of God, then it's an order to be obeyed by the Prophet and the companions alike. But if it is a personal opinion of the Prophet, then they can debate it, where the Prophet still would be the ultimate decider for what he sees the best for Muslims and Islam, which in many cases - like the incident we just mentioned - the final decision might not be the Prophet's initial suggestion.

Is amazing civility and true democracy of a Prophet of God in the seventh century not worth positively commenting on by the author of "The Truth About Muhammad"?!

The author covers another incident where, during the siege, one of Quraysh's warriors came out and challenged the Muslims for anyone to combat him. Ali Ibn Abi Talib, the cousin of the Prophet, went forward to combat him. The man, who was Amr Ibn Abd Widd, was an uncle of Ali. When God granted Ali victory over the Quraysh warrior,

222

the author tells us why he picked this specific incident out of the entire battle. On page 127, the author writes, in a dramatic fashion:
"Islamic loyalty was deeper than blood."

*True, to Ali Ibn Abi Talib an utmost loyalty to God was always deeper than blood, but neither Ali nor any Muslim would call it like what Mr. Spencer is trying to call it, "Islamic loyalty".
Muslims and all believers of God throughout history call it: "loyalty and obedience to God" that is above and beyond anything else.
Did Moses choose the Pharaoh family who sustained, protected, and raised him, over his obedience to God, his ultimate Sustainer? Was it totally the opposite, or was it that Mosaic loyalty was deeper than blood? The examples of the Prophets of God obedience to God, above and beyond anything; absolutely anything else, don't need any further comment.

On page 127 and 128, the author narrates how the Muslims, even though under the treachery of Banu Qurayzah and the tight siege around Medina, were able to break that siege through trickery and war deception. A new Muslim by the name of Nuaym Ibn Masoud, suggested to the Prophet that his Islam was not known yet to both parties of the siege, Banu Qurayzah and Quraysh, and suggested a trick that he can plant between the two enemy allies to break the siege.
And it was truly clever. He convinced Banu Qurayzah that they have more exposure by proximity to the Muslims and to the Muslim army than Quraysh, whom their fortunes are left behind in Mecca, and suggested that they request leaders of Quraysh as hostages till Muhammad (PBUH) is defeated, and then they would release them to protect themselves if Muhammad (PBUH) would win the battle. Then Ibn Masoud went to Quraysh and told them that Banu Qurayzah, because of their proximity to Muhammad (PBUH) in Medina, had decided to break their alliance and pursue a truce with Muhammad (PBUH) by offering him the heads of some of the Quraysh leaders. So when Banu Qurayzah made that demand after delaying their attack because of Sabbath, Quraysh leaders got worried about the request and refused. Then the aid of God came in with

a mighty sand storm that made it impossible for Quraysh to even keep their tents or fires in place. So their leader, Abu Sufyan decided to break the siege and return to Mecca.

Here is the author's nugget of hate-anything-Muslim at the end of every paragraph. On page 128, he writes:

"Nuaym's deception had broken the siege and saved Islam."

So it's not the clever plan of Nuaym and his war tactic. It was as if Nuaym deceived and lied to the innocent Banu Qurayzah and the sweet pagans of Mecca, who were sitting at their homes, sipping their tea in peace, while Nuaym was plotting his unwarranted despicable deception! The author himself writes on page 128 that Qurayzah wanted to take hostages from Quraysh leaders till:

"We will make an end of Muhammad."

*So, in the case of enemies of God that are laying siege around you with the intention of annihilating you, where you are forced to fight them to the end, whether your end or theirs; the solution of tactical deception seems somewhat immoral here to our author!

Maybe the author was disappointed in hoping for a lot of beheadings on both sides of which none had happened, thanks to that outrageously immoral deception!

"Dealing with the Banu Qurayzah"

On page 128, the author writes:

"After the successful resolution of the battle of the Trench, the angel Gabriel made sure that Muhammad settled accounts with the Qurayzah Jews."

Where is it mentioned in any acceptable source that "the angel Gabriel made sure that Muhammad (PBUH) settled accounts with the Qurayzah Jews."?!

Did Prophet Muhammad (PBUH) need heavenly intervention bring to his attention the treachery of the leaders of Banu Qurayzah?

What would any military leader in the world do to an ally who did not just break his covenant, but worse, at the time when your worst enemy had laid siege around you that ally joined forces with them till "the end of Muhammad"?

Would anyone give them his back ever again? Would you let them stay in the same town that your army, your women and children live in? Would any one risk that when the next siege is laid, that treacherous ally may have a better chance at achieving the goal that you are completely annihilated that time?!

On page 129, the author brings about a point that we addressed thoroughly before. He writes:

"The Holy Quran in three places (2:62-65; 5:59-60; 7:166) says that Allah transformed the Sabbath-breaking Jews into pigs and monkeys."

*As if "Sabbath-breaking Jews" are highly regarded and celebrated amongst Jews, and as if it is only the word of God that is harsh about them!

I would reiterate here what we explained earlier, that most Prophets before Prophet Muhammad (PBUH) were Jewish sent to all Jews. The Jews, who disobeyed God, fought and killed the Prophets of God, were condemned and promised torture in hellfire in the Old Testament before any other scripture, like those who commit the same abomination amongst any race or creed. And, on the other hand, the Jews, who believed in the Prophets of God, and obeyed God were promised paradise and God's utmost rewards, as any believers of God in any race or creed who have done the same. In the Holy Quran:

"And We have broken them (the Jews) **into separate nations on earth: some of them are righteous and some are less than that. And We tried them with good and evil in order that they might return** (to God).

Holy Quran, Surat (Al Aaraf) Ch (7) Verse (168)

225

وَقَطَّعْنَاهُمْ فِي الْأَرْضِ أُمَمًا ۖ مِنْهُمُ الصَّالِحُونَ وَمِنْهُمْ دُونَ ذَٰلِكَ ۖ وَبَلَوْنَاهُم بِالْحَسَنَاتِ وَالسَّيِّئَاتِ لَعَلَّهُمْ يَرْجِعُونَ (168)

So when God states an earthly punishment for those who disobeyed Him and fought his Prophets; that they were condemned to be pigs and monkeys, it is a punishment against the abomination committers and disobedience to God and never against a specific race, color, or creed.

As a matter of fact, one of the scientific miracles of the Holy Quran is that the only two animal species that the Holy Quran stated - 1400 years ago - that abomination committers, at one point in history, were condemned into were pigs and monkeys, which are the closest two animals to mankind physiologically and genetically!

On page 129 and after the Muslims have laid siege on the tribe of Banu Qurayzah for over 25 days, the author narrates (blaming the Muslims) for three choices that the Muslims actually did not offer, rather it was the leader of Banu Qurayzah, Ka'b ibn Assad - not the Muslims - had offered his people!

1. To accept Islam, save themselves and have the rights that Muslims have.

2. Expose their women and children to death by going and fighting Muhammad

3. Surprising the Muslims by ambushing the Prophet in the Sabbath.

But these were Ibn Assad's suggestions! <u>And the author is blaming the Muslims for them!!</u>

"The Qurayzah rejected all three, but chose to surrender to the Muslims," the author wrote on page 129.

We would like to add that what Ka'b ibn Assad had said were his own words, where in the beginning, as per the Prophet, on page 129, the author quotes Ka'b Ibn Assad saying:

226

"For by God it has become plain to you that he is a Prophet who has been sent and that it is he that you find mentioned in your scripture."

The author, of course, does not forget with that glaring admission of the knowledge of the leader of Qurayzah, that Muhammad (PBUH) is the last Prophet of God, to only blame Ka'b Ibn Assad of breaking the treaty with Muhammad (PBUH), as if the rest of the tribe were deaf mute playing bingo while their leader, on his own, was committing treachery putting them straight at war with Muhammad (PBUH) and the Muslim army!

The second thing is, again, it is Ka'b Ibn Assad's words, maybe to scare his people into surrendering, so that if they fought the Muslim, they would be exposing their women and children to death, which is not true, for Islamic Law states that civilians of all sorts, especially women and children, are not to be touched unless a woman is actually carrying a weapon and fighting herself. And as we see later, the women and children of the tribe were spared, unlike the norm in these treachery cases and times.

*We need to remind the reader here that, on the contrary it would have not been a surprise to any historian had Qurayzah and Quraysh defeated the Muslims, those Muslim women and children would have been slaughtered without a second thought.

Prophet Muhammad (PBUH), who was receiving a completely surrendering population of a treacherous ally, did not have to appeal to any considerations or politics than that of a victorious leader who's in absolute control. Yet, the Prophet did not want to make the judgment, obviously hoping for a more merciful judgment than his, for logically, he could have decided on his own to annihilate the entire tribe and no one could have blamed him. At least for that the Qurayzah, with their alliance with Quraysh, not only broke their covenant with him, committed treachery, but would have seen every Muslim slaughtered had they been victorious.

227

The Prophet decided to appoint a judge to decide on the fate of Qurayzah. He even let them chose a Muslim judge themselves!

Who would have blamed the Prophet if he chose someone who hated or participated in a war against the Jews previously?

The Prophet, on the contrary, appoints Saad ibn Muaz, to judge with a fair judgment, against the tribe of Qurayzah, who, of all people, had formed an alliance and did business with the Jews of Medina before.

Saad judged the warriors that would have killed the Muslims, had they defeated the Muslims, to be killed, and mercifully spared all the women and children.

In its research about the major world religions, "The Truth":

"While critics of Muhammad liked to point to this period of Muslim history as evidence that Muhammad was not a man of God, let us pause for a moment to recall the many "holy wars" started at the behest of Jewish prophets, as amply recorded in the Old Testament. Therefore, the Battle of the Trench, although an example of brutality, may be fairly understood for four reasons.

First, Muhammad already had been betrayed twice by the Jews in Medina. In the previous cases, he demonstrated remarkable restraint and mercy by releasing the Jews, particularly considering the brutality of the era. Thus, if you stopped to consider the barbaric nature of tribal warfare and the heinous code of ethics that reigned at the time, Muhammad's decision to "turn the other cheek" and spare the first two Jewish tribes was an unprecedented act of compassion and forgiveness.

Second, each time he was betrayed, Muhammad gave the remaining Jewish residents in Medina the benefit of the doubt. He continued to operate under the assumption that he could trust those Jews who chose to remain part of the Ummah (nation). Moreover, the Jews in Medina could leave at any time. Instead, they chose to betray Muhammad and the Ummah, which would be considered criminal treason even by today's standards.

228

Third, Muhammad had learned the hard way that if he released traitors of the Ummah, he might meet them again on the battlefield. He had no desire to release the third tribe of Jews just to fight them later, and it was evident that the Muslims and the Meccans would continue fighting until one group was dominant. From a strategic standpoint, therefore, it would have been foolish for Muhammad to release yet another tribe of defectors who might hurt his people in the future.

Fourth, despite this early disaster between the Jews and Muslims, the Jews would soon enjoy peace and prosperity in Muslim lands as illustrated in the appendix, the Muslim spirit of religious tolerance soon would produce a safe haven for the Jews, who were free to practice their religion wherever the Muslims reigned. Ironically, it was the Christians who became the primary Jewish antagonists. For the next thousand years, the Catholic popes and the Christian nations demoralized, expelled, and slaughtered millions of Jews and other "heretics."

"Thus, despite the current tensions between the Muslims and Jews, it would be wise for us to remember that historically, it is the Muslims who have been the Jews' greatest defenders and protectors."

The Oracle Institute in its research book, "The Truth", page 153-154.

On page 130, first when stating Saad's judgment, the author quotes Saad: "I give the judgment that their warriors should be killed and their women and children should be taken as captives." Then later, on the same page, 130, the author writes:
"In light of Saad's judgment to kill the men and enslave the women and children . . ."!

I have to stop here at a very important point, just to show the unimaginable civility and mercy of Islam and the law of God upon women and children, since "tolerance" is what brings tears to Mr. Spencer's eyes.

The author, who probably knows more than anyone else, how he takes things to extremes and totally out of context, does it exactly the same here. He used the word "enslaved" when describing the Muslims treatment to captives of war.

1500 years ago in a harsh desert laden with violence, the prevalent law is; whatever you can take is yours, and slave traders are everywhere, let's then assume also that the Muslims spared the women and children as they did, left them where they were, and went back to their homes in Medina. What would happen to the women and children of Qurayzah? It's simply one of three, and it will happen rather quickly:

1. They will die of starvation.
2. They will be captured by other men and enslaved to be sold.
3. They will be used in all sorts of horrible abuse and prostitution.

Even the possibility of the women and children traveling to other areas where they may join other tribes, like in Mecca, or further, to the Sham area, that would even put them into more danger of falling into the same three possibilities going through places and parts of the desert they might have never seen before; becoming a much easier prey.

What was the Islamic solution to the problem of war captives?

While it became totally forbidden for any man to enslave another man in Islam, as Prophet Muhammad (PBUH) says:

"Allah had said: There are three that I am their opponent on Judgment day; A man who was given in my name then betrayed, <u>a man who sold a free man and ate his price,</u> and a man hired a worker who fulfilled his job and didn't pay him for his work"
Narrator: Abu Hurayra. **Reference**: Saheeh Al Bukhary, **Number**: 2227.
Degree: Correct

Notice here the extraordinary nature and punishment for the three crimes committers of being categorized as opponents of God himself on Judgment day.

The Islamic solution to the existing slavery problem was absolutely ingenious and peaceful. A solution to the same problem of which failure to resolve, caused the American civil war; a civil war that caused the death of hundreds of thousands of people and trillions-worth of today's dollars in damages.

The Islamic solution was not only to dry the sources of slavery by forbidding enslaving people, but offered some of the highest rewards in paradise for whoever sets a slave free, or buy the freedom of slaves, in addition to allowing slaves to work away from their masters to earn money to buy their freedom back by "Al Mukataba", which in a record period of time minimized the problem without any bloodshed or civil wars. But then again, what was the Islamic solution for the women and children captives of battles? Even if the Muslims allowed these women and children to live amongst the Muslims in Medina without sponsors, and without any source of income to support them, they themselves would have been a cancer to society, as they would have been helpless towards theft, and illegal activities, including promoting prostitution, just to survive.

I don't have to go into detail to explain that this problem was always a guaranteed outcome of any war, anywhere.

Here is the Solution in Islam:

Islamic law offered three options for these women in general:

1- To set them free, and without paying any expiation, which was mainly dependent on the level of safety of the environment they were to be released to.

2- Paying expiation by which they are released. In the case of women, Islam mandated a three month period of "clearing" or "Istebraa" for women captives where their family or husbands may pay expiation for their release, and during which they cannot be touched by any man. If these women were abandoned by their families, or even were never claimed as family members, then one of the other two solutions could be applied.

3- Lastly the woman would be assigned as an additional wife without the title of a wife - for inheritance reasons - to a man who would agree to carry her responsibility; where she is treated exactly like a wife till she gives a birth to his child by whom she becomes automatically free to chose, and her baby would be legitimately named to his father.

Islam allowed men an exception at these times of war to take these women as additional wives, where the man would be responsible and providing her with the same living standard that he himself enjoys.

I cannot find a more telling quotation of the Prophet to show the mercy and tolerance of the law of God regarding these women than the following quotation in Sahih Al-Bukhari. The Prophet says:

"If a man taught a woman that he had (sponsored captive of war) **manners well, educated her well, then released her, and married her he would get two rewards…"**
(Prophet Muhammad (PBUH))
*Narrator: Abu Mousa Al Ashaary. **Reference**: Saheeh Al Bukhary,*
***Number**: 3446. **Degree**: Correct*

A woman who was the wife of a warrior, who not only hated Muslims but conspired, fought to kill them in battle, while she probably felt the same, yet the Prophet promises double the reward from God if she is taught good manners, treated well, educated, and not taken as an additional woman but as a wife.

Further - in a harsh desert 500 years before the dark Ages - the Prophet of God persuaded the believers to treat them well and educate them. And if they did that, they would have a tremendous reward in paradise. It is also worth mentioning that the Prophet would – amazingly - let an enemy combatant walk free if he taught 10 Muslims how to read or write.

Yet our truth-seeker uses the same language - "enslave"- that equates that unprecedented treatment with, for example, what happened to Africans kidnapped with no fault of their own from their homeland and put in the most horrible working and living conditions by their slave owners for centuries till they gained their freedom!

And what did Mr. Spencer write about the captives of the Muslim army: "enslave the women and children"!

On page 131, the author takes all the blame away from the devastating strategic decision errors of Medina's three major Jewish tribes, and try to blame their errors on the Prophet, as if the following never happened!

1. Banu Qaynuqa broke their covenant, attacked a Muslim woman, stripped her naked in their territory, and killed a Muslim man who fought for her. Did the Prophet of Islam kill them all? No. He allowed them all to leave with every possession they could transport, except their arms. If that is not merciful according to these conditions, then what is?

2. The leaders of Banu Nadir called the Prophet for a meeting and asked him to wait by a wall while their men were set to drop a rock on the head of the Prophet to kill him, and if it wasn't for the heavenly warning to the Prophet to leave immediately, it would have been not only the end of Muhammad (PBUH), but of Islam all together. Did the Prophet of Islam kill them all? No. He allowed them all to leave just the same. Did he even avenge the would-be assassins? No, he let them all walk free.

3. Banu Qurayzah broke the covenant and took allies of Quraysh laying siege around Medina for 3 weeks "till the end of Muhammad". Did Muhammad (PBUH) as the master of Medina ill treat them in any way before their treason? Not one bit.

"Finding excuses for a massacre"

On page 132, the author writes:
"The massacre of Banu Qurayzah has been understandably a source of embarrassment to Muslims."

Actually, understandably, not only wasn't it a massacre, but no real Muslim of minimal knowledge of either history or Islamic Law ever considered the treachery of Banu Qurayzah, and the aggression of Quraysh against the Muslims as any source of embarrassment to begin with!

Before we even try to shed light on the glaring-like-the sun historical facts of that war, we would have to reiterate the same point that we keep bringing, for the same absurd assumption the author keeps bringing up. Muslims use the guidance of an ultimate reference they measure up their actions to. It is the orders of the One Mighty God in the Holy Quran and in the "Sunnah" of God's last Prophet. Even the word embarrassment itself has no place in the vocabulary of a knowledgeable Muslim. In the famous quotation of Prophet Muhammad (PBUH):

"Every religion has a manner, and the manner of Islam is shyness"
Narrator: Abdu Allah Ibn Abbas. **Reference:** *Saheeh Ibn Majah,* **Number:** *3390.* **Degree:** *Good*

A Muslim would be embarrassed if, to other Muslims, he did something that was "Haram" (i.e. forbidden), something that was impolite or not befitting within the known righteousness of Islamic Manners. But then, still, it is the disappointment of one's self of failing to obey God. So the bad feeling should not be the tarnishing of one's image before the public, as if the public were the reference, but before God as the Ultimate Judge.

No wonder then, that the author and his peers of Islam-hating orientalist who are calling the war a massacre, to bring us a so-called Muslim scholar that we personally never heard of.

234

On page 132, the author wrote:

"various Muslim apologists have attempted to deny the incident altogether or to minimize the number of casualties. One Islamic Scholar, W.N. Arafat, published a lengthy article in 1976, arguing that the massacre never happened, chiefly for the anachronistic reason that it would have violated Islamic Law."

*The author had to go back and search in a span of thirty-five years to find one claimed scholar - who wrote an article and who evidently at this particular incident had neither, knowledge of history, nor of Islamic Law - to bring an excuse for an outcome to some war that requires no defending nor apologizing for!

In any court of law, in America and the world for that matter, if you kill someone in self-defense, you don't get prosecuted for murder. Even if the person who attacked you wasn't somebody that you knew you defended yourself, overcame and killed him - like he wanted to kill you - most likely you would walk tall out of that court room.

What embarrassment, what apologies, and what excuse would you ever need, if your attacker was someone that you allowed to reside in peace under your power, authority, and under your thumb?

An attacker, who you had struck a covenant of peaceful coexistence with for the purpose of spreading the peace that your religion mandates. An attacker who immediately took an ally of your worst enemy and laid siege upon you in a war that had one purpose that is to annihilate you physically and ideologically till the end, as the author himself brought it few pages ago: "till the end of Muhammad"!

The real question here, which the author covered from an opposite angle, is bringing some scholars, some of which I respect personally like Karen Armstrong, who argued that this was seventh-century politics and that it was the absolute norm of an outcome in such circumstances. The author objects to that by saying on page 132:

"That is true, but Armstrong misses the larger issue; as in all the incidents of Muhammad's life, he is still held up by Muslims around the world as "an excellent model of conduct" (Holy Quran 33:21)."

*Yes, Armstrong missed some of the larger issue, but what she missed was that the ruling of Muhammad (PBUH) was the ruling of the prophet of God, and for that, to the Muslims, it was and will always be the right thing to do if the same circumstances reoccurred. The fact that that was the norm of its time is true, but that was not why the rule was ruled as such. The rule was because this was Islamic Law according to the specific circumstances. But then looking at the real larger issue the author targets, I would ask the readers and anyone else, the real two questions that should be asked here:

The first; is never mind the seventh century, but even in any century, which victorious army, still agrees to a covenant of peaceful existence, to begin with, with another group of a certain minority after the first two groups of the same minority betrayed and violated their covenants with the ruling majority, by which one attempted to kill the majority's leader when he was their guest?

Which government or military is that, after two warnings would trust its own back to that group without going there occupying and taking it over when they absolutely could and should?

Only the Muslims under the law of God, the most merciful and the most gracious, would be that tolerant and still offer a covenant of peace to the third tribe.

The second question - even though its answer was already declared by Quraysh and Banu Qurayzah - is a question that is larger than any issue, then and today:

Had Quraysh and Banu Qurayzah won the war, what do you think would have happened to every Muslim soul in Medina, starting with Muhammad (PBUH) and ending with the youngest of infants?

You do not have to think of an answer or even make any guesses. Quraysh and Banu Qurayzah themselves had told us that it is a war to the end and total annihilation of anything Muslim, had they won the war.

236

Were Quraysh and Banu Qurayzah even the outnumbered, underequipped-underdog of the war? On the contrary, Quraysh on its own had never prepared a more equipped and larger army in any battle in its history than the battle of the Trench. The treachery of Banu Qurayzah allying with them, enforcing the three week siege, and closing the circle of the siege from within the outskirts of Medina, made it the worst of possible war outcomes for the Muslims.

While the author probably thinks that that mighty sandstorm that forced Quraysh to end the siege and retreat to Mecca, was just a coincidence of a bad weather report, the fact that the Muslims won the battle with the aid of God did not mean that, had Banu Qurayzah been successful, they would have let the Muslims walk free like happy campers, or even like Muhammad (PBUH) had allowed Banu Qaynuqa and Banu al Nadir do. It was a war with the goal of annihilating Muslims, with absolutely uncalled for treachery.

It was not some civil uprising, and definitely not that of a majority oppressing a minority.

If it was anything, it was a majority from a position of power accepting a peace treaty with a minority, and when that minority had the first chance to annihilate that majority, joined the majority's worst enemy in a war that laid a siege around their majority neighbor "till the end of Muhammad."

If Mr. "Preemptive Strike" thinks that Muslims need to be embarrassed, apologize, and find an excuse, for what Banu Qurayzah had brought upon themselves, then let him first denounce his extreme fascism, and, still face the fact that his argument doesn't make any sense either logically or historically.

On page 133, Mr. Spencer brings an interesting parallel to the Banu Qurayzah war that is; Israeli forces in 2007 preparing to move into Gaza, which meant military action and collective punishment for the civilians of Gaza, "in the wake of the kidnapping of an Israeli soldier by Hamas."!

Did the armless civilians of Gaza participate in laying a military siege around Israel and its fortified army by allying with Israeli's worst enemy?

Were the Israelis vastly outnumbered and underequipped and on their way to total annihilation, after the kindness and the civility of an Israeli covenant to the Gazans to coexist in peace?!

Usually, one would describe such an illogical comparison that: it is comparing apples with oranges. Here, it's so far-fetched that it is like comparing apples with baby crocodiles!

And when an unknown Muslim from a "British Muslim internet forum!" totally objected to the overwhelming blind military force of the Israeli army against civilian Palestinians in Gaza, our author writes, on page 133, of how come "no one accused him of illicitly importing seventh-century models into the present day."!

"The women of the Banu Mustaliq"

In this paragraph, the author brings the issue of the treatment of war prisoners of men, women, and children according to Islamic Law, but of course, specifically, in the case of women captives, which we have already explained and answered sufficiently in the previous pages.

Yet, our truth-seeker again omits the non-Muslims' horrible way, at the time, of treating prisoners of war altogether and specifically women.

So, he compares Islamic Law applied exceptionally to a case specific in a unique environment of 14 centuries in time difference, to the environment of today, and calls that fair!

As we have said earlier, the main reason of the Islamic law ruling at the time was for the benefit of the war captives themselves. And the main driving reason behind that is not the power of a winner over a war loser, or even to appease or give prizes to anyone. The fundamental reason is the environment in which these war captives, especially women and children, would have been released to, hadn't they been kept within the protective community of the Muslims.

While we explained that there were three alternatives to decide the end

238

result for the captives, meaning that keeping them was not mandated or the only rule, however any other alternative (other than being sponsored by the Muslim society at the time) would've had a horrible outcome to them. This outcome included enslavement and death, by murder or starvation, in the open desert. The author, in addition, totally ignores the rights that a woman captive was given by Islamic law when a Muslim man would accept her responsibility, which almost equated the rights of a wife. A Muslim man would totally provide for her and let her live in the same living standard that he lives in, i.e. eating the same food, wearing same level clothes, more importantly, her children would be legitimate children carrying his name within a general environment of treating her well, as per the quotation of the Prophet we provided just earlier. Simply, they were practically wives; only, for these exceptional times and circumstances, they were not given that title, so men would not use that as an excuse later to marry more than four women in normal circumstances, and to limit related inheritance rights to the existing wife. I would like to add here also, just in the case of any future truth-seeking, that the law was that the same woman was for the same man responsible for her, i.e. if he accepts her, then it is his responsibility, reputation and honor attached to her, exactly like a wife. Our author describes these conditions as taking them as "slaves"!

Another aspect is the point of view of the captives themselves. Yes they were the true casualties of war, but after the fact settles in, and realizing the horror that awaits them out there, the Islamic solution to their problem was the best thing that could have happened to them, short of if Banu Qurayzah leaders did not bring treachery and war upon their own families from the beginning.

Islamic law itself is universal and valid for every time and place, yet the flexibility in the law to yield exceptional measures to exceptional situations is one of the greatest fundamentals of the law.

Taking humane treatment in an exceptional situation in an exceptional era, and portraying it as the norm of the law, is anything but truthful or objective. The re-labeling of what things truly are, to fit them into a deceptive image that never existed, is really appalling when it comes to some Islam-bashers.

One example that comes to mind is one orientalist - in his to be published book - calling the gift to the bride that every Muslim man has to give his future wife, "the bride price," as if she was bought in a supermarket!

A Muslim lady that I know personally, who is an Arabic professor in one of the top 5 universities in America was asked to review the orientalist book in which this phrase was mentioned. The professor corrected the phrase that was personally offensive to her and corrected the rest of the errors of the book, to be shocked later that the book was published with her name on it, yet intentionally leaving "the bride price" as is!

It is not history or the truth; it is what fits the deceptive narrative!

All these rights given to the women-captives, most of whom did wind up being formally married to as wives, on the hands of our author, are being reduced to the statement of:

"Holy Quran permitted them to have sexual intercourse with slave-girls captured in battle…"

*This is as if the Muslims had multiple partner sex with them, left them alone in the deserts to die, and went back home!

And as if this void of any logic, objectivity, or fairness was not enough, the author starts the next paragraph by saying:

"If from a twenty-first-century perspective, this is one of the most problematic aspects of Muhammad's status as "an excellent model of conduct""

From the beginning, the author is telling us here, I am not truthful, I am not objective, and I don't care. How could you possibly compare two situations with absolutely and entirely different circumstances and claim that there's any hint of reference?

In the author's comparison, not only the circumstances are totally different in almost everything, but the author bypasses almost fifteen hundred years through time and over thousands of incidents with various levels of comparability just to avoid showing how merciful and

240

progressively ahead of its time the Islamic solution was toward captives in the 7th century, not in the 21st century!

In the Serbian war against the innocent civilians of Bosnia, which was actually an outright genocide against the civilian Muslims, the war captives, if I can even call it that, Muslim women were gathered in rape-camps for the Serbian soldiers and then they were left to either shame or death. The confessions of the Serbian war criminals showed their objective was not just to violate the Muslim women for pleasure, but to actually force them to give birth to Christian Serbian bastard babies.
Of course, that is not a comparison that our truth-seeker would want to make. Maybe because the Bosnians never laid siege around Serbia after violating a peaceful covenant that the Serbians gave them, or maybe the Bosnian civilians pursued allying with Serbia's worst enemy for the officially declared purpose of annihilating the Serbians!

Islamic Law's jurisprudence is fundamentally based on applying Islamic constants to the ever-changing circumstances of day-to-day life, to achieve the protection of life, properties, children, reason, and religion.
In the 21st century, where there are structured cities and towns, a victorious Muslim army would not only keep women and children and all population where they are, but in Islamic Law, the fact that you took over the town or the city and the fact that you are in control as a Muslim army, makes you responsible before God for providing for these civilian populations till a sustainable environment is achieved for them. In the quotation of Prophet Muhammad (PBUH):

"A woman was judged to hellfire by Allah for a cat that she had that died of starvation. Allah had said: You neither left her any food or water where you locked her nor allowed her to go out and seek her sustenance on Earth."
Narrator: Abdullah Ibn Omar. **Reference**: Saheeh Al Jamee, **Number**: 3995. **Degree**: Correct

Without going to hundreds of examples of the treatment of war captives generally under correct applied Islamic Law, the reader can make an easy comparison of how sinful would be the Muslim army for not providing for every human in a town or a city under their control.

The great Muslim ruler and companion of the Prophet of God Omar Ibn Al khatab said:

"If a sheep stumbled on a river bank in Iraq, I would have known that God would ask me: why didn't you pave the road for it, Omar?"

The author did not stop there, however, and actually dragged us to a subject of a comparison between how Islam deals with sexual deviance and how the rest of the world and the west generally deals with it.
First of all, we are still talking about a catastrophic and foolish decision that Banu Qurayzah took and by that, gambled their entire existence and the future of their children in Medina on the goal of annihilating Muhammad (PBUH) and the Muslims. Muhammad (PBUH) had a covenant of peace with them and no intention to violate it.
The author writes about women war captives:
"The treatment of women as war prizes, with no consideration of their will. Even a contemporary Islamic legal manual stipulates that when a women is taken captive, her "previous marriage is immediately annulled." If a jihad warrior takes her captive, she has no say in the matter."

In any army, in any time, does the term "war captive" mean in any language that you have free will? Not to mention that mysterious "Islamic legal manual" that has no reference or location that the author can enlighten us about. What is our U.S Army rule of engagement in these situations? Is it to let the war captives do whatever they want, move wherever they want, whenever they want? Or is it that you keep them under control, if not in closed buildings but in a tightly controlled and guarded locations where they are monitored 24 hours? Again, we ask the author to have an English speaking person explain the word "captives" to him.

242

We have previously displayed the three alternatives to release the captives. The "clearance" or "Al Istebraa" period which is three month for the relatives or the husband of the woman captive to pay expiation to have his relative released; in such period the woman is not to be assigned to a man to sponsor her. Yet according to an "Islamic legal manual" from a galaxy far, far away, that only the author knows, it is something different!

Without a doubt, we will not even dignify discussing how treacherous the desert environment for women and children was, had the Muslims left them there without protection and on their own. The only humane solution then would have been taking them with the Muslims and providing for them. The fact that the entire size of Medina at the time was smaller than the population of some of the smallest of villages today, and with no infrastructure of a social service, hospitals - even the Muslim treasury was not established then - how can you quantify and ensure that every soul of these captives is provided for, unless you would assign a group of these captives to able and providing men to care for them. Think about it. According to the circumstances of the time; that was the best solution.

Now, to practically deal with the "captives" free will, Mr. Spencer had tears for, let us ask: who would choose the other? And just to show how laughable Mr. Spencer's logic is: Would you set a table for the war captives to sit down and interview the Muslim soldiers, man after man, to choose whom they would like to provide for them and protect them? Or is it the other way around in the real world?

As a matter of fact, it wasn't even the other way around, for Prophet Muhammad (PBUH) assigned the responsibility of providing these captives according to what he saw of the different abilities of people to provide. The ultimate goal for the Prophet here was that these human souls that Muslims are accountable to God for, would be provided for, and I don't have to explain to you that assigning more women

243

captives to one individual is burdening him more with a long-term responsibility for them and their children than what the author is trying to portray of "pleasure". The author said shamelessly "the treatment of women as war prizes" as if their treatment was one night's stand and then they were left for dead.

And we explained in the previous page how these women had almost all the rights of a wife in Islam, unless our author thinks that economically and socially providing for let's say eight wives and their children is really a prize that every man looks forward to!

In England till 1882, twelve years before the turn of the 20th century, a woman was not even considered a legal entity. She neither could stand in court on her own, nor even own property in her own name. Our objective author, who's all the way back to the 7th century, in a harsh desert, does not praise the mercy of the law of God that mandated sparing the lives of innocent civilians, especially of women and children. He actually wanted a woman captive to decide which Muslim soldier she would want to pick to provide for her and protect her, as if the entire war that preceded it, was just for the purpose of marriage proposing and courting!

Here the author takes us to the core of the horrible misinformation about Muslim women's rights nowadays, and I would specifically quote the author when he so shamelessly said:
"even today, women are all too often treated as commodities in the Islamic world."

*"Treated as commodities"?! Really!!

*How huge is the prostitution, pornographic industry in Islamic countries? Is it in the tune of billions of dollars, as it is throughout Europe and North America? Or is it almost a statistical zero in Muslim countries, in comparison?

In that filthy industry, are western women treated just like commodities, even worse, like animals, or are they treated with utmost dignity?

244

*What are the rules of marriage overwhelmingly in Muslim countries? Is it that a young woman would keep dating and changing sexual partners till someone really marries her, or is it that, in Muslim countries, a woman cannot be touched unless there's a real man who would take the responsibility of a family and give her a right to walk in society like a lady and a wife with her rights protected and her children legitimate?

Is the treatment of women as commodities that our truth-seeker claims is all across the Islamic world, the main reason that AIDS and sexually transmitted diseases are almost non-existent in Muslim countries compared to the rest of the world? Or is it the civility and the cleanliness of the relationship between a man and a woman and the dignity and sanctity that Islam mandates for marriage?

*Is "all across the Muslim world" a new geographical term that means only the most poverty-hit and highest illiteracy rates rural areas in Pakistan and Afghanistan, where abhorring living and poverty conditions in some places are poking you in the eye? Or are 57 countries and 1.6 billion people around the globe what Mr. Spencer is constantly confusing it with?

*Is the fact that homicide as the number one cause of death for a pregnant woman usually committed by the boyfriend who wants to escape the responsibility of child support, a decade old statistic in Muslim countries, or unfortunately, in America?

I could go on mopping the floor with Mr. Spencer's nonsense about the issue, but I am more pained by the horrible conditions for some women in America that I would never bear to go any further.

The famous Arabic literature adage says: "She accused me of her own Ills, and then escaped."!

"Battle of Banu Mustaliq"

Oddly enough, the author contradicts himself and speaks about another battle: the battle of Banu Mustaliq, where the daughter of the leader of the tribe objected to the fact that she would be assigned to the cousin of the Prophet, whom she thought was beneath her social status. So, against all the misinformation that the author brought on the same page, the Prophet gave her the honor of marrying her himself, discharging her debt, which what the author correctly reported, even though he began the paragraph by claiming that the Prophet benefitted by gaining one woman captive!

What the author did not say is that she accepted Islam, and that the Prophet had the one exception amongst all Muslim men that a woman captive to him would be automatically declared a wife after she would have her first period. So, she accepted Islam and became the Prophet's wife, and because she was a Muslim, a hundred people of her relatives, and I repeat a hundred, became free of any debt, and became relatives of the Prophet. The author never mentioned that this captive was "mother of the believers, lady Jewayriya." He never mentions that she became a Muslim, a wife of the Prophet, and never mentioned her name - Jewayriya Bint Al Harith - that she is known by to date.

"Abdullah Ibn Ubayy and praying for one's enemies"

Having read the entire book of Mr. Spencer, the next paragraph was the most shocking to me, Mr. Spencer in this paragraph brings a well-known incident of how merciful and forgiving Prophet Muhammad (PBUH) was to his worst of enemies, not only that but Mr. Spencer narrated it with a 98 percent accuracy, which is more shocking than a 3-ft tall basketball player being the NBA's MVP!

Abdullah Ibn Ubayy was known to be the leader of the hypocrites, always scheming and plotting any possible campaign against the Muslims, never mind attacking the honor of Prophet Muhammad

(PBUH) himself as he was the promoter of the Ifk (fabrication) incident against the Prophet's wife, which we covered previously. That was one of two things that Mr. Spencer did not report in this paragraph. Ibn Ubayy's full name is Abdullah Ibn Ubayy Ibn Salool; he is well-known by Abdullah Ibn Salool. In the previous chapter, when the author discussed the Ifk incident, the author did not state his name as in this chapter, and I do not know if that was a mistake or intentional. Ibn Ubayy was well known for his plotting and hypocrisy, that many people offered the Prophet to kill him, including his son volunteering to kill his own father. The Prophet always refused to kill him, even visited Ibn Ubayy on his deathbed and wished him well, praying for God to forgive him. After Ibn Ubayy died, the Prophet performed the prayers of his burial himself against the opposition of his closest companions. What the author also did not mention was that the Prophet wrapped Ibn Ubayy's body in the Prophet's own shirt and carried him, laying him inside the grave himself.

How can that behavior of Prophet Muhammad (PBUH) be a characteristic of, "founder of the world's most intolerant religion"?!!

"The Treaty of Hudaybiyya"

The author starts this paragraph by claiming again that he has a historical precedence of being privy to the undeclared intentions and thoughts of Prophet Muhammad (PBUH). He wrote:
"Muhammad had a vision in which he performed the pilgrimage to Mecca, a pagan custom that he very much wanted to make a part of Islam."
As we just said, not only that Mr. Spencer did not know what Prophet Muhammad (PBUH) wanted or not, but pilgrimage was a not a pagan custom, for its founder was none other than Abraham (PBUH), who almost all of the Islam-hating orientalist writings never mention that the Kabaa, that building that all Muslims circle in their pilgrimage in Mecca, was built by Abraham himself. The house raised by Abraham in all Islamic literature means the one and only Kabaa. Pagans copied that

247

ritual from the previous Prophets of Islam and associated it with their idol worshipping.

Another misconception that many scholars, amongst which many orientalists also have is that; yes Quraysh worship idols, but it wasn't exactly like the pagans of Rome or Persia, their pagan idol-worshipping was a severe deviation from the original monotheistic Abrahimic teachings. In the Holy Quran:

"We were not worshipping them (the idols), except that they may get us closer to Allah."
Holy Quran, Surat (Al Zomar) Ch (39) Verse (3)

وَالَّذِينَ اتَّخَذُوا مِنْ دُونِهِ أَوْلِيَاءَ مَا نَعْبُدُهُمْ إِلَّا لِيُقَرِّبُونَا إِلَى اللَّهِ زُلْفَىٰ (3)

In the treaty of Hudaybyya that Prophet Muhammad (PBUH) signed, the agreement was a truce; a traditional truce agreement with an addendum that seemed totally unfair to Muslims. It stated that if a man from Quraysh accepts Islam and flees to Medina, then the Muslims should reject him and send him back to Quraysh. But if a Muslim man converted back to Quraysh, then the Muslims should not go after him.

The author himself displayed how easy to deal with and how flexible the Prophet was in negotiating the terms of the truce, as in the Prophet agreeing not to mention him as a Prophet of Allah, or that Islam is the true religion of Allah. The prophet agreed to Quraysh striking all that out of the treaty document, yet the author bypassed all that and went to the point when the truce was violated.

And I want to remind the reader here that Mr. Spencer, who was just shedding tears over the treatment of women war captives, only comes here just two pages later and objects to the fact that a Quraysh woman by the name of Umm Kulthum accepted Islam, fled to Medina, and Muhammad (PBUH) refused to give her back to Quraysh to be tortured for accepting Islam, violating the same treaty!

Not to mention that any decent man would do that without thinking, which what is really shocking that Mr. Spencer is even arguing this point, but he himself states that there was a revelation that was specifically revealed to the Prophet for this occasion, that if a woman who believed in God came to the Muslims, and the Muslims made sure that she is truly believing in God, that they should never bring her back to be tortured on the hands of infidels.

An entire revelation from God, an order from the Creator of Heavens and Earth, not to send a helpless believing woman to her demise, but in addition, to give her refuge and protect her from the infidels, even if that meant an entire war with many Muslim men to die as a result. How noble is that?

The author gives us his usual nugget at the end of the paragraph, by saying:
"Subsequent events would illustrate the dark implications of this episode."!

*Was all war truces ever signed never broken, and the Muslims truce was the world's first and last? Was risking a war just for helping a one helpless "woman commodity" after a specific revelation from God Himself to protect that woman, a "dark immoral implication"?!!

"The raid at Khaybar"

On pages 138 and 139, the author makes an apparent major error which we will see is evidently intentional. The author claims that the verses 18-20 in Surat Al-Fatah, Chapter 48, are about a promise that God and His messenger had given some claimed disgruntled Muslims over the treaty of Hudaybyya.
Even though there were points of objections raised by some of the companions towards the heightened leniency that the Prophet had showed, when negotiating the treaty of Hudaybyya with Quraysh, all records indicate that that was within the boundaries of the utmost respect

to the Prophet, most importantly, the utmost obedience to his final decision.

That objection, if any, is another indication of the constant consulting rule that the Prophet made an example of personally for Muslims, to use as a reference for "Shura," which is Islamic democracy. The fatal mistake that the author made, is that he confused the three above-mentioned verses, which talked about rewarding the early Muslims who had given the Under the tree allegiance to Prophet Muhammad (PBUH), with the treaty of Hudaybyya with Quraysh which had absolutely nothing to do with.

In confusing the two non-related events, the author made it as if there was some kind of rebellion against the Prophet, and that the only way that the Prophet could suppress it was by waging a raid and giving the rebellious companions more booty to silence them!

The misinformation of a well-known historical event and intentional fabrication of every aspect of the well-known battle could not be clearer an example as to how our author narrated the following battle; the battle of Khaybar.

The author, from the first line portrayed a false image of a revelation in the Holy Quran that God is indebted to some disgruntled companions of the Prophet for some booty, so Muhammad (PBUH) marched his army to a peaceful garden where the innocent farmers were walking in the morning with their baskets, when they ran back to their people screaming scared "Muhammad is here!" The author then brings you images of Muhammad digging for treasures and stripping these innocent farmers of everything that they have, just to pay off his angry "gang" members!

I will quote almost all the paragraphs that the author had brought to us narrating the battle of Khaybar, and I ask the reader to try to imagine how vast the difference is between the truth, and what the author narrated, and how that it is not just widely different, but absolutely and almost amazingly and totally opposite of the truth!

Facts:

1. The word "Khaybar" in the dialect of the people of that town meant "The fort."

    Was there one fort in Khaybar? No, Khaybar had eight forts, and you couldn't enter the town unless you passed through these forts. The forts were one after the other, and each one had its sufficient amount of weapons, stock of food, and water supply that could last in some places up to a year. You couldn't reach the second fort unless you went through the first one, and so on and so forth, you would not be able to reach into Khaybar unless you had pierced into the eight forts. The most fortified fort was the first one.

2. Khaybar or "The Fort" was not a small village. It had a population of almost ten thousand able-to-fight men. Beyond the forts were some of the largest palm tree-inhabited areas in the entire Medina area, one of which had about fifty thousand palm trees. So the little village that the author tried to impose as an image of Khaybar was actually the most fortified town, with some of the largest population, and economic independence in the entire region.

3. Khaybar was the place where most of the tribes of Qaynuqa and Banu Nadir settled in after being exiled when they broke the covenants with the Muslims. And Khaybar was a major center for plotting against the Muslims and Muhammad (PBUH). At the time, a man like Banu Nadir's leader Huayy Ibn Al Akhtab , whom we mentioned in the previous chapter, waved an entire sheep's skin filled with gold before the Muslims - promising them that all that gold would be used for shattering the earth the Muslims stood on - had then become a major player in Khaybar. History tells us that the treason of Banu Qurayzah, who laid siege around Muhammad (PBUH) and his army in alliance with Quraysh in the battle of the trench, was provoked and supported by none other than the leaders of Khaybar, including Ibn Al Akhtab himself.

4. What made it even more urgent for Muhammad (PBUH) to have to neutralize Khaybar, disarm them, and ensure that they would not be the spearhead in plotting to destroy the Muslims, was that the Muslims learned that Khaybar now is contacting the near two world powers at the time, which were the Romans and the Persians, trying to provoke them into attacking Medina and the Muslims.

5. Knowing that Khaybar was only eighty miles north of Medina, it would have been an act of committing suicide, if Muhammad (PBUH) waited around till Khaybar and its leaders were successful in their massive activity against the Muslims.

6. When Muhammad (PBUH) decided to move his army of fifteen hundred fighters to neutralize Khaybar with its eight forts and ten thousand fighters - and its innocent villagers with their morning baskets as per the author! - the leaders of Khaybar, with their existing growing web of plotting against the Muslims, had already promised Banu Ghatfan and their leaders Ibn Onayen the full harvest of the palms of Khaybar for an entire year if he comes with his three thousand soldier army and stop Muhammad (PBUH) from reaching Khaybar.

7. Let's use our logic here for a second. Is it easier to lay siege around a city that has an army of ten thousand, that is the most fortified around with enough stock of foods and water to last them a year while putting your fifteen hundred fighter army in a position of low altitude subject to their arrows; all that just to provide the author's imaginary disgruntled few companions for some imaginary war booty?!
Having stated all the above reasons, would you do it still if there weren't any disgruntled companions?

8. Prophet Muhammad (PBUH), on his way to lay siege around Khaybar, tried to offer the leader of Ghatfan half of the harvest of Khaybar, then the entire harvest of Khaybar, when he still refused to go back. Then the intelligence of the believers let them use a war tactic when they spread

the word inside the army of Ghatfan that Muhammad (PBUH) had dispatched another army to attack the then army-less tribe of Ghatfan. Ghatfan's army leader immediately turned his army around and went back all the way to protect his tribe and left Khaybar. Thus averting a huge battle without one drop of bloodshed.

9. Just to show how strong and fortified Khaybar was: it took the Muslims fifteen days of siege just to succeed in controlling the first fort with yet seven other forts left to go. At the end of the siege, when the people of Khaybar agreed to Muhammad (PBUH)'s conditions of disarming them, the total tally of casualties was sixteen of the Muslims and ninety-six from Khaybar, in mostly man-to-man duels.

10. When the Muslims emerged victorious, the terms of the covenant Muhammad (PBUH) struck with the Khaybar leaders did not include Muhammad (PBUH) forcing them to leave their homes or lands, for the covenant was the outcome of a fair battle before which Khaybar did not break a covenant with Muhammad (PBUH) and did not commit treason like Banu Qurayzah or Banu Nadir did. That was in spite of the fact that they posed significant danger in the past, but again, they did not commit treason.

11. Now let's see the amazing amount of facts and events that the author had omitted intentionally to impose - as per the author - the scared, armless villagers with baskets in the open gardens of Khaybar, who were attacked for no reason by the Muslim jihadists demons crazed for war booty!

On page 139, the author writes:
"Allah had promised the Muslims disgruntled by the treaty of Hudaybyya "much booty" (Holy Quran 48:19). Perhaps to fulfill this promise, Muhammad led them against the Khaybar oasis, which was inhabited by Jews - many of them exiles from Medina. One of the Muslims later remembered: "When the apostle raided a people, he waited

253

until the morning. If he heard a call to prayer he held back; if he did not hear it, he attacked. We came to Khaybar by night and the apostle passed the night there; and when morning came he did not hear the call to prayer, so he rode and we road with him . . . we met the workers of Khaybar coming out in the morning with their spades and baskets. When they saw the apostle and the army, they cried "Muhammad with his force" and turned tale and fled. The apostle said, "Allah Akbar! Khaybar is destroyed." "

Did the author mention anything about how fortified and strong Khaybar was? No.

Please pay attention to the fact that not only in actuality, Muhammad (PBUH) did not destroy Khaybar whatsoever, but also he never had the intention to do so. The outcome of the entire battle, which was the surrender conditions that he mandated, shows exactly what he intended by laying siege around Khaybar, which was nothing but to force them into a peaceful agreement by which they would not plot, attack, or impose danger against the Muslims in the future.

The author also, I believe, chose in his narrative to ignore the Muslim rule of engagement in battles ordered by Prophet Muhammad (PBUH) not to attack towns at night when the Prophet said:

"Leave in the name of Allah and by the religion of the Messenger of Allah, do not kill an old man, an infant, a child or a woman, and do not be excessive, pull your winnings together, be virtuous and good-doers for Allah loves the good-doers." (Prophet Muhammad (PBUH)) *Narrator: Anas ibn Malik.* **Reference**: *Takhreej Mishkah Almasabeeh* **Number**: *60/4.* **Degree**: *Good*

The author in many places in his book claimed to only have known the specific intentions and the thoughts of the inner mind of the Prophet, yet he would never mention a statement of civility about not killing women and children, even though he's narrating the exact same event. The reader might have also noticed that it is:

254

"one Muslim who remembered" who also doesn't have a name or reference. On the same page, the author follows by:
"The Muslim advance was inexorable." "The apostle, "according to Ibn Is'haq," seized the property piece by piece and conquered the forts one by one as he came to them."

*We will not comment again on why the author quotes only Ibn Is'haq. The amazing thing in here is that the author totally skipped Khaybar summoning the army of Ghatfan to fight Muhammad (PBUH), fifteen days of siege, all the way to the point when the forts as he said, started to fall one after the other. Not to mention that he never said anything explaining the existence of forts in that peaceful garden of the farmers carrying their morning mist baskets!
You can see clearly the false image of the innocent farmers being attacked suddenly by the Muslims. Yet the author, even in his own words, did not explain to us what kind of gardens of innocence are these that have one fort to begin with, never mind what he just told us, that they were many, one after the other or the days and weeks needed to go through them!

How truthful is the narration of the author when the Muslims laid siege, offered Islam and absolute equal rights to their opponents first and then asked for certain conditions by which the peaceful coexistence can happen before they attempt the battle and before any fighting, even if a siege would last weeks in a harsh desert and limited supplies for the Muslim army versus a well-supplied opponent in his own territory behind forts that spanned one after the other!?

A major fabrication followed, when the author claims that after Fajr prayer, the Muslims attacked and entered Khaybar. I do not know why the author made such a fabrication. Was it to associate Muslim prayers with attacking opponents in a battle? Or was it to give an impression that the Muslims never laid siege for 15 days, never offered terms, that the whole battle may have only lasted that one day, and that Khaybar just fell with its eight forts and 10 thousand fighters after just one morning of fighting?! Only Mr. Spencer knows the intentions behind what he is "narrating" to his readers!

What actually had happened is that after many days of siege and individual duels between some of the leading Muslim fighters, and their counterparts from Khaybar who left their forts to challenge in the duels, the first three forts fell down in the hands of the Muslims.

So there were still five more forts that the Muslims had to go through to get into Khaybar itself. The leaders of Khaybar, however, had already made another massive strategic mistake.

They stored their new, then state-of-the-art weapon, the Catapults, in the third fort, by which Muhammad (PBUH) could have filled them with burning tar and slammed the flames onto the rest of the forts and onto Khaybar itself. So what would the "Wrath of Muhammad", and the "destroyer of Khaybar" do?

Again, the goal for Muhammad (PBUH) was to force the people of Khaybar into peace. So he ordered his men to move the Catapult around to visible places so the warriors of Khaybar would see from their fortified positions, that Muhammad (PBUH) now has the capability of easily destroying Khaybar. Yet, Muhammad (PBUH) did not use any Catapults; not even once.

Muhammad (PBUH)'s plan worked when the leader of Khaybar offered him to surrender and accept peace, which Muhammad (PBUH) replied to with his agreement but under certain conditions. When Muhammad (PBUH) had control of Khaybar and when Khaybar surrendered to him, he was five forts away from Khaybar itself.

Now what did our author say about this?
On pages 139 and 140, the author wrote:
"Muhammad and his men offered the Fajr prayer, the Islamic dawn prayer, before it was light, and then entered Khaybar itself. The Muslims immediately set out to locate the inhabitants' wealth."!

*No Duels, no siege, no forts, just a walk in the park looking for wealth!!

Both parties agreed that half of the harvest of Khaybar would go to the Muslims, Khaybar would be a part of the Muslim state and the Muslim army would be responsible for the safety of the people of Khaybar after Khaybar is disarmed, and that its leader would pledge not to plot against the Muslim state.

Our author then brings a total abhorring fabrication by claiming that Prophet Muhammad (PBUH) ordered the torture of the leader of Khaybar Kinana Ibn Al-Rabi who supposedly, according to the author's claim, had knowledge of Banu Nadir's treasure that was only entrusted with him!!

At the time, not only that Banu Nadir's leader Ibn Al-Rabi was alive and well in Khaybar, but that treasure and any other treasure Banu Nadir might have had, the Muslims themselves allowed Banu Nadir to carry out with them when they forced them into exile from Medina. But I guess the image, and the smoky façade that the author is putting before the eyes of the American reader mandates a lost treasure and crazy pirates, who would torture anyone to get to the buried golden coins!

The author makes a worse fabrication by claiming that the people of Khaybar were sent into exile, which is not true as we have mentioned. He added that only a small part of the Khaybar population that were farmers were allowed to stay for giving half of their crop to the Muslim state. The rest of Khaybar, which was the majority according to the author - even though they didn't break any covenant or tried to kill the Prophet himself like Banu Nadir or Banu Qaynuqa, who were allowed to leave with all their possessions - our author claims that the majority of the people of Khaybar were allowed to leave just by leaving their gold and silver behind! The author heightened the fabrication by claiming that another lost treasure was found, and for that, Muhammad (PBUH) killed some of the men of Khaybar and enslaved their women and children, which is also not true.

The author never explained to us why the claimed majority of the people of Khaybar, which was basically a huge palm tree farm, were not given the treatment that Banu Nadir got, who posed more danger and tried to assassinate the Prophet himself. The author also does not explain why the town that he himself called "oasis of Khaybar", all of a sudden held a minority of farmers and a majority of gold and silver horders who surrendered, reaching a peace covenant with the Prophet, yet all of a sudden there are buried treasures, killed men, enslaved women and children, more than what is in a third-class pirates movie?

It is just sad how much misinformation is imposed on a reader in just one single book!

"The poisoning of Muhammad"

Zaynab Bint Al-Harith was a Jewish woman from Khaybar who poisoned a sheep shoulder, and presented it as a gift to the Prophet, who ate from it, as did a companion by the name of Bashar Ibn Baraa.

The Prophet spat the meat and declared that the bones of the sheep had told him it was poisoned. When the woman was brought in, she said that members of her family were killed in the battle of Khaybar and if the Prophet was a king he would have died and if he was a Prophet he would have been told it was poisoned.

As usual, Mr. Spencer has supernatural proprietary knowledge of the intentions and the inner thoughts of Prophet Muhammad (PBUH) when he wrote:

"Because she had thus obliquely confessed his Prophet-hood, Muhammad spared her life"

There is no reference whatsoever that the Prophet ever indicated or expressed this thought; obviously it is Mr. Spencer's usual attempt to empty the Prophet's forgiveness from its nobility by implying naively that it was for vanity! The Prophet of God, who made sure to eat sitting on the floor like servants, called himself, "**I am but a servant of Allah**", and ordered his companions to never stand up for him when he walked in, said:

258

"No one will enter Paradise if he had one iota of arrogance in his heart") Prophet Muhammad (PBUH))
Narrator: Abdu Allah Ibn Masoud. Reference: Saheeh Muslim, Number: 91. Degree: Correct

As per Mr. Spencer, this is someone who will forgive an assassin only because she hinted that he might be a Prophet!

But then what happened to Zaynab? There are two conflicting stories; one that she was forgiven by the Prophet and the other that she was executed. Which one is true? In my humble opinion, and that of some scholars, both are true. The Prophet had forgiven her initially, but after his companion died shortly of her poison, then according to the law of God she would have to be prosecuted for the man she murdered in cold blood, and she was then executed.

The author brings another weird story about gathering Jewish leaders around the poisoned sheep and asking them about right and wrong and hell fire!! Then, asking them about if the sheep was poisoned, with no verification of any source worth mentioning. I have more respect for the reader's time and mine to even comment on that.

"The spoils of Khaybar"

Saffyah Bint Al Akhtab was the daughter of the leader of Banu al Nadir and was taken captive in the battle of Khaybar when one Muslim soldier chose her for marriage or to carry her responsibility. When she objected as a first lady of the tribe to be matched with an average soldier, another companion reported the incident to the Prophet, who agreed to marry her after she accepted Islam. Later she told the Prophet that she had a dream that the moon fell into her lap and that her father interpreted that by slapping her on the face for dreaming of marrying Muhammad. Prophet Muhammad (PBUH) didn't marry her immediately but waited till after her next monthly period occurred, to consummate the marriage.

259

On page 142 the author narrates the same story but from the angle that the companion, who told the Prophet, didn't tell the Prophet about her refusal to marry an average soldier but that:
"We have not seen the like of her among the captives of the war"
And as per the relentless demonizing machine of the author, the Prophet ran after the lust - God forbid - and:
"Muhammad then immediately freed her and married her himself"!

Even though it was stated that the Prophet didn't consummate the marriage till she had her period, listen to the absurdity of a fabrication, on page 143 the author wrote:
"Saffiya's feelings on going from a wife of a Jewish chieftain, to widow, to captive, to wife of the Prophet of Islam in the course of a single day are not recorded"

Unless a woman can have her monthly period come and go in the same day, then of course this fabrication will never be recorded!

"Prophet Muhammad is not the greatest man that ever lived because he was the most merciful, gentle and righteous. Prophet Muhammad is not the greatest man that ever lived because he was the most powerful in fighting oppression. Prophet Muhammad is the greatest man that ever lived because he was simultaneously both"

Moustafa Zayed

Chapter Nine

"The conquest of Mecca"

Mecca was Muhammad (PBUH)'s hometown in which he was born and lived, till he had to flee to Medina for his life. Mecca was also where he and his early companions were persecuted, boycotted, starved, tortured, and many of them killed. The surrender of Mecca to the Muslims was a significant mark in the history of Islam.

When Mecca and its infidels surrendered without a fight to the Muslims and the Prophet of God:
*Did the Prophet of God have every right to bring the killers of his companions, prosecute them in a fair trial, and execute them for their crimes? Yes he did.
*Did he have every right to take back all the properties and impose payments to his companions for their properties seized by the infidels of Quraysh? Yes he did.
*Did he have every right to execute the leaders of the tribes who sent their men to kill the Prophet in his own bed before he fled to Medina?

Yes he did have every right to.

And when we say did he have the right, we have to understand that we're not talking about some individual who belonged to a victorious society, trying to get justice against the leaders of the defeated side. It was the right of the last Prophet of God against the most evil, vicious infidels responsible of the abhorrent crimes tyrannically committed against him and some of the best of his companions.

It was Muhammad (PBUH) and his Muslims, with all the horrific memories of which most had power, and ability to rightly avenge themselves against the infidels of Quraysh.

How would the "founder of the world's most intolerant religion" - as per Mr. Spencer - avenge himself and the victims amongst some of the best of believers of God?

Here is what the last Prophet of God did:

Muhammad (PBUH), with his army, came into the center of Mecca, where Quraysh's leaders were gathered awaiting a fate they knew was bleak at best.

The Prophet asked them: "**What do you expect me to do to you**?" Some of them replied: "You are a noble brother and son of a noble brother." The Prophet replied, "**Go, for you are set free**"

Again, "founder of the world's most intolerant religion" had given amnesty to every single soul in Mecca, including the leaders who harmed him personally, and conspired relentlessly to kill him.

A blanket forgiveness that even included the hired assassin who killed the Prophet's beloved uncle and great companion, Hamza Ibn Abdel Motaleb. Even "Wahshy" the assassin was given amnesty and forgiven!

Has this ever happened in the history of mankind, before or after?

A Prophet of God, a military leader, whom he himself was persecuted, harmed, battled and attempts to end his own life were committed by the worst of infidels; pagans who were then all under his thumb, yet he let them all go, forgiven?

That same Prophet of God, is the same one that our truth-seeker is calling the "founder of the world's most intolerant religion"?

And as absurd and laughable a statement this could be, I want the reader to look even further into the almost perfect discipline, that the manners of the religion of Islam afforded the soldier of the army of ten thousand Muslim men. Men who have seen horrors for years, living under the horrible oppression of the same infidels who were at that moment inches

263

away from the tips of their swords, yet they adhered to the decision of the Prophet of God, obeyed the orders of God, and did not avenge the crimes committed against them.

What is of the most importance to note is that these warriors are the collective human examples of Islamic manners to all Muslims throughout time and to date. These are the highest and noblest examples of a Muslim making "Jihad" or "striving" for the sake of God in the form of battling for God's cause when battling is a must for the nation.

Did the author enlighten his readers with that test of all litmus tests; about what Muslims are about?

Even though it was one of the brightest moments of human history, and evidence of the Prophet's absolute mercy, forgiveness, in pardoning the worst of criminals, it still should not be a surprise to the reader. For even Mr. Spencer himself had to show in a previous chapter - to our surprise - how Prophet Muhammad (PBUH) asked and prayed to Allah to forgive the leader of the hypocrites Ibn Salool. The Prophet visited him when he was sick, wished him well, performed the burial prayers upon his body, wrapped him in the Prophet's own shirt, carried him and laid him inside the grave himself.

That was the same Ibn Salool that provoked Banu Nadir to get into war against Muhammad (PBUH) after they broke their covenant, promising them two thousand soldiers that never arrived when the battle started, and was the same man that propagated the "Ifk" (fabrication) incident against Muhammad (PBUH)'s own wife; her honor and the Prophet's.

Not even the biggest of liars could come up with a claim that there was any hint of just one battle of resistance the Muslims had to go through to seize Mecca. Not even a two man duel.

And not even the "truth-seekers" of their time, could have fabricated stories about any killed by the Muslim army at the surrender of Mecca, any executed Quraysh leaders, warriors, any men, women, or even one soul.

264

Now, can Mr. Spencer, with a straight face, tell you the truth that is as glaring as the sun, of probably one of the most significant events of forgiveness and mercy in human history?

Why would our truth-seeker then, narrate the event by giving it the title "The Conquest of Mecca", even though not one Muslim sword needed to be raised?

Can the author go against his self-imposed "narrative" and say the words "the Prophet forgave them all" or "the Prophet totally tolerated their abhorrent crimes, and sat them and their families free"?

The author instead exhausts his readers about trivial individual stories that are irrelevant to the historically monumental pardoning of every Meccan.

On page 145, the author dances away from the blanket amnesty by either claiming things that never happened or, as usual, relying on another fabricated story of - you guessed it - Ibn Is'haq!

In probably one of the most, if not the most, significant events in the history of Islam and the Prophet, our author shows you the quality of his narrative by not quoting the micro-detailed events of the surrender of Quraysh within the leading Seerah references of Al-Bukhary, Muslim, Imam Ahmed, Al-Tarmazy, Ibn Majah, Al-Nasaey, Al-Tabary, or Ibn Katheer. He instead quotes a known fabricated story from Ibn Is'haq!

That Muhammad (PBUH) had forced Abu Sufyan, the leader of Quraysh, to become a Muslim under the threat of the sword, otherwise he would have his head chopped off!

Let's resort to logic here:

Why not kill Abu Sufyan, the leader of the infidels, who waged war against you, in Badr, in Uhud, and in the battle of the Trench? Why not kill him when you are more than justified to?

What benefit would the Prophet gain of him becoming a Muslim, knowing that according to Islamic law, if he declared Islam, he would have exactly the same rights that the companions of the Prophet had, and that he would get to keep all his properties, wealth, and walk free, not harmed and not losing one penny's worth of his wealth?

265

For the record, Abu Sufyan later turned to be one of the most sincere and respected companions of the Prophet himself.

On page 147 the author wrote:

"One of Muhammad's lieutenants, Abbas, responded to Abu Sufyan: "Submit and testify that there is no God but Allah and that Muhammad is the apostle of God before you lose your head." Abu Sufyan complied."!

Only two possibilities here: Either the nonsense of the author claiming that Prophet Muhammad (PBUH) is an intolerant, booty-seeking, blood-thirsty violent man is rubbish! Or the story is what it is, another one of his outright fabrications!

On page 145, the author starts by omitting that there was almost two years between the battle of Khaybar and the opening of Mecca to Muslims, and tries to make it look like a grand surprise to Quraysh!

After Khaybar, Quraysh became the imminent Muslims destination; a given that, for two years, was developing day by day in broad daylight. During these two years, Quraysh saw the number of people accepting Islam exponentially growing four-folds before their eyes, and with it, the size of the army of the Muslims reaching ten thousands from about only 1500 at the battle of Khaybar.

The real surprise would have been that the Muslims would not go back and take over the homeland of the Prophet, and not otherwise.

On page 145, the author writes:

"The surprise was almost given away by a Muslim who sent a letter to the Quraysh informing them of Muhammad (PBUH)'s plans; however the Muslims intercepted the letter."

The author then brings a translation of what he claimed was a translation of verses 1-4 of chapter 60 of Surat (Al-Mumtahina) yet he only translated verses 2-4 and omitted from his translation verse no. 1! Why?

He claimed that these verses were revealed about the person who sent that letter that was supposedly breaking the "surprising" news that every man knew for years, yet verse 1 that he omitted tells of the occasion and

266

the true context of the verses revelation which is general to all Muslims of all time. That is not to show kindness to those who fought Muslims and exiled them out of their own homes.

The first verse (omitted by the author) says:

"O, you who believe! Do not take my enemy or your enemy as an ally. You give them your kindness and they have disbelieved in what you were given of the truth, they exiled you from your homes because you believe in Allah your God, if you have left to strive for My Sake and hoping for satisfying me, then don't show them kindness and I am more knowledgeable of what you hid and what you displayed. And whoever does that amongst you, then he went astray of the straight path."
Holy Quran, Surat (Al Mumtahina) Ch (60) Verse (1)

يَا أَيُّهَا الَّذِينَ آمَنُوا لَا تَتَّخِذُوا عَدُوِّي وَعَدُوَّكُمْ أَوْلِيَاءَ تُلْقُونَ إِلَيْهِمْ بِالْمَوَدَّةِ وَقَدْ كَفَرُوا بِمَا جَاءَكُمْ مِنَ الْحَقِّ يُخْرِجُونَ الرَّسُولَ وَإِيَّاكُمْ ۙ أَنْ تُؤْمِنُوا بِاللَّهِ رَبِّكُمْ إِنْ كُنْتُمْ خَرَجْتُمْ جِهَادًا فِي سَبِيلِي وَابْتِغَاءَ مَرْضَاتِي ۚ تُسِرُّونَ إِلَيْهِمْ بِالْمَوَدَّةِ وَأَنَا أَعْلَمُ بِمَا أَخْفَيْتُمْ وَمَا أَعْلَنْتُمْ ۚ وَمَنْ يَفْعَلْهُ مِنْكُمْ فَقَدْ ضَلَّ سَوَاءَ السَّبِيلِ (1)

On page 146, the author pre-empts the amnesty that Prophet Muhammad (PBUH) had given to every single soul in Mecca by claiming:
"Many of the most notable Quraysh warriors now deserted and, converting to Islam, joined Muhammad's forces."

The author apparently confuses you between the exponential growth rate of men and women accepting Islam in Quraysh and more so in Medina, with a notion that during the night in which the Muslims camped out of Mecca, that many of the most notable leaders of Quraysh accepted Islam, converted and deserted to the Muslim army, before the morning had come!

So they converted, deserted Mecca and joined the Muslim army overnight, and were not forgiven as infidels when Mecca surrendered to the Muslims hours later!

And as illogical and unbelievable that is, apparently it could be nothing but an attempt to minimize the number of nobles that did not accept Islam, that Prophet Muhammad (PBUH) had shown his mercy, tolerance, and unparalleled leniency, not only upon them, but to the entire population of the infidels of Quraysh.

"Apostates to be killed"

The author starts this paragraph by another fabrication. He wrote: "When Muhammad (PBUH) "forced his entry" into Mecca according to Ibn Saad, "the people embraced Islam willingly or unwillingly." "!

Another trick used on the reader, who's not paying attention, where in the middle of the sentence the author said "according to Ibn Saad" and then quotes Ibn Saad, by which he confuses the reader as if the first part of the sentence was also a quotation of Ibn Saad (who is a military defector to be quoted of all people). In this case, the author also puts emphasis on "forced his entry," by putting quotation marks around it.

Where is it stated, even in one of the corrupt fabricated stories found in Ibn Is'haq's or any other reference, that there was any resistance even symbolized by one man raising one sword against the army of Muhammad (PBUH)? None.

Were there any force ever needed to enter Mecca? None.

But in the B movie of Spencer studios, Muhammad has to be a villain forcing his sword into anything, everywhere!

And that was why the author had to impose that sentence to begin with when narrating the Prophet entering a town that surrendered unconditionally before the Prophet had even entered.

The narrative of Mr. Spencer, as you know by now, is always crazy-jihadist-warriors with unparalleled violence, lusting for women and buried treasures, chopping off heads for entertainment, yet even in the moment that showed the highest amount of forgiveness, self-control, mercy and tolerance in the history of mankind, Mr. Spencer can only claim a quote of Ibn Saad, that people embraced Islam "willingly or unwillingly"; a claim that is against everything Islamic history stood for during 1400 years. Here are the orders of God:

"There is no compulsion in religion"
Holy Quran, Surat (Al Baqara) Ch.(2) Verse (256), and the verse,

لَا إِكْرَاهَ فِي الدِّينِ (256)

"Guiding them is not up to you, but it is Allah who guides whomever He wills"
Holy Quran, Surat (Al Baqara) Ch. (2) Verse (272)

لَيْسَ عَلَيْكَ هُدَاهُمْ وَلَٰكِنَّ اللَّهَ يَهْدِي مَنْ يَشَاءُ ۗ (272)

But according to Mr. Spencer, Muslims that day weren't following either the orders of God or his Prophet, but following the predetermined script of Mr. Spencer!

I ask the reader not only how the author, defector Ibn Saad, or any human being for that matter, knew what was in the hearts of people who accepted Islam at the time? And before we answer that question, I would ask the author and all his fabricated stories:
Did every single infidel or pagan in Quraysh accept Islam after the Muslims seized Mecca? The answer is such that even the author himself has to admit: No.
Did all Christians and Jews in the Arab Peninsula convert "willingly or unwillingly" to Islam when Mecca surrendered to the Muslims? Even the author himself has to admit: No.
What's a well-known historical fact is that, whoever did not want to accept Islam did not have to explain why, and did not have to apologize; he only had to declare it, just so that he would not be allowed to join the Muslim army as a Muslim. And by declaring that, he also had to

269

contribute to the community his share of tax (Jizyah), like the Muslims had to pay their (Zakah) tax, of which we have explained its rules sufficiently in previous chapters.

For his claim to be even something that is worth a paragraph in anyone's book, our author would have to show us the thousands of pagans, atheists, Christians and Jews that were mass-murdered in Mr. Spencer's "crazy-Muslim land" to show us how that at that point everyone in Mecca became Muslim" willingly or unwillingly"!!

The author then offends our intelligence - again - by bringing the issue of apostates.

Muhammad (PBUH) and all the Muslims were at war with Quraysh, till the day he seized Mecca and gave them all amnesty.

In a state of war, and I remind the reader that at the early stages of that war, when the Muslim army was at times not even one-fifth the army that Quraysh summoned, it was not a war to force surrender or to gain more land. It was a war to the annihilation of Muhammad (PBUH), the Muslims, and Islam altogether. During that state of war, when you not only convert back to paganism, but associate that with defecting to the enemy of Muslims itself, then that is military treason in capital letters, which is punishable in any court, in any country, in any time by death by a firing squad. If it was just espionage without declaring your defection, it would have been a life-sentence at best.

The author narrates for us the story of Abdullah Ibn Saad, who defected from the Muslim army to that of Quraysh, converting back to paganism. Before we narrate the incident - Abdullah ibn Saad, meeting with Muhammad (PBUH), when Muhammad (PBUH) settled as the ruler of Mecca - to decide his fate after his treason, I want to ask the reader to join me in asking Mr. Spencer, how is it that he skipped telling his readers as to how Muhammad (PBUH) entered Mecca and what had he done to his and the Muslims' worst enemies, persecutors, torturers, and killers of his best companions?

How it possible is that Mr. Robert Spencer - who is to enlighten us about the truth of Muhammad - intentionally doesn't say a word about the most important event of the history of Muhammad (PBUH) and Islam itself, at least so far in his chapter about "the conquest of Mecca"?

Was the fact that they were given all amnesty by the last Prophet of God, the reason why Mr. Spencer skipped everything to address first the case of two traitors who defected to Quraysh's army?!

But more interestingly; even the incident Mr. Spencer resorted to, showed - again - the mercy and forgiveness of the Prophet and the optimum civility of the law of God!

What was the judgment of the Prophet of Islam upon a military defecting traitor, who Mr. Spencer highlighted his story as 'an apostate to be killed"? The last Prophet of God let him and his brother walk free!

Abdullah Ibn Saad pled for his life and recited the certification indicating that he became a Muslim again. In any court of law, or wherever Mr. Spencer resides nowadays, that certification of allegiance to the same Islamic constitution that Ibn Saad had already betrayed defecting to its worst enemies, would have been worthless and a nonevent in determining his punishment. The Prophet turned his head away when Ibn Saad recited the certification for the first time, and the second time. But when Ibn Saad repeated it for a third time, Prophet Muhammad (PBUH) set him and his own brother free!

Applying the cardinal Islamic rule, that even the Prophet himself has no right to judge what is truly in people's hearts, and since there weren't any apparent crimes against Muslims or victims of the two brothers during the time of their defection to Quraysh's army, the Prophet would have not judged whether their repentance or their certification of Islam is true in their hearts or not. They were set free.

"Arabic Story of Abdullah Ibn Saad"

Our author, who totally omitted the Prophet forgiving all infidels of Mecca and giving them a pardon, comments on the release of the Ibn Saad brothers by saying, on page 147:
"Apostasy from Islam has always been for Muhammad a supreme evil."

Maybe defecting to the enemy's army in a state of war, which is punishable by death in every country in the history of the world that we're aware of, should, according to the author for some reason, be equivalent to only naughty-child play in Islam, and based on that assumption, he apparently blames Muhammad (PBUH)'s perception of military treason as a "supreme evil"!

I also want to remind the readers of the title Mr. Spencer chose for the Ibn Saad's subsection, **"Apostates to be killed"**!
Were they killed? No. Would the title be "Apostates pardoned" or "Apostates forgiven or released"? Absolutely not. This truth doesn't fit Mr. Spencer's narrative!

Still, and up till this point in the chapter, Prophet Muhammad's forgiveness upon the entire population of the largest city in the Arab Peninsula is totally trivialized and skipped out of the "Conquest of Mecca"! Instead, the author brings a story about defectors of the Muslim army, which we have explained, several times so far, that at that time officially declaring your apostasy - when no one forced you to declare what your heart's belief was - was an immediate act of confessed treason that was punishable by death, not only in the land of Islam but in any country at that time in history.

On page 148, the author narrates another story about another defection, and adds some of his own brand of spices. The story was about some Bedouin herders who claimed they accepted Islam and received support from the Muslims. Prophet Muhammad (PBUH) gave them permission to go to where the herd of charity camels were, and benefit from their milks. In rewarding the generosity of Islam and the help they received from the Muslims, as soon as the herders got away from Medina, they killed the camel shepherds, mutilated their eyes, stole the camels and renounced Islam in public. What is the punishment of premeditated murder and armed robbery coupled with defection or treason in any court of law nowadays?

If capital punishment wasn't specifically mandated for that kind of crime in any era worldwide, then for what other crime?

That kind of theft, treason, and murdering of innocent souls in cold blood fits into the crime of corruption in Earth, and not as the author translates it "in the land". Notice how the author claimed that the defectors released the camels to the desert after defecting so the theft crime would be taken out of the equation, which is not true, not to mention that even though there was absolutely no reason to kill the shepherds unless they of course wanted to keep the loot of the camels after their defection; defection, we might add, coupled with murder and theft, which are corruption on Earth crimes in capital letters.

Did anyone in the history of Islam call that crime anything but corruption in earth? No.

Did the Prophet call it anything different? No

And what does our author, on his own, call it for us after 1400 years of Islamic history? Apostasy!

The punishment in Islam is severe for the crime of corruption in Earth, yet at the end, it's not one iota more severe than the punishment of this crime in any country or any military, which is death. The punishment in Islam for corrupters in Earth is that an arm and a leg are cut diagonally, leaving them to die, in public, for everyone to be deterred from doing such robbery-murders in the future.

Such punishment in Islam is the same punishment for none other than the crime of terrorism which is a major corruption in earth crime.

What is more interesting is that the author chose to speak about the severe punishment with a bias to camel thieves, herder killers and not the main crime of terrorizing and killing the innocent herders, even when it fitted his most favorite subject of terrorism.

273

The spin that our author added is on page 148, when he wrote: "And their eyes put out with heated iron bars and that they are left in the desert to die. Their pleas for water, he ordered, must be refused."

*Which is an exception to the default punishment of that crime in Islam; because the killers did the same to the eyes of the herders they killed.
On page 148, our author also wrote:
"Muhammad legislated for his community that no Muslim could be put to death except for murder, unlawful sexual intercourse, and apostasy. He said flatly: "Whoever changed his Islamic religion, then kill him." "

*As usual, it's always the corrupted information that the author selects. First, not every unlawful sexual intercourse is punishable by death, only if the sinner is married.
Secondly, the quotation where the Prophet said to apply the death punishment on defectors was in his correct quotation:
"Whoever changed his religion, then kill him."
(Prophet Muhammad (PBUH))
Narrator: Abdu Allah Ibn Abbas. Reference: Saheeh Al Bukhary, Number: 6922. Degree: Correct

The author added the word "Islamic" on his own before the word religion. And while we know that the religion that the Prophet mentioned is none other than Islam, yet the clear difference between writing the history on the case of certain orientalists and Islam-bashers like Mr. Spencer, in comparison to the ethics of verifying historical events by Muslim scholars, are sometimes vast enough that when adding one letter or one word that was not there, it will discredit the entire story by a Muslim scholar, and sometimes any narration of the teller all together.

What is really interesting is that our "truth-seeker" of all people, writes at the bottom of the page:
"Unfortunately, this claim simply does not accord with the facts of Muhammad's life. That such assertions pass unchallenged only underscores the need for westerns to become informed about the actual

274

words and deeds of Muhammad - which make the actions of Islamic state much more intelligible than do the words of Islamic apologists in the west."

*Well, I can see it as if it's happening right now, that Mr. Spencer will call me an apologist! Let me ask the reader:
Did the so called Muslim apologists, who were hand-picked by Mr. Spencer, the ones that committed the action of fabrication, omitting part or whole verses of the Holy Quran, with misinformation and intentional mistranslation for a living hundreds of times, like an author that we all know? Who should be the apologist then?

The author made that statement as an answer to an American Muslim who stated that:
"There is no historical record, which indicates that Muhammad or any of his companions ever sentenced anyone to death for Apostasy."

*And while that statement is true, the author apparently intentionally confuses the generality of the meaning of apostasy with the specific crime of defecting to the enemy's army in a state of war.
Defection to the army of your worst enemy of Quraysh at that time could not just be minimized into apostasy or the one aspect of changing one's religion or belief. Changing your religion itself is impossible to prosecute according to Islamic law, unless you go ahead in a state of war, and stick your head inside the cannon of the law by declaring your conversion, butting heads with the Muslim state in contempt, to challenge and offend the constitution of the land, even though it is unlawful for anyone to ask you to declare what's in your heart!

What religion is that, that mandates its followers to plead to TV stations, or walk around knocking on everyone's door declaring that you have converted to a new religion? This is a totally different issue than the issue of freedom of religion; in our case it is simply and clearly the question of what level of dissidence is allowed in a state of war.

275

The author brings the story of a Christian Pakistani who could have worshipped quietly in his heart or in Churches - that by the way have existed in Muslim lands since the first day of Muhammad (PBUH)'s Prophet-hood - and lived his life following whatever doctrine he could choose. Yet, some in the West get fascinated by whoever tries to offend Muslims in their homelands and offend their constitution publicly. That's actually how we learned about the name of the man in America to begin with.

So, for a new Muslim who is thinking about accepting Islam, why would he take the chance and become a Muslim for if he wanted to change my mind later, he might be subject to be killed; why become a Muslim altogether? Correct? To the contrary, Islam is the fastest growing religion, not only in every corner in the world, but even in America.

In the recent statistic that was announced by CNN in 2009, it is stated that from the year 1990 to the year 2008, which is a span of 18 years, no religion, denomination, or faction of the major religions in America had percentage growth over the other groups, except for one religion. That religion growth, compared to the other groups, was not the surprise; the most amazing result, was that Islam was not only the only growing religion in America - which suffered two significant terrorist attacks that the media and the likes of Mr. Spencer tried to stamp on the forehead of Islam as a religion - the American Muslim population did not just grow, but actually doubled!

Does the author think that he's breaking news to us about the Hadeeth of the Prophet regarding the punishment of defection to the enemy's army, according to Islamic Law?

Does the author think that American Muslims who chose based on the correct knowledge of the religion of Islam itself, have just abandoned their jobs, their homes and ran to the hills to prepare for the clear and present danger of the apostasy rule in Islam, based on Mr. Spencer's breaking news?

It is a well-known rule, yet Islam is embraced and accepted on the face of the planet by tens of thousands, every single day.

276

"Muhammad at the Kabaa"

Another corrupted story: Muhammad (PBUH) stood before the Kabaa and recited the verse of the Holy Quran that stated that the right of Allah upon all people, is there to proclaim above all, and that falsehood is bound to vanish. Prophet Muhammad (PBUH) had ordered all the statues of all the idols to be knocked down and destroyed, in addition to the paintings that the pagans also worshipped. What did not happen was what the author claimed on page 149, when he said:

"He ordered that all the idols be burned except for an icon of Jesus and Mary."

Prophet Muhammad (PBUH) ordered every single item, painting, and statue, depiction of any idol, character, Prophet or angel to be destroyed. As a Muslim American scholar, and while I am well-aware of the reverence that Islam and the Holy Quran have for Jesus (PBUH) as a mighty Prophet of God, and for Virgin Mary as the greatest woman that ever lived and will ever live, I cannot stay silent to what the author tried to erroneously add to a historical fact. Not only that even the depiction of Jesus (PBUH) and Virgin Mary in any form is forbidden in Islam, but Prophet Muhammad (PBUH) himself forbade totally any depiction of himself, whether a picture or a statue be allowed; him and any other Prophet or companion.

In Islam, it is the message and the mannerism of the Prophets to be followed, not what they look like, especially when history is the witness of how extreme people may take the reverence of Prophets to the limit of the unforgivable sin of worshipping them, either alongside God, or worse, depicting them as God Himself.

Finally, the author admits the tolerance, forgiveness, and mercy of Prophet Muhammad (PBUH) upon the leaders of Quraysh and Mecca's entire population, when he narrated what we narrated in the beginning of the chapter; on page 149 he wrote the reply of Prophet Muhammad (PBUH)'s question to them:

""Oh Quraysh, what do you think that I am about to do with you?" They answered, "You are a noble brother, son of a noble brother." And it was so."

*And I would like to ask the author here, **"And it was so"** what?!

In the past four pages, the author gave us a splitting headache by analyzing apostasy, a military defector, a fabricated story about forcing Abu Sufyan to convert to Islam, and when the Prophet gives the entire population of Quraysh, including Abu Sufyan, a blanket amnesty and forgiveness, all that the author can enlighten us with about the "truth about Muhammad" is the lengthy statement of "And it was so"? Amazing!

Even on page 150, when the author narrated when Hind Bint Utba, the wife of Abu Sufyan - who hired Wahshy to kill Hamza, the uncle of the Prophet and mutilated his body - asked the Prophet to forgive her, which as you may expect by now, the Prophet did forgive her, our truth-seeker found no more than six words of extreme extrapolation about the tolerance of the Prophet to indicate that the Prophet did forgive the woman. The author wrote: "The homage of the women accepted,"!

The author then followed with Prophet Muhammad (PBUH)'s famous declaration of Mecca being a Muslim holy sanctuary forever, where no life should be taken: even trees couldn't be cut.

The same quotation of the Prophet is also one of the scientific miracles of Muhammad (PBUH)'s quotations when he clearly indicated the fact that trees have souls and responses to pleasure and pain; and in the case of cutting them down, extreme pain of the death of the tree, which scientists proved 1400 years later.

"The battle of Hunayn and mastery of Arabia"

On page 150, the author wrote:
"Muhammad was the master of Mecca, but there was one additional great obstacle between him and mastery of all Arabia."

What the author is implying here is clear; it is that Muhammad's goal was to be "master of Mecca", and as we explained and displayed many factual events that showed that all the burden, struggle and difficulties Muhammad (PBUH) had faced when he was then over 60 years of age, were only to invite to and protect the path of God.
Muhammad (PBUH)'s biggest sacrifice was his own self being in the first line of war, fighting tyrants who oppressed people not to worship their own Creator.

The next battle of the Muslims was the battle of Hunayn, and before we get to the author's narration of the battle, I would like to bring an example of the kindness, generosity, and mercy of the Prophet in one related event, that is in my opinion, unparalleled in the history of mankind, where the Prophet's mercy and forgiveness were given to people who were not even born then!

The battle of Hunayn was with the people of the city of Ta'if, which is south of Mecca. Ten years earlier, the Prophet used to visit a tribe after the other, to invite them to the righteous path of their One Mighty Creator. When Muhammad (PBUH) invited them, he did not ask them to surrender their properties to him or force them to make him their mighty leader, on the contrary, he would ask them to accept the basic manners of Islam; the Oneness of God, doing well by parents, not to steal, kill, lie, or cheat. Many tribes and many members of many tribes accepted Islam on the spot. Yet when it came to the tribe of Thaqeef of the city of Ta'if, they rejected the kindness and polite invitation of the Prophet so harshly and rudely that the Prophet walked, so saddened, a distance of more than ten miles till he started to gain consciousness of his surroundings again.

279

He reached a place called Qarn Al-Thaaleb at the time. In Sahih Al-Bukhari, it was narrated that the Thaqif tribe had hurt the Prophet so much that Arch-Angel Gabriel himself appeared to the Prophet and told him that God had ordered Gabriel to give the Prophet the choice that one of the angels crush the entire tribe between two of Mecca's mountains just for what they have done to his Prophet.

The last Prophet of God answered:

"No, for Allah might bring out of their offspring someone who may worship God and not associate a partner with Him."
(Prophet Muhammad (PBUH))

*Narrator: Ayesha. **Reference**: Saheeh Al Bukhary, **Number**: 3231. **Degree**: Correct*

The Prophet forgave them, even though they hurt him enough to have the angels descend from heaven with a license to punish them; all just to have mercy on a possibility of the children of the infidels' children becoming worshippers of God.

In the battle of Hunayn itself, and contrary to the author's claim that he wrote on page 151:

"The Muslims, despite their superior numbers, were routed."

*Allah had revealed in the Holy Quran that the reason was not despite of their superior numbers, but actually the superior numbers of the Muslims at that battle fascinated them into complacency in the beginning, as the main reason for their initial retreat in the battle.

In the Holy Quran:

"Allah has truly given you victory on many battle fields, and on the Day of Hunain when you rejoiced at your great number, but it didn't avail you and the earth, as vast as it is, was tightened upon you, then you turned back in flight"
Holy Quran, Surat (Al Tawba) Ch (9) Verse (25)

لَقَدْ نَصَرَكُمُ اللَّهُ فِي مَوَاطِنَ كَثِيرَةٍ ۙ وَيَوْمَ حُنَيْنٍ ۙ إِذْ أَعْجَبَتْكُمْ كَثْرَتُكُمْ فَلَمْ تُغْنِ عَنْكُمْ شَيْئًا وَضَاقَتْ عَلَيْكُمُ الْأَرْضُ بِمَا رَحُبَتْ ثُمَّ وَلَّيْتُمْ مُدْبِرِينَ (25)

As Allah had revealed in so many places in the Holy Quran, a severe punishment is given to people when they attribute the blessings that Allah had bestowed upon them, only to themselves and not ultimately to Allah as the Giver of all blessings. Worse, sometimes people are fascinated altogether with their ownselves and what they have, forgetting Allah - sometimes - altogether.

Then the author - again - refrains from calling clear matters by their names, and calls the aid that Allah revealed had given the Muslims, to reverse the tide of the battle in the Muslim's favor, by the word "supernatural help"!

The aid of God to His believers who are sacrificing everything they have, even their lives, for His sake, is not aid from God, but "supernatural help."

The author displays his mastery again on page 152. The mastery of emptying great events in the life of the Prophet of their content, Events that are telling of the utmost quality of his manners, belittling them, or redirecting their moral into irrelevant issues that fits his narrative.

He narrates the famous incident when Prophet Muhammad (PBUH) was distributing the spoils of the battle of Hunayn, when one Bedouin, who was new to Islam, objected rudely to the size of his share of the battle winnings. Prophet Muhammad (PBUH) had a very just system of distributing the spoils of war according to how bravely the man fought, and how many times he had been fighting with the Muslim army. The Bedouin yelled at the Prophet saying "Oh Prophet of Allah, fear Allah". And the Prophet replied politely, by saying:

"Am I not the most deserving of the people of earth to be fearful of God?" (Prophet Muhammad (PBUH))
Narrator: Abu Saieed Al khodrey. Reference: Saheeh Muslim, Number: 1064. Degree: Correct

Mind you that this was not only the last Prophet of God, but the leader of a huge army being offended and accused by a soldier. The companions of the Prophet jumped angrily in response to how offensive the Bedouin was to the Prophet of God. One of them was Khalid Ibn Al-Waleed, the great military leader who drew his sword, asking the Prophet for permission to kill the man. The Prophet answered with his usual leniency:

"Leave him. He might be a praying man." Khalid Ibn Al-Walid replied, "But how many praying men don't say with tongues what's in their hearts?" The Prophet Muhammad (PBUH) answered by his historical statement that not only became a cardinal rule in Islamic law, but one of the brightest moments of the history of the rights of mankind:

"Allah did not send me to dig into people's hearts or split their insides open to see what's in them."
(Prophet Muhammad (PBUH))
Narrator: Abu Saieed Al khodrey. Reference: Bayhaqy's Al sunan Al kubra, Number: 196/8. Degree: proven

The great meaning is that even the Prophet of God himself does not have the right to investigate people's intentions, or their inner beliefs under any circumstances, even in the case of an ignorant, rude Bedouin offending the Prophet of God himself.

How many times did some orientalists and Islam-bashers like Mr. Spencer claim that - apart from all people - they were so "supernaturally" privy to the intentions, motivations, and inner-thoughts of Muslims and the Prophet of God himself?

On page 152, the author comments on the status of the last Prophet of God amongst Muslims, where he is the ultimate human example of righteousness and Islamic manners. He wrote:
"His words and deeds exemplify their highest pattern of conduct forming the only absolute standard within Islam: anything sanctioned by the

example of the Prophet, with the sole exceptions of incidents such as that of the satanic verses, in which he was repentant, is good."

*The author uses what is known in the Arabic literature by the adage "mixing poison with honey," where he speaks about Prophet Muhammad (PBUH)'s great status amongst Muslims and then laces the paragraph with the reference to the "satanic verses" fabrication. He even adds another fabrication about the Prophet repenting of the fabrication of the satanic verses incident that never happened to begin with. Not only did we totally refute the satanic verses fabrication of the author in a previous chapter, but we would reiterate that the satanic verses fabrication, and consequently the claimed repenting of the Prophet of it, are not mentioned whether separately or together in any reliable Islamic source by the quotations of the Prophet, or any verified historical account of Islam altogether. If the author is trying to impose the infamous propaganda technique of repeating the lie so many times till it's perceived as truth, we will refute it for the author as many times needed till he is perceived as what he truly is worth as a researcher.

"Invitation to Islam"

The author moves to the era when Islam started to spread outside the Arab Peninsula. And as we said before, the number one duty and obligation of a Prophet of God was none other than to spread the invitation to the religion of God to his people, and in the case of the last Prophet of God, to all mankind.
With every Godly message, every Prophet of God is mandated by God to demand virtue and prohibit vice to the utmost of his ability. In the Holy Quran:

"Those whom if we enabled them on earth, they would establish prayers, give charity, demand virtue and prohibit vice, and to God all matters return"
Holy Quran, Surat (Al Hajj) Ch (22) Verse (41)

الَّذِينَ إِنْ مَكَّنَّاهُمْ فِي الْأَرْضِ أَقَامُوا الصَّلَاةَ وَآتَوُا الزَّكَاةَ وَأَمَرُوا بِالْمَعْرُوفِ وَنَهَوْا عَنِ الْمُنْكَرِ ۗ وَلِلَّهِ عَاقِبَةُ الْأُمُورِ (41)

The author describes this obligation on page 152, he wrote:
"...becoming the ruler of all Arabia. He began to set his sights on even larger quarry, eyeing the adjacent Byzantine and Persian territories."

*Notice the language of the author describing Prophet Muhammad's task as if it is eyeing worldly prizes or some sort of potential business expansion opportunity!
As a matter of fact, the bravery of Prophet Muhammad (PBUH) saying a word of truth to the leader of the largest and oldest empire in the world at the time is another undeniable proof of the unprecedented self-denying and sacrifice that the Prophet reached for the sake of God.
The Roman Empire spread throughout the three known continents in over 800 years. They had armies that can cover the entire Arab Peninsula and its entire population many times over. The deceptive statement that Mr. Spencer inserted in the first sentence, becomes important here.
On page 152 he wrote:
"The Prophet of Islam now faced little opposition,"

*What he meant was little opposition in the Arab Peninsula itself, but by any stretch of the imagination facing the Roman empire, was creating a stand-off with the largest army and biggest Empire in the world, which is anything but "little" and much more perilous than just an "opposition". On page 152, commenting on Hercules refusing the invitation of Prophet Muhammad (PBUH) to him and his people to accept Islam, the author wrote:
"Hercules did not accept Islam and soon the Byzantines would know well that the warriors of Jihad indeed granted no safety to those who made such a choice."

*Notice here that the Muslim army that controlled the entire Arab Peninsula is not an army in the eyes of Mr. Spencer, on the contrary they are some "warriors of Jihad" who are about to take on the largest empire in the world. Of course the Roman army consists of soldiers, but a Muslim army, No way!

The author's notorious false claim that non-Muslims lived under Muslim rule in subjugating conditions, is proven even more false by the author's previous statement. Even according to his claim, a second-class citizen is still a citizen, is still alive and safe, otherwise there would be no second-class citizens! How is it then an issue of "safety" or "no safety" to those who made such a "choice"?!
And since I am getting tired of refuting the absolute falsehood of the author's narrative, let me ask the question: what did some of the world's most prominent thinkers say about the subject?

"But we haven't heard - under Islamic rule - about any attempt to force non-Muslim communities to accept Islam, or about any organized oppression to eradicate the Christian faith. If the Muslim Caliphs had chosen any of the above two plans they would have swept Christianity with the same ease that Ferdinand and Isabella swept the Islamic faith out of Spain, that which Louis XIV had made the protestant faith followers punishable in France, or the same ease that Jews were exiled out of England for 350 years"
John Taylor Caroline (1753-1824) the American political Philosopher (Republican Jeffersonian)

"The eastern churches in Asia were already separated from the rest of the Christian world which was not to support them in any way considering them heretics of the religion. Therefore the sheer existence of theses churches today is in itself a strong evidence of the overall tolerance of Islamic governments towards them"
Sir Thomas Walker Arnold, the most prominent Orientalist in history

The invitation to Islam as we have mentioned earlier was one of three options, you accept Islam and you'd have every right Muslims have, or keep your religion, do not participate in the Muslim army that defends your home, but pay your due tax (Jizyah) like Muslims pay

(Zakah), or fight in the - bound to erupt any way - battle, man-to-man, face-to-face.

The third option however, in that specific case with the Romans was an apparent peril to the Muslims themselves. The Muslims were surely to be annihilated, in comparison to the gigantic Roman Army and its available resources. But to the last Prophet of Islam, and to his believers, inviting to the path of God was about fulfilling your duty to your Creator, no matter what the sacrifice was.

It was never about how big or how small the army they faced.

Another major factor is that all these battles with the Romans were about lands occupied by the European Romans, and not against the natives of these Asian or African lands.

How long the Romans occupied and oppressed the locals had nothing to do with the fact that these territories were not Roman lands.

I also want to draw the reader's attention to the fact that Muhammad (PBUH) was over 60 years of age then, and had been fighting almost all the time with unbelievable odds against him: odds that any brave man would have not dared to take on.

This fact in itself answers the earlier claim of Mr. Spencer about the pleasures that God afforded His Prophet. At that moment, Muhammad (PBUH) was drawing the attention, and was about to face the danger of taking on the largest empire in the world and its army!

On page 153, the author brings one of the famous quotations of Prophet Muhammad (PBUH), which showed one of the visions and miracles of the Prophet. In it, the Prophet predicted the fall of the two major world powers at the time, the Romans and the Persians.

A quotation, of an illiterate man with barely an army of 15 thousand predicted the fall of the two major powers that literally controlled the rest of the world and its armies.

The quotation, like the entire Prophet's, comes true in perfect detail. Do they comment about that? Do they ask themselves how is this possible for him to tell the future, and how could it have happened?

Even with some minimum objectivity, did they ask themselves; is there a possibility that this man is truly the last Prophet of God, after all his unparalleled achievements, predictions, and miracles since the day he was revealed as the last Prophet of God?!

It always amazes me, how much and how many times that Islam-bashers themselves, bring to their readers the proofs of the Prophet-hood and the divine protection of God to his Prophet Muhammad (PBUH), yet they don't believe! In the Holy Quran:

"And they said our hearts are sealed, but Allah had cursed them for their infidelity that they rarely believe"
Holy Quran, Surat (Al Baqara) Ch (2) Verse (88)

وَقَالُوا قُلُوبُنَا غُلْفٌ ۚ بَل لَّعَنَهُمُ اللَّهُ بِكُفْرِهِمْ فَقَلِيلًا مَا يُؤْمِنُونَ (88)

The author further ignores the religious duties of the Prophet, and the obligations given to him by God to invite to His path, and conjures this ultimate duty into a town hall meeting resolution.
On page 153 he wrote:
"The Prophet of Islam codifies this expansionist imperative as one of the duties of his new community."

The author then brings one of his famous misleading and erroneous translations, which is the verse in the Holy Quran that says
(our translation):

"Fight those who do not believe in God or the Last Day, do not forbid what God and His Messenger had forbidden, nor accept the manners of the religion of the truth amongst those of the people of the Scriptures, till they give the Jizyah with willing submission."
Holy Quran, Surat (Al Tawbah) Ch (9) Verse (29)

قَاتِلُوا الَّذِينَ لَا يُؤْمِنُونَ بِاللَّهِ وَلَا بِالْيَوْمِ الْآخِرِ وَلَا يُحَرِّمُونَ مَا حَرَّمَ اللَّهُ وَرَسُولُهُ وَلَا يَدِينُونَ دِينَ الْحَقِّ مِنَ الَّذِينَ أُوتُوا الْكِتَابَ حَتَّىٰ يُعْطُوا الْجِزْيَةَ عَن يَدٍ وَهُمْ صَاغِرُونَ (29)

I tried to find an excuse for the author, as to how could it be possible that he did not understand the simple verse in his own English translation. And I couldn't find an excuse.

The verse simply obligates the Prophet to collect the due taxes from non-Muslim citizens of the Muslim state, even if they were Christians and Jews (as the people of the scripture).

First, you cannot ignore, unless you intentionally want to mislead your reader, that the verse expresses that the people of the Scripture have a special treatment amongst all non-Muslims, and by that, when the verse mandated that the non-Muslims who have unethical behavior of doing what's forbidden or illegal, pay their taxes, it moved to the specificity of collecting the tax even from Christians and Jews.

What happens to an average fifth-generation all-American who's convicted of cheating the U.S government for taxes? Does the government empower itself with every right to search, arrest, and seize all properties of that person or not? Of course they do.

Does that make him a second class-discriminated and subjugated citizen?!

What would the case be - practically - for a minority who doesn't cheat on taxes but worse, actually, doesn't want to pay any tax at all?!

What the verse does really say in a most abbreviated sentence is simply this: **"People who do not pay taxes should be forced to pay taxes"**!

As a matter of fact, the investigation, and the consequent resignation of the former governor of the state of New York Eliot Spitzer - after an escort-service scandal - was initiated with an excuse by the IRS monitoring some of the NY governor bank transactions!

And when the IRS catches the tax-cheater - in our case evader - do they bring him in jail by providing him with a nice tuxedo, or in shackles? Do they make sure if he is of any significance in society, to be brought in handcuffs out of the location they arrested him, parading him before photographers and media cameras in "willing submission" or not? Of course they do.

Now, what would be the law for non-Muslims who not only do not believe in God to begin with and have the worst of manners as the verse stated, but who also refuse to pay their taxes at all?

Do they let them walk free without paying their fair share of taxes to their society? Or if they were of the people of the Scriptures, should they have an unheard-of privilege of living tax-free in their society?!

Mind you, that, as we explained the rule of the Jizyah before, it was 100 dollars worth per year per the able to fight non-Muslim man. This was a tax that wasn't applied to Rabbis, Priests, women, children, or any old men or women. In today's terms, it is two coffee lattes a month per family!

What's more amazing than the author pretension not to be able to read or understand a simple verse, is his interpretations and conclusions out of the simple English words. An example; where did the author come up with the word or meaning of a constant reminder of "their subordinate position"?!

Where is it in any tax law of any country in the world that tax evaders are not jailed and their properties not seized? Worse, who in his right mind would call that legal punishment, a "discriminatory regulation"?!

In what is known as the "Reddah" wars at the time of Caliph Abu Bakr - the first Caliph after the prophet passing away - the Muslim army had to fight Muslims who actually testified a certification of Islam, when these Muslims refused to pay their tax of the obligated charity "Zakah." They were fought by the Muslim army itself.

Would the same government then let non-Muslims in the same community not pay their proportionate tax obligations?

Is the author suggesting that for the tax-laws to be non-discriminatory, minorities should not pay taxes at all?!

Even when the author brings his translation of the word "Zemmey", he confuses the reader almost to a comedic level. On page 153 he wrote: "The Jews and Christians who agreed to pay the Jizyah were known as dhimmis, which means "protected" or "guilty" people."

The author, with his obviously not so-superb Arabic skills comments that the Arabic word means both "protected" and "guilty"!!

The word "zemmey" comes from the Arabic word "zemmah", which means the "account of" or "in the trust of." So a "Zemmey" is the person whose well-being is trusted with the Muslim state or the Muslims. It is like when I trust my children to my brother where, in that case, he is responsible for them or they are in his "Zemmah".

Our author spends an entire paragraph trying to convince his reader how a Zemmey - in his unique vocabulary - somehow means "guilty"!
Did the Arabs or the Muslims ever say in their language that Zemmey means "Guilty"? Never! In that paragraph, the author conjures up justifications that neither have basis in the Arabic language, or even in reality. He further tries to say that Zemmeys are only Christians and Jews, and not pagans! This is not true.
Zemmeys are any non-Muslims who live in a Muslim land, so all Christians and Jews are Zemmeys, but not all Zemmeys are Christians and Jews. The author then explains his made-up meaning of the word Zemmey - a new invention in the Arabic language - and justifies that they are guilty because they did not believe in God or his Prophet. Which is an imagination of the author as linguistically fictitious as - and I am serious here - claiming that the word Zemmeys, also means "Ice Cream".

It is worth mentioning here that in Islamic law there is no such a word that could mean "minority". Laws are applied exactly the same upon all people whether they are one of a kind or the entire majority of the land. An example is what we have mentioned in the event of the stolen shield of Ali Ibn Abi Taleb.

The author then refers to verse 33 in the same chapter "Al-Tawbah" without daring to bring the translation of the verse itself! He wrote:
"One Muslim jurist explained that the Caliph must "make Jihad against those who resist Islam""

*A question arises as to why not quote what the verse - selected by the author himself - is stating regarding the claim at hand instead of quoting that one unique Muslim jurist that doesn't have a name?
The verse says (our translation):

"It is He who has sent His messenger with guidance and the religion of truth to proclaim it over all man-made religions, even if the infidels detested it."
Holy Quran, Surat (Al Tawbah) Ch (9) Verse (33)

هُوَ الَّذِي أَرْسَلَ رَسُولَهُ بِالْهُدَىٰ وَدِينِ الْحَقِّ لِيُظْهِرَهُ عَلَى الدِّينِ كُلِّهِ وَلَوْ كَرِهَ الْمُشْرِكُونَ (33)

Why didn't the author bring the translation of the verse this time? Is it because it speaks not only just of the infidels, but also about peacefully proclaiming the true religion of God over all man-made religions? The author goes back and proves himself wrong again just a page ago, when he admits that Zemmeys were not just the Christians and Jews as he claimed. On page 154 he wrote:
"Muhammad also extended the Dhimma to Zoroastrians, a Persian religious sect."

*Even though Muhammad (PBUH) did not extend it, for that was the original rule; that all non-Muslims were Zemmeys.
Evidenced by the fact that one of the Muslim leaders of a territory as per the story that the author himself brought, asked about the Zemmey rule where he had Jews and Zoroastrians in his domain. That could not have been an indication of a rule that Jews and Christians were the only Zemmeys, otherwise he would have not asked. When the Prophet told

him, the Prophet was informing him of the rule itself, which is that all non-Muslims are Zemmeys.

And as if we did not have enough weird conclusions of the author in the past couple of pages, he shoots another pink elephant, flying high. The author claims that Prophet Muhammad (PBUH), in his writing to the Zoroastrians indicated, on page 154 that:
"The non-Muslim is unclean"!!

*How and where did the author come up with that conclusion? The author tells us because the Prophet "told them that Muslims would not eat meat that they had slaughtered."

When conservative Jews eat only kosher meat - Kosher meat is also Halal for the Muslims to eat - that is slaughtered according to a certain religious code, is that then sending the rest of the world a message that they're all unclean?
Even when an atheist American refuses to eat any regular supermarket beef, because, for example, he only eats organic beef, do the rest of us then need to take a shower?!

"The Tabuk raid"

The author insults the intelligence of his readers when he starts the paragraph with a statement that is presented like a given fact. The only fact related to his statement is that it is not true.

On page 154, the author wrote:
"After commanding his followers to make war against Christians, Muhammad resolved to set an example for his followers. In 631, he ordered the Muslims to begin preparations for a raid on Tabuk, then a part of the Byzantine Empire."

*Needless to say, the author and all Muslim-haters amongst orientalists could never come up with just one verse in the Holy Quran, or one correct Hadeeth of the Prophet that even as little as hints that either Allah or his Prophet had ever commanded the Muslims to wage a war against Christians because they were Christians. The author implied as if Muhammad (PBUH) had just decided to expand for the sake of expansion, and that it just happened that the Prophet decided to start with Tabuk. Yet, just in the following page, on page 155, the author himself admits the real reason why the Prophet wanted to attack Tabuk!

The author wrote:

"They found that the Byzantine troops had withdrawn rather than engage them." Pg. 155

So, there were troops at Tabuk that were ready to engage the Muslims. The Prophet prepared his army and decides tactically to attack them first, because it was then a looming danger for him and the Muslims. The fact that the Byzantine army that was to attack the Muslims from Tabuk, was of the majority of the Christian faith, had absolutely nothing to do with either the fact that they were an army that was about to attack the Muslims, or with the Prophet's reaction to that threat as an army leader defending his people.

Even though there was no battle, the author insisted on coloring the event with a materialistic goal he wanted to paint the Prophet of God with, regardless of the fact; which is obligating the residence of the area that has then become under Islamic rule, to pay their due tax to the government that was responsible for them.

On page 155 the author wrote:

"But the trip was not for naught: Muhammad accepted the submission of several of the area leaders, who agreed to pay the Jizyah and submit to the protection of the Muslims."

*Did we say enough times that "Islam" means "submission" to God and to no one else!

One of the interesting aspects of the author's narrative is that it is totally disconnected from not only reality in general, but mostly from the world realities of the seventh century itself!

The author will later admit the facts about the Jizyah that the Zemmeys were obligated to pay to the Muslim government, which, as we have mentioned before, was only one dinar!

Such tax is equivalent to about 100 of 2010 dollars, and that was due annually! Yet, the author makes the non-Muslims look like they were being taken advantage of, as if they never paid taxes to their oppressors or leaders before in their life, whether they were ruled by Romans, Persians, or Pagans in general!

Reality of the real world at the time was that the same Roman Empire, when occupied Egypt, had imposed 14 different taxes on the average Egyptian, which I assure you were more than one Dinar per year, and if the poor Egyptian didn't pay, the outcome he was to suffer would have been a totally different story!

Did the Roman Empire occupy the East for almost ten centuries because they wanted to travel from Europe to the East and donate gold to the local Arabs personally? Or so did the Persians?

As a matter of fact, during the 1400 years of Islamic History, the conditions of the Muslim states went in the normal historical cycles of strength and weakness, where major parts of the Muslim states were under constant attack from outside forces and, sometimes, were occupied for centuries, by non-Muslims. But the amazing factor that objective historians would attribute the huge populations of these areas keeping their Islamic faith at all times is the fairness, justice, and equality of Islamic law when it was applied upon them.

Here is another testimony:

"In their early years the Arabs never oppressed anyone for their religion and didn't push anyone to convert to their religion, therefore Semite Christians enjoyed freedoms after the early expansions of Islam that they never enjoyed for generations"
Leon Catani (1869-1926) The Italian prince and orientalist

A major example is the incident of Ukaider Ibn Abdel Malik, which demonstrates the relentless charade of forcing Islamic history into the preset "crazy Jihadist warrior" mold of Mr. Spencer.

He was a Christian ruler of an area called Daumat Al Jandal. The Prophet sent a faction of 420 soldiers led by Khalid Ibn Al Waleed to fold that area – ruled by the Romans at the time - into the control of the Muslim state. The Prophet told Khalid about the leader of that area:

"You will find him hunting for cattle"
(Prophet Muhammad (PBUH))
Narrator: Khalid Ibn Alwaleed. **Reference** *Sunan al bayhaqi,* **Number:** *187/9.*
Degree: Correct

Before the army had reached the fort of the area, Ukaider, their leader, awaiting the arrival of the Muslim troops, was tempted by wild cattle scratching the door of the fort with its horns, so he left his fort to hunt the cattle with his entourage including his brother Hassan. The two sides met and even though the Muslims outnumbered the entourage, Hassan challenged the Muslims and continued fighting to his death. Ukaider was brought to the Prophet where he agreed to keep his religion and pay his Jizyah as a citizen in the Muslim state while keeping his position as the leader amongst his people.
The Author claims on page 155 that:
"Jihad warriors led by the fierce Khalid Ibn Al Waleed captured him while he was hunting cattle: Ukaider's brother was killed in the Melee"

Please notice the key words that the author plants falsely in the story like - you guessed it!
"Jihad warriors" and "captured". The notion is that the rich Ukaider with his golden robe was "captured" by the wild warriors where his brother was killed in cold blood.
First of all, Ukaider was in his fort because the Muslims were on their way imminently.
Secondly, the entourage was fully armed, for definitely they weren't hunting cattle with just harsh words!
Hassan, Ukaider's brother made the decision that his brother refused to make, which was to fight the Muslims who vastly outnumbered them.
What was the Muslim soldier whom Hassan engaged to do, other than

295

engage him? But then what was the final outcome?

Ukaider was brought to Muhammad (PBUH) where he accepted the rule of the Muslims, no one forced him to change his religion, and agreed to paying the Jizyah which was much less that what the Romans imposed upon Daumat Al Jandal, occupied earlier not by the locals, or by Ukaider fighters, but by the Roman army.

The author then claims that verse 30 in Chapter 9 in the Holy Quran is directly related to the battle of Tabuk, which is not true; evidenced by the fact that in the author's claim the verse was among the harshest toward Jews and Christians!

On Page 155 he wrote:

"Revelations Muhammad received, referring to the Tabuk raid were among the harshest toward Jews and Christians than any that he had ever received before. They asserted that Jews called Ezra son of God, just as Christians called Christ Son of God".

Why is the glaring truth till today and stated by God, harsh?!

Does the majority of Christians believe that Jesus is son of God, or it is just a harsh and false allegation fabricated by the rest of the world?! And so was the claim of some of the Jews about Ezra. What is the meaning of the word "harshest" in Mr. Spencer's dictionary?

The Jews in addition, were not any part of the Roman army to be considered, not to mention that the verse speaks broadly about thousands of year's worth of violations amongst some of the Jews and 600 years of that amongst some of the Christians.

In the Holy Quran (our translation):

"Jews called Uzayr a son of Allah and Christians called Christ the son of Allah. That it is a saying with their mouths by which they imitate what the disbelievers of old used to say. Allah will battle them for how they were deluded away from the truth."

Holy Quran, Surat (Al Tawbah) (The Repentance) Ch (9) Verse (30)

Please note that in Islamic law, "Allah will battle them" means that Allah will battle them! Meaning that this is not a worldly order to Muslims to do it for God, for God doesn't need anyone's help, to say the least.

The author then brings the famous verses (31-32), where Allah had promised severe torture to those amongst the Jews and Christians who worshiped their Rabbis, Priests, or Saints.

And as we said before, the criticism that Allah specified to some of the Christians and some of the Jews was because they were blessed with true Prophets of God, with true scriptures of the word of God, and yet some of their leaders went astray to associate their own status and other humans with that of God Himself, taking their followers astray with them. Uday Ibn Hatem Altaeiy was a former Christian who heard the Prophet recites verse 31:

"They took their Rabbis and Priests as gods against Allah."
Holy Quran, Surat (Al Tawbah) (The Repentance) Ch (9) Verse (31)

اتَّخَذُوا أَحْبَارَهُمْ وَرُهْبَانَهُمْ أَرْبَابًا مِنْ دُونِ اللَّهِ وَالْمَسِيحَ ابْنَ مَرْيَمَ وَمَا أُمِرُوا إِلَّا لِيَعْبُدُوا إِلَٰهًا وَاحِدًا ۖ لَا إِلَٰهَ إِلَّا هُوَ ۚ سُبْحَانَهُ عَمَّا يُشْرِكُونَ (31)

Ibn Altaeiy wondered as a former Christian and asked the Prophet, "Oh Prophet of Allah, they were not worshipping them." ..Meaning that, as a former Christian, he did not see Christians bowing and worshipping the Priests. The Prophet replied, saying:

"No, but they made what was allowed by God forbidden, and allowed what was forbidden by God, and they (their followers) **still followed them, and that's their followers worshipping them."**
(Prophet Muhammad (PBUH))
Narrator: Addey Ibn Hatem Altayee. Reference: Saheeh Al Tarmazy, Number: 3095. Degree: Good

The meaning here is that one's practcal deity is whomever he follows and obeys in reality, against God's orders that were sent with His true Prophets.

The constant aspect of the narratives of Mr. Spencer, in which the author portrays a specific prejudice against Christians and Jews whether by Prophet Muhammad (PBUH) or even by God Himself, is as we explained several times so far, not only untrue, but actually the opposite of the truth. Jews and Christians, throughout the entire Holy Quran, are called by the noble name "people of the Scriptures".

The specific difference between some of the people of the Scriptures and others can be seen clearly in the Holy Quran, in Surat Al-Saff:

"Oh, you who believe, Be supporters of the Cause of Allah as said 'Eeesa (Jesus), son of Maryam to the disciples: "Who are my supporters in the Cause of Allah?" The disciples said: "We are Allah's supporters" Then a group of the sons of Israel believed and a group disbelieved. So We gave power to those who believed against their enemies, and they became the victorious "
Holy Quran, Surat (Al Saff) (The Row) Ch (61) Verse (14)

يَا أَيُّهَا الَّذِينَ آمَنُوا كُونُوا أَنْصَارَ اللَّهِ كَمَا قَالَ عِيسَى ابْنُ مَرْيَمَ لِلْحَوَارِيِّينَ مَنْ أَنْصَارِي إِلَى اللَّهِ ۖ قَالَ الْحَوَارِيُّونَ نَحْنُ أَنْصَارُ اللَّهِ ۖ فَآمَنَتْ طَائِفَةٌ مِنْ بَنِي إِسْرَائِيلَ وَكَفَرَتْ طَائِفَةٌ ۖ فَأَيَّدْنَا الَّذِينَ آمَنُوا عَلَىٰ عَدُوِّهِمْ فَأَصْبَحُوا ظَاهِرِينَ (14)

There were Jews who believed in the Prophets of God, and there were Jews that fought the Prophets of God.

The ancient conflict in Christianity itself between Christians following the true teachings of Jesus (PBUH) as a Prophet of God, and who believed in the Oneness of God, represented by the eastern priest Arius against the Pauline Christianity followers, where Jesus was considered the son of God and God - even though there is not one verse in today's any Bible where Jesus (PBUH) says "worship me" - represented by the followers of the eastern priest Athanasius. Both sides

accused the other side of blasphemy. In the previous verse of the Holy Quran, God Himself affirms that one of the factions is correct!
In The Holy Quran:

"...and you will find the nearest in love to the believers (Muslims) those who say: "We are Christians." That is because amongst them are priests and monks, and they are not proud.
And when they listen to what has been sent down to the Messenger (Muhammad (PBUH)) you see their eyes overflowing with tears because of the truth they have recognized. They say: "Our Lord! We believe; so write us down among the witnesses"
Holy Quran, Surat (Al Maeda) (The Table) Ch (5) Verse (82-83)

۞ وَلَتَجِدَنَّ أَقْرَبَهُمْ مَوَدَّةً لِلَّذِينَ آمَنُوا الَّذِينَ قَالُوا إِنَّا نَصَارَىٰ ۚ ذَٰلِكَ بِأَنَّ مِنْهُمْ قِسِّيسِينَ وَرُهْبَانًا وَأَنَّهُمْ لَا يَسْتَكْبِرُونَ (82)
وَإِذَا سَمِعُوا مَا أُنْزِلَ إِلَى الرَّسُولِ تَرَىٰ أَعْيُنَهُمْ تَفِيضُ مِنَ الدَّمْعِ مِمَّا عَرَفُوا مِنَ الْحَقِّ ۖ يَقُولُونَ رَبَّنَا آمَنَّا فَاكْتُبْنَا مَعَ الشَّاهِدِينَ (38)

Also, in the Holy Quran, Allah brings the Muslims a comparison that shows that fine practical manners are not monopolized by Muslims:

"Among the people of the Scripture is he who, if entrusted with a Qintar (a heap of wealth), will readily pay it back; and among them there is he who, if entrusted with a single coin, will not repay it unless you constantly stand demanding"
Holy Quran, Surat (Ale Omran) Ch (3) Verse (75)

وَمِنْ أَهْلِ الْكِتَابِ مَنْ إِنْ تَأْمَنْهُ بِقِنْطَارٍ يُؤَدِّهِ إِلَيْكَ وَمِنْهُمْ مَنْ إِنْ تَأْمَنْهُ بِدِينَارٍ لَا يُؤَدِّهِ إِلَيْكَ إِلَّا مَا دُمْتَ عَلَيْهِ قَائِمًا ۗ (75)

On page 156, the author repeats his statements that have nothing to do with the fact or even the subject at hand. He wrote:
"Muhammad's wrath would also extend to Muslims who ignored Allah's Messenger."

*Where is that wrath and where did the author bring it from? He talks about the famous incident where the Prophet ordered a mosque to be destroyed and burned; why? A verse was revealed to the Prophet about the plot that Mosque was built for by the Hypocrites, in addition to several correct quotations of the Prophet that narrated the incident in details. Even the identity of the hypocrites was stated by the name.

Why all these impeccable references weren't mentioned by Mr. Spencer and only the speculation of Mr. Spencer's "wraths", fury and imaginations?

The incident was when hypocrites, on their own, built a mosque where they gathered in to plot against the Muslims, mock and curse Islam and the Prophet. The Prophet didn't know of their actions to the limit that he promised them to lead prayers in their mosque, only just when he was about to go there to pray, a verse was revealed to him by God exposing the hypocrites. In the Holy Quran:

"And as for those who put up a mosque by way of harm and disbelief and to disunite the believers, and as an outpost for those who battled against Allah and His Messenger before, they will indeed swear that their intention is nothing but good. Allah bears witness that they are certainly liars"
Holy Quran, Surat (Al Tawbah) Ch (9) Verse (107)

وَالَّذِينَ اتَّخَذُوا مَسْجِدًا ضِرَارًا وَكُفْرًا وَتَفْرِيقًا بَيْنَ الْمُؤْمِنِينَ وَإِرْصَادًا لِمَنْ حَارَبَ اللَّهَ وَرَسُولَهُ مِنْ قَبْلُ ۚ وَلَيَحْلِفُنَّ إِنْ أَرَدْنَا إِلَّا الْحُسْنَىٰ ۖ وَاللَّهُ يَشْهَدُ إِنَّهُمْ لَكَاذِبُونَ (107)

Should the Prophet of God obey God and bring down a place that was built upon hypocrisy and damaging God's religion? Of course yes. Is it then the "wrath of Muhammad" or is it God himself exposing the hypocrites?

The author then adds the verses in Surat Al-Tawbah, where Allah criticizes the defectors of the Muslim army, which we covered earlier and we will not waste the reader's time explaining - again - as to how every country in the world treats their army defectors.

300

Then on page 157, the author, brings a claim of which he did not find a source to support, even amongst his worthless sources. He wrote: "Though Muhammad may not have needed the help, Jihad for the sake of Allah (Jihad fi-sabil Allah which denotes in Islamic theology armed struggle to establish the hegemony of the Islamic social order) is the best deed a Muslim can perform Quran 9:41".

*What is worse than the fact that this hegemony statement is totally fabricated and nonexistent in the entire Holy Quran and in the Sunnah of the Prophet, is that the transliteration the author quoted means literally "Jihad for the sake of Allah" where did the hegemony come from? My guess is from where all the blue elephants flys high every time!

The verse the author claimed proves that statement is verse 9:41!! The author only added its reference at the end of the paragraph and never quoted it!! I wonder why?

How possible is it that a claim as crucial to the validity of the author's entire narrative, which is that Jihad of the Muslims is to dominate the world under an Islamic social order, was not worth it for the author to bring the verse he claimed proved it?!

The answer is simple, because the verse that the author brought to us, which is verse 9:41, **has no relation to such claim.**
In the Holy Quran (our translation):

"Go forth, whether lightly or heavily-equipped, and strive with your monies and yourselves for the sake of Allah. That is better for you, if you knew."
Holy Quran, Surat (Al Tawbah) Ch (9) Verse (41)

انْفِرُوا خِفَافًا وَثِقَالًا وَجَاهِدُوا بِأَمْوَالِكُمْ وَأَنْفُسِكُمْ فِي سَبِيلِ اللَّهِ ۚ ذَٰلِكُمْ خَيْرٌ لَكُمْ إِنْ كُنْتُمْ تَعْلَمُونَ

(41)

Where is the mention of hegemony of the Islamic social order over the world, in verse 41 or anywhere in the entire Holy Quran?!!

From creating new meanings of Arabic words like "zemmey" to be meaning "guilty", now the author is making up verses out of his imagination to support his laughable claims!

The author, then follows by a weak hadeeth in which the Prophet stated that there is no deed a Muslim can do that can equal the reward of Jihad.

In the well-known "correct" Hadeeth of the Prophet, he was asked about the best deed that a Muslim can do in the sight of Allah. Jihad did not even make the first two! The Prophet replied:

"Establishing prayers on time, doing well by parents, and then striving for the sake of Allah."
(Prophet Muhammad (PBUH))
Narrator: Abdullah Ibn Masoud. Reference: Saheeh Al Bukhary, Number: 7534. Degree: Correct

In our preface of the book, we brought examples of other deeds that equal joining the army and fighting for the sake of God; only they are correct quotations of the Prophet, and not weak quotations, fabricated or from the imagination of Mr. Spencer.

"The sponsor of a widow or a needy person, is like the one striving for the sake of God, or Praying at night, and fasting at day"
(Prophet Muhammad (PBUH))
*Narrator: Abou Hurayra. **Reference**: Saheeh Al Bukhary, **Number**: 5353. **Degree**: Correct.*

When a young man wanted to join the Muslim army, the Prophet asked him if his mother was alive, when the young man said yes, the Prophet ordered him:

"Go and keep her company, for paradise is underneath her feet" i.e. serving his mother supersedes joining the army.
(Prophet Muhammad (PBUH))
*Narrator: Moawea Ibn Jahema Alsalmy. **Reference**: Al Albany of Saheeh Alnasaye, **Number**: 3104. **Degree**: Correct/Good.*

On page 157, the author refers to verse 43 in Surat Al-Tawba (9:43), the author wrote:

"He told Muhammad that true Muslims did not hesitate to wage jihad, even to the point of risking their property and their very lives."

By now, the pattern of excessively misleading verse translations is being coupled with the fact that such verses that have no relation to his subject are the ones that the author would not quote or even show his erroneous translations for!

In the Holy Quran, verse 9:43 says (our translation):

"Allah gave you grace, why did you grant them exemption till those who told the truth were seen by you and you have learned the liars?"
Holy Quran, Surat (Al Tawbah) Ch (9) Verse (43)

عَفَا اللَّهُ عَنْكَ لِمَ أَذِنْتَ لَهُمْ حَتَّىٰ يَتَبَيَّنَ لَكَ الَّذِينَ صَدَقُوا وَتَعْلَمَ الْكَاذِبِينَ (43)

Allah indicates to the Prophet that he pardoned too early those who stayed behind and didn't participate in battle before Allah had brought the truthful forward so the liars of those who were pardoned were known to the Prophet.

As a clear conclusion, the verse speaks of the leniency and the forgiveness of the Prophet towards hypocrites who stayed behind when the battle was about to start. Allah is telling us that the Prophet should have waited and not given his forgiveness till the truth of the liars was completely revealed. The verse talked about hypocrites who brought in false excuses so they don't join their nation's army that was heading to battle. In that specific battle, as the author himself admitted on page 155, the Roman army, and by that I mean the army of the most powerful empire of the world, camped at Tabuk with the evident intention of attacking the Muslims. If the Muslim army would not go to fight to defend themselves against the most formidable of enemies, what would the army then be in existence for to begin with?

And what would be the judgment upon those who have seen the army of the most powerful empire in the world about to attack their nation and chose to sit back?

303

Most importantly is the question: where in the verse does it say anything close to "wage jihad"? What is the meaning of the word "wage" used by our creative author, as if it was a Muslim provocation?
What does it mean in comparison to the truth admitted by the author himself that the Roman army was marching and camping outside the frontiers of the Muslim territory?

And if this specific incident does not fit the exact clear definition of striving for the sake of God, "jihad" that we have explained within the Holy Quran and the correct tradition of the Prophet several times already in this book, then what would be the true definition of jihad if it wasn't? Would trying to stand up, and defend your nation against the Romans ever suffice?

Was that "waging" an uncalled for war against the peaceful Romans? Or is it just about emptying truthfulness out of words, and packaging them in, with scary slogans that fit the author's scare crow narrative? The verse has nothing to do with the matter at hand, and no wonder the author did not quote it!

On page 158, the author wrote commenting on his translation of verses 73 and 74 of Surat Al-Tawba (Chapter 9):
"this "striving hard" was, in the context of Muhammad's circumstances, unmistakably a military command - particularly in light of the fact that Allah was guaranteeing paradise to those who would "fight in the way of Allah and shall slay and be slain" (Holy Quran 9:111)".

*The author drags us into having to explain rudimentary concepts about basic formations of societies! What the armies of every nation on the face of the planet are in existence for today?

Is it draining national budgets by the tunes of hundreds of billions of dollars? Or is it to defend not only against the nation's enemies, but in addition, protect national interests, whatever that may be, according to the liking of the politicians at the time? Our Pentagon for example has an annual budget that is pushing 600 billion dollars a year, I wonder why!!

Even as a universal concept, what is an enemy of any nation? I assure you that the definition at any given time does differ greatly. You will not even be able to put one simple line that you can claim fulfill that description to any nation in the world.

The definition of an enemy to be fought at any cost for the Muslim nation, however, is those who are enemies of Allah, Creator of mankind, heavens and earth. It is as simple as that.
That enemy of Allah is not a loose expression that would fit whomever the politician du jour would like it to be. The clear-cut definition in Islamic law is that an enemy of Allah is not an enemy who does not believe in Allah. Those, Allah will punish in this life and on Judgment Day when they stand before Him, and in a way such punishment no man-made punishment or war can equate. An enemy of Allah that Muslims should oppose is an <u>enemy to mankind</u>. Those who oppress the rights of the innocent, hurt the righteous, spread corruption and devastation on Earth, and take away mankind's God-given rights that are stated clearly in Islamic Law.

Simply put, according to Islamic law, you take violent actions against the justice that God had given mankind or oppress people; you are fought with every means possible as an enemy of God Himself. Having said all that, and as per the author's emphasis on the loose translation: what difference, "striving hard", medium, or extra-large against such an enemy is relevant, when it comes to that?
In the Holy Quran:

"Allah does not forbid you to deal justly and kindly with those who did not fight you for your religion and did not drive you out of your homes. Verily, Allah loves those who deal justly" [8]
"It is only in regards to those who fought you for your religion, have driven you out of your homes, and helped to drive you out, that Allah forbids you to befriend them. And whoever will befriend them, then those are the oppressors" [9]
Holy Quran, Surat (Al Mumtahina) Ch. (60), verses (8- 9)

لَا يَنْهَاكُمُ اللَّهُ عَنِ الَّذِينَ لَمْ يُقَاتِلُوكُمْ فِي الدِّينِ وَلَمْ يُخْرِجُوكُم مِّن دِيَارِكُمْ أَن تَبَرُّوهُمْ وَتُقْسِطُوا إِلَيْهِمْ ۚ إِنَّ اللَّهَ يُحِبُّ الْمُقْسِطِينَ (8

إِنَّمَا يَنْهَاكُمُ اللَّهُ عَنِ الَّذِينَ قَاتَلُوكُمْ فِي الدِّينِ وَأَخْرَجُوكُم مِّن دِيَارِكُمْ وَظَاهَرُوا عَلَىٰ إِخْرَاجِكُمْ أَن تَوَلَّوْهُمْ ۚ وَمَن يَتَوَلَّهُمْ فَأُولَٰئِكَ هُمُ الظَّالِمُونَ (9

In the same paragraph on page 158, the author brings one of the quotations of the Prophet that are very conveniently misinterpreted by Islam-bashers, and I would have been surprised if the author did not bring it. The famous quotation in Saheeh Al-Bukhari, where the Prophet had said:

"I was ordered to fight people till they testify that there's no God but Allah and that Muhammad is His Messenger, so if they said it, then they have forbade me their monies and blood, except by which is justified by the law. And their accounts are settled by Allah."
(Prophet Muhammad (PBUH))
Narrator: Abu Hurayrah. Reference: Saheeh Al Bukhary, Number: 2946.
Degree: Correct

The quotation of the Prophet is clearly about that if the conditions of war force the Prophet to fight, then he will fight till those who fought him are defeated or till they accept Islam - go back to the three offers that Muslims give before battle - the trick that is played in the English translation is the generalization of the word "people". As if Prophet Muhammad (PBUH) is commanded by God to fight every single non-Muslim till either they die or become Muslim!! Not to mention omitting the third possibility that the Muslims themselves are defeated or killed!

Before we show the correct translation of the exact Arabic word, I would like to ask the reader a very simple question: Did the Prophet do that in reality? Did the Prophet fight every single person that was not a Muslim till he killed them or till they converted?!! Had the Muslims even done that throughout history?
Even the author himself, with his "subjugating" and "second-class citizen" claims about non-Muslims in Muslim societies, cannot deny that

306

these claims themselves are an absolute proof that Muslims were not commanded to kill non-Muslims if they didn't accept Islam. Otherwise, all these supposedly second-class citizens would have been killed, and would have not existed at all to begin with! Here is another testimony:

"In Italy, many regions expressed to their oppressing rulers their hearty welcome to a Turkish (Muslim) invasion like the Balkan Christians did"
Maxime Rodinson; Historian (1915- 2004)

Why did the Muslims throughout history constantly enjoy that exceptional, impeccable record of tolerating minorities of all kinds? Or is it that the author's conclusion and translation are total fabrications?

The literal translation of the critical sentence of the quotation is "to fight the people". "The people" - in Arabic - here does not mean at all "all mankind" or "all people". It is like, for example, when you say to a teacher, "the students are here". That does not mean that every student on the face of the planet had come to attend that teacher's class! "The" in the Arabic language here is used to identify the group of students that both the speaker and the teacher know. A clear description of what the phrase "to fight the people" means "to fight the people I will fight." I.e. this referred to the pagans and the infidels that will fight the Prophet imminently and regardless. Even the claimed crazy "jihad warriors" that the author is relentless in being their sincere publicist; do not say "we will fight everyone on the face of the planet till we kill them or till they become Muslim"!! Only Mr. Spencer is claiming that!

"Collecting the jizya"

Even though we have discussed the Jizyah / Zemmey tax issue in details, but we will comment on the whole issue from the author's narrative. Before we start, I want to bring to the reader's attention that Mr. Spencer at this point, when we're about to get into the last chapter of his book, never called a member of the Muslim army by the name he would have called any member of any other army in the world, which is "soldier". In the eyes of the author, Muslims cannot be soldiers in their

307

own army, but only and always "jihad warriors"! Even when he described Prophet Muhammad (PBUH) on page 158 as "Muhammad was now the undisputed master of Arabia.", where the Muslim army was the dominant army in the entire Arab Peninsula, it's still not an army of soldiers, but an army of whatever his "jihad warriors" means.

On page 158, another fabrication, where the author again and again brings a fabrication that the Prophet told a messenger from a tribe who just accepted Islam, that if they didn't accept Islam he would have "thrown your heads beneath your feet."

*The reader by now knows that that never happened, that the options were accept Islam, keep your religion with paying your share of tax, or war, which as we have displayed earlier many times in the book and what Mr. Spencer admitted himself! The question to Mr. Spencer here is; what happened to digging for buried treasures, subjugating non-Muslims and calming the crazed Jihad-warriors-pirates claims of his? What did change the rules of Islam alongside his usual fictitious claims this time? Why to the Muslims that people accepting Islam is better than all the money in the world, all of a sudden this time? May be it is a fabrication in keeping with the only rule Mr. Spencer adheres to in his book?!!

On page 159, the same author who on just the last page said: "The inverse is also true: if they do not become Muslims, their blood and riches are not guaranteed any protection from the Muslims.", is now stating just one page later, that the Muslim army was instructed that if Christians and Jews refused to accept Islam, ", they were "not to be turned" from their religions."!!

With that clear admission of the fact by the author after the splitting headache that we had throughout his book that Muslims would wage war against you to become a Muslim or they would kill you, would the author change his narrative then?! Read on!

308

The author then makes the claim that the Jizyah was imposed upon every non-Muslim individual. As we have stated before, Jizyah in Islamic law is imposed only on men who are able to carry a weapon and fight. No women, children, old men or women, rabbis or priests are subject to pay Jizyah. The author however stated correctly the value of that huge, whopping, overwhelming amount the Jizyah tax was, which in his words was "subjugating" to non-Muslims! On page 158, the author imposes the Jizyah - on his own - upon every non-Muslim- he wrote:
"Must pay the poll tax for every adult, male or female, free or slave, one full dinar."

*The one full dinar equates less than a hundred dollars today and that's per year, per the able to fight man in the family if any!

Then the author brings an issue that is of surprisingly major interest to evangelists and Islam-bashers, which is that no non-Muslim worshipping establishments are allowed in the Arab Peninsula as per God's orders to His Prophet - and not wishes - as the author claimed.

Every religion has its own sanctuary where only that religion is worshipped within that specific area. I don't remember that either Muslims or Jews had ever complained that there are no mosques or Jewish temples in the Vatican, understandably because the Vatican is the sanctuary of Catholicism. And while no Jew or Muslim had ever dictated to the Pope of the Vatican as to how big or small the size of the Vatican borders of that sanctuary should be, it's really puzzling why some are so blind to the fact that the area that houses the holiest places for 1.6 billion Muslims is understandably God's choice of the sanctuary of the religion of Islam!

On page 159, the author comments about the Prophet of God's order to make the Arab peninsula the sanctuary of the religion of Islam. He wrote:
"He gave just such an order on his deathbed. Today the kingdom of Saudi Arabia neighbors labors zealously that the Prophet's wishes in this regard are scrupulously honored."

In the following paragraph, the author points to a phenomenon that is unique only to the Muslims! It is that the tax collected by a nation form its citizens is a source of income to that nation!!

On page 159 he wrote:
"The Jizyah tax was so important because, besides raiding, which produced inconsistent results, it was the Muslim's chief source of income."

In commenting again on the Jizyah tax, the author's clear imagination requires our clarification:

1. Non-Muslims can become Muslims, or if they choose not to, should pay the Jizyah tax, yet the author never said a word about the tax a Muslim is obligated to pay! The Zakah tax is two and a half percent of your unspent assets at the end of the year. So, naturally, Muslims paid their due tax to their government, but notice as well that the amount a Muslim should pay in tax is limitless, because the more money that a Muslim would make and the more assets he would gather, the limitless amount of taxes he would pay. Compare that to the fixed low amount of one dinar per able fighter per year, no matter how much assets that non-Muslim has.

2. The smaller number of non-Muslims compared to the overwhelmingly increasing number of people accepting Islam was minimal in the amount of tax raised from non-Muslims versus that obligated charity tax of all Muslims. That brings us to another nugget of wisdom of the author at the end of the paragraph on page 160, where he wrote:
"The onerous tax burdens that Jews and Christians in Muslim domains incurred for the privileges of being allowed to live in relative peace would become the key source of income for the great Islamic empires that carried Muhammad's jihad into Africa, Europe, and Asia."!

Really!!

Please notice the "onerous tax burdens" that the author claims collected from a tribe as a whole was 25% of just their income, not the assets. That "onerous" tax bracket would be a joy if applied to our author's income today, especially when we learn how much he makes in the business of bashing Islam and Muslims. In America today, my guesstimate is that he's closer to the 40% tax bracket. I think he would have done much better with Muhammad!

"The last pilgrimage, the rights of women, and the expulsion of the pagans"

On page 160, the author produces (again) a major mistranslation when the author brought a translation of the famous correct quotation of the Prophet in the last pilgrimage. The author translated the Quotation in the most bizarre but telling way of what his entire narrative against Islam is about. Here is the famous quotation in Arabic for reference:

'' فاتقوا الله في النساء ، فإنكم أخذتموهن بأمانة الله ، واستحللتم فروجهم بكلمه الله

Here is the correct translation (our translation):

"So fear Allah about your women, for you have <u>taken them</u> with the trust of Allah, and your intercourse with them was allowed to you by the word of Allah" (Prophet Muhammad (PBUH))
Narrator: Jaber ibn abdu Allah. Reference: Saheeh Al jamee, Number: 2068. Degree: Correct

What would our truth-seeker translate the word "take" as in Mr. Jones taking Mrs. Jones as a wife? To Mr. Spencer it means taking her as a "prisoner"!!

He wrote:
"Lay injunctions on women kindly, for <u>they are prisoners</u> for you having no control of their persons. You have taken them only as a trust of God, and you have the enjoyment of their persons by the words of God...."

On page 161, and in commenting on Mr. Spencer's misleading translation, the author brings a famous verse that Islam-haters always love to bring, and of course, without the clear context of the example of the behavior of Muhammad (PBUH) himself. The verse stated the steps of how to deal with a wife that is being suspected of wanting to cheat on

311

her husband.

Firstly, give her clear advice, as per the orders of Allah of the rights and obligations between the couple.

Secondly, if the wife would still disobey the orders of Allah that are applicable upon her and her husband just the same, then the husband should abstain from her in the same bed.

Thirdly, if the wife would continue with the same behavior, the verse dictates a psychological light beating that is less than a slap on the wrist, which most of the companions of the Prophet likened to slapping someone lightly with a toothbrush-like piece of branch on the wrist. Not only that "beating" is obviously more of a psychological impact upon the wife than any minimal physical impact might be, but which husband that will wait around till it reaches that stage? That extreme is clearly an absolute last resort of not losing to a final divorce. But does the author quote the people that received the verse, asked how it was applied during the life of the Prophet of God himself? The answer is no, for that does not fit the narrative of the author.

Taking Prophet Muhammad (PBUH) himself as the ultimate example of all Muslims: did our author and his unreliable sources, with all their satanic verses, and fabrications, bring one iota of an attempted fabrication that the Prophet had ever laid one finger or even said one foul word to any of his wives, no matter what the circumstances were? Never. Not to mention that at one point, the Prophet was about to divorce them all for them repeatedly asking him for materialistic things, yet in all circumstances, the Prophet was the kindest person they had ever seen.

Ayesha, the Prophet's wife, described the Prophet:
"He was the most lenient of all people, laughing and smiling."

Had the author mentioned anything about the fact that there is not one account of beating a wife in the entire body of the companions of the prophet? In a quotation of the prophet he expressed how repulsive beating a wife is:

" How is it that one of you may beat his wife in the morning and then have intercourse with her at night?"

On page 161, the author wrote:
"This was in accord with revelations Muhammad had received from Allah concerning women, which included the beating of disobedient wives."

The verse that the author had brought out is another example of misinforming the reader by omitting the facts included in the same verse that does not fit the author's convoluted narrative. The entire first part that shapes the general guideline of the relationship between a husband and a wife is totally omitted by the author without mention. Here is the first part of the verse that the author intentionally omitted from his translation in the Holy Quran (our translation):

"Men are the protectors and maintainers of women, because Allah has made some of them to excel over the others, and because they spend (to support them) from their means"
Holy Quran, Surat (Al Nissaa) (The women) Ch. (4), verses (34)

الرِّجَالُ قَوَّامُونَ عَلَى النِّسَاءِ بِمَا فَضَّلَ اللّهُ بَعْضَهُمْ عَلَىٰ بَعْضٍ وَبِمَا أَنْفَقُوا مِنْ أَمْوَالِهِمْ ۚ (34)

How significant is that in light of presenting Muslims as wife-beaters? The verse mandated men to protect and provide sustenance to their wives as a condition of attending to them. Yet, the truth-seeker on his own omits the words of God. He started his translation on page 161 by saying:
"So good women are the obedient, guarding in secret that which Allah has guarded. . . ."

Here's the correct translation of the entire verse, (our translation) in the Holy Quran:

"Men are the protectors and maintainers of women, because Allah has made some of them to excel over the others, and because they spend (to support them) from their means. Therefore the righteous

313

women are devoutly obedient and guard in the husband's absence what Allah orders them to guard. As to those women on whose part you see ill-conduct, admonish them (first), (next), refuse to share their beds, (and last) beat them (lightly, if it is useful); but if they return to obedience, seek not means against them .Surely, Allah is Ever Most High, Most Great."
Holy Quran, Surat (Al Nissaa) (The women) Ch. (4), verses (34)

الرِّجَالُ قَوَّامُونَ عَلَى النِّسَاءِ بِمَا فَضَّلَ اللَّهُ بَعْضَهُمْ عَلَى بَعْضٍ وَبِمَا أَنْفَقُوا مِنْ أَمْوَالِهِمْ ۚ فَالصَّالِحَاتُ قَانِتَاتٌ حَافِظَاتٌ لِلْغَيْبِ بِمَا حَفِظَ اللَّهُ ۚ وَاللَّاتِي تَخَافُونَ نُشُوزَهُنَّ فَعِظُوهُنَّ وَاهْجُرُوهُنَّ فِي الْمَضَاجِعِ وَاضْرِبُوهُنَّ ۖ فَإِنْ أَطَعْنَكُمْ فَلَا تَبْغُوا عَلَيْهِنَّ سَبِيلًا ۗ إِنَّ اللَّهَ كَانَ عَلِيًّا كَبِيرًا (34)

On page 161, the author makes a shocking contradiction to his own self and his own words, when he comments on Allah's order in Surat Al-Tawba, 9:1-2 to exile all the non-Muslims from the Islamic religion's sanctuary of Arabia. On page 161 he wrote:
"these unbelievers were pagan Arabs, not Jews and Christians, hence here there is no mention of the Jizyah option he had already offered to the latter. For Jews and Christians their choices were conversion, subjugation, or war; for the pagans the choices were only conversion or war."

As we stated before, the Jizyah was applied to every non-Muslim living within the Muslim society. It is laughable that the author claimed that a non-Muslim atheist living in the Muslim society is not asked to pay tax, while the Muslims, the Christians, and the Jews are paying their respective taxes! The issue that the author is discussing here was supposedly putting every non-Muslim out of the sanctuary of Arabia. So how is it - if the author is correct - that for all that time these "unbelievers pagan Arabs" had lived in the Muslim society without paying tax till the order came to exile all non-Muslims out of the Arab Peninsula?!

Did the savage Muslims kill them all because they were non-Muslims, then they came back to life and lived tax-free till they were exiled?!

The whole convoluted logic and mutilation of the fact is again an only resource available for the author to support his crumbling narrative that the Jizyah tax was some kind of prejudice against Jews and Christians, which the same author describes later as a benefit when he claims it was later "extended" to non-Muslims! Even worse, everything Muslim to the author is a cup half-empty and the other half is always filled with poison. On page 161, he wrote:
"Only conversion to Islam would save the lives of the unbelievers and only the hope that they would accept Islam would gain them mercy from the Muslims."

Why would the Muslims, who were a chapter ago pirates and gold-diggers, hope that non-Muslims become Muslims? Isn't it better to fight them, then seize their properties as spoils of war? Why would someone becoming a Muslim and worshipping God be a "hope" for Muslims over his money, his property, and his wealth if he didn't become a Muslim? Is it that their entire struggle is only for the sake of God and His reward, by freeing humanity from the oppressors and the rule of injustice?

An order was made that non-Muslims have four months to take all their property and move to wherever they want, whenever they want, out of the sanctuary of Islam. If after the four months during which a pagan was fully-protected by the Muslims, a non-Muslim stays, then he would be considered a law breaker and would be fought accordingly.

This was not a hidden deceptive rule, but the rule declared to everyone. So if you stayed behind after the four months, the only way you could be exempted from that rule - surprisingly according to the author's logic - is that if that non-Muslim had accepted Islam, and became a Muslim with the same rights of all Muslims living within the sanctuary of Islam! The author himself brought in a part of the verse that mandated that Muslims are ordered to accept the repentance and the conversion of a non-Muslim, even if they doubted his Islam. On page 161, the author brought the part of the verse (his translation):

315

". . . if they repent, and establish regular prayers and practice regular charity, then open the way for them, for Allah is All-Forgiving, Most Merciful." (Holy Quran 9:4-6)

On page 162, the author quotes a Hindu "historian", Sita Ram Goel, where he fabricated a record of abhorring war crimes supposedly committed by the Muslim army in India. On page 162, Mr. Goel lists some of which even our author himself could not fabricate or prove that such claimed abhorring warfare by Mr. Goel is even close to anything in the Holy Quran or the manners of the Prophet. Had Mr. Goel brought any reference - historic, reliable, or otherwise - other than his vivid Muslim-bashing imagination rant, we would have dignified his quote with a comment. But we won't.

"The murder of the poets"

On page 162, the author, again, makes claims about the Prophet's intentions or decisions that the author simply does not know and neither the Prophet nor his companions ever mentioned. He wrote: "Muhammad at this point was determined to wipe out every remnant of opposition to his rule. He set his sights on two poets, Abu Afak and Asma Bint Marwan, who had mocked him and his Prophetic pretensions and their verses."

Maybe the reader is now tired of us asking the truth-seeker, "Where did you get that from?" And who does the author, again, only quote for the two incidents? Again and again, none other than Ibn Is'haq.

"Muhammad's final illness"

On page 164, the author brings a weird irrelevant story about Ayesha having a headache and the Prophet wishing that he outlived her. Not only is the story not true, but to the issue of the death of the Prophet, any headache of Ayesha is totally irrelevant.

It is hard for me to even refute how low the author went in narrating the final hours of the Prophet of God.

The reason the author brought that fabricated story about Ayesha is for him to follow it with this: on page 164, the author used his "time-machine video camera" when he wrote:

"Ayesha responded to this with tart playfulness: "By Allah, I think you want me to die; and if this should happen, you would spend the last part of the day sleeping with one of your wives!" "

How absurdly low is this of the truth-seeker?!

The justice and fairness of the Prophet when he dealt with his wives was a model example for mankind. The Holy Quran is the only Scripture that has actual verses against multiple wives. In the Old Testament, Abraham had three wives, Solomon had hundreds of wives, even in Christendom and till the early 1300s; men having multiple wives was the norm in Europe. Only in the middle of the 20th century and particularly in 1952, the leading Rabbi of Israel, Yehuda Bin Greshom, mandated that Eastern Jews should stop the practice of having multiple wives and keep only one wife. In the Holy Quran:

"And you will not be able to be fair between wives even if you kept at it."

Holy Quran, Surat (Al Nissaa), (The women) Ch. (4), verses (129)

So using the license of multiple wives - up to four - in Islamic Law is an allowed exceptional remedy for exceptional situations with utmost fairness conditions. Prophet Muhammad (PBUH), with a unique license to marry more than four for the reasons that we have stated earlier, was the most fair in treating all his wives. Prophet Muhammad (PBUH) was so ill that when he made his last speech, they had to pour water on his face and he needed to be carried by two men to the mosque where he gave his last speech.

Prophet Muhammad (PBUH) was unconscious and when he gained his consciousness, he was at the house of Ayesha, where he asked for all his wives to be brought in her house to talk to them. When the wives arrived, totally taken by concern and fear, over not only their husband, but the last Prophet of God, they were shocked when the

317

Prophet - barely conscious - asked their permission to allow him to stay in the house of Ayesha during his sickness, for he hadn't the strength to even walk to their houses as he scheduled. During his last moments, and while the Prophet knew that he was dying, all what concerned him was to be fair and not take away the right of another wife upon him to be at her house according to the schedule that he had for them. This right was his wives' and not his, so the last Prophet of God requested their permission.

In his speech, which was the last speech the last Prophet of God would advise all mankind with, the Prophet gave three pieces of advice:

The first: was to always establish and never abandon prayers to God.

The second: was to always treat all women well, saying:
"By Allah, I leave a trust with you to treat women well."

And by women, the Prophet did not mean only the wife, but the mother, the sister, the daughter, as well as the wife.

The third: advice was to not let worldly, materialistic things distract believers so they will waste them and their deeds, like the nations before them that let materialistic things waste them by distracting them from their utmost duty - to worship God.

Let's now re-examine how low the author goes in depicting the last Prophet of God as a sick man, screaming and asking for the next wife's turn!

On page 164, he wrote:
"As his illness progressed, he grew anxious over the fact that he had to move, spending each night in the house of a different wife, as had been his practice ever since he began practicing polygamy. He would cry out anxiously, "Where will I be tomorrow? Where will I be tomorrow?" Finally his other wives allowed him to stay in the home of his favorite wife, Ayesha." Could Mr. Spencer stoop any lower?!

On page 165, the author claims that the Muslims gathered in his room, where the Prophet amazingly asked them to bring something to write on! The author wrote:

"So that I may write to you something, after which you will never go astray." Pg. 165

The fact that Muhammad (PBUH) died illiterate and never read or wrote a word throughout his entire life makes you wonder whom the author thinks reads his books! Not only that Muslims at the time of worrying about the sickness of the Prophet gathered in the mosque where Prophet Muhammad (PBUH) was carried and gave his final speech, but the story of him looking for something to write on, so suddenly, of which the believers would never go astray, a few hours before he was to die, is so laughable to even refute. The only correct quotation by which the words or the meaning of "I want to give you something, after which you will never go astray" is one of the most famous quotations of the Prophet, which he said in the day of the last pilgrimage. And it is amazing in two aspects. The Prophet said:

"I left amongst you two things that which if you took or worked with, you will never go astray: the book of Allah, and my tradition."
(Prophet Muhammad (PBUH))
Narrator: Abu Hurayra. Reference: Osoul Al Ahkam, Number: 251/2.
Degree: Correct

So, months before the death of the Prophet, the Prophet had said that the two things that will keep believers from deviating from the path of God are the two things that all the Muslims of their time already had; the entire Holy Quran and an entire 23 years of the quotations and the traditions of the Prophet.

The second interesting aspect is that the one time that a quotation of the Prophet is also mentioned by the letter in a Quranic verse, is what the Prophet had said in one of the greatest days in the history of mankind. Both the quote of the Prophet and the verse said:

"Today I completed your religion for you and I perfected the favor (which Allah had bestowed upon me) upon you, and accepted Islam as your religion."
Holy Quran, Surat (Al Maeda) (The table) Ch. (5), verse (3)

ۚ الْيَوْمَ أَكْمَلْتُ لَكُمْ دِينَكُمْ وَأَتْمَمْتُ عَلَيْكُمْ نِعْمَتِي وَرَضِيتُ لَكُمُ الْإِسْلَامَ دِينًا (3)

Islam, as a way of life and as a religion, was completed and perfected for all mankind at that great day in human history; the last pilgrimage of the last Prophet of God.

No other quotation of the Prophet has any wording or meaning of "I left you two things after which you will not go astray" other than the quotation and the verse that we just stated.

The claim that Muhammad (PBUH) on his deathbed anxiously tried to find a piece of paper to write a cure for all advice for the Muslims is beyond comedic, when we know that he was illiterate, and that the entire Holy Quran and the quotations of the Prophet were memorized verbatim from man to man through dictation during the 23 years of the Prophethood duration of Islam.

The two orders that the author claimed were given by the Prophet but not in that manner and definitely not on his deathbed; on page 165, the author wrote:
"Turn Al-Mushrikun out of the Arabian Peninsula; respect and give gifts to the foreign delegations as you have seen me dealing with them."

Why would the author mix timeframes and fabricate final moments for the Prophet? He tells us of his "noble" goal on page 165, when he wrote: "The unbelievers were much on his mind, even as he lay ill. Some Islamic traditions even claim that the Jews "bewitched" Muhammad. When some of his wives began discussing a beautiful church they had seen in Abyssinia, festooned with gorgeous icons, Muhammad sat up and said, "Those are the people who, whenever a pious man dies amongst them, make a place of worship at his grave and then they make those pictures in it. Those are the worst creatures in the sight of Allah." He

320

added: "Allah cursed the Jews and the Christians because they took the graves of their Prophets as places of worship." Ayesha observed that had Muhammad not said this, "His grave would have been made conspicuous." "

In just half a page, the author mixes facts and fabrications in totally different timeframes and tries to push them into the last hours of the life of the Prophet.

Of course, as we said, there's no such thing as Islamic traditions, which is a term used often for Christianity and other religions but a totally manufactured term for Islam by the author that could only mean to me, "made up" or "without any Islamic source or reference." The author claimed that some Muslims said that the Jews bewitched Prophet Muhammad (PBUH)! Not only is the Prophet of God protected by God Himself, but let's look at what the author claims they bewitched him to. It is a fact and a principle of Islam that associating, saints, priests, rabbis, or even any Muslim scholar with God, next to God, or as an intermediary between believers and God, is a form of "Shirk" or the ultimate sin unforgiven with God of associating a partner. Where is the bewitching here? In the correct quotation of the Prophet:

"Verily people before you did take the graves of their Prophets and righteous as Mosques (places of worship), so don't you take graves as Mosques, I forbid you to do that."
(Prophet Muhammad (PBUH))
Narrator: *Jandab Ibn Abduallah*. **Reference**: *Saheeh Muslim*, **Number**: *532*. *Degree*: *Correct*

Not only is it that the concept and the quotations are correct throughout the 23 year tradition of the Prophet, but neither was there any bewitching in the quotation, nor was what was claimed he said on his deathbed.

Then, needlessly, the author brings yet another fabrication about people gathering around the Prophet's bed forcing medicine into his mouth! Which is more untrue than it is irrelevant.

321

On page 166, commenting on the Prophet's most powerful command of the Arabic language, the author again mixes poison with honey when, in praising the briefness and powerful structure of the Holy Quran's phrases, indirectly claims that it is written by Muhammad (PBUH), since the topic is Muhammad (PBUH)'s language and obviously not the Holy Quran's!

A note from Moustafa Zayed:

There are two well-known, amazing features of the correct quotations of Prophet Muhammad (PBUH):

The first is that you cannot deliver the same meaning of his sentences with better expression or with a lesser amount of words. The second is that even though he had went through amazing tribulations, battles, victories, and experiences during his 23 years of Prophethood, all his correct quotations have the same structure and style that transcend time to the limit that you would think they were all said by the Prophet within the same day. Scholars attributed that to the revelation in the Holy Quran, that his commands to the Muslims are not uttered by his own self but are the revelations revealed to him, so even though they were said over 23 years time, they were all from the same one eternal source.

Objective scholars of all kinds not only agree that the language of Muhammad (PBUH)'s quotations is totally different than that unique language of the Holy Quran, but also that the language of the Holy Quran is so powerful and rich with amazing multi-dimensional structures that it cannot be of human source. I advise the author to start taking some basic Arabic classes that will greatly benefit him!

Commenting on the statement of the Prophet which we, again, had explained before, showed one of the forms of protection and support that God had given his Prophet and believers in all the battles, when the Muslims were overwhelmingly outnumbered. God struck fear of the Muslims in the hearts of the enemies of God, not to mention the angels that the Holy Quran stated had helped the believers of God in battles in

322

several occasions. Was it the ratio of 3 to 1 in favor of Quraysh's army in the battle of Badr that had made the Muslims so scary? Or was it God granting His persecuted believers their first victory?

Was Khaybar the most fortified city in Arabia that had warriors behind its forts seven times the number of Muslims, that what was terrorizing about the Muslims, or was it God striking fear in the hearts of the enemies of His Prophet, like He did with Moses, David, and many of his Prophets?

"You didn't kill them, but Allah killed them, and you have not thrown when you thrown, but it was Allah who threw, that He might reward the believers a good reward from Him. Verily, Allah is All-Hearer, All-Knower"
Holy Quran, Surat (Al Anfal) Ch (8), verse (17)

فَلَمْ تَقْتُلُوهُمْ وَلَٰكِنَّ اللَّهَ قَتَلَهُمْ ۚ وَمَا رَمَيْتَ إِذْ رَمَيْتَ وَلَٰكِنَّ اللَّهَ رَمَىٰ ۚ وَلِيُبْلِيَ الْمُؤْمِنِينَ مِنْهُ بَلَاءً حَسَنًا ۚ إِنَّ اللَّهَ سَمِيعٌ عَلِيمٌ (17

It's the author, again, just shoving the words, of terror, warriors, jihadists, etc. down our throats at any possible, relevant or irrelevant, occasion.

323

"After Muhammad"

The author makes another erroneous statement on page 166: "The Prophet of Islam left no clear successor; his fatal illness apparently came upon him too suddenly."

Even though Prophet Muhammad (PBUH) never ordered to make Abu Bakr his successor, and that is due to the obligation that God had ordered in the Holy Quran, which the Prophet himself had practiced and mandated throughout his Prophethood that is "Shura" or Islamic democracy, in the Holy Quran:

"And those who responded to their God, establish prayers, their matter is consulted amongst themselves and spent for the cause of God from what We have blessed them with."
Holy Quran, Surat (Al Shura) Ch. (42), verse (38)

وَالَّذِينَ اسْتَجَابُوا لِرَبِّهِمْ وَأَقَامُوا الصَّلَاةَ وَأَمْرُهُمْ شُورَىٰ بَيْنَهُمْ وَمِمَّا رَزَقْنَاهُمْ يُنْفِقُونَ (38)

Yet there was a clear succession command known to most people. The first and most important indication to who would be the successor of the Prophet was whom the Prophet assigned to lead prayers when the Prophet was sick. In that case it was Abu Bakr, and that was the prophet's vote for Abu Bakr, who was mentioned in the Holy Quran:

"And a second of two as they were in the cave, as he said to his companion "Do not be sad, for Allah is with us." "
Holy Quran, Surat (Al Tawbah) Ch. (9), verse (40)

إِلَّا تَنْصُرُوهُ فَقَدْ نَصَرَهُ اللَّهُ إِذْ أَخْرَجَهُ الَّذِينَ كَفَرُوا ثَانِيَ اثْنَيْنِ إِذْ هُمَا فِي الْغَارِ إِذْ يَقُولُ لِصَاحِبِهِ لَا تَحْزَنْ إِنَّ اللَّهَ مَعَنَا ۖ فَأَنْزَلَ اللَّهُ سَكِينَتَهُ عَلَيْهِ وَأَيَّدَهُ بِجُنُودٍ لَمْ تَرَوْهَا وَجَعَلَ كَلِمَةَ الَّذِينَ كَفَرُوا السُّفْلَىٰ ۗ وَكَلِمَةُ اللَّهِ هِيَ الْعُلْيَا ۗ وَاللَّهُ عَزِيزٌ حَكِيمٌ (40)

And even before the companions of the Prophet officially declared who the successor was after the death of the Prophet, you could even predict that the successor of the successor would be none other than Omar Ibn Al-Khattab.

The successor was decided in the (Saqefat banu Saeeda) where leaders of the largest Muslim tribes gathered to decide who the leader of Islam would be. Some of which were legitimately hoping to have the successor be from their own tribe. The matter was consulted amongst all of them with a major influence from Omar Ibn Al-Khattab supporting none other than Abu Bakr. It is worth mentioning here that the leader of a major tribe of khazraj in Medina, Saad Ibn Obada thought that the successor should be one of the original leaders of the Medina tribes, since they, from the beginning, provided the pivotal support, and incubation of the seed of the new Muslim state in Medina. Saad Ibn Oubada never gave allegiance to Abu Bakr, or Omar Ibn Al-Khattab after him and declared his opposition in public, yet no one had ever oppressed him or affected any of his businesses or social dealings.

On page 167, the author makes a weird supposition by presenting us with another untrue quotation. The author wrote:
"The one boy born to him, Ibrahim, whose mother was Muhammad's concubine Mariah the Copt, died at only 16 months old"
"If Ibrahim had lived, "Muhammad declared "I would have exempted every Copt from poll-tax" - that is, Jizyah.

Not only is the quotation untrue, evidenced at least by the fact that Copts of Egypt weren't obligated to pay any Jizyah at that point of time, for Egypt wasn't opened to Islam till after the death of Muhammad (PBUH) and Abu bakr, but think about it, was Prophet Muhammad (PBUH) saying that if I shall have a boy son from Mary the Copt, then I will exempt Copts from Jizyah? No. Ibrahim was already born and alive for 16 months as the author had mentioned. What was the Prophet waiting for to do that if the quotation was correct? Was he waiting for his son to be 17 months old or 17 years old? What was he waiting for according to the author's untrue quotation?

Is it a suggestion from the author that Muhammad (PBUH) wanted the successor of the leader of a Muslim state - as a rule - to be the son as if it is a kingship system?

325

All of the "correct" quotations and evidence state that the kingship system of succession was resented by the Prophet. In his famous quotation, the Prophet said:

"There will be guided governing in my nation for thirty years, and then after it, there will be kingship."
(Prophet Muhammad (PBUH))
Narrator: Safinah Abu Abdelrahman. Reference: Al Saheeh Al Musnady, Number: 440. Degree: Good

Not only that the quotation is a clear statement against the royal succession system according to the Shura rule of Islam, but also it is one of the Prophet's predictions that always came true with pinpoint accuracy. Thirty years exactly after the passing of the Prophet, the feud between Ali Ibn Abi Talib and Mouaweya Ibn Abi Sufyan became a full-fledged conflict with significant bloodshed that had many of the best companions killed, including Ali Ibn Abi Talib and the grandchildren of Muhammad (PBUH), Al Hassan and Al Hussein, themselves.

The author moves then to the issue of the supporters of Ali Ibn Abi Talib, who became the fourth caliphate, and totally confused the issue and the consequences of the death of Ali Ibn Abi Talib, with how Abu Bakr, then Omar Ibn Al-Khattab, then Osman Ibn Affan were appointed to lead the Muslims. There were no controversy as per if Ali Ibn Abi Talib was a contender to any of the three first caliphs. Immediately after the Reddah wars started - against Muslims who refused to pay the obligated charity tax (Zakah) - and after the passing of Fatima - the wife of Ali Ibn Abi Talib and daughter of Muhammad (PBUH) - Ali Ibn Abi Talib himself gave his allegiance to Abu Bakr, then to Omar Ibn Al-Khattab, and finally to Osman Ibn Affan, whom Ali succeeded as the fourth caliph.

The extremism and politicization of Ali Ibn Abi Talib and his two sons' tragic deaths started to get rampant - through time - with false claims and inventions about not only, the fact that Ali Ibn Abi Talib was the rightful leader of the Muslims and not Muahwiyah, which is true, but

326

also claims of Ali Ibn Abi Talib being the supposedly rightful immediate successor of Muhammad (PBUH) to begin with!

Even though the false claims were all results of the tragic death of Ali Ibn Abi Talib, Al Hassan and Al Hussein, yet they were never there before the tragedies. These false claims have even grown to the level of some of the Shiite factions elevating Ali Ibn Abi Talib to the status of the Prophet himself, and some went to the absolute extreme of even saying that Ali should have been the Prophet, not Muhammad (PBUH)!

Even though these are absolute minority groups, but they represent the level of extremism and false claims that this issue had caused.

The author, on page 167, comments on Ayesha; denying that the Prophet had left a will that stated that Ali Ibn Abi Talib should be the successor of the Prophet. Not only is it that the Prophet would never impose a successor upon the people, where the Prophet specifically indicated that he would not make that a tradition for the leader of the Muslims to impose which successor should come after him, but also because everyone knew that it was Abu Bakr that the Prophet always appointed to lead prayers in the Prophet's absence.

On page 168, the author comments on the ideological conflict that has been erupting every now and then between the Shiite Muslims and the rest of the "Sunni" Muslims who make a majority of 90% of the Muslims worldwide. The author, who never ceases to amaze me, ends the chapter with a statement that has nothing to do with the ideological disagreement between the two parties, or any logical relevance whatsoever. On page 168 he wrote:

"It is a legacy entirely in keeping with the attitudes and behavior of the Prophet of Islam."!!!

Did Prophet Muhammad (PBUH)'s behavior and attitude encourage Muslims to fight amongst themselves, or was it always to unite and always do things in harmony and for the best interest of the nation?

In the holy Quran:

"And hold fast, all of you, to the Rope of, and do not be divided among yourselves, and remember Allah's Favor on you, for you were enemies one to another but He joined your hearts together, so that, by His blessing, you became brethren (in Islamic Faith), and you were on the brink of a pit of Fire, and He saved you from it."
Holy Quran, Surat (Al Omran) Ch. (3), verse (103)
Or when the prophet himself (PBUH) said:

"you will not enter paradise till you become believers, and you will not become believers till you love each other; should I tell you about what if you would do you will love each other.. spread peace amongst your selves" (Prophet Muhammad (PBUH))
*Narrator: Abu Hurayrah. **Reference**: Saheeh Muslim, **Number**: 54.*
Degree: Correct

Did Prophet Muhammad (PBUH) preach to his followers to always fan the flames of their conflicts, and keep it going for centuries? Or did he suggest to them that he will not impose his selection of his successor, yet he will just imply his choice, leaving the ultimate decision to decide their leader after him?

I can only comment on the author's nugget of wisdom by saying it is a comment <u>entirely in keeping with the attitudes and behavior of a history- fabricator!</u>

"History makes it clear however that the legend of fanatical Muslims sweeping the world forcing Islam at the point of the sword upon conquered races is of the most fantastically absurd myths that historians have ever repeated"

Thomas Carlyle on Prophet Muhammad (PBUH), "Heroes and Heroines"

Chapter Ten

In the final chapter the author pushes the high lights of all his false allegations, into the high gear of one chapter. A thousand fascism zeroes, however, are still worth the same zero!

"The War on Terror"

With all the battles that the author narrated for us throughout nine chapters, can the author claim with all his unreliable sources, that Muhammad (PBUH) had declared jihad without the entire army of the Muslim nation and with every able-to-fight man participating?
In every battle, it was the entire Muslim nation fighting, mostly defending their own existence, and if it was an outside war, then it was mainly against a foreign occupation army that was imminently attacking the Muslims, and not the oppressed locals themselves. So to which reader was the author talking to when he said on page 169:
"...with the September 11, 2001 jihad terror attacks"?

How could a bunch of guys that (only God knows who gave them the ability to plan such a sophisticated attack and, have NORAD step down from covering our North American airspace exactly at the time of the attacks) be the entire army of Muslims or even that of the smallest Muslim nation to call it "Jihad" anything?

This was an attack claimed to be done by an acclaimed terrorist organization that operates out of Afghani caves!

How could killing hundreds of innocent Muslims amongst another three thousand innocent civilians victims of 9/11, even remotely be called an act of anything Islamic to begin with?

We have seen all the fabrications, crazy allegations, omitted and mistranslated verses throughout Mr. Spencer's book, so which verse of the Holy Quran or a quotation of the Prophet allows the killing of hundreds of innocent Muslims alongside three thousand innocent human beings?

You will not find an iota whether in the Holy Quran or the Quotations of the Prophet that substantiates the killing of one innocent soul, not to mention all the innocent victims of September 11th.

Where did the author find the audacity to claim that that criminal act be something that he says relevant to anything of the noble character of Prophet Muhammad (PBUH), while he knows of all people that a corruption-on-Earth crime in Islamic law is the most punishable in Sharia law, by execution in public to make an example of the criminals?

Was that because of whatever criminals associated with this abhorrent crime may have claimed, that they're Muslims or that they're doing this for Islam? Would that be the same justification that allows us to believe that God is responsible for the crimes that insane mass murderers commit, who even usually claim that God told them to do so? Had Jim Jones survived his massacre, would our author demand that he be left to walk free since he claimed that God had told him to do so?

The justification being that in Spencer land all insane mass murderers are credible and that they never lie!!

James Warren "Jim" Jones (May 13, 1931 – November 18, 1978) was the founder and leader of the Peoples Temple, which is best known for the November 18, 1978 death of more than 900 Temple members in Jonestown, Guyana along with the deaths of nine other people at a nearby airstrip and in Georgetown, Guyana.

Jones was born in Indiana and started the Temple in that state in the 1950s. Jones and the Temple later moved to California and both gained notoriety with the move of the Temple's headquarters to San Francisco in the mid-1970s.

The greatest single loss of American civilian life in a non-natural disaster until the events of September 11, 2001, the tragedy at Guyana also ranks among the largest mass suicides in history. One of those who died at the nearby airstrip was Leo Ryan, who became the only Congressman murdered in the line of duty in the history of the United States. [1]

On pages 15 and 16, the author wrote:
"...And it is not my intention, to insult Muhammad (PBUH), to deride him, to lampoon or mock him, or to write anything except a scrupulously accurate account of what he said and did about some key issues."

And the next paragraph would cement the level of truthfulness of Mr. Spencer. Here is the next subtitle.

"Pedophile prophet?"

The author naturally would not miss the famous incident where in one of the most trusted source of the quotations of the Prophet - Saheeh Muslim - reported that Ayesha said:

"The Messenger of God married me when I was six; my marriage was consummated when I was nine."
(Prophet Muhammad (PBUH))
Narrator: Ayesha. Reference: Saheeh Muslim, Number: 1422. Degree: Correct

Regardless of the apparent fact that the author tries his tired (poison / honey) mix again, by saying that this was the norm at the time of the Prophet, and that nobody thought ill of it then, even when the Prophet was fifty years of age; the truth remains that to Muslims and to the status of the last Prophet of God, the issue is totally different. Here is why:

If the Prophet of God had thought that at his age of fifty marrying a nine year old was righteous in whatever set of circumstances at the time, then it is, and it is accepted by every Muslim, and the issue here would be the

332

craziness of Mr. Spencer and his polite, well-mannered Mr. Vine thinking that their idea of right and wrong versus those of the last Prophet of God himself, could possibly be of any worth or value to Muslims.

1. Having said that, let's use logic, science, and history, before my own conclusion about the matter, can even be considered. The most important rule as to the age of marriage of females as per the majority of Muslim scholars is that the female had reached puberty and that she can mentally carry the responsibility of marriage. She has to be physically and mentally able to fulfill the duties of marriage. That combination varies dramatically from climate to another, from cities to rural areas, and from generations to others. A very telling part of the Hadeeth is the question; why was the Prophet waiting to consummate the marriage for three years? The answer is simple; for Ayesha to reach the acceptable combination of conditions for her to be accepted as a wife.

2. The second and important question is: what was the criterion for the scholars, Muslim and Al-Bukhari to verify to us that piece of information?
    The extremely difficult yet very simple criterion was that Ayesha did really make that statement. Here, the job of asserting the credibility of the quote as to Muslim and Al-Bukhari is completed, for she truly did say that. The most important question that many people are blind to, however, which is as simple and as clear as the sun, is; how did Ayesha know that she was nine at the time?!

3. Did Ayesha have her birth certificate in hand at the time? No. Was Ayesha looking at the calendar at the time? No. Was any one counting year after year watching her age, due to the need and importance of the info, maybe admission to kindergarten, vaccination table, or maybe, getting Ayesha an ID? No.

    The clear answer is that not only Ayesha was illiterate, did not know how to read, write, or calculate, but it was the middle of the seventh century, in one of the most rural areas of the planet at the time. So if Ayesha did not know the difference between nine and nineteen, and had no reference for her birth date whatsoever, how could she possibly know which age she was at?

4. Let's look at what happens - scientifically proven- in reality, not in the middle of the seventh century, but even in the 21st century in rural areas! An interesting fact that in world soccer youth championships - under seventeen years and under nineteen years' competitions - are usually dominated by African teams. Why?
The simple fact is that most of the African players are born in rural areas in Africa where there are no records of their birthdates whatsoever. The natural tendency is always to underestimate the ages of the children. So when these players are at the age of nineteen or even twenty-one, they think that they are under seventeen or eighteen years old, so when they meet more skillful European and Latin players, they have the overwhelming advantage of being three to five years older than their competitors at the time. So, they dominate. That advantage is totally washed away in regular men competitions, where being older by a few years is not an advantage since older players are also there on the other teams.

5. What many orientalists would not tell you is another piece of information in Sahih Al-Bukhari about Ayesha, who thought that she was six when she was engaged to the Prophet. The amazing piece of information is that she, at that supposed age, was formerly engaged to another man who was Jubair Ibn Muttaaem and then the engagement was broken! Which is virtually impossible, no matter what the author tries to allege that it is only an Islamic, or Arab cultural thing. An example, on page 172, is when he sheds tears for Afghani girls where he wrote:
"In early 2002, researchers in refugee camps in Afghanistan and Pakistan found half the girls married by age 13."
Mr. Spencer always forgets that his beacon-of-light examples that he paints 1.6 billion Muslims all over 57 countries with, are usually limited to the most exceptional of places like, refugee camps in his favorite sandbox of impoverished Afghanistan and Pakistan.
Refugee camps in non-other than rural areas of the 3rd poorest country in

the world, where, the same natural practices, prevail in other rural areas all over the world to date. Otherwise, why in a far, far away galaxy like the state of Alabama USA, the legal marriage age is only 14 years old! Last time I checked the fact that our good state of Alabama is not a war zone or occupied by a foreign country! And why not 1400 years ago but just 200 years ago the marriage age in the American state of Delaware was 12 years of age? I assure you not because they were crazy Jihadist Muslims!

6. Another scientific fact in reference to girls born in hot climates in the east, versus western girls born in cold climates, is that girls in hot climates reach puberty much sooner, sometimes five years earlier than those in cold climates.

7. Sociologists would tell you that maturity of boys and girls in rural areas happen much sooner than their peers in urban areas. The scarcity of people and the required additional manual activities teach responsibility at a much younger age.

8. Ayesha's marriage was 1400 years ago, where the life-expectancy of people was much less, almost by over twenty years than it is nowadays. Consequently, reaching puberty whether in the west or the east- at the time - happened naturally sooner.

9. The conditions of allowing a girl to get married in Islam is not that extreme example of the minority Iranian Shiite practice that the author wanted to paint 90% of the Sunni Muslims with. The condition is that the girl has reached puberty and that she is mentally and physically capable of carrying the responsibility of a marriage and a family. All quotations and historical context prove beyond doubt that Ayesha did fulfill both conditions. Ayesha once said to the prophet who most of the night was praying and worshipping God:

"أحب قربك ولكني أوثر عليه هواك"

"I love to be near you, but I prefer what you yourself like to do, over it."

335

Was that a little girl, or one of the wisest women you ever heard?

10. In the Prophet's famous quotation about sighting the moon to determine the beginning of the month of Ramadan:

"We are an illiterate nation, we do not know how to write or calculate . . ."
(Prophet Muhammad (PBUH))
Narrator: Abdu Allah Ibn Omar. Reference: Saheeh Al Bukhary, Number: 1913. Degree: Correct

So without a doubt, Ayesha's estimate of her own age had to be erroneous. Yet using all these scientific, social, and historical facts, what would be the most likely correct estimate of her age? Would she be much older or younger than she thought she was?

11. Again, I reiterate, had Ayesha been truly nine, in the circumstances of that time, and Prophet Muhammad (PBUH) accepted her for marriage, then that is accepted by every single Muslim, no matter how many self-proclaimed righteous haters rant!

"Misogynist?"

Even though we have covered the issue of the multiple wives of the Prophet before, we will answer what the author had added to his final attacks at the Prophet in chapter ten.
He starts on page 172 with a fabricated story, when he said:
"Gabriel brought a kettle from which I ate"

By which the story claims that the Prophet said that he had supernatural power. And as we have said before, the Prophet had one wife - Khadija- that was fifteen years older than him in a marriage that lasted a quarter of a century, where he did not marry again till she passed away. The Prophet was only married to her for a complete ten years after he had already been revealed as the last Prophet of God. The fact that needs to be mentioned is that, that ten years of Prophet-hood where the Prophet had only one wife that was Khadija, were the same period during

336

which he was ordered by God to invite to Islam in secret in the beginning, meaning that he could not publicly invite tribes to get into Islam and for that there was no need to marry into these tribes to forge peace and respect alliances. The other fact that we have mentioned several times but repetition is worthy here, is that the Prophet, even before he was revealed to be the last Prophet of God at the age of forty, was never known to have fornicated or committed adultery, even by the fabricators of his time. He was not known to be the one who sought materialistic things and chased lusts, even when he was tempted by the leaders of Quraysh offering him whatever and whoever he may want, just to give up inviting others to Islam.

On page 173, the author again interprets a famous verse in the Holy Quran in a way that is totally different from all the interpretations of the verse in any Islamic reference. In the Holy Quran (our translation):

"Your women are a tilth for you, so perform your tilth in whichever way you want to."
Holy Quran, Surat (Al Baqara) Ch (2), verse (223)

نِسَاؤُكُمْ حَرْثٌ لَكُمْ فَأْتُوا حَرْثَكُمْ أَنَّىٰ شِئْتُمْ ۖ وَقَدِّمُوا لِأَنْفُسِكُمْ ۚ وَاتَّقُوا اللَّهَ وَاعْلَمُوا أَنَّكُمْ مُلَاقُوهُ ۗ وَبَشِّرِ الْمُؤْمِنِينَ (223)

The verse addresses an incident when some of the companions of the Prophet asked him about a Jewish myth that if the intercourse happened in a certain position, the baby would be born cross-eyed. The verse later was revealed to indicate that as long as you're having natural intercourse with your wife, then you can have that intercourse in any position you want together. The verse never meant by any stretch of the imagination in 1400 years of Islam that a man can do to his wife whatever he wants. Mr. Spencer's interpretation is just that offensively absurd.

And as if the laughable fabrication crime that Mr. Spencer committed earlier in his book, where we exposed him was not enough, Mr. Spencer repeats verse 282 of Ch 2 (Al Baqara) again, where he claims that it pertains to witnessing rape crimes. This is after he omitted the first line of the verse that states that it is specifically for the matter of

337

taking debts in a financial transaction! He adds, on page 173: "It declares that a woman's testimony is worth half that of a man."

The rules of witnessing in Islam vary according to the incident. What is really interesting is that the author never mentioned the verses that specifically pertain to witnessing upon sexual deviance; the verses of "Leean" {Surat Al Noor (The Light), Ch.24 Verses 6 to 9)} where a wife's testimony is exactly equal to the husband. The author instead goes to the verse that specifically pertains to taking debts, omits that it is for taking debts, and then shed tears over the verse's inequality of witnessing rape incidents!!

In case of the taking debt verse, we explained that the purpose of two witnesses is solely for one to remind the other and that's why you don't have one man but two men and similarly you don't call one man a half a witness! So if there's no second man and no protection of women who would be forced to interact - to be able to be a witness - with men that may be foreign or forbidden for them to interact with, then that one man is replaced by two women, so they can independently remind each other as witnesses, while abiding by women protection laws of Islam.
The author then jumps again to the issues that we covered sufficiently before, of marrying up to four wives or marrying more in the exceptional case of women war captives at the time. It is interesting when the author himself even brings verse number 3 in Surat Al-Nissaa (The Women), where God clearly states the ultimate reference for a man's decision to marry more than one wife, which is dealing fairly and justly with them and avoiding injustice.
In the Holy Quran (our translation):

"But if you fear that you will not be able to deal justly (amongst them**), then marry only one, or that which your right hand possesses. That will be closer to preventing you from doing injustice."**
Holy Quran, Surat (Al Nissaa) Ch (4), verse (3)

فَإِنْ خِفْتُمْ أَلَّا تَعْدِلُوا فَوَاحِدَةً أَوْ مَا مَلَكَتْ أَيْمَانُكُمْ ۚ ذَٰلِكَ أَدْنَىٰ أَلَّا تَعُولُوا (3)

Of course, the sheer injustice of having multiple girlfriends, mistresses, one-night stands, with no rights or respect given to those women while dealing with them sometimes as sexual door mats, is supposedly to the author more respectable than giving women rights as wives, respecting them and their legitimate children publicly in the Islamic system.

The author jumps again as if he is in a race to jam this page with as many accusations, unfounded or not, as possible by going to the inheritance issue, which we also covered before. Where, in one case of inheritance, the son inherits double the daughter, yet in the other thirty cases of inheritance, the female potentially inherits exactly like a male, and in three of them she inherits more. This is only with the caveat that according to Islamic law the father, then the brother, then the husband, then the son, are always financially responsible for the female; at the same time, her inheritances are only hers!

Another jump to another mistranslation where the author quotes verse 34 in Surat Al-Nissaa - as usual - mutilating the first line that says (our translation):

"Men are to attend to women with what Allah had preferred one of them over the other and with what they spend of their monies (supporting them)"
Holy Quran, Surat (Al Nissaa) Ch (4), verse (34)

الرِّجَالُ قَوَّامُونَ عَلَى النِّسَاءِ بِمَا فَضَّلَ اللَّهُ بَعْضَهُمْ عَلَى بَعْضٍ وَبِمَا أَنْفَقُوا مِنْ أَمْوَالِهِمْ ۚ (34)

The author, instead, made it as if men are in charge of women, and as if a wife is a piece of property, to the contrary of all what we have stated of correct quotations about the reverence of a mother and that the best of men in Islam are the best to their women. Naturally the wives included; also, the issue of claiming that husbands is to beat their disobedient wives, which we have covered just in the past chapter. And as if all these crammed false accusations in just one page -173 - were not enough to have the intelligent reader appeal to Mr. Spencer to retire from any profession that has anything to do with credibility, the author adds

339

another mistranslated quote of the Prophet at page 174:
"I have not seen anyone more deficient in intelligence and religion than you. A cautious, sensible man could be lead astray by some of you."

The translation is totally erroneous; the Prophet said:

"I have never seen ones that lack reason and religion that could make a firm man lose his mind than you."
(Prophet Muhammad (PBUH))
Narrator: Abu Saeed Al Khidry. Reference: Saheeh Al Bukhary, Number: 304. Degree: Correct

The quotation means simply that, a woman is naturally more guided by emotions than reason: look at any mother and her relentless, limitless, love and care for her babies above and beyond any logic, need, or personal comfort, and try to explain that with cold logical reasoning. That illogical emotional kindness in itself is a mercy from God upon the human race in the form of our mothers. In addition, the fact that women, due to their monthly period and pregnancy, naturally have the license to pray and fast less than a similar aged man, which is a natural fact of being a woman, consequently gives women less religious duty (but not lesser reward). What is more interesting is the second part of the same quotation, where the Prophet testifies to the intelligence and the skill of a female's ability to manipulate a cautious, sensible man, which in itself is praise.

And the final gem of wisdom comes when the author writes on page 174: "With statements like these from the Holy Quran and Muhammad, it is no wonder that women in Islam and in the Islamic world suffer such inequalities."

In chapter (8) we have covered an objective comparison between the rights of a Muslim woman in Islam, and in the Muslim world and that of many women in the west, however, I would like to add, that with fabricated mistranslated verses and quotations like those the author crammed page 173 with, it is no wonder that women in the west are deceived into scarecrow narratives like that of Mr. Spencer, that they are blinded to the birth-given rights that God had afforded them in Islam.

"Draconian punishments?"

The author here addresses the issue of capital punishment in Islam, which we have also covered previously:
"Stoning for adultery and amputation for theft" are the two punishments that the author focuses on here, on page 174. But he goes to describe them as "emblematic of its pre-medieval harshness and unsuitability for the contemporary world."

The author then brings up the issue of stoning as a punishment for adultery in the Torah, which we have also covered earlier:

When we proved that the order for stoning is in the Torah, evident by the famous tale in today's Gospel of John, when people gathered to stone a woman who committed adultery, and Jesus (PBUH) said that whoever was without a sin should <u>cast the first stone</u> at the woman. Hadn't it been a rule to stone as a punishment for adultery, why would Jesus try to persuade the people not to? Why, for example, did he not warn them that they are about to commit murder, unless stoning was the law?

"If a man be found lying with a woman married to a husband, then they shall both of them die, both the man that lay with the woman, and the woman: so shall you put away evil from Israel"
King james bible, Deuteronomy 22:22

Yet, in Islamic Law, it's not what was in the original Torah or not. The fact that the Prophet had ordered it and declared it as a rule in Islamic Law is more than enough for it to be as such for all Muslims; in the Holy Quran:

"Whatever the Prophet had brought you, then take, and whatever he forbade you, then abstain from."
Holy Quran, Surat (Al Hashr) Ch (59), verse (7)

(7) ۞ وَمَا آتَاكُمُ الرَّسُولُ فَخُذُوهُ وَمَا نَهَاكُمْ عَنْهُ فَانْتَهُوا ۞

341

The conditions for prosecuting, and stoning married adulterers, however, are so difficult that it is more of a deterrent of such a crime than it is a capital punishment in itself. Evident by the historical fact that in the first 1000 years of Islam, stoning for committing adultery was applied only three times upon voluntary insistent confessions of the committers, and not on e single rime due to catching any adulterers in the act itself. The fact remains that it is - even though in reality more theoretical than practical - a part of Islamic Law for 1400 years and to date. How the rule is applied; justly or not, accurately or not, is a responsibility upon the shoulder of rulers applying the law and their integrity. That responsibility is applicable upon any law and whoever is responsible for applying it, anytime and anywhere.

But in over a millennia of Islam, which I might add a closer millennia to successful application of Islamic Law than the second millennia, there was not one single case of executing by stoning, a couple caught during the act of adultery.

How much knowledge do some Muslims have about Islamic Law, and how accurately they may apply it in some tent village somewhere on planet Earth is irrelevant to the efficacy of the law itself.

On page 174, the author again resorts to:
"Islamic apologists in the West," whom he claims "like to point out that the Holy Quran does not contain this command."
Never mind if these specific apologists do exist, or they are just a product of the author's imagination; they are the last to speak about Islam, not to mention defending it. For as per the cardinal rule of Islam represented by the verse we just quoted, correct quotations of the Prophet of what's allowed and what's forbidden are as obeyed as any command in the Holy Quran itself.
So when these "unnamed" apologists claim that the stoning rule does not exist because it's not in the Holy Quran, while it's repeatedly ordered by the Prophet in his correct quotations, they should be questioned first

about having any minimal knowledge of the basics of Islamic Law to begin with, not to mention speaking for or defending Islam!

In the next paragraph, the author's comments truly represent the devastating ills of ignorant men creating man-made laws that have brought devastation to their societies, while so naively claiming civility and righteousness in fighting the laws of the Creator of all mankind!

On page 174, the author writes about the penalty of stoning for adultery, that it "can be mitigated. However, that hope is illusory."

Is adultery a good thing that the law of God inconceivably punishes harshly for?

How much do sexually-transmitted diseases cost every year the secularly-ruled countries that do not punish for adultery?
How many millions of lives lost to AIDS alone so far worldwide?
How many families were destroyed because of the irresponsible no-deterrent of the "two consenting adults"?
How many children suffered the lack of one of their parents or both around them in their upbringing because of adultery? More importantly, look at the vast gap between the cost and the devastation of adultery in the West, versus their counterparts in Muslim countries even the poorest of them.

I want to ask pragmatically, practically and even from an absolute scientific secular standpoint: are these gigantic, devastating costs and ordeals worth three stonings by confession every 1000 years?

The author then brings the famous hadeeth of Omar Ibn Al Khattab, who reinforced the law of stoning married adulterers, where he mentioned a verse that was revealed to the Prophet; but then God ordered the Prophet after it was known to the companions to reveal the verse in Chapter 24, number 2 that describes the lashing of non-married couples. In many instances of revealing the Holy Quran, and to bring attention to certain laws for their importance and significance to the Prophets and the Muslims, God would reveal changes of position or additions to certain verses on a Muslims-need to basis and as the reminding occasion of the final form of the verse. A major example of that is when God revealed the verse about the difference of reward between those who fought for the cause of God in battle and those who had a legitimate excuse to stay behind. Then Ibn Oum Maktoum complained that he was blind and there was nothing that he could do to be able to join battle. That was the occasion where the verse was revealed that the same rule applies, except for those who are physically unable. Please note that both verses are valid and independently relate to each other.

The author then creates his own problem and then criticizes Islam for it! On page 175, he creates a new group called: "Islamic reformers" and then states that:
"It is difficult, if not impossible, for Islamic reformers to make headway against this, when Omar specifically warns against them."

While "religion reformers" are more than a well-known term in political and Judeo-Christian religious denominations, it is not a valid or a meaningful term according to Islamic Law.
Islamic Law in its principal is the collective commands in the Holy Quran and the commands of the Prophet himself, and not the collective man-made laws within a body overwhelmed with man-invented theology mainly influenced by a certain environment of a certain age.
So when times change beyond the comprehension of these men, reform throughout Europe and later in America became an unstoppable necessity. Reform in Islam has always successfully been purifying the original laws of God and the commands of the Prophet from inventions and man-imposed errors, mainly due to unjust rulers' influence or that of corrupt and weak scholars; an effort that has mostly been honestly adhering to the well-known black and white Islamic Law fundamentals guided by a word of God that was never tampered with and the correct Quotations of the Prophet. So reform as an indication of a process of betterment does exist and, not to mention is actually mandated by Islamic Law, but by definition it is regaining the purity of the perfect laws of God - not altering or changing them according to Mr. Spencer's business ambitions - that endured all tests of time for the past 1400 years and

344

where it was the primary reason of the constant thriving of the Muslim nation and expansion of Islam itself. At the same time, Islamic reformers, as per the definition of the author, may be nothing but wolves of promoting secularism, in Islamic-activists' sheep's clothes.

The author comments on the capital punishment of theft, which in Islamic Law is cutting off the hand. While this law is within the context of the responsibility of the Muslim treasury of providing the poor with their sustenance no matter what the condition is, still, in cases of famine and the inability of the Muslim treasury to support and protect people from hunger and poverty, the law is suspended. An example is in the case of the year of Ramadah (a year of famine), under the rule of Omar Ibn Al-Khattab when the rule was suspended. The severity of the punishment which has to be done in public is mainly a deterrent for people to commit theft than it is to punish.

The reaction to this law in some circles is a clear indication of how short-sighted and sometimes blind people are when they attempt to control societies and the ills of man through the limitations of their comprehension without ever being able to grasp the consequences of the big picture of society. In the Holy Quran:

"And in punishment there is life for you, O, you who comprehend, so that you may fear (God)."
Holy Quran, Surat (Al Baqara) Ch (2), verse (179)

وَلَكُمْ فِي الْقِصَاصِ حَيَاةٌ يَا أُولِي الْأَلْبَابِ لَعَلَّكُمْ تَتَّقُونَ (179)

Watching the harsh capital punishments and even the knowledge of the existence of such potential punishments is the best crime-fighter and deterrent of future criminals. A time-tested simple fact.

As per the US government, there are 6.6 million violent crimes committed in the US each year. It is hard objectively to claim that at least half of these crimes would have not been committed had there been a belief of the entire population that the Islamic punishment is there and is that severe.

345

When comparing the number of armed robberies that result in permanent injuries and loss of life to the victims as a percentage of the population to the similar ratio in a society like Saudi Arabia, the ratio is vastly overwhelming in favor of the safety of the Saudi citizen.

And if you apply the ratio in a wealthy, diverse with foreign labor society like the society in Saudi Arabia to the number of violent crimes that are committed annually in the U.S, you would discover that millions of injuries and tragic deaths could have been prevented had Islamic Law been applied correctly in the U.S.

Amazingly and interestingly, if you look at the abstract statistics objectively and scientifically, Mr. Spencer and his likes are doing nothing but protecting tens of thousands of violent criminals and thieves from punishment, at the expense of millions of injuries and deaths of their victims every single year!

Copying the author, at the end of the paragraph with his a nugget of sad words of wisdom, I will repeat them, only sincerely thanking God with his same words:

"the binding words of Allah, applicable then, now, and forever."!

"Warrior prophet?"

In this paragraph, the author lists the battles that the Prophet had participated in, and as usual confuses the fundamentals of forming any society, with the overriding principal of peace in Islam.

The contradiction is really extreme. On page 178, he wrote:

"here again, Muhammad's example is normative."

*What better example should the Muslims take as reference than the last Prophet of God? Richard Nixon?!

According to the author's logic, every battle that the Prophet fought, most of which the Muslim army was severely outnumbered and fighting for their very existence, is somehow a type of violence!

A cop is a police officer and a praised, valued member in any society and, if Muslim, he is one who might be "linked to violence"!!

346

A general or a soldier of a national army is a hero or a fallen hero if he is killed in battle, but if Muslim, they are jihadist-warrior terrorists going crazy for killing, and for buried treasures!

How practical is it for anytime in our modern time, that anyone of society be totally army-less and defenseless in the name of hypocritical peace?
How absurd is it if I ask the author to find one country that does not have an army, or even one small-sized city that does not have a police department?
Are the guns that police officers carry all over the world there to help commit violence or to protect the innocent from violence and keep peace?
How "normative" that rule is throughout the world; why would it be an oddity in the case of Muslims? God sends the Muslims, and all mankind a perfect human example as a model of guidance to live by righteously in the real world. But instead, the author's argument is that, unless the preferred "normative" for the Muslims is to surrender your sovereignty and your natural resources to fictitious-wars crusaders; otherwise, the Muslim's religion cannot be called by the same crusaders a "religion of peace"?! How absurd.

Is the goal to deter Muslim countries from standing up for themselves against oppression, otherwise they are stamped with the Jihadist crazed terrorist Spencer stamp? Or is it to further scare the western population into oppressing the exponential peaceful growth of Islam in the west?

The author again invents false Islamic rules then accuses the Muslims of them! On page 178 he wrote:
"It is difficult, if not impossible, to maintain that Islam is a religion of peace where warfare and booty were among the chief preoccupations of the Prophet of Islam."

Not only is it that booty is a consequence of any war, and was never in any quotation of the Prophet, or any verse of the Holy Quran, a

347

prime target by any stretch of the imagination, but war itself was an obligation upon the Prophet to defend the newly born Muslim state, and fight oppression by defending against the imminent attacks of tyrannical rulers around the Muslims. Hadn't that been the case, the author would have fabricated a flying elephant conclusion about any hint of such booty drive. if there was even a fabricated story about! In the Holy Quran:

"And if they leaned towards peace, then lean towards it and rely upon Allah, for He is the most knowledgeable and the most listening."
Holy Quran, Surat (Al Anfal) Ch (8), verse (61)

وَإِنْ جَنَحُوا لِلسَّلْمِ فَاجْنَحْ لَهَا وَتَوَكَّلْ عَلَى اللهِ ۚ إِنَّهُ هُوَ السَّمِيعُ الْعَلِيمُ (61)

"And fight for the sake of God those who fight you and do not transgress, for Allah does not like the transgressors."
Holy Quran, Surat (Al Baqara) Ch (2), verse (190)

وَقَاتِلُوا فِي سَبِيلِ اللهِ الَّذِينَ يُقَاتِلُونَكُمْ وَلَا تَعْتَدُوا ۚ إِنَّ اللَّهَ لَا يُحِبُّ الْمُعْتَدِينَ (190)

In the second verse, not only is it forbidden to attack people for no reason, but even when you are allowed to fight whoever fought you first, it is that you do it only for the sake of God.

Fighting just for war and booty is the furthest thing from the cause of God. I ask the author again, how "truthful" is it of him to fabricate a false statement that "war and booty were among the chief preoccupations of the Prophet of Islam" in light of the above two verses that he - always - never quotes to his readers?

How did the author know a preoccupation of Muhammad (PBUH) that Muhammad, the Holy Quran, and all the Prophets' companions did not know about?!!

The author then on page 177 - being the wise man he is - advises his Islamic reformers as to how to retreat from "that Muhammad's example as an all ways normative."

I myself advise his Islamic reformers to work diligently with Mr. Spencer himself to convince him to stop fabricating Islamic rules and Islamophobia that have been, and are, causing horrible bloodshed of Muslims around the world a thousand folds more than his beloved terrorist attacks ever did.

"Islamic tolerance?"

On page 177, the author subconsciously revealed a part of his prejudicial, racist, and fascist ideology. He wrote about the Muslims: "They have painted an ironic picture of Islam's respect for its sister "Abrahamic faiths" and thereby have given many Jews and Christians confidence that Western countries can accept Muslim immigrants in large numbers without any significant disruptions to their pluralistic societies."

In Mr. Spencer's fascist-land, people of all faiths, no faiths, and ethnicity from around the world can immigrate; only Muslims should be interrogated at the gate about their religious beliefs, otherwise they may disrupt Mr. Spencer's pluralistic societies! A South Korean or Northern Irish, a West Indian or a Zambian can immigrate to America, but only a Muslim may slip through the cracks if he was not questioned about his religious beliefs!
While the author is openly challenging the existence of Muslims today in America and the west altogether, I wonder what hypocrisy may be about, if he in the next paragraphs, will try to critique the peaceful existence of Christians and Jews, freely and clearly worshipping according to their own religions in Muslim lands of the 7th century?!

Amongst the three Abrahamic religions, which one religion of them mandates the belief in all Prophets of God, the original scriptures given to these Prophets by God, and all the angels of God? Only Islam does so as a fundamental of the religion, 1400 years before America was blessed with the existence of Mr. Spencer.

349

I am not breaking any news that in Judaism, Jesus (PBUH) is an imposter and Virgin Mary - God Forbid - was a sinner, not a virgin, and in both Christianity and Judaism - contrary to what's in the original scriptures - Muhammad (PBUH) is not a Prophet of God!

The Muslim, who believes in all the Prophets and scriptures of God, however, should be the ones kept at the gate of Spencer land!

In the following pages 177 and 178, the author severely contradicts himself after praising the West's pluralistic societies and provoking them against Muslim immigrants. He shows an uglier side of fascism when he lists a difference in ideology and Islam's criticism of deviated Christians and Jews.

As a laughable evidence of what he claims Islamic intolerance to be, how is an ideological Islamic criticism of the man-made deviance of some of the Jews and Christians, which is no matter how you slice such a difference in opinion - in the pluralistic, and free, democratic society of Mr. Spencer - be an evidence of intolerance, which is a practical behavioral crime?

How could a difference of opinions and beliefs - in a democracy - automatically become a crime of intolerance?

It is really amazing that in a lecture of Mr. Spencer's, where he was defending the crusades of all topics! - that caused six million Muslim victims - where he had to stop and apologize for the first action the crusaders did after entering Jerusalem, when they went to the nearest synagogue, shut its doors and burned the innocent Jewish worshippers inside alive! What's more amazing than the inhumane crime the crusaders committed against the Jews, is also the comparison of Islamic tolerance of the same synagogue and its congregation built in peace where Jews worshipped in freely under Muslim rule!

And we all, supposedly, should learn tolerance from Mr. Spencer who in addition of teaching us his crusader brand of tolerance, is the same one to also enlighten us as well about "the truth" about Muhammad!

On page 178, the author again mistranslates verse 51 in Chapter 5 (Al Maedah) (The Table) in the Holy Quran, may be to try to push hatred between people. The author translated the word "Aouliaa" which in the context of the verse means "war or political allies", so in the case of battle, Islam forbids that Muslim nations get into alliance with non-Muslims, and again because of the special status that Christians and Jews have above all non-Muslims; the verse specifically said not to take even Christians and Jews as allies because they have more allegiance amongst themselves than what they may have with the Muslims (read history). So from forbidding a nation taking another nation as an ally, the author changed the word "ally" to "friend" to force a political rule in a state of war between nations down to the personal level between just individuals! As if no Muslim can have a Christian or Jewish friend; I have laughed hard enough already.

Even using the translation of the author, which is erroneous at best, if Muslims did not have a tendency to have alliances with Jews and Christians, why would the verse specifically prohibit alliances with non-Muslims, even if they were Christians and Jews, if Muslims weren't naturally open to have allies with Christians and Jews? And why dance around the bush and concoct stories, mistranslations, and fabrications about what the verse would make Muslims do? Why wouldn't the author show us where Muslims may have committed a massacre in cold blood against Christians and Jews who lived in peace in Muslim lands? The answer to that question is, absolutely not. On the contrary go back to what the Crusaders, for example, did to Muslims and Jews under their rule.

Muslims know of the highly-revered position of Jesus (PBUH) in Islam. Muslims await not the coming of Muhammad (PBUH) at the end of time, but actually, they await the coming of Jesus (PBUH) at the end of time, who will not only descend from Heaven, but will also kill the Anti-Christ and pray with the Muslims after destroying the forbidden practices that men added, and mutilated his message with centuries after he was ascended to heaven.

About the second coming of Jesus, the author writes on page 179 t: "He will return to end the dhimmi status of non-Muslims in Islamic societies, not by initiating a new era of equality and harmony, but by abolishing Christianity and imposing Islam upon everyone."

Not only is it that Muhammad (PBUH) never said that Jesus (PBUH) will impose anything upon anyone, but the quotations the author brought did not even mention imposing or forcing anyone to anything! As a matter of fact, as per Muhammad (PBUH)'s famous quotation about the coming of Jesus (PBUH):

" I swear with whom my soul is in his hand, son of Maryam is about to descend amongst you a fair judge and a just leader breaking the cross, killing the pig, abolishing Jizyah, and money will overflow till no one will want it"
(Prophet Muhammad (PBUH))
Narrator: Abu Hurayra. Reference: Musnad Ahmed, Number: 93/14. Degree: Correct

The only thing abolished in the quote is the Jizyah tax, which the author made us swim in a river of his tears about throughout his book. The "dhimmi" status that will be canceled after the coming of Jesus (PBUH) is evidently due to the fact that his followers will not be called Christians anymore, for the true teachings of Jesus (PBUH) were his teachings as a mighty Prophet of Islam. So when Jesus restates his Islam, which was the case from the beginning, then Christians and Jews for that matter will become Muslim and abandon drinking liquor, and eating pork as a practice of some Jews and Christians. The author then, on page 180, writes:
"Combine this stripping away of all legitimacy from Judaism and Christianity with Muhammad's exhortations to fight against Jews and Christians, and it is no wonder that the Islamic world has been at odds with Jews and Christians through the centuries."

Where is that exhortation by the Prophet (PBUH) to fight against Jews and Christians? Can the author show us once just one verse that says just that, or a correct Hadeeth that does the same? And if he will never bring any, then where did he come up with these claims and to

352

what kind of readers he thinks that these insane statements can ever make any sense? What legitimacy does the author talk about when the Christians follow Jesus (PBUH) teachings directly from him in the second coming? If Jesus (PBUH) declares that he is a Prophet of the One Mighty God - which he never declared otherwise in any true Gospel – and declares his Islam (Submission to the One Mighty God) which Muslims believe was the case all along, then what the Muslims believe in is the true legitimacy of the true Jesus (PBUH) and his true teachings. The same thing goes for the Jews, for the one major issue that separates a Jew from a true Christian is that Jews do not believe that historical Jesus, son of Mary, was the real Messiah they await his coming. So when he does come, and they're mandated in their own scriptures to follow him, then that actually bridges the gap that was there for over two thousand years so far, which will unite the true beliefs of Jews and Christians once and for all towards the worshipping of the one mighty God whom Jesus is His mighty Prophet.

Yet according to the author, that wonderful moment in the history of mankind, when people would follow the true Prophets and their true teachings, and not the man-made theology of those who misguided their beliefs away from the true worshipping of the One Mighty creator throughout history, and separated them into opposing factions among the one religion. That glorious moment when Jesus (PBUH) will spread light, peace, and justice throughout the world, where everyone is united in the true religion of worshipping the same one mighty God, that moment that is all led, initiated and powered by the descent of Jesus (PBUH) from heaven, has to only be seen through the "hate anything Muslim" prism! That wonderful moment in the history of mankind the author calls a "stripping away of all legitimacy from Judaism and Christianity"!

As if the severe difference between Judaism and Christianity that is almost in a clashing opposition of ideologies is the legitimacy of the two religions! So when Jesus (PBUH) brings about the truth and ends the controversy forever, then according to Mr. Spencer, Judaism and Christianity are not legitimate anymore.

The real interesting statement of the author is when he wrote: "No wonder that the Islamic world has been at odds with Jews and Christians through the centuries."

As per the Jews, we have demonstrated repeatedly that if it wasn't for Islam and its tolerance of Judaism and the protection that the Muslims provided for the Jews to worship and co-thrive freely, there would have not been Judaism today. Christianity was even more protected by Islam. True Islamic history that the author does not quote, states that even during the Crusades that resulted in the death of six million Muslims, and even though the Crusaders falsely declared that they were committing their abhorrent crimes in the name of Christ, there were no retaliatory acts of Muslims whatsoever against native-born Christians in surrounding Muslim countries.

The author then introduces a really interesting quote. He quotes a Saudi Sheikh by the name of Marzouq Al-Ghamdi. When the author said that Al-Ghamdi gave that quote four years ago, the long quote included that non-Muslims should not ride horses and that they should feed Muslims if they pass by their homes for three days and so many other things that there's no room to quote! And my question is; which society it is that, four years ago, still used horses for transportation?! At the same time, the rights and the laws that govern non-Muslim citizens in an Islamic society are already etched in stone by the Prophet, the Holy Quran, and centuries of unparalleled tolerance within any context you choose. Why would you go to a Saudi or non-Saudi individual and seek a controversial quote - to say the least - if you had any intention to really tell your readers the laws that are already clear in the Holy Quran, quotations of the Prophet, and 1400 years of history?

Was that Saudi sheikh who made that statement four years ago, the only human being that can decipher the complex codes of the Holy Quran that no one seemingly could comprehend, or the extra-terrestrial, unknown language of the Prophet, and for that we have to use that one opinion as our one and only universal reference of Islamic tolerance? Why is it that throughout Mr. Spencer's book that facts are, not the

354

absolute apparent truth and as clear as black and white, but always his hand-selected contemporaries who are quoted for their weird statements and bizarre opinions that contradicts the very same clear and apparent Islamic truth?

The author, again, tries desperately to find any trace of intolerance with Muhammad (PBUH) by pushing for the same lame conclusion that:
"We have already seen how insistent Muhammad was about the collection of the Jizyah."!

The statement is as ridiculous as claiming that all Muslims should pay taxes, but in the same Muslim society, non-Muslims should live tax free! Or as ridiculous as asking why the U.S. government is so adamant about collecting taxes!
The author repeats again the issue in verse 9:29 and quotes only the end of the verse. On page 181 he wrote:
"Meanwhile, the second-class status for Christians and Jews mandated by Holy Quran 9:29's stipulation that they "feel themselves subdued," was first fully articulated by Muhammad's lieutenant Omar during his caliphate (634-644)"

What the author has failed to tell his readers is that those who are to "feel themselves subdued" are nothing but tax-evaders, where the verse tells the Prophet to collect the tax from non-Muslims even if they were Christians and Jews. And they should – till they pay what they cheated or evaded to pay - that they pay it when they are subdued. We previously commented on that, that the IRS treats "first-class" citizens who cheat - never mind evade - on their taxes much worse than that!

Throughout my book, I didn't have the room to even make comparisons between Islamic laws and similar conditions in the surrounding real world at the time, or display facts in the objective light of "compared to what."
I always displayed Islamic law in the absoluteness of it that transcends

355

time and place, regardless of the ease to compare it to the others.
One historical fact that comes to mind is that the Roman Empire - that was Christian at the time - imposed over 14 different kinds of taxes upon Christian Egyptians! Feeling "humiliated" when caught by the Romans cheating on taxes was a dream compared to what happened to the Egyptian that got caught evading taxes altogether!

Another issue that the author quoted the Saudi Sheikh for is that non-Muslims should not wear the distinctive attires of Muslims, which was true yet it wasn't a matter of classes. The matter was that non-Muslims were not to participate in the Muslim army, where the official army-attire was the traditional Muslim man-attire, so that rule was an "army uniform rule" i.e., not to cause confusion in battles about who is a Muslim soldier and who is a non-Muslim civilian.
On pages 181 and 182 the author brings a corrupt document about the status of non-Muslims in a Muslim society. Even though the author claimed that it was an imposed order from Omar, the great companion of the Prophet and the great second caliph after Prophet Muhammad (PBUH), the language of the document the author quoted is amazingly a statement or a pledge made by non-Muslims, and not an order by the Caliph or the Muslims themselves!
The real Caliph Omar document however, which is known by the "Omarian document," is etched in stone to date in Jerusalem, was offered to the non-Muslims of Jerusalem when the whole city surrendered peacefully to the rule of Muslims, with its leaders insisting that they would only surrender it to the great Caliph Omar in person: It states as follows:

"This is what the servant of Allah, Omar, the Caliph of believers, had given the people of Illia (Jerusalem) of security, he gives them safety of themselves, monies, churches, crosses, its ill and healthy and its entire denominations. That their churches will not be used for housing, that they will not be destroyed, that nothing is taken from them, or their monies, that they are not forced against their religion, and that none of them is harmed. That Jews are not forced to live with them, and that they pay Jizyah as much as the swelters of

cities pay and that they are obligated to exile thieves and Romans out. Whoever chooses to move to another town then he and his monies are safe till he reaches his destination and whoever decides to stay then he is obligated to pay his Jizyah…"

Omar, that the author tries to impose intolerance upon of all people, is the great Muslim Caliph who, when was visiting Christian leaders in one of the largest churches in Jerusalem (Church of Qyama) and noon prayer was called, refused to pray inside the Church, and left to pray outside, stating that he did not want any man to come after him and claim the Church as a mosque for the Muslims, with the excuse that Omar was seen praying there one time.

On page 182, and after commenting on an apostasy case of a Kuwaiti citizen in 1990, the author resorts again to his rock-solid statements about the illusionary things that only he can see.
"It is nothing short of staggering that the myth of Islamic tolerance could have gained such currency in the teeth of Muhammad 's open contempt and hatred for Jews and Christians, incitements of violence against them, and calls that they be converted or subjugated."

!! Hello!!

I thought that this book was about the truth about Muhammad?

It is Muhammad (PBUH) who had said that:

"Whoever killed a Zemmey will never smell Paradise"
(Prophet Muhammad (PBUH))
Narrator: Abdu Allah Ibn Amro Ibn Alas. Reference: Saheeh Al Bukhary, Number: 3166. Degree: Correct

Is he the same Muhammad (PBUH) that the author had just talked about, or does the word "truth" nowadays mean "illusions"?

Where is that piece of truth that the Holy Quran, correct quotations of the Prophet, and all scholars of Islam have missed in the

357

past 1400 years, and where did Prophet Muhammad (PBUH) ever openly incite violence against any innocent non-Muslim?!

Where does Muhammad (PBUH) say 'convert,' or 'be subjugated'? Was it ever said that if you become a Muslim, you're not paying any tax, and when you remain a non-Muslim, you're forced to pay Jizyah tax?!! Can a hundred dollars a year per family be considered subjugation to any American minority community? Or did the author mean to say cheat, don't pay taxes, otherwise if you pay taxes to your Muslim government you're a second-class citizen?

Here is a repeat for history's leading thinker/orientalist quotes about the subject for the second time!

"We have not heard that - under the rule of Islam - about any predetermined attempt to force non Muslim factions to convert to Islam, or about any deliberate organized oppression to eradicate the Christian faith. If any of the Caliphs chose to execute any of the two plans they would have crushed Christianity with the ease that Ferdinand and Isabella eradicated the religion of Islam from Spain, that made Louis XIV ordained that the protestant faith followers punishable in France or like the way that Jews were exiled of Britain for 350 years"
John Taylor Caroline (1753-1824) the American political Philosopher (Republican Jeffersonian)

"The eastern churches in Asia were already separated from the rest of the Christian world which was not to support them in any way considering them infidels of the religion. Therefore the sheer existence of theses churches today is in itself a strong evidence of the general tolerance of Islamic governments towards them"
Sir Thomas Walker Arnold, the most renowned orientalist in history

The author throws again one of his nuggets of delusion, stating, on page 182: "And Muslims can, of course, act as tolerantly as anyone else, the example of Muhammad, the highest model of human behavior, constantly pulls them in a different direction."!

It is a blessing of God for any Muslim to be pulled constantly in the direction of the last Prophet of God. The man, who forgave his enemies, granted them their freedom, wished them well, and prayed to God to forgive them. And wasn't not just one enemy, but he forgave an entire city of them. With our author himself, who's up to this point clearly and definitely clinically senile of what he himself wrote in the previous chapters, when the Prophet let an assassin who sneaked upon him to kill him, walk free, when he forgave the leader of the hypocrites and plotters against Islam, wrapped his body with his own shirt when he passed away, laid him in his grave himself, and supplicated to God to forgive him. Muhammad (PBUH), the same man that the author himself stated that the ultimate punishment he gave a man who committed apostasy, and joined the enemy's army, was nothing but to let him walk free! Would I want to be pulled towards the example of that man? I pray to God, absolutely yes, please have me swept all the way in that direction.

The author, at the end, complains that the Western analysts oversee his delusional conclusions and accuse them of believing what they wish to believe: that Islam is a religion of peace and that the Prophet is the Prophet of tolerance. Here's the joke. Are you ready?
Robert Spencer is claiming that:
"People can be convinced of something they wish to believe, regardless of overwhelming evidence to the contrary."
I can only comment by the famous Arabic adage that we quoted before:
"She accused me of her own ills, and then escaped."

"A kinder, gentler Muhammad"

The author here brings a whiff of objectivity when he now quotes some of the correct quotations and descriptions of the Prophet; that won't last long though. We will bring the quotations without comment.
On page 183, "The one whose "heart was filled with intense love for all humankind irrespective of caste, creed, or color" "

"The one who had "the opportunity to strike back at those who attacked him, but refrained from doing so" "

"One of his companions described him as "neither rough nor harsh. He is neither noisy in the markets nor returns evil for evil, but he forgives and pardons." "

"He "was not a reviler or a curser nor obscene." "

The author then brought the quotation of Anas ibn Malik, who served the Prophet for ten years, saying (our translation):

"So I served the Prophet for ten years; he had never said to me for anything I did: why did you do that, or for anything I didn't do: why didn't you do that?"
(Prophet Muhammad (PBUH))
Narrator: Anas Ibn Malik. Reference: Ibn Taymyah's dare Altaroud, Number: 420/8. Degree: Correct

That surprise of the rare incident of the author bringing more than one correct quote within one page ends quickly when he, between the quotes, brings an irrelevant incident of an American professor who founded what is called the "Student's Islamic Movement of India" (SIMI), which the author claims was implicated in the Mumbai bombings of July 2006. The author quotes the professor, wondering as to how that some members of that movement could commit such crime of violence against innocent civilians in the name of Islam.

The amazing fascism logic, which allows you to punish people by stretching suspicion to an extreme of conviction without any evidence, is really apparent here: what is the innocent professor to do with the behavior of totally different human beings living in another continent?
Who in their right mind can even dare to claim that if I found any social organization, then every member would automatically become a human angel, and if one of them commits a crime on his own for whatever reason, then amazingly somehow, that professor should be implicated?!

As a matter of fact, one of the most laughable, yet saddening expressions that is always repeated when any Muslim man or woman is harassed or falsely arrested without evidence lately, is the expression that he or she is "linked" to whatever claimed terrorist organization du jour!

Most of the time, that "linked to" accusation is as strongly supported by evidence as my genetic link to Elvis Presley!

The courts' garbage cans are where most of these cases wind up!

The author then does not surprise us when he, on his own, decides that the myriad of forgiveness and merciful actions of the Prophets and the testimony of all his companions were nothing but a "magnetism" and "charm" tricks that he must have used to gather all these people around him! Even worse, the author brings a well-known quote that does not surprise any Muslim, yet it is surprising that Mr. Spencer himself would bring it, which is the correct quote of the incident, when the Prophet stood up in respect to the passing of a funeral, and when one of his companions indicated to the Prophet that the deceased was not a Muslim but a Jewish man, the Prophet of all mankind answered, "Was he not a human being or did he not have a soul?"

The amazing comment on that apparent noble mannerism of the Prophet is when the author claimed that it must've been in the early days when the Prophet wanted to invite Jews to Islam!!

Not to mention that the quote that the author brought states that the Prophet was surrounded by companions who were all Muslims, was the Jewish man raised from the dead to become a Muslim?!

On page 184, the author moves to another incident, when Prophet Muhammad (PBUH) stated what he had stated throughout his hadeeth and what God had revealed in the Holy Quran, that the only religion accepted by God is Islam, which in itself is a purification of the true teachings of the Prophets of Christianly and Judaism enhanced by the additional laws that God had revealed to all mankind through his last Prophet. The author quotes the incident of another passing away of a Jewish man, when he wrote:

"A Muslim recounts that, "The bier of a Jew passed before the messenger of and (the members of the family) were wailing over him. Upon this he said: you are wailing and he is being punished."

In many historical incidents of which we have mentioned several in this book, Prophet Muhammad (PBUH) displayed an ability given to him by God to tell the fate of certain people on Judgment day, including a brave soldier in his army who the Prophet said was destined to hell fire. The companions then witnessed the man committing suicide in the battle. When the Prophet tells of the fate of another man Muslim or non-Muslim, it can only mean simply that it is about foretelling that specific man's fate. Yet if it is Mr. Spencer who is narrating the story, the conclusion would automatically be that it is only because the man is Jewish!
Did Prophet Muhammad (PBUH) say that? No.
Is it entirely a baseless wild guess of Mr. Spencer? Yes.

What the author also did not mention is that screaming, or wailing over the deceased is forbidden in Islam.
The author then claims that his so-called Muslim apologists - when they speak about the mercy and the forgiveness of the Prophet - don't mention his battles and raids against the infidels.
So when it is upon the Prophet to fight evil and oppression, he fought them, for the cause of God, sacrificing his life like no man ever fought. And when it was the normal day to day life, he was the most merciful, forgiving, kindest man that people had ever seen. When the author confuses the most vicious of infidels, who were out there to destroy the religion of God, with just political opponents or some sort of ideological opposition, then it's not the apologists who are not telling the whole story, but it is Mr. Spencer who is insistently resisting any hint of understanding it, worse, accepting its existence!

What I think, is that most of the readers with any common sense do understand the perfectness of the character of the Prophet as a real life example for all mankind in dealing with both sides of the spectrum of life; Good and evil.

362

Even in his previous comment, the author wondered about what he called the conflict between Muslims, Christians, and Jews throughout the centuries. Christian/Christian wars in central Europe that victimized 10 million according to some estimates (French Voltaire is one), not to mention that France and England pillaged Muslim countries for centuries, yet you would think reading the books of Mr. Spencer and his likes, that it is the Iraqis who are occupying America and that it is the Afghanis occupying England, while the Palestinians are wreaking havoc upon German Zionists in Europe. Maybe it became a true conflict recently, but it is a conflict of oppression, where Muslims in their own homelands are plain victims all the time, and by the millions.

"The veneration of Muhammad"

Prophet Muhammad (PBUH) himself, when he was asked about the purpose of God sending him with His message to all mankind, answered:

"I was sent but to complete the most noble of manners."
(Prophet Muhammad (PBUH))
Narrator: Abu Hurayrah. Reference: Al selsilah Al Saheha, Number: 45.
Degree: Correct

"And you are but with great manners."
Holy Quran, Surat (Al Qalam) (The Pen) Ch. (68), verse (4)

وَإِنَّكَ لَعَلَىٰ خُلُقٍ عَظِيمٍ (4)

The entire religion of Islam as defined by the Prophet of Islam himself - and not extreme nameless commentator's millennia later - is about nothing but noble behavior and manners.
God Himself in the Holy Quran made the ultimate reference of that noble mannerism pursuit of the Prophet of God in the above mentioned verse. For Muslims then to follow the mannerism, the ethics and the character quality of the Prophet of God is in itself a blessing of not only achieving the highest level that satisfies one's hope of an accepted stance before God, but more so achieving that according to the precise record and the

clear reference of the Prophet himself.

For specifically, that reason and to the benefit of all mankind, it is no coincidence that the most accurately quoted man in history is Prophet Muhammad (PBUH), not to mention that he's the most biographed man in history as well. Having said that, it is he who said:

"Do not praise me like the Christians praised Eissa son of Maryam but say (call me) **a servant of Allah, and his messenger"**
(Prophet Muhammad (PBUH))
Narrator: Omar Ibn Alkhatab. Reference: Ghayat Al Muram, Number: 123.
Degree: Correct

It is him who made sure to always eat on the floor like servants, and used to help his wives in their house chores, including cooking, milking the sheep, sewing his garb and generally serving himself.

It was him who forbade his companions, who loved him more than they loved their ownselves, from ever standing for him when he walked in, and it was also him who could never have been identified as the last Prophet of God by any hint of arrogance or posture in the way he sat amongst his companions. If you did not know him, you would have had to ask about what he looked like, for you could never tell his status as the ultimate man of god by his modest behavior.

One famous incident is the incident of the insemination of the palm trees in Medina.

The Prophet was walking in Medina and he saw some men inseminating palm trees; the Prophet said to them, **"Maybe this is not the right thing to do."** Which was a suggestion by the Prophet, yet the result was that the palm trees that were not inseminated did not bring fruit the following season, and then some Muslims came to the Prophet inquiring about that negative outcome.

The Prophet explained to them that what he meant was a thought that could have gone either way, and that they are more knowledgeable about the matters of their business and their world. The Prophet added:

"But if I told something about Allah then take it, for I never lie about the account of Allah; all praises and greatness to Him"
(Prophet Muhammad (PBUH))
Narrator: Talha Ibn Obaid Allah. Reference: Saheeh Muslim, Number: 2361. Degree: Correct

This incident is of great significance in Islamic Law and the religion itself.

Firstly, in many other occasions and in his general behavior that supported Shura (Islamic democracy of consulting) that always opened the door for people with knowledge to decide upon their matters of life, in the sense that Islam provides the general solid structure of long-term stability and protection to Muslims' God-given rights. Yet, within the same structure, it is the Muslims themselves who have to manage, compromise, decide in whichever way they want to pursue their happiness within the guidelines of that Islamic Law structure; as the matter of fact, one of the definitions of Islamic jurisprudence (Fiqh) is that it is applying the guidance of God to mankind via the comprehension of reality. There is no rigidity in Islamic Law.

Secondly, is that, in pursuing the do's and don'ts of the religion itself, where the "Sunnah" or the tradition of the Prophet is a key component as equal and as important as the commands of Allah in the Holy Quran, "Sunnah" is not copying every single thing that the Prophet had done. The Prophet clearly stated that his sunnah is what he said to do, and what he said not to do, his behavior about doing the same things in question, and agreeing or disagreeing with things, whether verbally or by gesture. However, the absolute personal preferences of the Prophet when he never said, you have to do this or you shouldn't do this, like his personal preferences of food, clothes, pattern of travel, etc. are not a part of the Sunnah of Islamic law; and when you go as far as emulating these non-mandated by the Prophet preferences, it becomes an individual choice and preference to you as an individual, but not a mandated law.

An example is that the local custom at the time was that many men did braid their hair. That was the manly look of the time. Yet, while Prophet Muhammad (PBUH) ordered Muslim men to grow their beards, he never said or ordered Muslim men to braid their hair. The beard is a universal part of sunnah for every Muslim man, while the second part was a local custom that changes, where the only preference to that is that a man should look like what a man should look like during the time or within the culture he lives in - unless it violates a clear forbidden matter - and the same for women. Another example is that the Prophet, preferred to eat squash and it was one of his preferred foods. You will not find Muslim scholars today of any worth that would tell you it is mandated that every Muslim should eat squash, as if it is a part of the tradition of Prophet Muhammad (PBUH) or his manners.

To the contrary, and out of a huge volume of work of the respected Muslim scholar Abu Hamed Al-Ghazali, where he, on his own, according to his own comprehension, was so fond of the Prophet when he said, what the author quoted on page 185:
"The key to happiness is to follow the Sunnah and to imitate the messenger of God in all his coming and going, his movements and rest, in his way of eating, his attitude, his sleep, and his talk."

That statement is simply a personal preference and opinion of a Muslim scholar that is only substantiated by his own unique individual perceptions and preferences to achieve religious happiness. And as we have stated before, a cardinal jurisprudence rule of Islam is that "the comprehension of men is not a revelation of God."

How would that personal preference of Al-Ghazali about happiness be a mandate upon Muslims, if Muhammad (PBUH) himself did not mandate it upon Muslims that way?
Please note also, it is so clear that Al Ghazali was clearly speaking about his own personal preferences.

366

Can the author differentiate between personal choice and perception of one man or a group of men versus the generality of Islamic Law and its rights/obligations upon all Muslims?

Having said that, even doing it like the scholar Al-Ghazali has preferred is not wrong according to Islamic Law, yet the accuracy of the law and the civil rights of people clearly differentiate between what you are obligated to do and what preferences you may have according to your own liking.

The author, instead of discussing what true scholars of Islam have said about taking the great manners of the Prophet as an example, or what the Prophet himself has said about it, he as usual resorts to the most extreme of minorities of which some are not even Muslim to begin with, like when he wrote on page 185:
"Likewise, a modern Arab writer opined that Allah "created Muhammad 's body in such unsurpassable beauty as had neither before him or after him been seen in a human being." "

That Arab writer that the author hand-picked to quote - Annemarie Schimmel - not only is not a Muslim, nor an Arab, but is a German orientalist, but her opinion is not supported by the Holy Quran, the quotation of the Prophet himself, nor any majority of Muslim scholars. That however, is irrelevant of the fact that Schimmel might have thought she was praising the Prophet.

According to Islamic Law, the physical looks and appearances of the Prophet are of absolutely no importance to the manners of the Prophet or the religion itself. Even depicting a picture or a statue of the Prophet is totally forbidden by none other than the Prophet himself! Another source of how extreme and unreliable the sources of the author are, is again not a major scholar of Islam, not a quotation of the Prophet himself, not a part of the Seerah of the Prophet, nor the Holy Quran itself, but a Persian Sufi mystic poet, Mansoor Al-Hallaj, who of all people, was overwhelmingly accused of blasphemy by the scholars of his time, including not just Sunni but Sufi ones, and was convicted as such!

367

The author quotes him, when he wrote on page 185: "Perhaps reasoning from his study of the Holy Quran, said that Allah "has not created anything that is dearer to him than Muhammad and his family." "

There is nothing in the correct quotations of neither the Prophet nor the Holy Quran itself that pertains to that quote, specifically in regards to Muhammad's family. The status of the family of Muhammad (PBUH) is revered to all Muslims and its repeated in every prayer that Muslims pray for Allah's Praise of Muhammad (PBUH) and his family, as they do praise Abraham (PBUH) and his lineage, but how dear or not dear that family is to Allah is just a speculation that was rampant to date in the minority of Sufi mysticism and Shiite Muslims, who are in many ways factions that sometimes commit grave sins; similar to the ideology of raising saints to the status of the Prophets of God in some factions of Christianity, and sometimes even supplicating and praising them as much.

Why resort to mysticism in minority Sufism? Even to the one who died accused of an extremely rare conviction of blasphemy? Then why you want to go as far as "perhaps reasoning from his study of the Holy Quran," if it is in the Holy Quran itself, then show it to us, and if not, then, why travel to the outer space of mysticism if you are telling your readers any "truth" on earth about Muhammad?

The answer is, because the clear truth of the manners of Muhammad (PBUH) - which is at hand in his clear correct quotations, biography, and the Holy Quran - is to the opposite of the narrative of Mr. Spencer that can only be supported by "the perhaps reasoning" of extreme blaspheming Sufi mystics!

"Imitating Muhammad today"

On page 186, the author makes a statement that I do not know if was meant to be the joke it is or not; however, regardless of his intention, it is really laughable. He wrote:

"When Muslims look to imitate him, they look to the same sources I have used in this book: the Holy Quran, the Hadeeth, and the Seerah."!!

Really?! In the last page, when quoting Islam and Muslims about the exemplary model of the manners of the Prophet, and how to follow them for individual Muslims, the author did not quote one verse from the Holy Quran, one quotation of the Prophet, correct or not, nor anything that has anything to do with the Seerah, which is the biography of the Prophet. As a matter of fact, the closest - time wise - reference to the Prophet was a quote of a Persian, Sufi, mystic Mansoor Al-Hallaj, who lived four centuries after the Prophet and died accused and unanimously convicted of blasphemy!

Does the author think that his readers have the memory of a fly, or maybe that they take long vacations every other page? Not to mention that throughout his book, none of some of the major references of Seerah and Holy Quran interpretations were ever used even once. And the overwhelming reference that the author relies upon is the most corrupt, unverified, and unfiltered source of the biography of the Prophet, which is Ibn Is'haq: where the author almost exclusively quoted only the well-known, proven fabrications of them.

On the following pages, from page 186 all the way to page 190 and building on the joke that the author claimed Muslims used as a reference for their emulation to the manners of their great Prophet, the author brings several cases of quotes, incidents of some Muslims that of course are hand-picked by him as if it is the consensus of 1.6 billion Muslims. Naturally, I would challenge the author in any allegations that he has against Islam and Muslims. But I would not dignify generalizing, out of context quotes of individual deviation cases, with a discussion or a comment as if it is any indication or any representation of Islamic Law or the manners of the Prophet himself.
For every case, every quote, and every individual action that the author may quote, even if they were by the thousands, I, or anyone else can bring a thousand times more horrendous, worse actions and crimes - never mind quotes - that belong to the fascist-right for whom which Mr.

Spencer is proudly a mouthpiece. And if terror is so abhorring in Islam and considered a corruption-on-Earth crime, which is described in Islamic Law as "terrorizing safe people" - where people here means all people of any kind for that matter - then, if the author exhorting us in his crusade against terrorists, the least honorable and objective pursuit should be standing against those who terrorize, kill and torture the innocent using fictitious wars, awkwardly empty slogans, to afflict collective state terrorism upon entire Muslim nations and not just individuals. Or is it that the entire demonize-Muslims, Jihadist warriors campaign is the needed justification to commit real abhorring state terrorism?

When the author finds us that one Muslim country, that just for fictitious reasons, have invaded and occupied a non-Muslim country, killing its civilians whether directly or indirectly by the hundreds of thousands, then let's hear his laughable theories about jihad, Mystics, illusionary traditions, and warrior terrorists. When terror is imposed on a daily basis upon the innocent civilian population of Palestinians, Iraqis, Afghanis, with a total of millions displaced out of their homes, hundreds of thousands killed, natural resources and infrastructure pillaged or destroyed, then I would dignify his examples with an answer.

On page 190, the author comments:
"Most western governments and law enforcement officials would dismiss all this and similar examples and others as manifestations of the twisting or hijacking of Islam. But we have seen that all the words and deeds of Muhammad, which the jihadists prefer are amply attested in early Islamic traditions. Nor is there a wealth of material in those traditions offering a radically different view of Muhammad"

As we have commented on this previously, the author comes again, beating the same dead horse. The fact is, in America, there are charitable organizations that spend billions of dollars in alleviating pain and suffering of poor people around the world in a gigantic practical act of mercy. I am proud to add here that America is the most charitable nation in the world. These wonderful efforts by the American people do not make a radical difference or a dual personality of America, when also it is the biggest nation in spending on arming local police departments and on jails in the world. A perfect example is when a person fights with every strength that he has when fighting is a must, but when the circumstances are the normal then expressing and acting as merciful, as forgiving and giving as much as he can is just as normal. The example of Muhammad (PBUH) sacrificing himself for the cause of God against oppression and against the infidels who, through force and tyranny, wanted to destroy the righteous and the path of God, is actually more noble than any act of charity itself, for when you do that - protecting the innocent who cannot protect themselves - you are sacrificing the most valuable thing you have: your life. In America we don't call them falling heroes for nothing.

Yet the author refuses and blinds himself to see the difference between a state of war and a state of peace, which every nation and every individual goes through in life, with different reactions and ever changing priorities.

A police officer, a fire fighter or a soldier is the hero of any society, but if they were Muslims; to Mr. Spencer they are all linked to violence!

In the end of this section, the author makes a statement that, in my opinion, should have had him sued by not only every Muslim organization in America, but by any civil rights organization that is true to its message. On pages 190 and 191, the author wrote:
"Such officials often placed themselves in the peculiar position in maintaining that Muslim supporters of terror are only a tiny minority, but acknowledging at the same time that this tiny minority controls the leadership of virtually every significant Muslim body, and evidently the vast majority that rejects jihad, violence can do nothing to dislodge them from these positions of power"

Very few fascists and totalitarian systems would dare to have the absurdly stupid word of "every" added to such a naïve, awkward

371

accusation, and I repeat, Mr. Spencer, our objective truth-seeker- who claims that he somewhat represents the best interest of not only the American people, but the west in general - has just alleged that virtually every significant Muslim body is ruled by "supporters of terror"!

In fascist Spencer-land, only he does know them all, know their intentions all, accuse them all, judge them all, and by an allegation like terror, demand to get rid of them all!

Mr. Spencer has to be paid very well for his relentless efforts in framing the leaders of 1.6 billion people into his demonized terrorists sham, yet an allegation like this against a minority population of Muslims in a society like America today, makes him unfortunate of not being born when an employer like Hitler would have paid him much more handsomely for the same efforts!

"Frightening reality"

The real, frightening reality is allowing the history of evil to repeat itself, just under a different label, using the same excuses and the same declared goal of hurting the innocent by suspicion or for whatever religion, race, and association they may have.

It is frightening that people forget that when Hitler wreaked havoc on earth, causing tens of millions of deaths, he never said, I am a fascist-crazy dictator who has the least regard for any human decency. Hitler ranted about Germany defending itself against its enemies and against conspiracies targeting the Germans from every direction.

The atrocities that he committed in the name of God, country, and attacking the enemies of Germany, before they attacked Germany will always be indication of the same consequences Mr. Spencer is happily a first-in-line mouthpiece for.

The fascist and blatant goal, in broad daylight, to discriminate, oppress, crush Muslims, their beliefs and their ideology of right and wrong into a tenth class world citizens is openly disclosed throughout Mr. Spencer's writings, this book, and specifically in its last pages.

We have made it so clear with true evidence: by history, and testable evidence, that the entire horrible image that the author imposes upon every Muslim and upon the last Prophet of God is an outright pitiful fabrication, mutilation, and omission of the facts. Yet, regardless, the western democracy which Mr. Spencer describes by "a pluralistic society by definition" in itself prohibits the persecution of a group of people's ideology or difference of opinion. Yet, in a fascist society and ideology that Mr. Spencer clearly subscribes to, all you have to do is find a criminal or a group of crimes and vaguely impose an association between those crimes and that entire population you want to persecute, or worse, eliminate, and there goes any God-given or even civil right that that population may have ever had.

The belief in Islam, God, and the last Prophet of God, regardless of what Mr. Spencer and his likes believe in, is a God-given right to a quarter of the planet's population to believe in it whatever way they want to believe in. In any society a Muslim may live, even a society that is not ruled by Islamic Law, Islamic Law mandates that if you are a Muslim and accepted to live in such a non-Muslim society for over three days, then you have accepted without doubt the application of the local law of the land upon yourself. Should you commit any crime that is prohibited by the law of the land, then you have to adhere to it and bear the consequential punishment for it. Should a Muslim think that such a law or laws are unfair, then he had no excuse if he lived there more than three days. The meaning here is that when a Muslim commits a crime, whether in a Muslim or non-Muslim land, he should be punished according to the relevant laws. As simple as that, the same rule applies upon any human being in general and in any civilized society.

The fact that you take one person or one group's crime whom only God knows who is pulling their strings, and who's benefiting from the "scare the herd" chaos of their crimes, and impose that upon hundreds of millions of people, is a fundamental definition of

373

discrimination in totalitarian systems that are the opposite of the democratic and pluralistic society that the author claims he speaks for.

In February 2010, Joe Stack, an obviously unstable US citizen hater of the IRS and the US Government, flew a plane in a suicide mission, slamming it into the federal IRS building in Texas, killing himself in the process. Seventy six percent of Americans who participated in the online survey on the homepage of CNN.com declared that this was not a terrorist attack!

On Friday the 19th of February 2010, and on the popular talk show of Bill Maher on the cable channel HBO, Bill Maher asked one of his guests, "What if the suicide attack perpetrated by Joe Stack was perpetrated by a Muhammad Stack?" His guest answered with a laugh, saying, "Oh, then it would be a terrorist attack!"

When a man carrying a machine gun walked into an fitness gym in Pennsylvania, killing about a dozen people for no apparent reason but that he just chose the place as a theatre for his massacre, no one asks which Church he goes to, what ideology he subscribes to, and whether he was Christian, Jewish, Buddhist, or as to how Jesus (PBUH), Moses (PBUH), or Buddha's influence affected his character and shared the responsibility in the massive murders.

This is the discrimination and the propaganda of hate that Mr. Spencer is not even shy of imposing and perpetrating upon the American people. So at the end, the "pluralistic society" and the democratic West would impose a fascist-like ultimatum upon their Muslim citizens and worse, on Muslims worldwide! Apparently because Mr. Spencer can poorly fabricate tales!

On page 191, the author writes:

"The jihadists know better. Instead, their only hope of succeeding, as slim as it is to acknowledge and confront the words and deeds of Muhammad and the doctrines of Islam that teach jihad violence and Sharia supremacism and to construct a case for the rejection of Holy Quranic literalism and the definitive discharging of these teachings."

*Mr. Spencer wants Muslims to disband their defense armies of fifty-seven countries since that is the definition of jihad in Islam, and literally discharge their entire religion and its teachings down the tubes. Should they then hope to be treated better in the next Abu Ghariab, Master Spencer?!!

How could anyone in his right mind dare to even make the request that denigrates 1.6 billion people that way, and with whose authority?

What kind of wars and clashes worldwide that such an absurd, irresponsible claim is to generate if it is brought even to minimal action. Is the Mr. Spencer and the goal of whom he represents, the clash of civilizations in itself and the trillions generated by fictitious wars, based on extreme ideas of a Western supremacy that parallels that infallible Aryan racism of Hitler Nazism?

And what is Sharia supremacy? As a Christian or as a Jew, when I believe for example that the doctrine of my religion that I belong to is the best way of life for me to live, would that mean, for example, that Orthodox Jews are supremacists as let's say the KKK or Skin heads?!

Did any of the Muslim scholars, other than the author's mystic Sufi Jihadist warriors in some cave somewhere, say that let's impose our ideology by forcing Catholics for example, to denounce the literality of their Scripture and discharge the Bible of the teachings of Jesus (PBUH), while imposing the denouncing of some basic tenets of their faith on every Catholic Church?

But that's what the author is asking to be done to the Muslims, in writing and in broad day light!

If what the author is demanding is not supremacy in its worst condition; imposing his ideology not only upon the minority within a country's grasp of its Muslim citizens, but worse, upon the majority citizens of fifty-seven countries in the world, if this is not similar or even worse than Nazism and fascism itself, then what is?

As an American, I have to warn every American brother and sister of the consequences of letting that ideology prevail and be

375

presented as if it is a representation of the western society, for the consequences, throughout history are always the same. The German population that let Nazism speak for them is the best to tell of the consequences.

"The wolf of fascism is blind. When you stay silent watching it attacking others; it will still be blind when it imminently turns chasing viciously after you."

"What is to be done"

Here the author, without shame, puts his fascist agenda based on the illusion of the scarecrow he thought he concocted out of thin air.

On page 192, he wrote:

1- "Stop insisting that Islam is a religion of peace. This is false and falsehoods are never productive."

*Mr. Spencer is stating a unique philosophy that "falsehoods are never productive"? Was he awake and conscious when he omitted entire verses of the Holy Quran, mutilated parts of them and intentionally mistranslated the rest?
Wasn't he aware that he has falsified tens and hundreds of accounts of the Prophet by bringing laughable lies and conclusions based on stories Muslim third graders know are untrue?
Even when some religion or someone claims that he is for peace - Mr. Spencer does not even qualify - why should we fight that? Is that because it's better that the same person would say I am for war, worse behave accordingly? Is it that so war profiting can have another trillion-dollar fictitious war bonanza against the next defenseless small country?
The most famous rule in the American legal system is that the accused is innocent till proven guilty, while the burden of proof lies upon the plaintiffs or the prosecutor.
Every citizen is peaceful and innocent till he is proven without doubt that he is otherwise. That fundamental foundation of the "pluralistic society's" legal system is what the author wants to destroy to start his

376

wars against Muslims. Another surprise is that this is the first thing that the author is demanding, which in itself is clearly demanding war, no matter how peaceful their conduct and how many calls of peace Muslims make to the world.

The author not only wants to impose his dictatorship of brainwashing Muslims and denying them their right to defend their lands, but he is even imposing himself on the Western leaders by asking them not to express their own opinion, and to limit what they say about Islam to only his own personal invented claims! He wrote about western leaders: "they would be much wiser to limit themselves to declaring that their foes wished to impose Islamic Sharia rule upon their countries and the world, and that they are going to lead resistance to that."!

The author, a page ago, wanted to impose atheism upon 1.6 billion Muslims by discharging the literal teachings of the Holy Quran, denouncing taking the Prophet of God and Islam as any example, yet he demands that the leaders of the West declare: that instead, it is his unknown "foes" that want to impose their ideology of Sharia upon the West! So even if it was true, that some cave residents somewhere in the world, who are "exclusively" quoted by the "selected few" in the Western media, have this crazy notion of imposing Sharia law upon non-Muslim countries and that is what the crazy jihadist warrior lunatics demand, then what is the excuse of Mr. Spencer, the civilized beacon of light of the pluralistic Western society demanding committing even worse upon the population of fifty-seven Muslim countries?!

The Sharia law, by the admission of Mr. Spencer himself, allowed Christians and Jews, even atheists to practice their religion and keep their identity intact whichever way they wanted it, and however they wanted it, as citizens in a society where the obligation was through a taxation system that was fair, objective, and applicable upon them as it was applicable upon the majority of Muslims themselves.

Compare that to the truth-seeker's statement of literally deleting the entire religion of Islam as ideology and as a practice by imposing and invoking the west against 1.6 billion Muslims.

Question of the day: define "absurdly insane" for us!

2- On page 192, he wrote:
"Imitate a full-scale Manhattan Project to find new energy sources."

Here, any psychologist would tell you that Mr. Spencer's subconscious has just told the truth. Mr. Spencer's solution to what he thinks is the problem of the West buying oil from the East by paying money for their natural resource is to create a nationwide program for alternative sources of energy. And out of the hundreds of the nationwide programs or campaigns that America had created in modern times, like the space exploration program for example, the author chooses the secret Manhattan project that produced the atom bomb which outcome was the incineration of the hundreds of thousands innocent civilian population of two major Japanese cities! Can it be any clearer than that? I can see even theoretical fascists running to the hills from being associated with Mr. Spencer.

I am the number one supporter of alternative sources of energy, especially solar and water-produced hydrogen fuels, yet I support it for a totally different reason than Mr. Spencer's. Mr. Spencer sees the revenues of oil sales to Arab countries as a negative according to the narrative of hate-anything-Muslim, discredit-anything-Muslim, and hurt-anything-Muslim. Yet even according to that imposed façade of what "oil money" does, I'd like to explain to the readers some of the oil-games that are perpetrated upon the entire population of the Earth. The largest industry as far as international trade is arm sales, and no wonder when the biggest supplier of such arms is America itself, and the largest two customers out of the top three are none other than Saudi Arabia and the United Arab Emirates, who, combined, buy tens of billions of dollars of arms, which they never use and most likely will rust in the desert.

Aside from the rest of the Arab countries buying similar amounts of such arms; there is the entire preference of the gulf oil-producing area of American multi-national industrial products. What even supersedes that entire systematic process of recycling American oil dollars back again through arms and multi-national sales revenues in the Middle East, is that the obviously artificially inflated oil price itself is a mechanism to mob back the massive inflation pressures caused by the enormous costs of factious wars and government failed programs. These wars and waste programs are financed by printing additional dollars. Oil is traded in dollars and the higher the price of oil, the more demand for dollars worldwide, which would, to a certain extent eliminate the effect of printing trillions of dollars in debt without added asset value or true positive economic activity. These dollars are recycled back with trillions of dollars worth of arm sales and multinational corporations' Middle East revenues. Is it planned that way, I don't know, but it is the way it is.

3- On page 192 he wrote:
"make Western aid contingent upon renunciation of the jihad ideology."

All the declared aid programs throughout the West and America are for the common goals of the United Nations and mankind of alleviating suffering, supporting growth and prosperity in under-developed and developing countries within an overall perspective of supporting world peace. Here, Mr. Spencer wants to disrupt all that to impose his personal dictatorship upon countries that are in need of international support. Throughout the book, we showed beyond any doubt that Mr. Spencer had invented himself a perception of a crazy ideology that he gave the title of "Jihad Ideology", which is not only different in its entirety than the concept of jihad in Islam, but in many aspects totally the opposite. So let's say that jihad to a Muslim nation is its army of its own people, defending themselves and their national interests, like any nation in the world, which is a true definition. While some crusader in the west decided, according to his invention, that jihad is a form of (let's say) cannibalism, or eating newborn babies alive, and chose an Arabic word as a title for it.
Should Muslim countries then disband their armies and live defenseless,

379

just because one man in America has the pitiful ability to boldly fabricate, blatantly lie, and believe himself?

Or maybe, one of the Muslim organizations that he claims are all led by terrorist supporters should sue him for all the fabrications and omissions of their holy book, in addition to threatening their existence in their own country, as American citizens and the future of their children. Which country that has any sovereignty would accept aid based on imposing an ideology that literally wants to destroy its own? How would world peace and the stability of the world in its entirety be like, if fifty-seven countries that are Muslim are denied international aid or cooperation because their identity did not adhere to Mr. Spencer's little-Hitler fascism?
Would the result be, again and again and again, instability and war?
Is there a reason why this is where Mr. Spencer's road of fascism leads to all the time?

4- On page 193 he wrote:
"Call upon American Muslims advocacy groups to work against the jihad ideology. Instead of endorsements of the US Constitution and American values, Islamic institutions in the United States are filled with Jihadist propaganda against Jews and Christians."

Here the author uses the fascist technique of discrediting and suspecting citizens' citizenships and loyalty to their countries, and mandates only one way to validate their allegiance to their societies by adhering to an imposed oppressive system of Mr. Spencer's invention, that is neither mandated by the constitution, the law, and totally against any hint of civil rights.

And in the exercise of the McCarthyism "linked to" system of destroying people's reputations and threatening them with laughable suspicions, the author attacks one of the leading peaceful Muslim civil rights organizations in America (CAIR) by just declaring on his own - as if he is any Islamic ultimate source of truthfulness - when he said, "This is not surprising given the pedigrees of such groups, for example, emerged from the Islamic Association of Palestine, a Hamas front."

How simple a technique is that? Blow the horn about a certain hated crime and then link anyone who opposes you, or worse, that you do not like, to that crime using the most ridiculous and absurd false accusation, to persuade the public to destroy them for you!

Here is Mr. Spencer acting his ideology in the practicality of a thug's behavior. On page 193 he wrote:
"Courageous officials and politicians, if any exist today, should challenge these groups to put up or shut up to produce genuinely moderate and reformist initiatives that teach against Muhammad's warlike example, or to stop posing as moderate groups."

Even when he amazingly asked law enforcement agencies - which is disastrous under any minimum sense of what civil rights are about, that some of our American local and national law enforcement agencies allow someone like Mr. Spencer to speak and lecture law enforcement officers, trained and funded by Muslim tax payer money - that they "should accordingly stop regarding these U.S Muslim groups as trustworthy, loyal moderate who accept Western pluralism without reservation." And by the way would someone in the whole entire world explain to me on whose authority anyone can force me to believe in anything without reservation, I really would like to know!!

By that, he destroys any quality of pluralism itself, so when the citizens of any society have any reservations or suggestions about how to improve a system which more than one third of the population believes is corrupt, people are prohibited of attempting to improve or even demand the improvement of that system. So, of all American citizens, Muslim citizens and their social organizations, even as sincere Americans, are forbidden to get involved in the politics or in the process of the betterment of their own country!
And of all citizens, they have to accept what is served to them regardless of their opinions, maybe as inmates of their own Spencer land country!

So Mr. Spencer's pluralism "without reservation", is that Muslim citizens are a "to put up or shut up" in his totalitarian system enforced - by our own law enforcement agencies!

5- On pages 193 and 194, he wrote:
"Revise immigration policies with the jihad ideology in view."

In this last demand, Mr. Spencer demands that only Muslims would be asked questions about their personal beliefs, specifically questions in the regard of his crazy jihadist Pinocchio. Some of the questions – aside from the fact that no Muslim would oppose that any immigrant to America be asked background questions, as long as they're asked to everyone indiscriminately - are:
"questions about the applicant's pluralistic societies, religious freedom, women rights, and other features of Western societies challenged by elements of Muhammad's teachings and Islamic Law."
If it is mandated upon every immigrant to be asked these questions, then every Muslim immigrant should oblige by them. But here, it's not just a matter of discrimination and targeting a specific group, not only for whatever belief they may have, but for a totally fabricated baseless accusation of Mr. Spencer himself.

Within that screaming criminal discrimination attempt, there is another notion that we proved laughable throughout Mr. Spencer's book. Here is a quick review:

Islam opposes pluralistic societies.

Prophet Muhammad (PBUH)'s leading companions were Abu Bakr and Omar the Arabs, Bilal the black African, Salman the Persian, Suhaib the Roman, and Abdullah Ibn Salam the former Jewish Rabbi Leader, whom the Prophet not only consulted with all on a consistent basis, but applied their advice against his own opinion in many and most important occasions as well. Fundamental mandates of Muhammad (PBUH)'s teachings and Islamic Law, not only allowed or protected the rights of Christians and Jewish citizens to worship freely according to the tenants

382

of their own faith in Muslim lands, but in itself at the time was the only resort of safety and justice in the entire world. The history of Islamic tolerance of non-Muslims at the time of the prophet, in comparison to the Crusades, the Inquisition or the abhorring treatment of Jews throughout Europe in general, is one comparison that the author can attempt to undertake at the risk of whatever is left of his credibility if any!

Religious freedom

If it wasn't for the protection of Jews in Muslim countries, there would not have been Judaism today. Islamic Law is the only religion and faith-based law that prohibits the questioning of anyone's beliefs, even openly-declared enemy of Islam.

Women Rights

Compare the size of prostitution and pornography industries that are based totally on the exploitation of women, between Western countries and Muslim countries. And while you're at it, compare mandated inheritance rights of Muslim women from their men relative around them, between the two camps, then compare divorce rates, domestic violence cases, and the number of victims of AIDS amongst females, then let the results be enough of an answer about true women rights, all of which are results of the blessed teachings of Muhammad (PBUH), the last Prophet of God.

While there are 6.6 million violent crimes committed in America annually, of which the pain and suffering of their victims is as sinful as the pain and suffering of any similar terrorist crime, the author wants every politician in the West to engage in the discrimination, oppression, destabilization of world peace and international trade to eventually bring a clash and optimally, according to the author, wage war against one quarter of the population, basically in retaliation for the three thousand innocent victims of September 11th, of whom hundreds were Muslim. The terrorist attack that happened under the watch of some elements of the U.S. government ten years ago, while at the same time our "pluralistic society" - that Muslims should accept without reservation - allows 45 thousand innocent Americans to die every year who are denied their basic human rights of healthcare, over 30 thousand deaths a year caused by drunk driving, in addition to hundreds of thousands of victims, families, and hundreds of millions of dollars of economic loss due to the licensing of liquor, intoxicants, and carcinogenic tobacco products.

On page 194, the truth-seeker writes:
"If no western politicians can be found who are courageous enough to grasp this nettle, Western countries will eventually pay a stiff price, when the Jihadists they have admitted carry out successful Jihad attacks, or inspire native-born Muslims to do so – or when they advance Sharia provisions by peaceful means."

America has already paid the stiffest of prices in the history of mankind by allowing the spread of the hatred and hate-mongering propaganda of the likes of Mr. Spencer, where our US Treasury and the future of our own children were pillaged and are still being pillaged of trillions of dollars to pay for a fictitious war against a country that has never done anything to us, causing the deaths of hundreds of thousands of innocent civilians in the process, in our own name, and benefitting what I doubt to be the real employers and motivators of Mr. Spencer's "defense" contractors and oil multinationals.

On page 194 the author writes again:
"The words and deeds of Muhammad have been moving Muslims to commit acts of violence for 1400 years now."

The acts and teachings of Muhammad (PBUH) have taught the world to stand up to oppression and fight for the cause of God those who want to pillage countries of their natural resources and impose their crusading, ruthless fascist oppression that have absolutely *nothing* to do with any decency of the teachings of all Prophets of God and the true teachings of Jesus PBUH, who, on Judgment Day would be the first to renounce them and call them by their name: which is none other than

384

"evil-doers." Even the last sentence of Mr. Spencer's book is one of the biggest lies that you can claim about the teachings of Muhammad (PBUH)

In his most famous quotation, Prophet Muhammad (PBUH) taught:

"Deeds are judged by what they were done for, so whoever his immigration was for a world to gain or a woman to marry, then his immigration is to what he immigrated and whoever immigrates to the sake of God and his messenger, then his immigration is to them."
(Prophet Muhammad (PBUH))
Narrator: Omar Ibn Al Khatab. Reference: Saheeh Al Bukhary, Number: 3898. Degree: Correct

No Muslim ever raised the sword in the name of Prophet Muhammad (PBUH) personally. He is the first to forbid it, for he himself sacrificed his entire life throughout an enormous 23 years struggle, for one purpose only: that is for the sake of the one mighty God.
It was Muhammad (PBUH), who forbade Muslims to have pictures of him, or perform even the smallest hint of associating him in any remote capacity with God Himself.
It was Muhammad (PBUH) himself who declared to his followers that no matter what they think of his good deeds, he will only enter paradise by the mercy of the One Mighty God, and not by the Prophet's own righteousness.
It was Muhammad (PBUH) himself who declared that all Prophets of God are his own brothers and gave a trust to every Muslim who would be alive when all Muslims witness the second coming of Jesus (PBUH) from heaven; the trust is to give Jesus PBUH, Muhammad (PBUH)'s greeting of peace.

The truth-seeker's last statement was:
"The sooner this is done, the safer all will be. But as long as the manifold problem continues to be ignored, Muhammad (PBUH) will continue to inspire his followers to wield the sword in his name."!

"He preferred migration to fighting his own people. But when oppression went beyond the pale of tolerance, he took up his sword in self-defense. Those who believe religion can be spread by force are fools."

Lamartine, "Historie de la Turquie," Paris 1854

Finally:

Stealth Fascism

The latest phase of the terrifying ideology the author subscribes to is what I call "stealth Fascism!"
You are an innocent citizen or a charitable organization, which practically and publicly promote and hope for peace, yet you are Muslim! And Mr. Spencer cannot find anything to "link" you or associate you with any of his terrorist, scare crow acquaintances; what is the solution then? What can the "defensive crusader" do with the overwhelming majority of Muslims who are peaceful and peace spreading as mandated by their prophet and religion?

The solution is "stealth" allegations! That even though there isn't one iota of any proof or any hint of any wrong doing whatsoever, in Spencer land which makes Disney land looks like a very serious place, the evidence and the proofs are right there!

Muslims in the west are plotting and are about to attack us viciously to take away our, liberty, freedom, and cookie dough Ice cream! Only it is in a "Stealth" mode.

A stealth mode that only the author and his likes can know about, see and scream, demanding persecuting all Muslims for!

In the beginning of the book I mentioned that in Mr. Spencer's eyes, "Muslims are guilty till never proven innocent"!
If you are innocent or not, you call for peace or not, an ideal citizen or not; if you have a hint of a difference of opinion, or that they cannot "link" you to any of their boogie men, then they have their patriotic undisputed "stealth" evidence ready for you, with the little caveat that it is invisible and intangible, that no one else can see, or sometimes understand except the defense contractors' patriots! After all it is the evil Muslims who have it hidden in that tricky "stealth" dimension!

So not only, and as we have proven, that his Jihadist, terrorism fabrications against Islam are absurdly false, but these accusations are entirely baseless not because they are, but because only him and his peers can see the invisible "evidence" that proves them true, hence, there are now "stealth Jihad", "stealth terrorism", "stealth warriors" who are all first cousins to Harvey the rabbit!

But I do agree with Mr. Spencer, for truly the terrorists are here, the supremacists are here, and with blunt and in your face screaming evidence, they are attempting to take over America!
Only they are Mr. Spencer and his new Fascists - stealth or otherwise - who are relentless in taking America to lower than the inhuman abyss the inquisitions have taken Europe to:
"We will torture you to death to purify you of the blasphemy you are denying, but if you confess, we will be merciful enough to drown you to death quicker; you are free to choose."!

Is the goal to deter Muslim countries from standing up for themselves against oppression, otherwise they are stamped with the Jihadist crazed terrorist Spencer stamp? Or is it to further scare the Western population into oppressing the exponential, peaceful growth of Islam in the west?
You need to answer that pressing vital question yourself!

"The wolf of fascism is blind. When you stay silent watching it attacking others; it will still be blind when it imminently turns viciously chasing after you."

Ask the Germans.

Moustafa Zayed

Theliesaboutmuhammad@gmail.com

تم بحمد الله

Accomplished with the blessings of Allah.

July, 2010

Index of Answers to Allegations

Muhammad and his experiences

14. Muhammad had knowledge of Zoroastrian scriptures and Hinduism that he borrowed the images of Jannah from. P 97.

15. Muhammad saw the wife (Zaynab Bint Jahsh) of his adopted son and divorced her from him to marry her for himself. P 102

16. The story of Ifk, or the false accusations against the honor of Ayesha, the wife of Muhammad. P 108

17. Muhammad evidently believed the rumors about Ayesha. P 109.

18. Muhammad seems to have retreated from the claim that Israa and Miraaj was a bodily journey. P 141

19. Zaynab Bint Al Harith, who tried to poison the Prophet, was forgiven first because she said that Muhammad is a prophet of God. P 259

20. The thieves who killed the Muslim herders and stole the charity camels were killed for apostasy and not for corruption on earth. P 274

21. Muhammad's goal was to be the master of Arabia. P 309

22. On his death bed Muhammad looked to write his last advice for Muslims. P 320

23. Muhammad left no clear successor before he died. P 325

24. Was Muhammad a pedophile prophet? P 333

Muhammad and Quraysh

25. Muhammad reacted to the infidels of Qurayesh's rejection to Islam with Fury. P 79

26. Muhammad personally threatened the Pagans of Qurayesh if they didn't convert to Islam. P 129.

27. The torture that Qurayesh committed against the early Muslims was a "strike back". P 129.

28. Muhammad had anger and frustration over his failure to convert the Qurayesh pagans and threatened he will slaughter them. P 130

29. The description of Masjid Aqsa that Muhammad gave the pagans of Qurayesh as proof for the Israa and Miraaj Journey was not accurate. P 141

30. Muslim relations with the Jews dictated the Muslim relations with Qurayesh. P 170.

31. In the opening of Mecca, Muhammad had forced Abu Sufyan, the leader of Quraysh, to become a Muslim under the threat of the sword. P 266

32. Qurayesh was the reason why all other tribes accepted Islam when they did. P 50

Islam/Muhammad and War

33. Muslims were supposed to fight for the prophet of Islam, not God. P 171.

34. Muslims kill women and children at battle. P 157

35. In the beginning of the battle of Badr, Muhammad didn't expect these numbers and cried out to Allah in anxiety. P 172

36. There is a possibility that Muhammad never participated in the battle of Badr.   P 173

37. The execution of Uqba Ibn Moyeet and Al Nadr Ibn Al Harith. P174.

38. Two young Muslims murdered Abu Jahl as he was walking amongst people in the battle of Badr. P 175

39. In Badr, Allah fought for the Muslims. P 176

40. Beheading hostages and war captives is an Islamic practice, then and now. P 176

41. Allah warns the Muslims not to consider booty won at Badr to belong to anyone but Muhammad. P 180

42. Muhammad was given victory by awe that is worth the rally in battle of one month. P 182.

43. The battle of Badr was the first practical example of what came to be as the Islamic doctrine of Jihad. P 182

44. In battle, Muslims are ordered to go for the kill all the time. P 185.
45. At the battle of Uhud, the Muslims were confused and fighting each other. P 198.
46. Muhammad allowed mutilations of dead bodies in battle. P 200
47. Muhammad (PBUH) had frequently insisted that Allah Himself had been fighting for the Muslims. P 201
48. The aid that God gives to his Muslim believers is "super-natural intervention" P 204
49. Muslims won the battle of the Trench by deception. P 225
50. The battle of Khaybar. P 250
51. Muhammad married Saffyah Bint Al Akhtab in the same day of the battle of Khaybar. P 261
52. The Muslims, in the battle of Hunayn, despite their superior numbers, were routed P281
53. In Tabuk, Muhammad ordered his army to attack the Roman army because they were Christians P 293
54. The first blood to be shed in Islam is when Saad Ibn Abi Waqas defended himself against intruders. P127
55. Muslims enslave war captives of women and children. P 230
56. The Nakhlah raid was a terrorist attack. P 155
57. It is difficult, if not impossible, to maintain that Islam is a religion of peace. P 348
58. Warfare and booty were among the chief preoccupations of Muhammad. P 348

The Quran

59. Holy Quranic verse numeration is not standard. P 36
60. Quranic texts are difficult to understand even when translated from Arabic. P31
61. Quran is also named Um al-kitab. P 38.

62. Quran is not the word of God because there are verses in the Quran that say (God willing). P 38.
63. The Quran is not self explaining of some of the verses and needs to have context provided. P 39.
64. Quran is a sketchy text. P 44.
65. There are some indications in Islamic history that the Quran was altered. P44
66. Quran is not the word of God. P 66.
67. Stories of the Quran are copied from Bible and the Old Testament! P 73
68. There are differences between the stories of the Quran and the stories in the Bible. P 73
69. The story of Qabeel and Habeel of the Quran is copied from the Talmud. P 76
70. Some charged that the Jews taught Muhammad the Quran. P 86.
71. Warqa Ibn Nawfal taught Muhammad the Quran. P 86
72. Many of the verses of the Quran were to manifest Allah's anxiety to grant his Prophet his heart's desires. P 100
73. The story of the Satanic verses. P 135
74. The language of the Quran is discursive and prosaic. p 145
75. The laws in the verses of the Quran revealed in Medina were copied from the Jews. P 145
76. Muhammad composed for the Muslims a brief prayer known as the Fatiha that became the corner stone of Muslim prayer. P 150
77. Quran permitted Muslim men to have sexual intercourse with slave-girls captured in battle. P 241
78. In the Quran a woman's testimony is worth half that of a man. P 338
79. The order of stoning adulterers in Islam is not in the Quran, so it is not true. P 343

80. Muhammad repented of the "satanic" verses incident. P 283
81. Muhammad received revelations through his dreams at night. P 58
82.

Male Superiority

1. The Muslim husband takes his wife as a prisoner. P 312
2. Muslim husbands beat their wives up. 314
3. Husband can do to his wife whatever he wants sexually. P 338
4. Women in Islam are deficient in intelligence and religion. P 341
5. Muslims gave a treatment of women as war prizes, with no consideration of their will, and where their previous marriages are annulled. P 243
6. Today, women are all too often treated as commodities in the Islamic world. P 245
7. The sight of an unveiled woman – to Muslims - is so distressing, so deeply sinful, that it causes even the angels to flee. P 60
8. In the Quran a woman's testimony is worth half that of a man. P 338

Muslims and Jews

1. Islam is anti Jews or Judaism. P53
2. Muhammad was strongly influenced by Judaism, situating himself within roster of Jewish Prophets. P 146
3. Muhammad continued to appeal to the Jews to accept his Prophetic status. P 161
4. There is a sharp distinction between Jewish and Islamic concepts of compassion. P 164.

5. The incident of exiling the Jews of Banu Qaynuqa. P 187

6. The Prophet of Islam directed his anger at the Jewish poet Ka'b Ibn Al-Ashraf. P 192

7. After the murder of Ka'b, Muhammad issued a blanket command, "Kill any Jew that falls into your power." P 195

8. The Banu Al Nadir standoff. P 205

9. The execution of Banu Qurayzah 'warriors.' P 225

10. Allah transformed the Sabbath-breaking Jews into pigs and monkeys. P 226

11. The three conditions offered to Banu Qurayzah were offered by the Muslims. P 227

12. The massacre of Banu Qurayzah has a source of embarrassment to Muslims. P 235

13. The mission of Muhammad was to kill the scholars of the Jews. P 52

14. Muhammad respected Jewish tribes around Mecca and sought their approval of his Prophetic mission. P 72

15. Muhammad condemns Jews to hell fire. P 348

Hadeeth and Scholars

1. There is no way to know what is correct and what is not correct of the Hadeeths. P 42

2. Hadeeth is overwhelmed with false information. P 44

3. Muslim scholars' opinions differ sharply from the opinions of some orientalists. P 45

4. Hadeeths of the Prophet (PBUH) are the Sunnah itself. P 40

5. Many incidents in the Prophet's life, including ones that became influential in Islamic history, have no supporting sources. P 43

6. Some modern scholars contend that Warqa actually rejected Muhammad p 88

Islam and Other Abrahamic Religions

1. Islam mandates a death penalty for Christian converts. P 28
2. Islam is copied from Christianity and Judaism. P 71
3. Muslims believe in Islam supremacy. P 74
4. In Islam, God was embarrassed to have his prophet Jesus die in shame on the cross, that's why Muslims do not believe in the Crucifixion. P 93
5. The nature of Jesus and his ascension to God in Islam was an attempt by Muhammad to end the conflict between squabbling Christian groups. P 95
6. Jews and Christians as sinful renegades is cornerstone of Islamic thought regarding non-Muslims. P 148
7. Muhammad was never mentioned in the Old Testament. P148
8. A Muslim should avoid Christians and Jews for the Fatiha criticizes them. P 150
9. Muhammad kept an icon of Virgin Mary and Jesus in the Kaaba. P 277
10. Jesus being son of God is a harsh accusation by the Muslims. P 296
11. The nature of Jesus and his ascension to God in Islam was an attempt by Muhammad to end the conflict between squabbling Christian groups. P 94
12. Allah told Muhammad to consult with the Jews and Christians if he doubts the truth of what he has been receiving. P 82
13. Islam asks Muslims to never befriend Christians and Jews. P 189
14. In Islam the return of Jesus is to abolish Christianity and impose Islam upon every one. P 351

15. Muhammad exhorted Muslims to fight against Jews and Christians. P 352
16. Muhammad had open contempt and hatred for Jews and Christians, incitements of violence against them, and calls that they be converted or subjugated. P 357
17. There was a conflict between Muslims, Christians, and Jews throughout the centuries. P 357
18.

Jihad

1. Jihad is holy war. P 147
2. Warriors of Jihad indeed granted no safety to those who did not accept Islam. P 284
3. Jihad of the Muslims is to dominate the world under Islamic social order. P 301
4. The September 11th, 2001 attacks were jihad terror attacks. P 330
5. The teachings of Muhammad persuade committing violence because "Jihadists" use the Prophet as an excuse. P32

Non-Muslims under Islamic law

1. Non-Muslims under Islamic law live in subjugation as inferiors under Islamic law. P 132
2. Islamic loyalty is deeper than blood. P 223
3. Jizyah is a discrimination against Christians and Jews. P 287
4. Non-Muslims are unclean because they don't eat Halal meat. P 294
5. Jizyah was Muslims' chief source of income. P 312
6. Islam forced non-Muslims not to wear distinctive Muslim men attire. 358

Islam Today

1. Avenging Insults via rioting is universally accepted by Muslims. P 31.
2. Outlawed Organizations are a representation of Islam. P 31.
3. Racism against Islam is not like Anti-Semitism. P 33
4. The Danish cartoons controversy shows the limited freedom of speech and expression in Islam.   P 34
5. Saudi Arabia doesn't allow churches as a discrimination against Christians. P 311
6. The controversy between Shiite and Sunni Muslims is in keeping with the attitudes and behavior of the Prophet of Islam. P 329
7. Capital punishment in Islam is pre-medieval harshness and unsuitable for the contemporary world. P 343
8. Islam needs Islamic reformers. P 346
9. Muslims should be limited from immigrating to the west. P 351

Misc

1. The mention of Judgment day, even though it didn't happen yet. P 45
2. Allah of the Arabs is a tribal God and not the One Mighty God. P 50
3. Fitnah in the religion means seduction. P 131
4. All Muslims in Medina were not treated equally. P 146
5. Allah is ready to command what will please Muhammad. P 219
6. Hajj was a pagan custom that Muhammad wanted to make a part of Islam. P 249
7. Zayd Ibn Harithah invited the prophet to enter Zayd's home while Zayd wasn't there. P 107

8. Cutting the hand of the thief as a punishment for theft. P 347

Total allegations: 155.

Other books by Imam Moustafa Zayed:

"Muhammad Said"

www.muhammadsaid.com

To be released soon:

"Does America need Islam?"

VISIT US AT:

WWW.THELIESABOUTMUHAMMD.COM

YOU CAN ALSO INTERACT WITH US ON:

FACEBOOK

AND ON:

TWITTER

Made in the USA
Charleston, SC
25 October 2010